# GLOBAL HEALTH SECURITY

# GLOBAL HEALTH SECURITY

## A BLUEPRINT FOR THE FUTURE

### LAWRENCE O. GOSTIN

Harvard University Press

CAMBRIDGE, MASSACHUSETTS & LONDON, ENGLAND

2021

Library of Congress Cataloging-in-Publication Data

Names: Gostin, Lawrence O. (Lawrence Ogalthorpe), author.
Title: Global health security : a blueprint for the future / Lawrence O. Gostin.
Description: Cambridge, Massachusetts : Harvard University Press, 2021. |
    Includes bibliographical references and index.
Identifiers: LCCN 2021006385 | ISBN 9780674976610 (cloth)
Subjects: LCSH: World health. | Communicable diseases—Prevention. |
    Biosecurity. | Public health. | Security, International.
Classification: LCC RA441 .G67 2021 | DDC 362.1—dc23
LC record available at https://lccn.loc.gov/2021006385

*I dedicate this book to my two wonderful grandchildren,
Aviva and Ellis,
who symbolize a future of global health with justice*

# Contents

# Abbreviations

AFRO    Regional Office for Africa—One of the World Health Organization's (WHO's) six regional offices around the world. It serves the WHO African Region, which comprises forty-seven WHO member states, with the Regional Office in Brazzaville, Republic of Congo.

AMR    antimicrobial resistance—The ability of microbes to survive by rendering ineffective medications that once could successfully treat them.

BWC    Convention on the Prohibition of the Development, Production and Stockpiling of Bacteriological and Toxin Weapons and on Their Destruction—This treaty, outlawing the development, production, stockpiling, transfer, and use of biological weapons, was the first treaty to ban an entire category of weapons.

CCMs    country coordinating mechanisms—National committees that submit funding applications to the Global Fund to Fight AIDS, Tuberculosis and Malaria and oversee Global Fund grants.

CDC    Centers for Disease Control and Prevention—The central US public health agency and part of the Department of Health and Human Services. Through developing and sharing expertise, promoting public health, responding to disease outbreaks, and more, it works to ensure the health and safety of Americans. Its unmatched expertise also makes it a valuable partner in containing disease outbreaks abroad. Some other countries' national public health agencies are also called centers for disease control and prevention.

CDIFF    *Clostridium difficile*—This bacterium can cause infections of the colon that are life-threatening. It is the most common hospital-acquired infection in the United States, and one that the CDC has deemed an urgent antimicrobial resistance threat.

CEPI    Coalition for Epidemic Preparedness Innovations—This public-private coalition stimulates research and development for new vaccines for diseases with pandemic potential.

COVID-19    Coronavirus disease 2019—This infectious disease, caused by the SARS-CoV-2 virus, was first detected in Wuhan, China, in late 2019, and within months had become a pandemic that reached nearly every country in the world, causing huge loss of life and economic and social disruption.

CRE    carbapenem-resistant *Enterobacteriaceae*—Bacteria that have developed resistance to multiple antibiotics, including carbapenem, and are considered a top antimicrobial resistance threat by both the WHO and the CDC.

CRISPR    clustered regularly interspaced short palindromic repeats—Sequences of DNA in bacterial genomes that are derived from DNA fragments of viruses that had previously infected the bacteria. They are part of the bacterial immune system, used to detect infections of similar viruses. This genetic machinery and associated enzymes have become the basis of a gene-editing technology that can be used to remove, change, or insert new genetic sequences with far more precision than previous techniques.

DDT    dichlorodiphenyltrichloroethane—An insecticide used to control mosquitoes that, although low-cost and effective, has been the subject of public skepticism due to its potential effects on health and the environment.

DG    director-general—The WHO's director-general has considerable authority as the head of the organization's Secretariat.

DRC    Democratic Republic of the Congo—A country in central Africa, by area the largest in sub-Saharan Africa. It has been plagued by misgovernance and decades of conflict.

DURC    dual-use research of concern—Research that can be beneficial but might also be used for technologies that pose a significant threat, including to public health and safety, the environment, or national security.

ePPP    enhanced potential pandemic pathogens—Pathogens that do not occur in nature, but instead are developed as part of research aimed at better understanding and preparing for potential threats. These pathogens are expected to be both highly transmissible, enabling rapid and uncontrolled spread among people, and highly virulent, causing significant levels of death and disease.

EU    European Union—A political and economic bloc consisting of twenty-seven countries in Europe, with a total population of more than 400 million. The EU can issue regulations that bind member states.

EUA    emergency use authorization—A mechanism to facilitate the use and availability of medical countermeasures, including vaccines, during a public health emergency. In the United States, the Food and Drug Administration may grant an emergency use authorization to unapproved medical products, or unapproved uses of medical products, in an emergency to diagnose, treat, or prevent serious or life-threatening diseases or conditions.

FAO    Food and Agricultural Organization of the United Nations—This specialized agency of the UN leads international efforts to end hunger and improve nutrition and food security, and contributes to global health security through its information-sharing and standard-setting functions.

FBI    Federal Bureau of Investigation—The domestic intelligence and security service of the United States and the principal US federal law enforcement agency.

FDA    Food and Drug Administration—A federal agency of the US Department of Health and Human Services. It is responsible for protecting US public health by regulating food and drugs.

G7    Group of Seven—An intergovernmental organization consisting of the seven countries with the largest advanced economies: Canada, France, Germany, Italy, Japan, the United Kingdom, and the United States. Its leaders meet annually to address economic and other issues.

G20    Group of Twenty—A forum of the G7 countries, twelve other countries with some of the world's largest economies, and the European Union. The G20 focuses on economic issues but also addresses other issues of international concern.

Gavi    Gavi, the Vaccine Alliance—Originally called the Global Alliance for Vaccines and Immunisation, this public-private global health partnership provides funding to increase low-income countries' access to vaccines.

GDP    gross domestic product—A standard measure of the size of a country's economy; the monetary value of all finished goods and services made within a country during a given time period.

GHEW    Global Health Emergency Workforce—A WHO network consisting of first responders to infectious disease outbreaks and other emergencies with health consequences. It includes emergency medical teams and members of the Global Outbreak Alert and Response Network.

GHSA    Global Health Security Agenda—Launched in 2014, this initiative has grown into an international collaboration that includes more than sixty countries, along with international organizations, nongovernmental organizations, and private companies that work together to strengthen capacities to prevent, detect, and respond to infectious disease threats.

GOARN    Global Outbreak Alert and Response Network—A network supported by WHO that consists of hundreds of technical and public health institutions, laboratories, NGOs, and other organizations that work to observe and respond to threatening epidemics.

GOF research    gain-of-function research—Research to modify pathogens in ways that provide them with traits they do not have in the wild, increasing their transmissibility, virulence, or both. It is a type of dual-use research of concern.

H1N1    A strain of influenza virus, more precisely designated (H1N1) 2009 or H1N1v, that caused a global influenza pandemic in 2009–2010. It was also known as "swine flu" because the virus included genetic material that was known to circulate in influenza viruses that infect pigs.

H5N1    A strain of influenza virus that mainly infects birds; also called avian influenza (or "bird flu"). H5N1 has a very high lethality rate in people, but infections and human-to-human spread are rare. The first known human infections were in 1997.

H7N9    A strain of influenza virus, more precisely known as avian influenza A(H7N9), that had previously been detected in birds and was first seen in people in 2013. Most people infected experience severe illness, with a high mortality rate, though person-to-person transmission is rare.

HHS    US Department of Health and Human Services—A cabinet-level department of the US federal government whose mission is to protect the health of all Americans by providing essential health and human services and contributing to advances in medicine, public health, and social services.

HIV/AIDS    human immunodeficiency virus/acquired immunodeficiency syndrome—AIDS is a chronic, potentially life-threatening condition caused by the HIV virus, which interferes with the immune system. The disease was first identified in the early 1980s and initially killed virtually everyone infected. Infected persons were (and sometimes to this day still are) subject to intense discrimination. It has infected and killed tens of millions of people globally, yet thanks to powerful advocacy by people with HIV/AIDS and the work of scientists, highly effective treatment (antiretroviral therapy) now exists and enables people who receive treatment to live a normal life span.

ICESCR    International Covenant on Economic, Social and Cultural Rights—This is the core UN treaty guaranteeing economic, social, and cultural rights, including the right to health, and defining governments' responsibilities for fulfilling these rights. It is part of the International Bill of Rights, along with the Universal Declaration of Human Rights and the International Covenant on Civil and Political Rights.

IHR    International Health Regulations—The member states of the WHO in 2005 adopted the latest version of this legally binding agreement, which significantly expanded the scope of earlier versions. Through the IHR, countries have agreed to measures to build their capacities to detect, assess, and report public health events. The agreement also gives WHO the authority to declare public health emergencies of international concern, and establishes a framework for national public health measures, including measures to protect against the spread of disease, that seek to protect public health while respecting human rights and not unnecessarily interfering with trade or travel.

IMF    International Monetary Fund—An intergovernmental organization of 189 countries that was created in the aftermath of World War II with the primary purpose of ensuring a stable international monetary system.

IP    intellectual property—A category of property that includes intangible creations of the human intellect and that the law protects from unauthorized use. Forms of intellectual property include copyrights, patents, trademarks, and trade secrets.

IPCC    Intergovernmental Panel on Climate Change—An international UN body that provides objective scientific information related to climate change. Its reports draw on scientific literature, with thousands of scientists contributing.

IRS    indoor residual spraying—A malaria control measure that involves spraying insecticide that lasts for an extended period of time ("residual") on the interior walls and other surfaces of homes to kill mosquitoes, in order to prevent malaria transmission.

ISR    International Sanitary Regulations (ISR)—Predecessors of the International Health Regulations, the member states of the WHO adopted the ISR in 1951 to provide a single set of rules to protect the world from the spread of plague, cholera, yellow fever, smallpox, typhus, and relapsing fever. The ISR consolidated twelve international sanitary conventions and related agreements, the first developed in 1892.

ITN    insecticide-treated bed net—Bed nets that have been treated with an insecticide that kills or repels mosquitoes. People use nets when sleeping to protect against mosquitoes.

JEE    joint external evaluation—Evaluations of countries' capacities to prevent, detect, and respond to public health risks, as required under the IHR. This is a voluntary process where, following a national assessment, an international team of experts evaluates a country's core public health capacities and develops a final report after discussing its findings with host country experts.

LAI    laboratory-acquired infection—Infections acquired through laboratory or laboratory-related activities.

LLIN    long-lasting insecticidal net—A type of bed net treated with insecticides that offer protection from malaria for at least three years. LLINs are one of the main strategies for protecting people from malaria.

LMICs    low- and middle-income countries—Countries classified as low- or lower-middle-income, or upper-middle-income countries by the World Bank. As of 2020, these included 138 countries with per capita incomes of up to $12,375.

MDR-TB     Multidrug-resistant tuberculosis—A form of tuberculosis infection caused by bacteria that are resistant to treatment with at least two of the main first-line medications for TB, isoniazid and rifampin.

MERS     Middle East respiratory syndrome—An infectious disease, caused by a coronavirus, that was first identified in Saudi Arabia in 2012.

MRSA     methicillin-resistant *Staphylococcus aureus*—A bacterium that is resistant to methicillin and other antibiotics. It is a major cause of health care–related infections, and is also transmissible in community settings.

NAM     National Academy of Medicine—One of the three components of the US National Academies of Sciences, Engineering, and Medicine, which operates under an 1863 charter from the US Congress for the National Academy of Sciences. NAM is a nonprofit organization that aims to provide authoritative scientific and policy advice on issues concerning human health. Until 2015, it was known as the Institute of Medicine.

NDCs     nationally determined contributions—Under the Paris Agreement on climate change, the goals that countries are required to set for themselves to progressively reduce their carbon emissions.

NGO     nongovernmental organizations—Nonprofit organizations that are independent of any government. They include organizations that advocate for a social or political cause and that provide services.

NIH     National Institutes of Health—A part of the US HHS and the main US government agency for conducting and supporting medical research. It includes twenty-seven institutes and centers that address different areas of health.

NSABB     National Science Advisory Board for Biosecurity—A panel of experts established in the US HHS that provides advice on biosecurity and dual-use research.

OIE     World Organisation for Animal Health—The intergovernmental organization responsible for improving animal health globally, including through sharing information and developing standards.

OIHP     Office International D'hygiène Publique—An organization whose responsibilities included overseeing the international sanitary conventions. Founded in 1907 and adopted into the World Health Organization when WHO was created.

PEF    Pandemic Emergency Financing Facility—The PEF, housed at the World Bank, provides funding to lower-income countries to respond to infectious disease outbreaks, particularly cross-border, large-scale outbreaks that have a risk of becoming pandemics.

PHEIC    public health emergency of international concern—A formal declaration by the WHO of an extraordinary event determined to constitute a public health risk to states outside the place of origin through international disease spread, potentially requiring an international response. The IHR provide WHO the authorities, and state parties the duties, to respond to a PHEIC.

PIP Framework    Pandemic Influenza Preparedness Framework—A non-binding international agreement, endorsed by the World Health Assembly, that has the dual aim of improving information sharing on influenza viruses with pandemic potential and increasing developing countries' access to vaccines and other lifesaving products during a pandemic.

R&D    research and development—Studies and other activities to create new or improved products or services, such as new medicines.

SARS    severe acute respiratory syndrome—An infectious disease caused by a coronavirus. After emerging in China, it led to a worldwide outbreak in 2003.

SARS-CoV-2    severe acute respiratory syndrome coronavirus 2—The virus that causes COVID-19, a coronavirus (CoV) with similarities to SARS.

SDGs    Sustainable Development Goals—United Nations member states adopted these seventeen goals, including one specifically on health and others closely connected to health, in 2015. Generally covering the period through 2030, these goals set the global sustainable development agenda for the next fifteen years. They aim to end poverty, ensure people's essential needs, protect the environment, and advance peace and prosperity.

STIs    sexually transmitted infections—Infections, which can be caused by viruses or bacteria, that can be transmitted via sexual activity. They include hepatitis B, herpes, HIV, and the human papilloma virus (all causes by viruses) and chlamydia, gonorrhea, and syphilis (all caused by bacteria).

TB  tuberculosis—An infectious disease caused by the bacterium *Mycobacterium tuberculosis,* which usually attacks the lungs and is spread through the air. It affects millions of people annually (10 million in 2018), killing more than a million (nearly 1.451 million in 2018).

TRIPS agreement  Trade-Related Intellectual Property Rights agreement—A binding treaty, developed through the World Trade Organization, that provides minimum standards that countries are supposed to adhere to in order to protect intellectual property. The agreement permits countries to take measures necessary to protect public health, and to grant licenses to patented products without authorization of the patent holder in certain circumstances.

UHC  universal health coverage—A system where all people have access to the health services and resources they need, when and where they need them, without financial hardship. It includes the full range of essential health care services, as well as basic public health necessities like clean water and sanitation.

UN  United Nations—The international organization that is the focal point of international law and cooperation. Founded in 1945 and currently comprising 193 member states, its central purposes include maintaining international peace and security, achieving international cooperation, and protecting human rights.

UNAIDS  Joint United Nations Programme on HIV and AIDS—A UN agency that was established in 1996 to coordinate UN work on HIV / AIDS, and now encompasses eleven co-sponsoring agencies. It leads global HIV / AIDS work through advocacy, strategic direction, coordination, and technical support, seeking to catalyze global action.

UNFCCC  United Nations Framework Convention on Climate Change—A 1992 international environmental treaty that set the goal of avoiding dangerous human-induced climate change. The Kyoto Protocol (1997) and Paris Agreement on climate change (2015) were protocols to the UNFCCC.

UNICEF  United Nations International Children's Emergency Fund—A UN agency is responsible for providing humanitarian and developmental aid to children worldwide.

VRE vancomycin-resistant *Enterococcus*—Bacteria that are resistant to the antibiotic vancomycin. VRE infections are a significant health care–associated infection in the United States, Europe, parts of Asia, and several countries in other regions. These bacteria are also resistant to a number of other antibiotics as well, making them very difficult to treat.

WHA World Health Assembly—The highest governing body of the World Health Organization. It is comprised of health ministers from all WHO member states, and meets annually, including to set policy, adopt agreements, and approve WHO's budget.

WHO World Health Organization—The specialized UN agency charged with being the directing and coordinating authority on international health, with the goal of enabling everyone to achieve the highest possible standard of health. This intergovernmental organization, whose constitution was adopted in 1946 and came into force in 1948, currently has 194 member states.

WTO World Trade Organization—An intergovernmental organization established in 1994 as a forum for negotiating international trade agreements and settling trade disputes. It currently has 164 member states.

XDR-TB extensively drug-resistant tuberculosis—A type of multidrug-resistant TB that is resistant to isoniazid and rifampin, as well as to fluoroquinolone and injectable second-line drugs. Treatment is successful in only about one-third of cases.

YF yellow fever—An ancient disease caused by a virus that is spread through mosquito bites. People with yellow fever develop a fever, and some then develop more serious symptoms including jaundice, hence the disease's name. The disease can be deadly for people with these more serious symptoms, which also include deteriorating kidney and liver function and significant bleeding.

ZIKV Zika virus—A virus transmitted by mosquitoes that causes a disease, Zika, that came to global attention with an outbreak that began in Brazil in 2015. People with the disease generally have no or only mild symptoms, but infections that occur during pregnancy can cause birth defects, including microcephaly, a potentially fatal congenital brain condition.

# GLOBAL HEALTH SECURITY

# Introduction

## The Great Coronavirus Pandemic of 2020

**We may never fully understand** the exact origins of the Great Coronavirus Pandemic of 2020, but here is the prevailing theory. In early December 2019, probably even earlier, a resident of Wuhan, China, visited the Huanan live seafood and animal market and became infected by a novel coronavirus that had "jumped" species. The World Health Organization (WHO) later classified this microbe as severe acute respiratory syndrome coronavirus 2 (SARS-CoV-2), which causes coronavirus disease 2019 (COVID-19).[1] SARS-CoV-2 is a beta-coronavirus like MERS-CoV and SARS-CoV, which originates in bats.[2] A pangolin, or scaly anteater, might have been the intermediary host, the "missing link."

Whatever the zoonotic origin, this microscopic virus began to rapidly circulate in Wuhan City and the rest of Hubei Province, silently passing from person to person before beginning a relentless march across the globe. SARS-CoV-2 is almost the perfect biological specimen. It is ruthlessly efficient, and highly contagious. SARS-CoV-2 doesn't cause symptoms right away and asymptomatic carriers can transmit the virus, preventing us from knowing if the person sitting next to us is infected. The case fatality rate for COVID-19 has varied widely in different parts of the globe, and has evolved, usually lessening, as treatments become better and health workers better understand the most effective care. But it is highly lethal, especially in the elderly and vulnerable. Unlike SARS, MERS, or Ebola, though, SARS-CoV-2 does not kill most of its hosts.[3] The combination of rapid asymptomatic spread, complex and serious symptomology, and a moderate death rate make the virus a formidable foe.

The virus is also an unpredictable foe. Many people barely notice COVID-19, and many experience only mild symptoms at most. For others it is devastating and incapacitates multiple bodily functions, not just respiration (breathing), but also muscular, gastrointestinal, and the senses of taste and smell.[4] It can cause so-called "long-COVID"—enduring debilitating symptoms like breathlessness, persistent cough, joint and muscle pain, and chronic fatigue. Most of the healthy and young are spared serious symptoms, but not all. Young children rarely fall ill from it, yet some can develop multisystem inflammation. And this foe strikes so unfairly, preying on the vulnerable—the elderly, people with chronic health conditions, migrants, racial/ethnic minorities, and the poor.

Like most viruses circulating in a large population, such as with HIV and influenza viruses, SARS-CoV-2 has undergone genetic mutations. In other words, viruses adapt to survive, seeking to evade our defenses.[5] One mutation identified by the United Kingdom in December 2020 appeared significant, making the virus more transmissible. South Africa identified a similar genetic variant around the same time, and Brazil identified another at the end of January 2021. All of these variants, and more, spread to other countries and regions. Most SARS-CoV-2 mutations are harmless, but others can make the virus more transmissible, more pathogenic, or even make vaccines less effective.

We don't have clarity about the exact timing, but the scale and speed of the global spread of SARS-CoV-2 has been staggering. COVID-19 swept through mainland China and by early to mid January 2020 began its relentless march through Asia (e.g., South Korea, Japan, Singapore, Hong Kong, and Taiwan).[6] Barely a month later, the disease arrived in force in Europe (with Italy, Spain, and the United Kingdom experiencing some of the highest levels of infection and death). From Asia and Europe it spread to the United States, which became the global epicenter by the spring of 2020 and would later experience a massive surge in the fall and winter. COVID-19 also affected much of Latin America, notably Brazil and Mexico. The virus swept through Africa, the Indian subcontinent, the Middle East, and most of the rest of the world.

Within months a microscopic novel coronavirus traveled from a wet market in central China to have devastating effects on every continent except Antarctica. And in December 2020, a COVID-19 outbreak on a Chilean Antarctic research station meant that the virus had engulfed the entire planet.

We can only stand in awe that nature is capable of creating a microbe that is invisible to the naked eye and can jump from a single animal to a single human being, and then be propelled worldwide to billions of people within months.

And so began the Great Coronavirus Pandemic of 2020. Before COVID-19 emerged, I had written in Chapter 1 of this book that a novel virus would one day "jump" species from an animal to a human, becoming rapidly transmissible and highly pathogenic. This novel virus would cross oceans and borders to become a pandemic catching the world unprepared. I imagined how a virus would overwhelm health systems, with devastating health, social, and economic impacts on civilizations. In this pandemic, the vast bulk of humanity lived, and many people died, in the reality of a pandemic that caught the world utterly unprepared. Even though we knew this kind of event was coming, we still failed to prepare and respond. Why?

## Social and Economic Devastation

The COVID-19 pandemic is first and foremost a global health crisis, but its social and economic devastation has been just as consequential. COVID-19 changed the world and transformed the lives of nearly everyone on Earth.

Perhaps the most visible personal impact is what we *didn't* see: crowded streets, family celebrations, social gatherings, and people busily shopping or enjoying themselves at restaurants, concerts, and movie theaters. Borders were shut and airlines stopped flying to many parts of the world. The implementation of "social distancing" began where the virus originated in China, where the government imposed a *cordon sanitaire* (a guarded area where no one may enter or leave) in Wuhan and other cities in Hubei on January 23, commonly referred to as the "Wuhan lockdown." The unprecedented action kept 57 million people confined to their homes.[7] The sheer scale of the lockdown was beyond anything we could have imagined, but the director-general of WHO commended China for decisive action, "unprecedented in public health history."[8] Yet later investigations revealed that SARS-CoV-2 was likely circulating in Wuhan hospitals for several weeks or even months before the lockdown.[9]

The Wuhan lockdown was enforced through intrusive surveillance and social control, almost uniquely possible in China—including smartphone location tracking and restricting movement, citizen informers enforcing stay-at-home orders, and armed police patrolling the city.[10] China forcibly removed thousands of infected or exposed people to isolation centers. It wasn't until April 8 that China finally lifted the restrictions, after the people of Wuhan had experienced more than two months of hardship, social deprivation, and loneliness.

After the lockdown, COVID-19 cases dropped dramatically in Hubei Province and throughout mainland China. They stayed low throughout the pandemic. Would China's centralized authoritarian governance become a global model? It would be a mistake to conclude that ruthless efficiency does not have a high cost. China suppressed independent scientists, journalists, and civil society, causing critical delays in reporting and responding to the novel coronavirus. In early December 2019, weeks before China's initial report to WHO, Dr. Li Wenliang posted in a group chat with other medics about patients exhibiting a SARS-like illness.[11] Chinese authorities reprimanded him for "spreading rumors." He became a global symbol as a heroic whistleblower when he later died of COVID-19.

Liberal democracies hardened through experience with SARS or MERS fared well using traditional public health tools: widespread testing, contact tracing, isolation/quarantine, and social distancing (a protocol called Test/Trace/Separate). Many Asian nations (e.g., South Korea, Taiwan, Singapore) avoided prolonged lockdowns by acting early and aggressively. Island nations, like Australia and New Zealand, performed particularly well. Highly populated federalist jurisdictions in the heart of Europe, like Germany, locked down early, which suppressed transmission, enabling some semblance of normality. Yet even in Germany, the virus came roaring back in the winter of 2020.

Many countries' COVID-19 responses, however, were highly dysfunctional, as if they hadn't anticipated a catastrophic biological event. Rich nations with world-class scientists and health systems seemed utterly unprepared. In Europe, COVID-19 overwhelmed countries like Italy, Spain, France, and the United Kingdom. But COVID-19 hit hardest in the world's richest nation, the United States, home to public health treasures like the National Institutes of Health (NIH) and the Centers for Disease Control and Prevention (CDC). When comparing what worked and what didn't, there is one key lesson: Invest/Prepare/Prevent. And use science as the singular guide to action.

In the spring of 2020 about half of the world's population was locked down under some kind of restrictive order. The Wuhan lockdown was unprecedented, and yet it was surpassed in sheer scale by India, which ordered 1.3

billion people to shelter in place.[12] Iconic cities from London, Milan, and Paris to Rio de Janeiro and Mexico City locked down, repeatedly. In the United States, three out of every four residents were under some form of lockdown at the height of the pandemic. With schools closing in most countries, the global system for educating children virtually collapsed, with nearly 90 percent of the world's children (over 1.5 billion) unable to attend school.[13] The education achievement gaps exploded during the pandemic, with the poor left behind. Universities, the drivers of societal innovation, shifted to online classes where possible. As COVID-19 cases soared again in the fall of 2020, governments reinstated lockdowns across regions like Europe and the Asia Pacific, desperate to regain control of the virus. Yet cases continued to climb, and many areas braced for a dark winter.

### The "New Normal": Social, Cultural Shifts

It was not only public health orders that shifted human behaviors. The coronavirus made people fearful, as we watched patients struggling for breath in intensive care units. We worried also about contracting and then transmitting the virus to vulnerable loved ones. A "new normal" arrived where many of us hesitated to step outside our homes, forwent shaking hands or hugging, wore masks to the grocery store, stocked up on necessities like toilet paper, and stood several feet apart in checkout lines. We stopped going to restaurants, malls, theaters, and sports events. Traveling all but shut down. The Olympic committee postponed Tokyo 2020, the first time the Olympics were delayed since World War II. Tokyo 2021 proceeded but without fans from abroad.

Pandemics can bring out the best, and the worst, in humankind. The COVID-19 pandemic spurred many of us to look out for the most vulnerable, through both public and private initiatives, to combat hunger, illness, and even loneliness. But the fear of the pandemic also found roots in misinformation spread by traditional and social media, leading to dangerous behaviors like hoarding supplies, placing blame, and discriminating against people of Asian descent. Countries too turned on one another, casting blame on one another.

### Economies and Livelihoods

The economic impact of COVID-19 is likely to be long and intense. Macroeconomic forecasts estimated global GDP declines of 4.9 percent in 2020, with the United States and Eurozone contracting 8.0 percent and 10.2 percent, respectively.[14] However, macroeconomic measures don't begin to convey the compound hardships among the poor.[15] The US unemployment rate registered at nearly 15 percent in April 2020, the highest level since the Great Depression.[16] It clawed back many of the losses in employment, but agonizingly slowly.

The US and Europe were able, at least, to pass trillion-dollar stimulus plans, and central banks also intervened. But low- and middle-income countries could not simply print money and were already burdened with enormous foreign debt. Lockdowns and a loss of remittances pushed hundreds of millions of people into extreme poverty.[17] The number of people experiencing acute hunger was projected to double.[18] Higher-income countries would need to provide up to a trillion dollars to build health systems and assist those afflicted by the virus and harmed by its economic consequences.

## The Health System: "Flattening the Curve"

Each night in cities around the globe, people tethered to their homes sang songs, applauded, and rang bells for the heroes of the COVID-19 pandemic: educators, social workers, grocery store employees, delivery personnel, and sanitation workers, and most importantly, health workers. Like so many other epidemics, health workers risked their lives caring for COVID-19 patients, often without adequate personal protective equipment (PPE), like N95 masks, goggles, gloves, and gowns.[19] And many essential medical resources, including test kits, ventilators, and intensive care beds, were in short supply. Shortages were most acute in lower-income nations, but even in the world's richest countries, many health workers went unprotected.

We came to understand the term "flatten the curve"—a phrase that became commonplace, the idea of keeping the daily number of new cases at manageable levels, even if the total number of cases remained about the same over time. The point of this was to ensure that health systems could effectively manage the influx of patients from COVID-19 on top of their routine patients. But across the globe, as countries each day experienced tens of thousands of new COVID-19 cases and thousands of deaths, the path toward flattening the curve was often a devastating sharp rise in cases, often beyond the capacity of health systems to keep up.

Hospitals were overwhelmed or at the brink of collapse. In Italy, Spain, and New York City, hospitals' intensive care units were stretched beyond their maximum capacities. In the face of critical shortages, doctors and nurses were forced to make life-or-death treatment decisions. Many jurisdictions shifted to so-called crisis standards of care, where priorities are set for which patients can receive life-saving treatments. So many died. Morgues and crematoriums were also overwhelmed, struggling to manage the number of bodies. In some cities, like Sao Paolo, we saw images of hastily made graves with the bodies of those who had died from COVID-19.

## Global Solidary: WHO Caught in a Geopolitical Power Struggle

Global solidarity unraveled as well. WHO became a major casualty, caught in the middle of a geopolitical power struggle between the world's two most powerful nations. China promoted conspiracy theories that the US military had created the coronavirus. The United States countered that SARS-CoV-2 was released from the Wuhan Institute of Virology. (Scientists have concluded that there is very high likelihood the virus was naturally occurring, with a zoonotic origin.)

President Donald Trump accused China of hiding the virus's origins and failing to promptly notify the world.[20] He accused WHO of siding with China and failing to investigate thoroughly and report transparently. For the first time in history, in May 2020 the meeting of the World Health Assembly (WHA) took place virtually. It was also devoted to a single issue, the pandemic.[21] Chinese President Xi Jinping called for unity, donating $2 billion to the global response, whereas President Trump did not attend the meeting at all. He sent a long letter to the director-general of WHO, Tedros Adhanom Ghebreyesus, threatening to withdraw US funding and even US membership if WHO did not undertake vaguely specified reforms.[22] In July 2020 President Trump submitted formal notice that the United States would end its relationship with WHO. That move was reversed by President Biden on his first day in office.

The WHA's most consequential decision was to support an independent inquiry into the COVID-19 response.[23] In September the director-general appointed a panel to review WHO's coordination of the COVID-19 response, saying the panel would have full access to internal UN agency documents. Former Liberian president Ellen Johnson Sirleaf and former New Zealand prime minister Helen Clark co-chaired the panel.

By November 2020, WHO released a plan to investigate the origins of the pandemic, which the United States quickly condemned as lacking transparency.

Western governments raised concerns that China would not grant WHO scientists unimpeded access to vital sources of information. It wasn't until January 2021 (a full year after the pandemic started) that a team of ten international scientists traveled to Wuhan to investigate the origins of COVID-19. On February 9, 2021, WHO concluded that the initial outbreak in Wuhan was naturally occurring (rather than laboratory-derived), but also gave credence to the hypothesis that the virus could have arrived in Wuhan from a transnational animal shipment. Following the Wuhan investigation, there still remains uncertainty about the scope of WHO's access to key geographic locations, complete data, and open discussions with Chinese health workers and scientists. This was a moment in human history of deep consequence, and yet it will likely remain shrouded in mystery.

It all remains a history still in the making. We do not know when the COVID-19 pandemic will finally end, or how many lives will be lost before it does. It is uncertain when—or even if—life will resume as it was before the outbreak. We do not know which governments will ultimately put politics aside to unite. We need a robust global health leader like WHO; therefore, giving it ample powers, funding, and political support will be crucial to global health.

## Human Ingenuity and the Race for a COVID-19 Vaccine

There is one unparalleled human achievement that emerged from the pandemic. I spoke earlier about feeling awe at nature's ability to unleash a microscopic pathogen that would affect virtually every person on the planet. But that microbe has been met with an equally awe-inspiring force—human ingenuity. In less than a year, the world witnessed breathtaking scientific achievements. Scientists mapped the entire genomic sequence of the virus, explained the modes of transmission, developed accurate diagnostic tests, and deployed therapeutic interventions like antiviral medications, immune-based therapies, and adjunctive therapies.

But the singular scientific achievement was the development of safe and efficacious vaccines. By March 2021, researchers were testing seventy-one vaccines in human clinical trials, with twenty having reached the final Phase 3 trial stage. China, Russia, and the United Arab Emirates authorized emergency use of Chinese and Russian vaccines in mid/late 2020. Stringent regulatory agencies in Canada, the European Union, the United Kingdom, and the United States all granted emergency authorization for two messenger RNA (mRNA) vaccines in December 2020. Both the Pfizer/BioNTech and the Moderna mRNA vaccines were found to be up to 95 percent efficacious in preventing symptomatic disease. More immunizations were headed toward regulatory approval in early 2021, including adenovirus vaccines from AstraZeneca/Oxford University and Johnson & Johnson.

In the United States, an ambitious public/private vaccine partnership called Operation Warp Speed[24] propelled development of safe and efficacious vaccines. The task facing the United States and the rest of the world was to smoothly roll out mass vaccination campaigns amid supply shortages, vaccine hesitancy, and huge logistical hurdles. The early vaccines were two-dose, and the Pfizer/BioNTech vaccine requires storage in arctic temperatures of −70°C. The United States and much of the world had to grapple with how to equitably and efficiently distribute scarce vaccine supplies, with most prioritizing health workers and nursing home residents, followed by the elderly and the most vulnerable.

And beyond domestic allocation, it became evident right from the start that low- and middle-income countries would be left behind when it came to lifesaving vaccines. WHO, Gavi, the Vaccine Alliance, and the Coalition for Epidemic Preparedness Innovations (CEPI) launched the COVAX Facility, designed to make vaccines affordable and accessible in low-income countries. But rich countries quickly bought up advance vaccine supplies, threatening the success of COVAX. French president Emmanuel Macron warned of a "two-speed world," while South Africa's government viewed those rich-country deals as creating "vaccine apartheid."[25] Dr. Tedros called the inequities a "catastrophic moral failure." As a result, lower-income nations may not be able to vaccinate their entire populations for years, perhaps not until 2024, whereas high-income countries might return to near normal by the end of 2021. The sense of injustice is unmistakable, with the poor once again being left far behind.

As COVID-19 rages on, the world remains vulnerable to other global health threats. We don't know the exact pathogen or the timing, but we do know that another pandemic is coming. And because we cannot know the answer, we must prepare for all health hazards.

### No Time to Lose: Preparing for Threats beyond COVID-19

This book will span the range of infectious disease threats, primarily novel and fast-moving pathogens like SARS-CoV-2. We know that bats harbor a host of viruses, including coronaviruses. From novel influenza viruses to

Ebola viruses, most emerging infectious diseases have zoonotic origins. This book will also look at growing threats, from humanity's biggest killer, mosquitoes, to a host of infections spread human-to-human.

And I will cover threats of modernity, ones that involve ancient pathogenic killers but are new to, or amplified in, our era. These include the risks of bioterrorism and accidental release of pathogens from laboratories; antimicrobial resistance, as microbes evolve to elude our treatments; and the climate crisis. As the planet warms, it brings a plethora of dangers, including expanded ranges of pathogens and conditions ripe for the spread of waterborne diseases.

I then turn to key elements of our response, from the role of international institutions and legal frameworks to the importance of strengthened health systems and accelerating research and development of vaccines and medicines to protect and treat us. COVID-19 has highlighted all the major challenges of mounting a robust national and global response to disease threats. The leading global health institution, WHO, has been sidelined and castigated. Legal frameworks, such as the International Health Regulations (IHR), have not worked well as countries have simply disregarded their norms. Countries have at times been reluctant to share critical biological information, including virus samples and genetic sequencing data. The WHO's Pandemic Influenza Preparedness (PIP) Framework was irrelevant to the COVID-19 pandemic because it fails to even apply to coronaviruses. And the preparedness and resilience of health systems have been tested. Even the most sophisticated health systems in Europe and the United States were unable to cope well.

This book offers a new paradigm for preparing for pandemic threats on a global level. Instead of narrow, reactive silos of national health policy and aid, global health security requires sustained economic investment, robust international institutions, resilient national health systems, targeted research and development, and effective risk communication with affected populations. We must guide future action with values that include cooperative action, shared responsibility, equity, and fairness. We must agree to global norms that will be respected and enforced. And above all, preparedness requires sustained financial investments and political will, both of which are in short supply.

## A Blueprint for a More Secure Future

This book offers a blueprint for a more secure world, which includes four major action agendas.

### 1. National Health Systems at the Foundation

Robust national health systems are the foundation for a safer world. The international community is only as secure as its weakest link, so strong and resilient health systems are required in every country. The IHR—a binding treaty—requires all 196 states parties to develop "core" health system capacities: to rapidly detect, report, and respond to novel outbreaks. Key capacities include surveillance, laboratories, a health workforce, and medical countermeasures. Yet most countries have not fulfilled their legal obligations under the regulations. The world remains vulnerable because many, if not most, countries cannot be relied upon to quickly detect and report a novel infectious disease. As the COVID-19 pandemic has demonstrated, delays in detection and notification can prove deadly. With each passing day, a novel pathogen will spread—possibly beyond national borders—and will be harder to contain. At a certain point, keeping an outbreak under control becomes nearly impossible.

What's required is an independent global monitoring mechanism of outbreaks and strong, system-wide, in-depth tracking and assessment of outbreak management efforts. For example, the Economist Intelligence Unit, with partners, has developed the Global Health Security Index to assess a country's technical, financial, socioeconomic, and political capabilities to prevent, detect, and rapidly respond to epidemic threats.[26] A further illustration is the National Academy of Sciences' Framework for Monitoring Pandemic Preparedness and Global Health Security.[27]

### 2. The World Health Organization at the Apex

If national health systems are the foundation for global health security, at the apex is an empowered World Health Organization, along with other international organizations. WHO's Constitution designates WHO as the lead agency for global health, charged with directing and coordinating the international response, especially in health emergencies. The COVID-19 pandemic revealed deep structural problems, including WHO's reliance on states' largely voluntary funding and cooperation, that can constrain WHO from putting health and science ahead of politics. Perhaps WHO's most visible flaw was not having the power to independently verify China's reporting. In the early days, China blocked WHO from entering the country to objectively investigate the pandemic's origins and likely trajectory. As mentioned earlier, WHO's investigation of the virus's origins did not even begin until a full year after the first report of a novel coronavirus circulating in Wuhan, China.

Even before COVID-19, the West African Ebola epidemic (2013–2016) revealed deep flaws in WHO's ability to lead and coordinate a coherent international response. Its delays, dysfunctional emergency response, and poor communication and coordination allowed the outbreak to spin out of control. By the time another Ebola outbreak emerged in the Democratic Republic of Congo (2018–2020), the agency performed far better, even though its staff were impeded by political violence and community distrust. Despite major post-Ebola reforms, WHO's budget is still wholly incommensurate with its global mandate, and its governance remains antiquated. A clear governing framework and leadership are needed to ensure coherent efforts and a functional global system.

### 3. Research and Development for Top-Priority Medical Countermeasures

Resilient health systems and an empowered WHO, while essential, still require modern medical tools to fight epidemics. Developing an armory of diagnostics, vaccines, and medicines to prevent, identify, and treat novel infections requires a new strategy for research and development (R&D). R&D needs to start long before an epidemic so that clinical trials or emergency deployment can begin swiftly. At present, pharmaceutical companies rarely invest in technologies to counter novel pathogens that break out suddenly and without warning. Safe and effective vaccines, for example, can take ten years to develop.

WHO is working on "platform" technologies to counter top-priority pathogens, so that clinical trials can be launched at the first signs of an outbreak. CEPI is using an innovative funding model to fund early vaccine R&D. It has coordinated with WHO in the research and development of a COVID-19 vaccine, and in March 2020 it issued an urgent call for $2 billion to support these efforts.[28] Despite a promising start, sustainable funding and incentives for high-priority research are well below the level needed to stay a step ahead of fast-moving epidemics.

And yet, the world can create the most remarkable vaccines and treatments when there is the political will. Even though successful vaccines often take years, if not decades, to develop, COVID-19 vaccines were created in record time. The competition to develop a COVID-19 vaccine resembled the "race to the moon," pitting political rivals against one another. It has been a huge biotechnological and logistical undertaking, but one with enormous payoffs for human health.

## 4. A "Peace" Dividend

Virtually every global health expert has urged sustained investments in national health systems, WHO capacities, and research and development. This not only is wise as a guarantor against wide-scale illness and death, but also promises economic benefits. Prevention is far more efficient than stemming out-of-control epidemics. The World Bank estimates that investing in pandemic preparedness for zoonotic diseases alone could yield between $11.6 and $26.6 billion in global benefit. The benefits may even be far higher, considering that the United States alone has appropriated trillions of dollars toward the COVID-19 response. Furthermore, countries with reduced burdens of devastating diseases, such as HIV/AIDS, tuberculosis, and malaria, have more robust economic growth—a more productive workforce, enhanced consumer spending, and fewer demands on health and social services.[29] Healthy and safe nations are more stable and secure.

What level of economic investment is required to ramp up preparedness? In 2012 the World Bank estimated that $1.9 to $3.4 billion was required to upgrade zoonotic disease prevention and control systems in developing countries to meet World Organisation for Animal Health (OIE) and WHO standards. In 2016 the Commission on a Global Health Risk Framework proposed what I call a "peace" or "security" dividend—an incremental additional investment of approximately $4.5 billion per year. This would include:

- $3.4 billion for upgrading national pandemic preparedness capacities;
- $1 billion for R&D for vaccines, therapies, diagnostics, personal protective equipment, and instruments to combat emerging infectious diseases; and
- $130–$155 million for the WHO Contingency Fund for Emergencies, World Bank Pandemic Emergency Financing Facility, and proposed WHO Center for Health Emergency Preparedness and Response. (As we will see in Chapter 7, actual funding needs for the Contingency Fund for Emergencies and the Pandemic Emergency Financing Facility are higher. WHO did not create the proposed Center, but it did establish a Health Emergencies Programme.)

Just 60 cents per person per annum would buy the world far greater security.[30] The enormous economic toll of the COVID-19 response might have been largely avoided through far smaller investments in prevention and preparedness.

The blueprint and ideas presented in this book are based on my thirty years of experience in global health, including directing the WHO Collaborating Center on National and Global Health Law and serving on two global commissions evaluating the Ebola response in West Africa. I've been privileged to serve on key WHO expert committees over the years, including on smallpox, pandemic influenza, viral genomic sequencing, and universal health coverage. The blueprint I offer also follows a strong consensus in the global health community of the importance of preparedness, with robust national health systems, innovative research and development, and sound global health leadership and governance.

Injecting new urgency into global health security to make progress in each of the four global health security action areas will require action from all sectors. I have therefore written this book for a diverse readership. It aims to inform and motivate policymakers so that national and global norms are based on strong scientific evidence and good values. I also hope to reach scholars, advocates, and students who are interested in understanding the pressing threats to global health security and how the world needs to respond to make us all safer.

The world's future depends on well-informed leaders and policymakers, and the voters who elect them. Global health security depends on ongoing evaluation of what works and what doesn't, which values are crucial (equity and justice) and which are harmful (stigma and blame). It requires an empowered civil society that will insist on the truth and hold leaders to account. In this book, I hope to arm all these key actors with the knowledge and ideas they need to advocate for change.

For teachers and students of global health security, this book distills key challenges in pandemic preparedness and response and provides an understanding of the responses required. For policymakers in national governments and international institutions, it offers a roadmap for future action and investment. For civil society activists and for all informed citizens, this book provides a valuable foundation for understanding impending threats to global health security and determining how best to engage, ranging from policies to advocate for to demanding that global health security be placed higher on the political agenda.

We turn next to the major threats before us.

# PART I

# GROWING THREATS

# CHAPTER I

# The Impending Threat

**We are at a historic crossroads** in global health security. Our scientific tools to protect us—vaccines and antiviral medications—have never been more potent. And yet, as the COVID-19 pandemic painfully showed, the world is ill-prepared to respond effectively to infectious disease threats. In fact, much about today's world—congested cities, mass travel, and close contact with animals—enhances the dangers pathogens pose. Climate change is drastically altering the world's habitats, so human beings are more likely than ever to encounter animals that carry exotic microbes.

Consider how a virus circulating among bats took a zoonotic leap to infect one human, before spreading to millions and taking countless millions of lives around the globe within just months.[1] Models of other potential pathogens predict even worse outcomes: the Institute for Disease Modeling simulated a modern-day, lethal airborne and highly contagious pathogen, like the 1918 Spanish Flu, and found that nearly 33 million deaths worldwide would occur in just six months.[2]

Despite this bleak prognosis, today we are situated better than ever to respond. The delay in detecting and reporting early COVID-19 cases (see Chapter 2) forced countries and global institutions to be reactive—trying in vain to separate infected persons from the population, whether through quarantines, cordons sanitaires, social distancing rules, business closures, or travel restrictions.[3] Yet it need not have been this way, as we have the biomedical tools available to be proactive.

Public health organizations are capable of sophisticated, even if imperfect, surveillance—meticulous tracking and monitoring of infections worldwide. Visit the emergency operations center of the US Centers for Disease Control and Prevention (CDC)—real-time data is tracked on novel infections in every corner of the globe. Similarly, WHO detects around 3,000 signals a month. While very few ever pose a threat, some do and could become mass killers.[4] We can now see these threats as they unfold.

New therapeutic agents and technologies allow scientists to ever more rapidly identify pathogens' weaknesses and develop medical countermeasures. Within weeks after the first reported cases in Wuhan, Chinese scientists sequenced the entire genome of the coronavirus, sharing it with scientists around the world. New methods, such as the gene-editing CRISPR (clustered regularly interspaced short palindromic repeats) technology, hold great promise for developing vaccines and treatments, as well as innovative methods of stemming disease vectors, such as reducing mosquito populations.[5]

Biomedical countermeasures have rendered dreaded pestilences largely relics of the past. WHO eradicated smallpox in 1980 and is on its way to doing the same for polio. WHO resolution WHA66.12 could signal the end of neglected tropical diseases, such as dracunculiasis (guinea-worm), leishmaniasis, and human African trypanosomiasis (sleeping sickness).[6] Through vaccines, modern medicines, and controlling mosquito populations, dangerous diseases like yellow fever and malaria can be prevented.

Scientists quickly brought to market an effective vaccine for influenza A (H1N1) during the 2009 pandemic and are developing a Zika vaccine in the aftermath of the 2016–2017 epidemic in the Americas.[7] In 2018 WHO deployed a "ring" vaccination strategy to halt the spread of a disconcerting Ebola outbreak in the Democratic Republic of Congo (DRC). In 2019, Ebola virus disease (EVD) re-emerged in the war-torn Eastern Congo and became the second largest Ebola epidemic in history, but we now have a highly effective vaccine and new ways to treat patients with EVD. The 2019 COVID-19 outbreak generated vaccine development at an unprecedented speed. On March 16, 2020, the first COVID-19 vaccine candidate entered human clinical testing, just over two months after the virus's genomic sequence was released, and vaccines were approved for emergency use by multiple countries within a year.[8]

Along with medical countermeasures, we have robust institutions, like the US CDC and WHO, that have actively engaged in epidemic response.

WHO's Health Emergencies Programme supports the Global Outbreak Alert and Response Network (GOARN), a global network of institutions that respond to potential public health emergencies of international concern. The CDC's Global Rapid Response Team has a surge capacity of more than 400 public health experts to respond to outbreaks wherever they occur.[9]

Despite these gains, the COVID-19 pandemic has shown that the global hazard level is extraordinarily high. Patterns and trends of modern life counter these momentous scientific advances. While globalization and economic development bring enormous social benefits, there are also hidden costs: Hypercrowded cities, rapid air travel, mass migrations, and intense human / animal interchange alter how pathogens emerge and colonize, amplifying the risk and severity of outbreaks. Conflict zones unravel health systems and spur exoduses, as has happened in Syria, Yemen, and the DRC. The expansion of human populations into new geographic areas, climate change, deforestation, intensive farming, and food production shift the web of interactions between humans, animals, and the planet as never before. We need to recognize these diverse drivers of disease, and plan and respond accordingly.

### Rising Populations, Megacities, and the Loss of Natural Habitats

A major feature of modern human civilization is an ever-increasing population, migrating en masse to cities. In 2007, for the first time in history, more of the world's population lived in urban areas than in rural areas, with Africa and Asia urbanizing faster than any other regions.[10] Ever greater urbanization is the clear trajectory for the twenty-first century.

In crowded cities, dense populations of humans and animals often live in close proximity, fueling transmission of novel viruses that "jump" from animals to humans, and then human-to-human. In late 2019, COVID-19 emerged when a virus circulating among bats evolved to become transmissible between humans, and through another animal intermediary, the virus jumped to a person in a wet market (a live animal market) in Wuhan, in China's Hubei Province. SARS, MERS, and Ebola all started under similar circumstances.

Natural habitats are lost through deforestation and extractive industries, like logging or mining, to ensure vast populations have food, potable water, and abundant energy. Dams, irrigation, and deforestation increase vector-borne diseases such as malaria and Rift Valley fever. "Backyard" chicken flocks, wet markets, and intense animal husbandry (poultry, pigs, cows) create troubling risks of zoonotic leaps to humans, such as avian influenzas H5N5 and H7N9. As domesticated animals infect wild birds (and vice versa), microbes travel on avian transcontinental migration routes.[11] The threat from zoonotic diseases cannot be overstated, constituting the majority (over 60 percent) of emerging infectious diseases.[12]

Although there is no single cause of a zoonotic leap, these factors can combine to create a perfect storm for novel infections. COVID-19 likely stemmed from a wet market, where humans and animals that would never meet in the wild come into close contact. The rise in Ebola outbreaks since 1994 is associated with drastic changes in forest ecosystems in tropical Africa, and "extensive deforestation and human activities in the depth of the forests may have promoted direct or indirect contact between humans and a natural reservoir of the virus."[13] The "index" case of the West African epidemic was most likely a young boy having eaten bush meat—Ebola thus being a case of pestilence literally emerging from the jungle.

## Rapid Travel and Trade

Globalization propels travel and trade, as microbes span the globe at vast speed. Through globalized trade, infected animals transmit zoonotic diseases to new reaches. In 2001, diseased animals spread foot-and-mouth disease from the United Kingdom to Ireland and the Netherlands, resulting in billions of dollars in economic losses.[14] Likewise, the rise of affordable air travel has resulted in the increased potential for a pathogen to transmit through an unsuspecting host, as it is possible to travel anywhere in the world within twenty-four hours. Meanwhile, the world is undergoing a historic migration crisis, as refugees and asylum seekers flood across borders from conflict zones. Not since World War II has the world seen this level of forced migration, as people fleeing political and economic meltdown in Venezuela and conflicts from South Sudan to Syria to Afghanistan.[15]

Consider these cases: In January 2020, China imposed a mass cordon sanitaire of 60 million people in Hubei Province—the epicenter of the COVID-19 epidemic—but in the weeks before the lockdown, 5 million travelers had left for elsewhere in China and international destinations;[16] by early 2020,

COVID-19 had spread to every continent but Antarctica. In 2015–2016, the continental United States reported approximately 5,500 travel-related cases of Zika coming from the Caribbean and Latin America, compared to fewer than 300 locally transmitted cases.[17] In May 2015 a man returning from travel to the Middle East introduced MERS to South Korea, resulting in three dozen deaths, ultimately leading to the fall of the government. Mexico reported the first cases of novel influenza A (H1N1) in April 2009;[18] by June 11, WHO had raised the alert level to a full-blown pandemic, and nine weeks after the first reported case, every WHO region reported cases of H1N1. Mass travel will continue to rapidly propel disease, underlining the need to enhance global health security.

## Climate Change

Changes in climate and the environment can also unleash pathogens. Increased rainfalls multiply mosquito breeding grounds and overwhelm sanitation systems.[19] Global warming expands the geographic range of disease vectors, prominently mosquitoes, and enables them and the diseases they carry to spread to new regions, subjecting previously unexposed populations to infections, such as Chikungunya, dengue, and Zika. Warmer temperatures also affect the life cycles of certain pathogens. Waterborne diseases, such as cholera, become harder to fight with rising temperatures and flooding. In 2019, Yemen, a country ravaged by war and on the brink of famine, faced the worst cholera outbreak in the world. United Nations relief workers brought cholera to Haiti in 2010, and the nation is still in the grips of an unrelenting epidemic.[20]

Arctic thawing from climate change could release long-dormant bacteria and viruses that have been trapped in ice and permafrost for millennia and for which humans have no immunity. In August 2016 in the Yamal Peninsula within the Arctic Circle, a twelve-year-old boy died, and at least twenty people were hospitalized, after being infected by anthrax. A historic heat wave that summer had thawed a long-dead reindeer infected with anthrax bacteria, leading to this rare anthrax outbreak.[21] There are even more worrying possibilities. Anthrax outbreaks occur occasionally, primarily from cows, goats, and other herbivorous mammals.[22] Smallpox was eradicated more than four decades ago, but could it return as warming exposes the corpses of people who died in a smallpox epidemic in Siberia more than a century ago?[23]

## Fragile States

Climate change, which has been unleashing nature's fury in the form of historic hurricanes, droughts, and other cataclysmic weather events, is one of many factors affecting states' stability. The world recently experienced the worst humanitarian crisis since World War II, with 20 million people facing starvation and famine in northeastern Nigeria, South Sudan, Somalia, and Yemen. Where states collapse or cannot govern, basic public health safeguards are decimated, sanitation systems cease to operate, immunization programs are disrupted, and health systems erode.[24] As a result, diseases can spread or re-emerge, like wild polio has in unstable countries, including Afghanistan, Nigeria, Pakistan, and Syria.[25]

The mass movement of families fleeing violence propels diseases across borders, while refugee camps congregate people closely in unhygienic conditions. In April 2020, local transmission of COVID-19 was reported by 122 refugee-hosting countries.[26] In high-density refugee camps it is practically impossible for people to practice recommended measures to avoid viral transmission, like social distancing and frequent handwashing. As vulnerable populations flee conflict zones, drought, or flood, they bring microbes with them. As temperatures change, rainfall slows, and soil erodes, food production can precipitate famines, forcing people to flee in search of food. Often this leads to destruction of forests and other natural habitats to grow crops.

## Antimicrobial Resistance

Many scientists view antimicrobial resistance (AMR) as the most disconcerting threat facing the world.[27] As people use—and overuse—antibiotics and other antimicrobials, microbes' genetic mutations enable them to survive and spread. Once-treatable infections (e.g., hospital-acquired *Staphylococcus aureus*, malaria, and tuberculosis) are becoming resistant to all known treatments, harkening back to the days before the advent of antibiotics and antiviral medications.[28] Today the world's most disadvantaged people face the highest burden from hard-to-treat infections. Several hundred thousand people die every year from multidrug-resistant and extremely drug-resistant tuberculosis (TB), perhaps humankind's oldest microbial nemesis. Most of these deaths occur in sub-Saharan Africa, South Asia, and the Indian subcontinent and could climb into the millions every year.[29] Antimicrobial resistance occurs in even the richest countries and world-class health facilities; tens of thousands of Americans die every year from antimicrobial resistance.[30] Can we even imagine a world where even common infections become untreatable, bringing us back to the dark times when people could die from a simple infection?

But the proliferation of antimicrobial-resistant organisms is avoidable, the result of discrete and destructive ways in which we have developed, or not, our health systems and farms—prophylactic antibiotic use in farmed animals, indiscriminate medical prescribing, and poor hospital infection control. The vast global networks in substandard or falsified medications pose another major risk. The illicit sale of substandard and falsified medicines is as widespread, if not much more widespread, than trafficking of illicit drugs such as cocaine, heroin, and opioids. Falsified and substandard medications often contain sub-therapeutic doses of a drug's active ingredient. When patients buy these drugs unknowingly in a street market or on the internet, ineffective dosages enable microbes to become resistant.[31] In short, human behavior is what enables "superbugs" to thrive.

### Ethnocentric Nationalistic Politics

Behavior of a very different sort adds to today's threat of infectious diseases. Populist politicians rail against the very values needed for global health preparedness: international cooperation, robust international institutions, rules-based international relations, and mutual solidarity. Preparedness is more than a national project. It is a global responsibility. Yet populist leaders are more likely to be inward-looking than to provide ample technical and financial assistance to poorer countries. Instead, hypernationalists erect walls, literally and figuratively, putting country "first," ahead of the world's population and the planet we inhabit. They renege on promises of humanitarian assistance and global climate change solidarity; they undermine international organizations, and they blame "the other."

These pivots away from mutual solidarity are certainly dangerous for political relationships, but also for global health. Cooperative action is in every country's national interest. No legal or physical barrier can impede the spread of microbes. The COVID-19 pandemic began in a single person in a single municipality in Hubei Province, but within months the novel coronavirus had infected millions of people in over 210 countries across six continents.[32] Fighting a pathogenic threat where it arises is far less expensive and more effective than waiting until the pestilence reaches our shores.

## The Economic Costs of Epidemics

Infectious diseases are also a serious economic concern. During the COVID-19 pandemic, the International Monetary Fund (IMF) estimated that government spending measures adopted through mid-April 2020 to sustain economic activity amounted to $3.3 trillion, with loans, equity injections, and guarantees costing an additional $4.5 trillion.[33] We have already blown past pre-COVID projections from the National Academy of Sciences (NAS) that novel infectious diseases will cost the global economy $60 billion per year, amounting to $6 trillion through the twenty-first century.[34] What makes these data (both COVID-19 estimates and NAS projections) chilling is that these estimates are direct costs only; they do not account for the vast impact of epidemics on global trade, travel, tourism, and worker productivity, which are harder to accurately estimate. And the toll on families and communities can unravel social support networks.

Economic models predicted much higher costs, but predictions still fell far short of the actual (and still fast-accruing) costs from COVID-19. The World Bank estimated potential losses from a severe influenza pandemic—a once or twice in a hundred years event—at $3 trillion in global direct and indirect losses, or 4.8 percent of global GDP.[35] The National Bureau of Economic Research projected a figure of $490 billion that includes mortality costs. A further approximation suggested the annual global cost of moderate-severe to severe pandemics is roughly $570 billion, or 0.7 percent of global income.[36] In mid-April 2020 the IMF estimated that due to the COVID-19 pandemic, the global economy, which only months beforehand the IMF had expected to expand by 3.3 percent in 2020, would instead shrink by 3 percent.[37] World trade was expected to fall by 13 to 32 percent.[38]

In 2017 the CDC assessed the economic vulnerability of the US export economy posed by trade disruptions in forty-nine global health security priority countries.[39] US exports of goods and services to these countries exceed $308 billion annually, supporting more than 1.6 million jobs. These exports represented 13.7 percent of all US export revenue worldwide and 14.3 percent of all US jobs supported by all exports. The agency concluded, "Economic linkages between the US and global health security priority countries illustrate the importance of ensuring that countries have the public health capacities needed to control outbreaks at their source before they become pandemics."[40] The National Academy of Medicine came to a similar conclusion that the US economy is vulnerable to novel epidemics.

The economic toll of past epidemics was more in line with predictive models. The 2003 SARS outbreak cost East Asia $54 billion, annual seasonal influenza costs $30 billion, and Ebola caused Guinea, Liberia, and Sierra Leone at least $2.2 billion in lost economic growth.[41] Global losses due to the six major zoonotic disease outbreaks in 1997–2009 cost on average $6.7 billion per year.[42] We do not yet know the full economic impact of COVID-19, but we have seen financial markets plunge as companies and supply chains face damaging disruptions—already well beyond the economic costs that any model had predicted, as the pandemic continues on.

At the societal level, catastrophic pandemics like COVID-19 shutter businesses and leave people out of work. During the COVID-19 outbreak, the United States saw its highest unemployment rate since the Great Depression.[43] Researchers projected that the outbreak could yield 20 million jobs lost across Africa and that the number of people living in extreme poverty globally, after decades of progress, could rise by hundreds of millions.[44] Pandemics like HIV/AIDS also dampen productivity as sickness and death remove workers from the workforce. Children are robbed of their parents, prompting knock-on effects on economic growth. Often their parents' condition means children cannot access education, leading to worse job prospects. Economic activities such as farming are disrupted, undermining food security. Access to vital services like health care is diminished, and chronic conditions go untreated. In fact, during the Ebola outbreak in West Africa, more people died of treatable causes—such as malaria, cardiovascular disease, and complications of childbirth—than from Ebola, because people avoided health care facilities and many health centers closed.

The costs are amplified by fear. As Tedros Adhanom, the director-general of WHO, recently put it: When an outbreak hits, there are two epidemics— "one caused by the virus, and the other one caused by fear." For instance, while SARS claimed 800 lives, its economic costs were extensive.[45] Tourism, for instance, often suffers as vacationers seek to avoid infected areas. In Sierra Leone, hotel occupancy plunged from 70 percent to 13 percent in one year during the Ebola outbreak.[46] In 2018, Chinese travelers had made 150 million visits overseas, a rise of 14.7 percent from the previous year.[47] Virtually all of that travel ceased in early 2020, though, as dozens of countries erected travel bans or quarantines against Chinese travelers, while most global air carriers suspended flights. As COVID-19 spread out of China and into other parts of the world, travel bans and flight suspensions were greatly expanded— yielding further losses in tourism.

Fear of disease and the closures mandated by fearful governments also lead consumers to avoid retail stores, sports and music events, and cinemas. Although trade often moves online, outbreaks primarily affect local, small sellers. COVID-19 placed millions of small businesses across the world at risk of closing permanently. Hindsight has demonstrated that the closures, quarantines, and travel bans for COVID-19 were largely justified to prevent the spread of disease, but governments might sometimes overreact and impose unnecessary, economically harmful restrictions. But even rational government action can take an economic toll. For example, the mass culling of chickens to prevent the spread of avian influenza deprived individuals of private property, often without compensation.

## The Cost to Justice

Even though people everywhere are at risk for infectious diseases, public health gains are inequitably distributed, raising major issues of justice. Low- and middle-income countries (LMICs) bear most disease burdens, exacerbating health disparities. One study found that LMICs suffer 95.7 percent of disability-adjusted life-years (DALYs) due to AIDS, TB, and malaria. Overall, infectious diseases account for over 300 million DALYs lost in LMICs, with an estimated $1.695 trillion in lost productivity.[48] It remains unknown how many lives will be lost in LMICs from COVID-19, but the outcome likely depends on the amount of support their fragile health systems receive from other countries and institutions to confront outbreak.

Global inequalities of wealth and scientific resources critically undermine epidemic preparedness and response. Despite improvements, hundreds of millions of people lack access to clean water, adequate sanitation, and resilient health systems. Even if vaccines or medicines are available in high-income countries, people in low- and middle-income states often lack access to them. Global health security requires mutual solidarity.

Health security also requires countering deep, structural issues that produce domestic inequalities. In the United States and elsewhere, COVID-19 disproportionately affected already marginalized populations. In the United States, for instance, blacks and other people of color suffered disproportionately high levels of death and infection, caused by such factors as a lack of health care and employment in jobs deemed essential, such as grocery store workers.[49] The effects extended beyond infection and disease itself to people who could no longer afford food or fell into poverty.

The COVID-19 pandemic has exposed the interconnectedness of humanity: an outbreak anywhere puts us all at risk. It would be profoundly mistaken to ignore the lessons of social epidemiology and view health as individual matter. Efforts to reduce and eliminate health inequalities promote not only health justice but also a more health-secure world.

## New Ways of Operating

This is a pivotal moment for the future of global health security—the COVID-19 pandemic has prompted renewed momentum. The world awoke in 2020 when our inability to control a localized outbreak before it exploded into a pandemic was exposed. This inability to control an outbreak persists despite previous reforms to global health institutions following the 2014–2015 West African Ebola epidemic. In 2018, when the next urban Ebola outbreak occurred in the DRC, WHO's new Health Emergencies Programme sprang into action, with international partners quickly on the ground, and WHO's director-general immediately calling an Emergency Committee under the International Health Regulations. Yet even a reformed WHO couldn't quickly bring a second 2018 Ebola epidemic under control in the DRC. Nor has it managed to gain the political support and funding to control the COVID-19 pandemic. The lessons are clear. We need to fully understand the extraordinarily high risk we all face, along with the reasons the risk is so high. We do know how to prevent and control outbreaks, but we need to be prepared. And the task is urgent, because we cannot know when the next pandemic will occur. In the next chapter, I will start by exploring the COVID-19 pandemic, and the factors that allow contagious and deadly pathogens to spread so easily between humans.

# CHAPTER 2

# The Human Link

Just over a hundred years since the Spanish influenza pandemic infected a third of the planet and killed at least 50–100 million people, another novel virus, SARS-CoV-2, revealed that the world remains deeply vulnerable.[1] In many ways, SARS-CoV-2 emerged as the perfect storm for transmission: because it is a novel virus, no one had immunity to it. It spread more readily between humans than other coronaviruses like SARS or MERS. And while SARS-CoV-2 is highly pathogenic, it is also less deadly than SARS or MERS, enabling contagious carriers with mild or no symptoms to continue human interactions that enable the disease to spread exponentially. A year into the pandemic, the United Kingdom, South Africa, and Brazil reported genomic variants capable of spreading even more rapidly. Those variants, and possibly many others, spread quickly around the world. Given these characteristics, it would have required early detection and action to prevent a localized outbreak of COVID-19 from ultimately becoming a pandemic.

But the world was not prepared for COVID-19, and our failure to act early resulted in severe and ongoing human and economic losses. It is likely COVID-19 will become endemic in countries around the world. This chapter starts by examining a timeline of the COVID-19 pandemic, identifying how we failed to detect and contain the outbreak before it got out of control. But COVID-19 exemplifies only one path in which an outbreak can ignite and spread. This chapter also looks to other risks posed by the human link, including lack of water and sanitation, inadequate hygienic practices, cultural behaviors, and the systems that support them. We offer key strategies to significantly reduce epidemic risks, so that we can detect and control future outbreaks long before they become pandemics.

## How COVID-19 Became a Pandemic

On the last day of 2019, Chinese authorities informed the World Health Organization that a number of pneumonia-like cases had appeared in Wuhan, a city in Hubei Province, with an unknown cause.[2] Most of the forty-four initially identified cases were tied to the Huanan wet market, where live animals are traded, and the market was quickly shut down. A week into the new year, China identified a novel coronavirus as the cause of the outbreak.[3] Scientists believe that the virus likely originated in bats and, after possibly passing through an intermediary host, evolved to be able to infect and be transmissible between humans.[4] WHO sent a team of scientists to Wuhan a year later in January 2021, and the team concluded that the virus had natural, rather than laboratory-derived, origins. Yet it is likely that we shall never be sure of the zoonotic or other origins of COVID-19.

The virus spread quickly, despite the Chinese government's severe measures, including locking down 60 million people in Hubei Province in a cordon sanitaire.[5] It was reported that some 20 million people left Wuhan before authorities ordered the lockdown. By mid-January, China was reporting its first related deaths. On January 14, WHO disseminated a report from Chinese authorities that there was no efficient SARS-Cov-2 transmission between humans, despite growing evidence to the contrary. It also would soon emerge that Chinese authorities had punished physicians for spreading "rumors" about the virus's severity; one of the physician whistle-blowers, Li Wenliang, would himself fall victim to the virus.[6] On January 22, WHO confirmed human-to-human transmission, with over 200 cases worldwide, including among health care workers.[7] Only eight days later, when WHO declared the virus a global emergency, there were over 10,000 cases and 200 deaths in over a dozen countries.[8] Many countries began applying strict travel restrictions on people coming from China.

During February the virus began spreading exponentially. China still remained the epicenter (with tens of thousands of cases and thousands of deaths), but cases outside of China rose steadily. On February 28 a WHO-China Joint Mission on Coronavirus issued its report,[9] while beginning to work with the pharmaceutical industry on therapeutic countermeasures. In a press conference, WHO relayed warning signs: there was already a severe global disruption in the market for personal protective equipment worn by health care workers, with demand 100 times higher than normal.[10] WHO director-general Tedros called the virus "a very grave threat for the rest of the world," and warned that the window to contain the virus was narrowing. Around the same time US president Donald Trump downplayed the threat, saying that COVID-19 was not any worse than seasonal influenza, and would pass by quickly.[11]

The virus did not pass quickly, but escalated at an alarming rate. In March, COVID-19 cases skyrocketed to over 700,000 globally, and deaths surpassed 30,000.[12] Totals of infections and deaths outside China surpassed those inside China. The United States became the new epicenter, with more cases than any other country. On March 11, Director-General Tedros declared COVID-19 a pandemic, imploring countries to take urgent and aggressive action.[13] Countries enforced lockdowns, travel restrictions, business and school closures, and other social distancing measures. Some also passed stimulus packages as economies plunged and families and businesses struggled. Before long, governments had appropriated trillions of dollars to aid businesses and persons out of work.

As COVID-19 cases began to rise in Africa, India, and Latin America, so did serious concerns on how it could impact countries' fragile health systems. Income losses across low- and middle-income countries were projected to surpass $220 billion.[14] Following a virtual summit on March 27, G20 leaders released a statement on commitments to strengthen health systems globally.[15] But around the same time the United States and the European Commission took measures to redirect global shipments of personal protective equipment and other medical gear back into their own countries. To this day, there is scant funding for robust national health systems to rapidly detect and respond to novel outbreaks.

In April, global cases of COVID-19 surpassed 1 million, and they would hit 3 million before the end of the month.[16] Deaths soared past 200,000. Roughly 2,000 Americans died from the virus each day. The global economy faced its worst slump since the Great Depression. The global market for ventilators and other medical equipment became largely depleted. Meanwhile, in Africa, in countries already short on medical resources, COVID-19 cases neared 50,000 and deaths 2,000.[17] Perhaps even more concerning were the effects that lockdowns and economic losses were having on many of the world's most vulnerable people, including a warning that the number of people around the world suffering from acute hunger could double.[18] The United Nations appealed for billions of dollars for assistance to refugees, internally displaced persons, and other vulnerable populations in sixty-four fragile states.[19]

WHO launched a task force to dramatically scale up supplies for poorer countries.[20] But when global solidarity was needed more than ever, US president Trump announced he would suspend WHO funding, citing its slow and "China-centric" response.[21] Director-General Tedros begged world leaders not to politicize the virus, but to instead come together and unite to overcome COVID-19 as the common enemy.[22] In May 2020, global cases surpassed 3.5 million and deaths 250,000.[23] Epidemiologists predicted reoccurring spikes in cases, hospitalizations, and deaths over the next year, with the possibility of a far larger wave of cases and deaths in the fall of 2020.[24] Yet even in countries with rising cases, governments began reopening businesses and lifting stay-at-home orders. In the United States, President Trump pressed states to reopen their economies despite CDC predictions that the daily death toll would reach 3,000 in June, with 200,000 new cases each day.[25] In July, President Trump notified the United Nations that the United States would withdraw from WHO, effective in July 2021, falsely accusing the agency of "siding with China" and hiding the true nature of the outbreak in China.

Sadly, predictions of escalating cases and deaths largely came true. The United States, India, and Brazil experienced massive COVID-19 waves during the summer of 2020. After cases declined in late September and October, there was another rush to resume in-person schools, businesses, and social gatherings. On September 26 the White House hosted a gathering to celebrate Supreme Court nominee Amy Coney Barrett, which would ultimately be recognized as a superspreader event that infected President Trump and many persons around him. Across Europe, mounting COVID-19 cases in late October and November prompted renewed lockdowns in countries like France and Germany. Yet the United States by far fared the worst, with cases skyrocketing in November and December, reaching more than 200,000 new cases and thousands of new deaths each day. Globally, in just a year's time, by December 2020, over 80 million people became infected with and nearly 2 million people died from COVID-19.[26]

As I finished this chapter one year on since the pandemic began, the world was more hopeful than at any earlier moment in this pandemic. Immediately following his inauguration, President Joseph Biden signed documents expressing intent for the United States to rejoin WHO and announced that henceforth the US response to COVID would be based on science. Stringent regulatory authorities in the United States, Europe, and the United Kingdom approved two highly efficacious messenger RNA vaccines manufactured by Pfizer/BioNTech and Moderna. The UK approved an AstraZeneca vaccine, and Western governments were on the verge of approving new vaccine candidates. Multiple countries were already giving their vaccines to millions of their residents, and the number of new COVID-19 cases per day were finally beginning to decline steadily (see Chapter 10).

And while there remains vast uncertainty about the future, a few things are clear: An outbreak of a novel virus can take an enormous toll on human lives and economies everywhere—from the wealthiest to the poorest nations. Even the best health systems can be overrun. Delays in detecting and reporting outbreaks—whether due to system failures or cover-ups tied to political and economic interests—are a missed opportunity to avoid the severest harms. Placing blame on other countries or WHO only impedes the response, where strong leadership guided by science is essential. The Great Coronavirus Pandemic of 2020 vividly demonstrates the urgent need to invest in public health preparedness and health systems, which could empower us to confront the multitude of threats that spread between humans. Next, we turn to some additional, and just as important, threats arising from the human link.

## Water, Sanitation, and Hygiene

In the mid-nineteenth century, John Snow identified a water pump as the source of a devastating cholera outbreak in Soho, London. Closing the Broad Street pump brought the outbreak to an end. Just as John Snow's investigations led to vast improvement in London's water system, it is still vital today to ensure safe water, sanitation, and hygiene. In intensely congested megacities, sanitation and water systems are not just overtaxed, as seen in Haiti's recent cholera outbreak, but also often missing in large areas. Yet solutions are not a mystery, and with adequate funding and expertise, infrastructure improvements can dramatically reduce the risk.

## Haiti in the Time of Cholera

In January 2010 a catastrophic earthquake struck the island of Hispaniola (comprising Haiti and the Dominican Republic). The earthquake's proximity to the Haitian capital of Port-au-Prince, combined with the country's poor-quality infrastructure, caused mass devastation: 200,000 people died and 1.5 were million displaced. The international community acted quickly. The United Nations and nongovernmental organizations (NGOs) such as Partners in Health embedded in Haiti working to rescue and rebuild residents' lives. Yet despite good intentions, one element of this response actually increased the suffering of the Haitian people.

UN peacekeeping troops from Nepal arrived nine months after the earthquake, setting up camp on the Artibonite River, a major waterway. Camp residents disposed of human waste in the river, which flowed downstream to Meille, where villagers collected the contaminated water for drinking and cooking, launching a major epidemic that continues to this day. The water was contaminated with vibrio cholera. Eight years later the cholera epidemic had infected more than 800,000 Haitians, killing nearly 10,000—all of this having been unwittingly caused by UN troops.[27]

Cholera has persisted in Haiti due to weak water, sanitation, and health systems. Only a quarter of the population has access to decent toilets, and only a half to clean water.[28] The disease's symptoms—explosive diarrhea and vomiting—accelerated its diffusion. Because Haitians had never before experienced cholera, they lacked immunity to it.

Despite clear epidemiological evidence confirming the UN camp as the outbreak's source, the UN denied culpability for years, refusing to pay compensation. Finally, in December 2016, the secretary-general apologized for bringing cholera to the island. But the UN has continued to deny compensation to individual victims.[29] UN troops withdrew from Haiti less than a year later, in October 2017. And to date, UN member states have failed to contribute the $400 million that would fund a two-pronged plan to end the epidemic: an intensified response and longer-term infrastructure improvements. An impoverished country continues to suffer from a fully preventable infectious disease.

## Sanitation Systems

Haiti's epidemic starkly illustrates the devastation of fecal-oral disease. Globally, 4.2 billion people lack safely managed sanitation, and 2.2 billion lack access to safely managed drinking water services.[30] Diarrheal diseases account for 1 in 9 child deaths worldwide—killing 2,195 children every day—more than AIDS, malaria, and measles combined. The Sustainable Development

Goals (SDGs) (see Chapter 7) promise universal access to safe water and basic sanitation by 2030, but the challenges are formidable. Both the extent of unsafe water and sanitation systems and variable conditions impede solutions. And there is precious little funding, even though ensuring rotavirus vaccination, breastfeeding, safe water, and hygiene and sanitation, and preventing diarrheal and other waterborne diseases is not only possible but cost effective: every $1 invested yields an average return of $25.50.[31]

A project in Maputo, Mozambique's capital, illustrates what can be achieved. Less than 10 percent of Maputo's population have a sewer connection and most fecal waste is unsafely managed. Waste from pit latrines and septic tanks is routinely buried in backyards or dumped into storm drains. The city piloted a project with the World Bank in a densely populated district. Stakeholders developed improved services with equipment that could be carried through narrow urban alleyways. After two years, viable sewage businesses remained operational.[32] Advances in clean water and sanitation systems can markedly reduce waterborne diseases.

## Health Care–Associated Infections

Like people living in areas with poor-quality water and sanitation systems, people who are hospitalized face heightened risk of infection. Hospitalization carries major risks of acquiring infections, many of which are highly resistant to treatment. Hospital-acquired infections result in prolonged hospital stays, long-term disability, loss of income, and even death. They vastly increase health care costs and fuel antimicrobial resistance.[33]

While all countries experience health care–associated infections, low- and middle-income countries bear the highest burdens. In Europe and North America, 5 to 10 percent of all hospitalizations result in potentially serious infections.[34] In Latin America, sub-Saharan Africa, and Asia, the rate is 40 percent.[35] The very old and the young are most susceptible. Patients in intensive care and those undergoing invasive procedures also are at higher risk.

Health care facilities can vastly reduce risk by altering the physical environment. Key interventions include clean water for drinking and handwashing, ventilation, sterile storage, personal protective equipment, and safe disposal of medical waste.[36] WHO and UNICEF provide resources to guide health professionals.[37] Overall, hospitals must adopt a "systems" approach where cleanliness and safety are built into the culture.

## Changing Behaviors

Human behavior propels pathogens. Changing people's conduct to lower risks of transmitting or acquiring infections is a core public health strategy. Risk behaviors range from the routine, like a lack of personal hygiene or not washing hands, to those deeply ingrained in politics and culture. In the United States during the COVID pandemic, simple risk mitigation measures like wearing masks or social distancing took on a distinctly political posture, often aligned with support for, or opposition to, President Trump. Human behaviors are also deeply ingrained culturally, and health officials must understand traditional beliefs and the subtlety of language to enable effective risk communication. The Ebola case study below offers a striking example of how local leaders influenced a community where international experts had failed.

## Laying Hands on the Deceased

In December 2013, a two-year-old boy acquired a disease from a fruit bat.[38] This was the start of what became the West African Ebola epidemic. Between humans, the Ebola virus is spread through direct contact (via broken skin or mucous membranes in the nose, mouth, or eyes) with the blood or bodily fluids of a person who is ill with or has died from Ebola. The virus spread to the boy's family, then to people in surrounding villages, ultimately arriving in Guinea's capital city.[39] But the cultural practices of people living along the Guinea/Sierra Leone border accelerated transmission into a full-blown epidemic that would soon cross the Liberian border 300 miles away.

In the early days of the outbreak, a popular healer named Mendinor treated Ebola patients in the border region between Guinea and Sierra Leone by rubbing their bodies with tree-leaf mud packs.[40] She contracted the virus and died. In accordance with local custom, her family and neighbors prepared her body for burial by washing, grooming, and dressing the corpse.

Unbeknownst to her family and neighbors, the viral load (the amount of virus within a person) reached its peak at the point of death; the corpse can remain highly infectious for a week.

Hundreds of people attended Mendinor's funeral and laid hands on her, unknowingly exposing themselves to high concentrations of the Ebola virus. Fourteen women, including Mendinor's niece, became infected at Mendinor's funeral, and they then transported the virus to Liberia's capital city,

Monrovia. In all, preparations for the healer's burial, and her funeral, were linked to thousands of Ebola cases.

In response to unsafe burial practices, health officials buried corpses quickly in body bags, foregoing traditional burial rituals.[41] They were met with distrust and popular backlash. To avoid Ebola clinics, some families retreated to the forest, which increased the disease's spread. In frustration, health officials sought help to change burial customs: chiefs, imams, pastors, and local healers, with community members, supported safe burial rituals that were sanitary while respecting mourners' traditions. Burial workers in protective gear dressed corpses in special clothing and inserted jewelry in the body bag as payment to ensure a successful journey to the afterlife.[42] A nuanced appreciation of culture, combined with scientific understanding, devised practices that helped communities become better at stemming the epidemic.

## Sterile Injection Equipment to Fight HIV and Hepatitis

Risk behaviors are fueled by laws that impede people's ability to help themselves or get help, as well as by local cultures. Sharing or reusing injection equipment transmits bloodborne infections such as HIV and hepatitis B and C. Injection drug users share needles and syringes out of practical necessity because sterile injection equipment is often scarce or inaccessible. In many countries, carrying or possessing needles and syringes incurs a harsh criminal penalty. Drug users also share equipment as a social ritual, a form of personal bonding. Yet even a miniscule blood residue on a used needle or syringe can transmit infection, and infected persons can then transmit the virus to other needle-sharing and sexual partners.

Sterile drug injection programs such as needle exchanges are highly effective,[43] enabling people who use drugs to swap used injection equipment for new. Combining exchanges with health exams, testing, counseling, and addiction treatment is most effective.[44] Evidence of effectiveness is overwhelming. Australia introduced the first needle exchange in 1986, saving thousands of lives. Elsewhere there has been fierce political resistance, with politicians stubbornly refusing to dismantle criminal laws banning needle exchanges, fearing that "harm reduction" programs increase crime and drug use. But the opposite is true: needle exchanges bring people into treatment.[45] Today, needle exchanges exist in over forty countries,[46] saving lives and money.

## Safer Sex

Another area of transmission requiring a change in human behavior is sexually transmitted infections (STIs). STIs are so old they are mentioned in the Old Testament.[47] They are spread during vaginal, oral, or anal sex, through semen, vaginal fluid, or other bodily fluids. Globally, more than 1 million people every day acquire an STI—syphilis, gonorrhea, chlamydia, trichomoniasis, hepatitis B, herpes, HIV, and human papillomavirus.[48] Today the United States is experiencing a surge in STIs, driven by such factors as opioid use, which contributes to increased high-risk behavior, and lack of access to health care, particularly among people who are poor, along with reduced funding for public STI programs.[49] Currently vaccines can prevent human papillomavirus, hepatitis A, and hepatitis B. Vaccines for other STIs are under development, including for herpes simplex virus.

Safer sex is a vital harm reduction strategy. Instead of teaching abstinence, it is essential to teach young people the importance of proper condom use. Thailand's 100 percent condom programme, for example, mandated condom-use in all brothels. The campaign also emphasized decreasing sex worker visits by Thai military recruits, mass media campaigns, and community mobilization. The campaign was a resounding success, widely credited with averting an HIV epidemic in Thailand. The rate of Thai military recruits having sex with commercial sex workers decreased from 57.1 percent to 23.8 percent in a four-year period. For recruits who continued to attend brothels, condom use increased from 61 percent in 1991 to over 92 percent in 1995. Safer sex campaigns globally have reduced STIs and unintended pregnancies.[50]

## Detecting and Responding to Outbreaks

When outbreaks do arise, early detection and rapid response are vital. In an era of mass travel and migration, global solutions are critical. Yet a lack of will and funding threaten global health security.

Consider the failures to rapidly contain SARS in Canada and Asia, followed by strong action that stemmed the outbreaks. The initial reports of SARS arose in November 2002 in Guangdong Province, China. By February 2003 SARS had become a global epidemic propelled by travel and trade. Beginning in March 2003, WHO issued increasingly dire global alerts and recommendations to restrict travel, and states ordered school and business closures and mass quarantines.

By July 2003, WHO declared the global epidemic over. In total, more than 8,000 people became sick and 774 died.[51] Economic losses were estimated at $40 billion.[52] The total losses were far less than those that would result from the COVID-19 pandemic. This is partially attributable to SARS's lower transmission rates and higher death rates. Still, the 2002–2003 SARS outbreak similarly sparked widespread fear and panic among nations, while governments restricted individual rights. The global panic over SARS led WHO to reform the International Health Regulations in 2005.

## Global Surveillance

Public health officials are now capable of sophisticated surveillance—meticulous monitoring of infections worldwide. At the CDC's emergency operations center, real-time data on novel infections are tracked in every corner of the globe.[53] Beyond official reporting of novel diseases, health officials can now track and analyze "big data" sources, including from web searches, social media, and news reports. Genomic surveillance is also important to rapidly identify any significant mutations of a virus. Disease surveillance (the ongoing systematic collection and analysis of health data) is essential for planning, implementing, and evaluating public health interventions.

Effective surveillance is only as good as its inputs, and each level in the health system plays a vital role. Health providers report patient data to health authorities. Health authorities run or confirm laboratory tests, while collecting and analyzing data. WHO sits at the apex of global surveillance. The International Health Regulations (2005) require states to report certain novel pathogens, such as smallpox, polio, and SARS. Other diseases that present an unusual risk—such as cholera, viral hemorrhagic fever, and biological, radiological, or chemical events (see Chapter 7)—may also be reportable.

This pyramid structure of disease surveillance depends on each nation developing its own system of detection and reporting, and then complying with reporting requirements. The COVID-19 pandemic revealed that if a country withholds accurate case counts and fails to disclose the severity of an outbreak, this can leave WHO relatively powerless to act to reduce global spread of the pathogen. Alternatively, the 2013–2016 Ebola epidemic revealed that many countries do not have the capacity for disease surveillance. In Guinea, Liberia, and Sierra Leone, the health systems were in shambles after years of poverty, neglect, and conflict. Community health centers did not have even the most basic equipment to collect clinical data.[54] The failure to collect accurate data was exacerbated by underreporting and insufficient contract tracing.

Failures in coordinating and ensuring surveillance can also stymie rapid public health responses. For COVID-19, WHO could have taken more aggressive action earlier if the agency had been given accurate information on the number of cases circulating in China, and had known of the virus's transmissibility between humans. During the 2013–2016 Ebola outbreak, WHO failed to declare a public health emergency of international concern until more than four months after international spread. Initially, WHO delegated its response to the burgeoning crisis to the regional offices, which were unable to accurately track Ebola patients and transmission pathways.[55]

## A Systems Approach

Rapid detection and response to novel infections requires a systems approach, with sustainable funding and resource mobilization: ensuring good sanitation and hygiene; understanding and respecting local cultures; changing risk behaviors and unhealthy rituals; social distancing such as avoiding congested areas (like mass transit, sporting events, schools); ensuring essential needs like clean water, food, and medicines for people under quarantine or in isolation; and medical countermeasures (such as pharmaceuticals, vaccines, and personal protective equipment). Above all, strong health systems are needed for surveillance, response, and health care.

More often than not, though, these fundamental pillars of epidemic preparedness are not in place. Many governments fail to invest in these proven interventions or lack the capacity to do so. Meanwhile, higher-income countries fail to help build capacities in lower-income countries. The West African Ebola epidemic took place in three countries with weak health systems. Despite a known risk of Ebola in sub-Saharan Africa, there were no vaccines or medical treatments available. What a difference a few years made. In two Ebola outbreaks in the Democratic Republic of Congo (DRC), WHO partnered with the Gavi, the Vaccine Alliance, to deploy highly effective immunizations. International partners and the DRC rapidly developed logistical systems for transport and cold storage of the vaccine even to remote villages.

For COVID-19, it remains to be seen whether wealthy countries like the United States will change course and support WHO's work to control the pandemic in low- and middle-income countries. The development of vaccines and medical countermeasures has thus far been remarkably successful, but it is uncertain whether they will be shared equitably across the globe. When the world fully funds and thoroughly prepares for dangerous outbreaks, it is highly likely that dangerous pathogens can be rapidly brought under control. If we neglect the threat, wait until it is too large to stop, and then panic, many lives, and dollars, will be lost. Most of the human and economic suffering is preventable. That is the lesson of national and global preparedness.

# CHAPTER 3

# Humanity's Biggest Killer

**In our increasingly urbanized world**, it is a daunting task to try to halt a virus that spreads readily between humans, like SARS-CoV-2, the virus that causes COVID-19. Yet some of the world's deadliest threats spread their destruction using an entirely different vehicle: the mosquito.

In the early summer of 2012, emergency rooms in Dallas were overrun with patients experiencing fevers and stiff necks.[1] By mid-July more than 50 patients a week turned up in doctors' offices; some were being carried into ERs paralyzed or comatose from brain inflammation. After nine people died in early August, Dallas County declared a public health emergency. By the year's end, 19 were dead, 216 hospitalized, and 1,162 tested positive for what turned out to be West Nile virus. West Nile outbreaks had occurred periodically in the United States, but the outbreak in Dallas began a national epidemic. How did this happen?

Mosquitoes are a contradiction: they appear small and fragile, yet they can be deadly. Isaac Asimov once observed, "Human beings can easily destroy every elephant on earth, but we are helpless against the mosquito."[2] We are not truly helpless, thanks to effective prevention strategies and some available medical countermeasures. But Dr. Asimov's observation feels apt for a foe that remains so deadly despite the fact that it is low on the food chain, is easily swatted, and has a life span measured in days. When temperatures drop, temperature-sensitive mosquitoes slow down, eventually coming to a hibernation-like halt. And without stagnant water, the eggs of mosquitoes cannot hatch. Any disruption to the water's surface can be damaging, if not fatal, to eggs and larvae. But given the right environment, mosquitoes thrive, like they did in the Dallas winter of 2012. Warming Dallas winters allowed the mosquitoes to awaken from their seasonal hiding spaces. It takes as little water as the rain collected in an overturned bottle cap for mosquitoes to lay up to 3,000 eggs; imagine what an increase in rainfall and temperature can do to the numbers and distribution of mosquitoes that transmit serious diseases. In recent years, mosquito-transmitted disease has more than tripled in the United States.[3] This is but one example of a growing risk to the public's health spurred by unpredictable weather patterns.

The mosquito is the world's deadliest animal, taking hundreds of thousands of lives every year, mostly from malaria.[4] More than half the world's population lives in areas inhabited by the deadly *Aedes aegypti* mosquito, which transmits diseases such as Zika, dengue fever, chikungunya, and yellow fever. Dengue is the world's most common mosquito-borne viral disease, with about 390 million cases a year.[5]

Mosquito-borne diseases overwhelmingly impact the world's poor, particularly children, and they also exacerbate poverty—inflicting a relentless cycle of suffering and debilitation, lowering quality of life, and diminishing human capabilities. As climate change takes hold, the menace of mosquitoes stands to become still more far-reaching, claiming more lives. It is not too late to limit climate change—and the spread of mosquitoes.

With effective methods to vastly reduce the mosquito population and prevent human exposure, we can sharply reduce enormous amounts of suffering and death. To understand the solutions, however, we need to understand mosquitoes, their life cycle, and the environments in which they breed. What are the most effective strategies for mosquito control? What are the obstacles, and how we can overcome them? Mosquitoes certainly will remain a constant part of the ecosystem, but it is within our power to dramatically curb mosquito-borne diseases.

Of the 3,500 mosquito species, only a few spread human diseases (see Table 3.1). These diseases are known as arboviruses, which are viruses transmitted by arthropod vectors (e.g., mosquitoes, ticks, and sandflies). The word "arbovirus" is an acronym—"arthropod-borne virus"—and not a family name or taxonomic description. The CDC lists 600 arboviruses,[6] of which only about 130 can infect humans and a smaller fraction yet can cause severe illness.[7] Arboviral infections tend to be asymptomatic, though they can also lead to symptoms ranging from mild febrile illness to life-threatening encephalitis.

**Table 3.1.** The Killers

| *Anopheles* mosquitoes[1] | *Aedes* mosquitoes[2] |
| --- | --- |
| • *Anopheles* mosquitoes are the only vector for transmitting malaria—an ancient scourge. Among 430 *Anopheles* species, only 30 to 40 transmit malaria. They are widely distributed across the world, including in places where malaria has been eliminated but could be reintroduced, such as the eastern United States. Female *Anopheles* can lay 50 to 200 eggs at one time. The eggs hatch within 2 to 3 days. Most *Anopheles* are nocturnal or crepuscular (active at dawn or dusk). Common preventative measures focus on reducing human exposure during these times, specifically while people are sleeping. Bed nets can be highly effective, along with improved home construction. Destruction of breeding sites to interrupt the *Anopheles* egg-laying cycle and indoor residual spraying (IRS) are also effective. | • Although 900 species of *Aedes* mosquitoes inhabit the world, the *Aedes aegypti* and *Aedes albopictus* are most notorious. They are the primary vectors for yellow fever, dengue, Zika virus, chikungunya, West Nile virus, and eastern equine encephalitis. <br><br>• Viruses such as yellow fever and dengue generally depend on another reservoir species, such as nonhuman primates, for sustained transmission. Diseases such as chikungunya and Zika include other reservoirs—such as rodents or birds—but usually rely on human-mosquito-human transmission. <br><br>    *Aedes aegypti* prefer living near humans, in and around living spaces and refuse sites. They need only a minute amount of water—as little as what fits in a bottle cap—to lay their eggs, and often depend on water left in artificial containers such as abandoned tires and trash cans. Similarly, *Aedes albopictus* was once a forest species and has evolved to live in rural, suburban, and urban human environments. Their eggs can survive for long periods without water, even in arid conditions, and become viable months later when exposed to water. Unlike *Anopheles* mosquitoes, *Aedes* are active biters throughout the day. From an evolutionary perspective, they are an ideal vector—hardy, active feeders, and deeply rooted in human habitats. |

[1] "Anopheles Mosquitoes," CDC, https://www.cdc.gov/malaria/about/biology/index.html.

[2] Kara Rogers, "Aedes," Britannica Encyclopedia, https://www.britannica.com/animal/Aedes; Darvin S. Smith, David J. Marino, and Micah L. Trautwein, "What Are Characteristics of the *Aedes* Mosquito Species That Transmit Dengue?," *Medscape*, May 3, 2019; Julie Beck, "The Other Zika Mosquito," *The Atlantic*, May 2, 2016; "Transmission of Yellow Fever Virus," CDC, https://www.cdc.gov/yellowfever/transmission; "Zika Virus—Modes of Transmission, "CDC, https://www.cdc.gov/zika/hc-providers/preparing-for-zika/clinicalevaluationdisease.html; CDC, "How to Prevent the Spread of the Mosquito That Causes Dengue," https://www.cdc.gov/dengue/resources /Vectorcontrolsheetdengue.pdf.

Arboviruses generally maintain zoonotic transmission cycles between hosts (e.g., birds and small mammals) and their arthropod vectors. Human infections are incidental. However, there are important exceptions where humans become the source of virus amplification and subsequent arthropod infection. These viruses may spread from people to arthropods, and then from arthropods to people, as in the cases of yellow fever, dengue, Zika, and chikungunya.

In this chapter I take a closer look at the five deadliest diseases carried by mosquitoes—yellow fever, dengue, Zika, chikungunya, and malaria—and consider strategies to combat them. Yellow fever, one of the oldest arboviruses, has persisted in killing tens of thousands for decades, despite the existence of a cheap, effective vaccine. Dengue is the heir apparent, having spread quickly, with built-in immune complications. A vaccine exists, but WHO recommends using it only in areas with high levels of infection (high seroprevalence). Chikungunya is another rising menace; although it rarely causes death, its debilitating symptoms can ruin lives. Zika has transitioned from being ignored to being dreaded; its ability to cause congenital neurological defects in newborns has struck fear among poor pregnant women. Malaria is the most lethal of the arboviruses. Cases of malaria are declining—so is treatment effectiveness, due to widespread antimicrobial resistance.

## Yellow Fever

Scientists speculate that the first human yellow fever (YF) cases date back to 1000 BCE, originating in Africa. As global commerce expanded during the Age of Discovery, the YF virus was transported via barrels of water containing mosquito larvae and by infected slaves. The first recorded yellow fever outbreak occurred in 1648 in the Yucatan Peninsula; subsequent outbreaks occurred in the late seventeenth century in the urban port cities of New York, Boston, and Charleston. By the late nineteenth century, YF was killing thousands of Americans; New Orleans reported 26,000 yellow fever deaths between 1839 and 1860, and the deaths from YF among US soldiers during the Spanish-American War triggered the formation of a Yellow Fever Commission, chaired by Major Walter Reed. Reed proved correct Cuban physician Carlos Finlay's 1881 discovery that mosquitoes transmitted the disease, enabling the commission to launch successful mosquito control programs in Cuba, and later in the Panama Canal Zone.

Initial symptoms of YF include fever, muscle pain (prominent backache), headache, loss of appetite, shivers, and nausea or vomiting. Many people who contract YF recover during this phase, but 15 percent of those infected progress to a second, toxic phase. These individuals develop fever, jaundice (hence the name "yellow" fever), and abdominal pains and vomiting. Kidney and liver functions deteriorate quickly, and bleeding may occur from the eyes, nose, mouth, or stomach; blood may appear in vomit and feces. The case-fatality rate among toxic-phase individuals is 20 to 50 percent, with death occurring within ten to fourteen days. Treatment for either form of yellow fever focuses on treating the symptoms, because no cure has yet been found for it. With symptoms similar to other diseases, YF, like most arbovirus infections, is difficult to diagnose. The only way to definitively diagnose YF is through laboratory tests.

In 2017 Brazil experienced the largest outbreak of YF the world had seen in decades. Cases surged throughout the rainy season from January to April. During peak months, Brazil and neighboring countries were gripped by fear, as mosquitoes infected with YF left jungle habitats and moved ever closer to the large metropolitan areas of Bahia and Rio de Janeiro, stopping at villages and towns along the way. The start of 2018's rainy season ushered in a rapid increase in YF cases in major cities, including São Paulo and Rio de Janeiro. With more rainy, hot months ahead, Brazil undertook an ambitious vaccination campaign, reaching nearly 22 million people, on top of more than 13 million people already vaccinated. During the 2017–2018 YF season, 1,376 cases had been reported, but only 75 cases were confirmed during the 2018–2019 season, suggesting that the vaccination program has been effective.[8]

The Brazilian outbreak came on the heels of YF outbreaks in Angola that spread to the DRC, Kenya, Uganda, and China in 2016 and into 2017, leading to the chilling prospect of YF epidemics in densely populated Asian countries. Vaccine supplies were too scarce to cover such a large population. Yellow fever is endemic in South America and sub-Saharan Africa, but Asia had never reported cases until March 2016, when eleven YF-infected Chinese nationals flew home from Angola.

Even though YF is endemic to 45 countries (32 in Africa and 13 in Central and South America), the outbreaks in Brazil and Angola demonstrated the urgent need for continued preparedness. Despite ongoing WHO vaccination campaigns with a much-needed emphasis on routine infant immunizations, tens of thousands of people die from YF every year.[9] As YF spread in the aftermath of the Angolan outbreak, the demand for vaccines surged, and due to global shortages WHO and the United Nations International Children's Emergency Fund (UNICEF) resorted to fractional dosing—administering one-fifth of the normal dose. The United States experienced manufacturing difficulties, leading to a complete depletion of YF vaccine supplies for US travelers.[10] YF vaccine shortages will continue to be a concern, especially if a major spike in cases reoccurs.

Mosquito control, through breeding site elimination and adulticides (insecticides that kill adults), is effective in minimizing YF transmission. Successful mosquito control campaigns that targeted breeding sites by draining swamps and emptying standing-water receptacles helped eliminate *Aedes aegypti* from most of Central and South America, though these mosquitoes have recolonized in urban areas. Insecticides such as dichlorodiphenyltrichloroethane (DDT) became prevalent after the turn of the twentieth century, and by the end of World War II were a crucial component in controlling YF. The development of a YF vaccine in 1937 by Max Thieler offered lifetime immunity and has since become a key tool for preventing and controlling outbreaks.

Dense urban settings, combined with the ubiquity of *Aedes* mosquitoes, leads to increased transmission and makes urban YF outbreaks a major threat. YF transmission is complicated by the fact that humans can transmit infection to mosquitoes before exhibiting symptoms. Mass vaccination is therefore vital. This requires ample stockpiles, effective distribution, and an emphasis on routine infant immunization in countries where VF is endemic. The full vaccine dose is extremely safe and affordable, and conveys lifelong immunity. To address cross-border transmission, WHO's International Health Regulations grant countries the right to require that travelers provide YF vaccination certificates.

Because mosquitoes act as a reservoir for YF, eradication is not feasible. With appropriate surveillance, mosquito control, and vaccination, however, the world's poor—who are disproportionately affected by YF—could be considerably safer.

## Dengue

In 2017 Sri Lanka was struck by an unprecedented outbreak of a different arbovirus: dengue. The monsoon season brought heavy flooding in places with poor sanitation, and garbage piled up, creating ideal mosquito breeding grounds. As a result, from 2010 to 2016 the country saw four times the number of dengue cases compared to the average number.[11]

The outbreak overwhelmed hospitals, forcing them to turn away patients, and required the deployment of the armed forces.[12] Health authorities underestimated the prevalence of dengue, while poor surveillance and education posed huge obstacles to successful control. One analysis explained:

> Sri Lanka has witnessed a series of dengue epidemics over the past five years, with the western province, home to the political capital of Colombo, bearing more than half of the dengue burden. Existing dengue monitoring prevention programs are exhausted as public health inspectors . . . cope with increasing workloads and paper-based modes of surveillance and education, characterizing a reactive system unable to cope with the enormity of the problem.[13]

Similarly, that year in Dhaka, Bangladesh, a sudden flare-up of dengue took a heavy toll. Many patients suffered complications or died due to wrong or inadequate treatment.[14] Without access to affordable broadband internet, surveillance and reporting become burdensome and inaccurate. Technology has the power to vastly improve disease identification and response. Consider the power of geospatial mapping to track disease spread, or the use of artificial intelligence to analyze data and deploy resources efficiently.

Dengue, or dengue fever, has long been a human scourge. This ancient arboviral disease is transmitted by *Aedes aegypti* and caused by four closely related strains of the same virus, which appear to have independently "jumped" from monkeys to humans between 100 and 800 years ago in Africa and Southeast Asia. Epidemics of dengue-like illnesses are reported to have taken place in the French West Indies in 1635 and in Panama in 1699, and continued throughout the eighteenth and nineteenth centuries. World War II wartime shipping transported mosquito eggs, further dispersing the dengue's vector and expanding the dengue endemic zone. Widespread use of DDT, originally intended to eradicate malaria mosquitoes, was eventually applied to *Aedes aegypti* and led to the near elimination of dengue by the late 1950s. Dengue resurged in the 1960s, however, following the end of the malaria eradication campaign (discussed below) and as DDT became widely unpopular due to concerns that it was harmful to humans and the environment.

People may be infected by any of four dengue serotypes (strains). Recovery from infection by a particular one provides lifelong immunity for that serotype but only temporary and partial immunity to the other three serotypes. A person who becomes infected a second time with a different serotype is at risk for developing severe dengue, also known as dengue hemorrhagic fever.

Dengue fever is characterized by high fever and two or more of the following symptoms: severe headache, joint and muscle pain, pain behind the eyes, nausea, vomiting, rash, and swollen glands. Symptoms can last for two to seven days. Most patients recover when their fever declines, but for some patients a decline in fever may be accompanied by fluid accumulation, severe bleeding, plasma leakage, respiratory difficulty, or organ failure. This is dengue hemorrhagic fever, which may further progress with severe abdominal pain, restlessness, fatigue, persistent and bloody vomiting, rapid breathing, and bleeding gums. This critical stage of infection generally lasts 24 to 48 hours and requires proper medical care to reduce the risk of death.

Today dengue is endemic in more than a hundred countries, with Southeast Asia, the Western Pacific, and the Americas most affected. Incidence is climbing rapidly. The dengue virus is now the most widespread arbovirus, causing widespread social and economic disruption in South America and Southeast Asia. In fact, dengue accounts for the highest human morbidity and mortality compared with West Nile, YF, or Zika. Children carry the highest burdens.[15]

In addition to the *Aedes aegypti*, the *Aedes albopictus* mosquito—which has expanded its endemic zone from Southeast Asia to Europe and North America via the international trade in used tires—can also spread dengue. *Aedes albopictus* mosquitoes are highly adaptive and can tolerate cool weather. Transmission occurs year-round, though peak transmission occurs during rainy seasons. Droughts or decreased rainfall and human behavior influence dengue transmission dynamics; for example, increased water hoarding in response to drought can accelerate mosquito densities. The rapid spread of dengue due to unplanned urbanization, increasing globalization, high temperatures, erratic rain spells, and human behavior is exacerbated by the lack of resources for effective, eco-friendly mosquito control.

Like YF, there is no specific treatment for dengue fever. There is a vaccine, though it has proved controversial (see below). Severe cases of dengue fever generally require body fluid replenishment, and individuals who recover can experience fatigue and weakness for months.

## Chikungunya

In 2004 a new strain of chikungunya emerged from coastal Kenya and began to circulate in the Indian Ocean islands. The outbreak in La Réunion, a French overseas department, is best remembered for the sheer volume of cases—300,000, or 1 in 3 persons—and as one of the earliest, most severe epidemics. The strain spread through South Asia, causing major outbreaks affecting millions of people. Travelers brought chikungunya to the Western Hemisphere, where the virus began circulating among mosquitoes and people.

Europe reported its first cases of chikungunya in 2007, when more than 200 people were infected. At the time, the cautious stance was that the "*possibility* of introducing" chikungunya into Europe could not be "ruled out."[16] Just ten years later, France experienced its third chikungunya outbreak. In an incredibly short time, chikungunya went from the disease you've never heard of, confined to the Global South, to an expected disease wherever *Aedes albopictus* and *aegypti* mosquitoes are endemic.

Chikungunya, an arboviral, has more recent origins than YF or dengue, though it could be older than reports indicate. It was first reported in 1952–1953 in the border area between Tanzania and Mozambique. Retrospective studies suggest, however, that chikungunya epidemics may have taken place as far back as the late eighteenth century but were miscategorized as dengue due to similarities between the two diseases' symptoms.

A person infected with Chikungunya will usually begin to show symptoms within three to seven days after being bitten by an infected mosquito. Chikungunya is characterized by the rapid onset of fever, frequently accompanied by joint pain, joint swelling, muscle pain, rash, and headache. The disease is rarely fatal, but the joint pain it causes can be debilitating and persist for months, or even years. Most patients will recover within a few weeks and are then immune to future infections.

WHO has identified chikungunya in over sixty countries, mostly in Africa, Asia, and the Indian subcontinent, although Europe and North America have experienced outbreaks. Latin America and the Caribbean have also seen widespread chikungunya epidemics. Global interconnectivity now guarantees that all regions where mosquitoes can transmit the disease face a heightened and ongoing risk. The emergence of chikungunya is a major global health threat, underscoring the urgency of developing a safe and effective vaccine. Several vaccines are being tested, but none are licensed.[17] As with YF and dengue, there is no specific treatment.

## Zika

In the lead-up to the 2016 Summer Olympic Games in Rio de Janeiro, organizers faced a daunting challenge: how to ensure the health of athletes and spectators in the midst of a Zika outbreak. Panic among athletes and spectators alike cast a dark shadow over the Games, bringing even more of the world's attention to the specter of Zika. And of course, local residents, especially impoverished women, bore the greatest risk.

Zika is the most recent of mosquito-borne human threats. It is named for the Zika Forest outside of Entebbe, Uganda, where it was first discovered in monkeys in 1947, and then in *Aedes africanus* mosquitoes in 1948. The first human cases were detected in Uganda and Tanzania in 1952. Initially detected only in equatorial Africa, and frequently associated with mild or asymptomatic illness (usually a non-itchy rash that covers the body), isolated cases of Zika were detected in several countries in Asia beginning in the 1980s. Until 2007 there were no Zika outbreaks and only fourteen confirmed cases of disease.[18]

The totality of the signs and symptoms of Zika are not entirely known, as the disease and the virus appear to be evolving. The known symptoms of the Zika virus are fever, muscle and joint pain, headache, skin rashes, conjunctivitis, and malaise; these symptoms are mild and can last for two to seven days. WHO has concluded that Zika infection during pregnancy can cause congenital brain abnormalities, including microcephaly, in fetuses. Zika is also a known trigger for Guillain-Barré syndrome, a disorder where the host body's immune system attacks parts of the nervous system and weakens muscles. At present, scientists and public health researchers are investigating links between Zika and a wide range of other neurological disorders.

Once disregarded, Zika has now garnered political attention. Zika virus (ZIKV) has changed since its discovery more than seventy years ago: its endemic zone has spread dramatically, and the symptoms have transformed from benign to severe. The speed of these changes has taken scientists by surprise and caused public alarm.

Like other arboviruses, ZIKV circulates between nonhuman primates and mosquitoes in tropical biomes in Africa. This cycle is not established anywhere else, though scientists are concerned that it will become established in other regions. The disease has spread globally in recent decades due to the ubiquitous *Aedes aegypti* and *Aedes albopictus* mosquitoes. It is essential to increase countries' capacity for surveillance, mosquito abatement, and risk communication. Barrier protection (i.e., wearing clothing covering the body) and mosquito repellents are effective, as is preventing mosquitoes from entering homes by using screens, closed doors, and mosquito nets. Destruction of breeding sites and using adulticides are also important strategies for controlling Zika.

ZIKV is also transmissible via sexual activity. In regions where ZIKV is actively transmitted, WHO recommends that sexually active men and women use condoms, and that pregnant women practice safer sex or abstain from sexual activity during pregnancy. In regions where ZIKV is not actively transmitted, WHO recommends that persons returning from ZIKV-endemic regions practice safer sex or abstain from sexual activity for six months. During the height of the Brazilian outbreak, the CDC even recommended that women in outbreak areas postpone pregnancy.

The Brazilian outbreak came less than a decade after the first large outbreak in 2007 on the Micronesian island of Yap, when 73 percent of the island's 11,250 residents became infected. Yap did not report any deaths, hospitalizations, or neurological complications. In 2013–2014, additional Pacific island outbreaks resulted in thousands more cases. Still, scientists regarded Zika as a mild disease that did not warrant urgent action.

Then came Brazil. In March 2015 the northeastern states of Brazil reported a mysterious illness characterized by skin rash, afflicting 7,000 people. By May, Brazil had identified samples as positive for Zika and confirmed ZIKV transmission throughout the country. In July the link between Zika and Guillain-Barré syndrome emerged. By November, Brazil had reported 141 cases of microcephaly in newborns from Pernambuco state. The subsequent detection of ZIKV in the babies' blood shocked the world: Zika, the once-benign infection, was causing infants to be born with severe congenital deformities.

Since then the virus has spread throughout the Americas, up to the southern edge of the United States. On February 1, 2016, WHO declared Zika's neurological consequences a public health emergency of international concern. That November WHO discontinued the state of emergency. While it downgraded the outbreak's status and allayed fears, there was also another subtle, disconcerting message: Zika was "here to stay," and emergency containment would be replaced by long-term efforts to understand, prevent, and protect.

Not only is Zika here to stay; so are its consequences: a generation of babies living with neurologic abnormalities. Many of the families caring for Zika-affected children are poor and in desperate need of education and services. Governments must work to provide not only vaccines and prevention, but also family and community support. There is an ethical duty to provide services to enhance the quality of life for everyone Zika touches.

## Malaria

Imagine a parasite that has adapted perfectly to humans, requires a human body to replicate, and attacks while its host is sleeping. This parasite has killed hundreds of millions of people and resisted all attempts to destroy it. Unlike arboviruses, malaria is caused by a single-celled intracellular parasite: *Plasmodium falciparum, P. vivax, P. ovale,* and *P. malariae.* Globally, *P. falciparum* and *P. vivax* are the most common malarial infections. Infections with *P. falciparum* pose a greater health concern because these infections can be more severe or fatal. A fifth species, *P. knowlesi,* circulates primarily in macaques, but is rarely (yet increasingly) reported in humans. The parasite circulates between mosquitoes and humans. Human malaria transmission is quite different from arboviral diseases. Arboviral infections in humans are incidental, as the viruses depend on nonhuman hosts as their reservoirs. But for malaria parasites, humans *are* the reservoir.

Malaria is an ancient, resilient disease that has plagued humans for thousands of years. Malaria-like symptoms have been documented since 2700 BCE, in records from ancient China, Greece, and Rome. In 1880 Dr. Alphonse Laveran, a French military doctor posted in Algeria, uncovered the cause, after discovering malaria parasites in a patient's red blood cells. In 1897 Dr. Ronald Ross, a British officer serving with the Indian Medical Service, discovered malaria parasites inside an *Anopheles* mosquito that had recently bitten an infected patient. He went on to demonstrate the role of mosquitoes in the transmission of malaria.

The life cycle of the malaria parasite is complex. When feeding on humans, a female *Anopheles* mosquito injects 10 to 100 sporozoites (spores of the malaria parasite) into the bloodstream; some of these spores survive the immune system and invade liver cells. The liver stage is not characterized by disease, though is the stage where the most advanced malaria vaccine, RTS,S/AS01 (see below), works by blocking sporozoites from entering liver cells, preventing replication. After five to sixteen days of sporozoite maturation, the infected liver cells rupture, releasing 10,000 to 30,000 merozoites into the bloodstream, where they invade red blood cells and further reproduce. Blood-stage parasites are usually the target of drug research because they are responsible for disease symptoms and because they are more easily manipulated within the laboratory. A small percentage of merozoites differentiate into the sexual form of the parasite, called gametocytes. These circulate in the host's blood until they are taken up by a feeding female mosquito, leading to their further development and, ultimately, to sporozoites, which can once again infect people.

Malaria symptoms can be uncomplicated or severe. An attack of uncomplicated, or classical malaria, can last six to ten hours. The attacks, which repeat every few days, generally consists of three stages: a cold stage, characterized by shivering or chills; a hot stage, characterized by fever, vomiting, and headache; and a sweating stage, characterized by sweating, tiredness, and a return to normal temperature. Uncomplicated malaria can also take the form of a combination of symptoms: sweats, fever, nausea and vomiting, headaches, chills, body aches, and general malaise.

Severe malaria involves serious organ failure and other abnormalities. Cerebral malaria is the most common complication and cause of death due to *P. falciparum* infection. Other manifestations of severe malaria include severe anemia due to red blood cell destruction, acute kidney failure, and hypoglycemia (dangerously low blood sugar levels).

Malaria is endemic in close to ninety countries across Africa, Asia, and the Americas.[19] There were an estimated 228 million cases of malaria and 405,000 malaria deaths worldwide in 2018.[20] About 93 percent of cases were in Africa. Children under five accounted for 67 percent of worldwide malaria deaths.[21] Almost half of the world's population is at risk.[22] Despite the enormity of cases, from 2010 to 2018 global malaria incidence actually declined by 24 percent, and mortality rates by 39 percent.[23]

Two antimalarial treatments—artemisinin and quinine—have been used for centuries. Both of them target blood parasites. Artemisinin, which is derived from the sweet wormwood plant, also known as the Qinghao plant, has been in use since the second century BCE. It is still used in artemisinin-based combination therapies, and researchers have now tripled the artemisinin naturally produced by sweet wormwood leaves by genetically modifying the plant.[24] The bark of cinchona trees, which contains quinine, was used by the indigenous peoples of Peru, Bolivia, and Ecuador in teas as a muscle relaxant before it was discovered to be an effective treatment against malaria in the seventeenth century. There are also more modern treatments; the appropriate medication (or combination treatment) depends on the species of *Plasmodium*.

Antimalarial resistance poses a serious threat to global efforts to control and eliminate malaria (see Chapter 5). *P. falciparum* has formed resistance to previous generations of medicines, such as chloroquine and sulfadoxine-pyrimethamine, ultimately torpedoing WHO's malaria eradication campaign. Today resistance to artemisinin-based drugs has been detected in five countries within the Mekong subregion.[25]

Resistance is perhaps the greatest threat today to the goal of eradicating the disease entirely. This goal was established in the mid-twentieth century, after the world witnessed the success of DDT against malaria. In 1955 WHO launched the Global Malaria Eradication Program (GMEP) at the eighth World Health Assembly (WHA) with the stated goal of eradicating the disease entirely. As part of its strategy, the GMEP employed vertical interventions that primarily consisted of indoor residual spraying with DDT and other insecticides. Traditional strategies aimed at controlling malaria, such as eliminating breeding grounds, were abandoned as more resources were channeled into eradication efforts. To receive international funds, countries were required to adopt the goals and means of the GMEP.[26]

Despite initial successes, many countries where eradication had seemed promising experienced resurgences of malaria starting at the beginning of the 1960s, in large part because mosquitoes developed resistance to DDT and to malaria medications. In 1969, at the 22nd WHA, the world recognized that eradication was not feasible with the means available. Though the GMEP failed to achieve its goal, it did succeed in eliminating malaria from 37 of the 142 malaria-endemic countries, and from two continents: Europe and Australia.[27]

Today there is renewed interest in eradicating malaria. In 2015 the WHA adopted the Global Technical Strategy for Malaria 2016–2030, through which WHO member states commit to a "bold vision of a world free of malaria."[28] Learning from past failures, the Global Technical Strategy moves away from the vertical methodology employed by the GMEP and instead aims to strengthen health systems and address drug and insecticide resistance. It also reiterates the importance of vector control.[29] The Global Technical Strategy's goals are ambitious, but achievable: eliminate malaria in thirty-five countries, reduce incidence and mortality by 90 percent, and prevent resurgence in malaria-free countries, all by 2030.

Eliminating malaria by 2040 "could save an estimated 11 million lives and unlock an estimated $2 trillion in economic benefits."[30] WHO's Global Technical Strategy offers a blueprint for doing so. Malaria is a stubbornly persistent but beatable foe. Decisive action could achieve one of history's greatest global health victories.

### Advances in Mosquito Control and Disease Prevention

As the centuries-old battle between humans and mosquitoes rages on, the health community pursues traditional approaches while developing new ones to control the vector and prevent deadly diseases.

#### Environmental Management

Environmental management, a traditional technique, aims to eliminate mosquitoes' breeding grounds. Because most mosquitoes lay their eggs in pools of stagnant water, including ponds, lake edges, or water that has accumulated in potted plants, roof gutters, and discarded plastic containers, actions to keep water from accumulating in these locations reduces sites for mosquitoes to lay their eggs, thereby reducing the overall mosquito population. Eliminating stagnant water is a key mosquito control strategy. It played a vital role, for instance, in controlling the 2016 Zika epidemic in Brazil.[31]

#### Chemical Control

Another traditional strategy is chemical control. Insecticides are used to control mosquito populations either by larvicide or by adulticide. Adulticide targets adult vectors through indoor residual spraying (IRS), which involves coating walls and other surfaces inside peoples' homes. It aims to reduce mosquito density, longevity, and transmission parameters.[32] IRS techniques saved hundreds of millions of lives in Europe, Asia, and the Americas between the 1940 and 1980s, and increasingly has been used successfully in Africa.[33] Larvicide, by contrast, targets larvae to reduce adult populations by preventing the mosquito larvae from maturing. The effectiveness of this intervention, however, is limited because larval habitats vary greatly. WHO therefore recommends larvicides as a supplementary intervention where mosquito larvae are few, fixed, and findable.[34] The method should also be restricted to containers that cannot be removed or otherwise managed.[35]

Although chemical control has been shown to be useful and cost-effective, it has its difficulties. First, drinking water must be treated carefully to reduce potential toxicity for humans.[36] Second, insecticide resistance to the chemicals must be monitored to ensure that chemical treatment continues to be effective.[37] And third, public skepticism can be a barrier to using chemical control. For example, DDT is an insecticide that, although low-cost and effective, has been criticized due to its negative effects on human health and the environment. Still, it remains one of twelve WHO-recommended insecticides for malaria prevention and, in the absence of comparably effective alternatives, will remain an important option for disease control.[38] The Stockholm Convention on Persistent Organic Pollutants places restrictions on the use of DDT but permits its use in IRS, given its effectiveness in controlling vector-borne diseases.[39]

## The Bed Net Revolution

Bed nets are a core, cost-effective prevention strategy for protecting people from mosquito-transmitted diseases, most notably malaria. Bed nets act as physical barriers to prevent mosquitoes from biting people while they sleep. There are two main types of nets: insecticide-treated nets (ITNs) and long-lasting insecticidal nets (LLINs).

Bed nets are most effective when treated with insecticides that repel, injure, or kill the mosquitoes.[40] Ordinary ITNs are a powerful tool, but they require regular retreatment to remain effective. The protection that LLINs offer, by contrast, is meant to last at least three years (the life span of the net itself), thus eliminating the need for retreatment.

WHO supports the use of LLINs and, in the Global Technical Strategy, sets a goal of universal coverage for all people at risk of malaria.[41] In 2016, 54 percent of the at-risk sub-Saharan African population slept under LLINs. Although 80 percent of households owned at least one net, only 43 percent of households had enough nets.[42] Moreover, health authorities often distribute LLINs and other ITNs without providing education on their proper use.

Mosquitoes can become resistant to the insecticides used on treated nets. Consequently, in 2017 WHO recommended a change in insecticides used to treat LLINs in areas where malaria-transmitting mosquitoes have developed resistance. Further testing is required to ensure the effectiveness of these nets.[43] In addition, researchers have discovered that saturating bed nets with antimalarial drugs can block the development of the *P. falciparum,* the most dangerous mosquito parasite, preventing further transmission. This new approach to using bed nets to fight malaria has the potential to extend the effectiveness of bed nets as part of malaria control strategies.[44]

## Vaccines

Vaccines have great potential to transform the battle against infectious disease, especially malaria, yet few vaccines exist for vector-borne diseases. Vaccines for YF and Japanese encephalitis are the only two examples of effective vaccines, though a recent study has seen promising results for a new dengue vaccine and a pilot study has begun for a malaria vaccine.[45]

The dengue vaccine must be tetravalent to effectively protect against the four dengue viruses (serotypes 1–4).[46] In 2016 Sanofi's Dengvaxia (CYD-TDV) became the first dengue vaccine to reach the market. But in 2017 the company announced a major problem. Although the vaccine lowered the risk of hospitalization for severe dengue infection in children who had already had at least one bout of the disease, it elevated the risk for children who were vaccinated before ever having dengue.

When the Philippines rolled out plans to vaccinate one million children, it increased the risk of severe illness in previously unexposed children. Amid widespread public anger, the government suspended the vaccination program and threatened legal action against Sanofi. Public confidence in all vaccines plummeted in the wake of the controversy.[47] WHO then recommended that the vaccine be given only to children who had previously been infected with dengue.[48] But currently no point-of-care rapid test for prior infection is available, and having to test before vaccination complicates mass vaccination campaigns. Although other vaccines are now in development, public trust may be difficult to restore.

Pharmaceutical companies and foundations are also attempting to develop a vaccine for malaria. The RTS,S/AS01 vaccine, developed by GlaxoSmith-Kline Biologicals and the PATH Malaria Vaccine Initiative, is the world's first malaria vaccine and acts against *Plasmodium falciparum*, the deadliest of the malaria parasites.[49] It provides partial protection, reducing malaria cases by approximately one-third.[50] In 2019 a large-scale pilot implementation program began in Ghana, Kenya, and Malawi, where the vaccine is being administered to young children through routine immunization programs.[51]

Research is also being conducted to create a vaccine that provides broad protection against all mosquito-borne diseases. NIH scientists began Phase 1 clinical trials in 2017 to test an investigational vaccine, AGS-v, which, rather than targeting specific viruses and parasites, is designed to trigger an immune response to mosquito saliva.[52] Scientists hypothesize that this vaccine could also control mosquito populations by causing mosquitoes who bite vaccinated individuals to die or become unable to reproduce.[53]

## Gene Editing and Irradiation

Eliminating mosquitoes' ability to transmit infection holds the promise of eliminating malaria. Genetic engineering, particularly using CRISPR (clustered regularly interspaced short palindromic repeats), is at the center of this effort. This gene-editing tool, which now dominates much of biological research, allows scientists to cut targeted DNA sequences, then use the cell's own repair system to add or delete genetic material or replace a DNA segment with a customized sequence. Scientists are using CRISPR to delete targeted genes in mosquitoes to make the mosquitoes resistant to malaria parasites.[54] Recently scientists used CRISPR to test for gene drives to suppress the reproductive capability of mosquitoes.[55] Gene drives are gene-editing techniques that allow the desired genes to spread throughout the population; targeting genes that reduce reproductive capability could therefore eliminate an entire population. A study reported in 2018 used a gene drive to eliminate an entire caged mosquito population within seven to eleven generations, which was the first time this technology successfully suppressed a whole population.[56]

Before it can be used outside the laboratory, this technique must be rigorously tested in larger spaces that mimic ecological conditions and must overcome public skepticism of genetic engineering.[57] Despite WHO, CDC, and FDA assurances of safety for certain genetic modification techniques, the public has still been resistant to genetic technologies. In 2016, for example, residents of Key Haven, Florida, opposed by a margin of nearly four to one a genetic program to reduce wild-type *Aedes aegypti*.[58] The public expressed concerns about the impacts on the environment, human health, and genetic modification more generally. There was also an overlay of distrust in government.[59] For genetic technologies to become viable, public trust will have to be restored. If ongoing testing demonstrates safety and effectiveness, genetically modified mosquitoes could play a vital role in vector control.

Another approach now being tested combines irradiation with the force of numbers. A pilot project in South Africa uses radiation to sterilize male mosquitoes and then releases mass-produced sterile males in numbers that overwhelm the wild population. Before launching the project, a malaria awareness campaign was implemented to ensure community support.[60]

## Bacterial Assistance

Along with vaccines, gene editing, and irradiation, scientists have discovered another mosquito control technique: *Wolbachia*, a bacterium that occurs naturally within many insects but not in *Aedes aegypti*. When scientists infect male *Aedes aegypti* with *Wolbachia* and release them into the wild, infected males breed with uninfected females. Eggs from those clutches (groups of eggs produced at a single time) do not hatch, reducing mosquito populations. When two infected adults breed, the eggs will hatch, but the offspring are infected with *Wolbachia*, which will lead to further population reductions, as the offspring may be infertile or produce eggs that do not hatch. Moreover, *Wolbachia* blocks dengue virus replication within mosquitoes, which is potentially a major advancement toward eliminating dengue.

### Protecting Humanity against Its Greatest Killer

Even as new mosquito-borne infections continue to arise and ancient ones persist, we are better equipped than ever to combat them. An array of mosquito control strategies already exists, along with lessons on their effective use. Adding to this arsenal through further vaccine development, like the malaria vaccine implementation program currently under way in sub-Saharan Africa and advances in gene editing and the potential of gene drives, brings us closer to the goal of making the world far safer from humans' smallest but most lethal nonhuman enemy. Any optimism should be tempered, however, by the limits of traditional strategies, hurdles still to overcome for newer possibilities (from scientific challenges to skeptical publics), and the weaknesses of the health systems in many of the countries where the burdens of mosquito-transmitted infections are greatest (see Chapter 9). Growing antimicrobial resistance and climate change pose further challenges to dramatically reducing the toll of these diseases (see Chapters 5 and 6).

History teaches us to proceed cautiously. As we learned from Zika, diseases that we think we understand can change, becoming a major public health threat. The future remains rife with uncertainty: Might science one day wipe out the mosquito? What would such a world be like? Will we someday live in a world without malaria or arboviruses? Will our efforts to genetically modify mosquitoes present unforeseen human or ecological risks? Will these diseases instead gain new footholds as climate change accelerates? One thing is certain: without increased efforts to control and defeat the mosquito, humans will continue to fall victim in massive numbers to the world's deadliest creature.

So instead we must continue to invest in scientific research to further realize its potential in areas ranging from vaccine development to gene editing. But the battle against mosquitoes and the diseases they carry will have to be waged on many fronts, as diverse as strengthening health systems, building public trust, and limiting resistance, much less curtailing climate change. As ever, we must not disregard the magnitude of the threat from the tiny mosquito, but rather be humble in our efforts to protect humanity against this small foe.

# CHAPTER 4

# Disease by Decision

## Human-Induced Threats to Biosafety and Biosecurity

On October 2, 2001, Robert Stevens, a sixty-three-year-old photojournalist at American Media Inc., was hospitalized in Florida after experiencing shortness of breath and vomiting. While doctors first suspected meningitis, he was later diagnosed with inhalational anthrax, caused by the naturally occurring yet deadly bacterium *Bacillus anthracis* entering the lungs. Days later, Stevens would become the first person to die during the 2001 anthrax attacks.

Around September 18, 2001, five anonymous letters laced with deadly anthrax spores were mailed to major news media. America was already on high alert following the terrorist attacks on 9/11. On October 9 two more anthrax letters were sent to senators Tom Daschle and Patrick Leahy. The anthrax attacks ultimately caused five deaths (two postal workers, a hospital worker, a journalist, and an elderly woman whose mail was cross-contaminated) and infected at least seventeen other people, including a seven-month-old infant.

In response, the Federal Bureau of Investigation (FBI) launched the "largest and most complex" investigation ever.[1] It involved over 10,000 interviews, 6,000 pieces of evidence, 5,000 grand jury subpoenas, and 5,000 environmental samples. Nearly nine years passed before the FBI formally closed the case in 2010, naming Dr. Bruce Edwards Ivins, a scientist at a US biodefense laboratory in Fort Detrick, as the suspected perpetrator. Dr. Ivins took his own life before any charges were filed. However, an independent review by the National Academy of Medicine (NAM) in 2011 cast doubt on the scientific evidence connecting Dr. Ivins's laboratory to the anthrax found in the letters.[2] Their report found that it was not possible to draw definitive conclusions about the origins of the anthrax, because the available data did not rule out other possible sources.[3] A second report in 2014 from the Government Accountability Office reached a similar conclusion on the basis that the FBI employed poorly designed sampling and statistical methods in its investigation.[4] Unanswered questions remain about this deadly biological attack.

The malevolent use of pathogens as weapons of terror is not new. In ancient Athens, for example, a city leader poisoned the local water supply with the toxic roots of the *Helleborus* plant.[5] Yet globalization and scientific advancement have created unprecedented threats in the modern age. Technological advancements in computing power, tools to synthesize and edit long tracts of DNA, and heightened understanding of biological systems promise enormous benefits in areas ranging from health and medicine to agriculture, energy, and the environment. Researchers can now study infectious agents by synthesizing dangerous pathogens from scratch (as done with smallpox in 1994) or enhancing the transmissibility of microbes (as in the case of influenza H5N1 in 2012). In 2019 scientists at the CDC created a synthetic version of the Ebola virus strand that was circulating in the Democratic Republic of Congo to develop and test medical countermeasures.[6] Meanwhile, the proliferation of information that is openly available on the internet has "democratized" science, enabling amateur and professional scientists alike to pursue research experiments in makeshift laboratories or even their own homes.

It is not difficult to imagine how the same tools that promise solutions for health threats could lead to global catastrophe if they end up in untrained or malicious hands. Instead of being used to prevent or cure diseases, the technique of gene editing could be used to make a dangerous pathogen even more lethal or transmissible. Instead of enhancing vaccine development for diseases like COVID-19, pathogens could be strengthened to evade countermeasures. Major social and ethical challenges arise regarding what information should be publicly shared, who should have access to genetic sequencing data, and who should be authorized to make information-sharing decisions. How can we harness the benefits of modern biotechnology without unleashing potentially catastrophic threats to biosecurity and biosafety?

"Biosecurity" refers to actions to protect humans, animals, and the environment against the spread of harmful biological substances.[7] It includes precautions to prevent the intentional removal of toxins or pathogens from research laboratories for malicious, harmful, or unlawful purposes. It also covers policies relating to "dual-use research of concern" (DURC), which is research that offers knowledge that could be misapplied to pose significant threats to public health and safety.

"Biosafety" refers to the maintenance of safe conditions in biological research facilities to prevent the accidental escape of hazardous materials that could harm laboratory workers, communities, or the environment. The physical sharing of viruses between laboratories has always come with inherent risks of contamination, but more recent developments such as sharing genetic sequencing data, the ability to recreate or enhance dangerous pathogens, and the democratization of biology require scientists and policymakers to rethink what it means to be biosafe.

At times the potential for misuse has led policymakers to pause or even ban some types of biological research.[8] In other cases, policymakers require "hardened" research sites, where dangerous pathogens cannot escape into the environment or into the hands of a bad actor. Even the possibility of biothreats has fueled distrust between countries: during the COVID-19 pandemic, US secretary of state Mike Pompeo alleged that the SARS-CoV-2 virus came from a Chinese lab, whether manmade or through an accidental escape. That the virus could have been manmade contradicted all evidence from scientists and intelligence agencies that signified the virus was a product of nature, and the intelligence community and epidemiologists considered it highly unlikely that the virus had escaped from a laboratory.[9]

To avoid global catastrophe, regulations for biosafety and biosecurity must be informed by the intricacies of the science itself, as well as the tremendous potential to improve human health and the environment. Through proper regulations, risks can be universally monitored, mitigated, and addressed. This chapter explores how national governments, international organizations, and scientists can engage in a regulatory process that advances biosafety and biosecurity to maximize the discovery of promising scientific advancements as well as global health security.

### Emerging Benefits and Risks of Biological Research

Biomedical research is valuable for its potential to generate information that can save, improve, and extend human lives. Research and development are essential for discovering new vaccines, antimicrobials, and other medicines needed to respond effectively to novel diseases. The availability of investigational vaccines and treatments for Ebola, for example, was instrumental during the first outbreak in the DRC in 2018, and ultimately helped control the DRC's second 2018 Ebola outbreak, in the country's war-torn eastern region, though only after more than two years and several thousand deaths.

New technologies are opening up new possibilities. In the past few decades, advances in gene-sequencing technologies have allowed scientists to "read" DNA segments like sentences in a book. More-recent gene synthesis technologies have enabled scientists to "write" or edit genetic sequences by stringing together As, Gs, Cs, and Ts—DNA's bases, whose order constitutes our genetic sequence. CRISPR, whose promise against malaria we saw in Chapter 3, has brought these technologies to new heights. Scientists have even discovered ways to create genetically engineered bacteria (in the form of synthetic microbiomes) that can act as drug-making factories inside the human body upon ingestion.[10]

Some forms of biomedical research are controversial. "Gain-of-function" (GOF) research, for example, involves modifying a pathogen to acquire traits it does not possess in the wild, including to increase its pathogenicity or to enable more efficient human-to-human transmission.

These technologies, if used responsibly, can help scientists better prepare for, detect, and respond to emerging infections. More-sophisticated understanding of microbes can also help develop vaccines and other countermeasures against threats—such as COVID-19 and the 1918 Spanish influenza—that would otherwise overwhelm the human immune system. Imagine the benefits of being able to predict the next pathogenic shift, enhance surveillance, and have countermeasures on hand to end an outbreak at its earliest stages.

In an effort to accelerate scientific advance, an open science movement has gradually taken hold internationally, encouraging scientific advancement by making research available to all. The European Commission's national funding agencies, for instance, require grant recipients to make their research freely and publicly accessible.[11] The coalition that enabled this change intends to expand the model globally. Openness of research methods, data, and findings promotes key values of scientific freedom, integrity, and transparency.

Yet publishing certain research, like GOF research, carries considerable risk, leaving many to question the wisdom of sharing data publicly. With a simple DNA fragment or genetic sequencing data, anyone with the requisite expertise can potentially recreate a dangerous pathogen, with scant regulatory oversight. In 2002, for example, researchers recreated poliovirus in a test tube after mail-ordering genetic segments and chemically stringing them together.[12] In 2005 the *Guardian* placed an online order for a DNA fragment of the smallpox virus, exposing the ease with which basically anyone can obtain dangerous biological materials.[13]

The "democratization" of biological tools and information stimulates new and exciting opportunities to improve human health and the environment, but may exacerbate the potential for the misuse of research. As more people become engaged in and have access to biological research, the risk of dangerous errors and misuse grows, with potentially devastating consequences.

Consider an incident involving H5N1, or "bird flu," an avian influenza virus that causes severe and highly infectious respiratory disease in birds. Its lethality, endemic presence, and large host reservoir make H5N1 a pandemic threat, and billions of dollars have been spent on studying it. In humans, H5N1 is thought to have a 59 percent case fatality rate—nearly double that of smallpox. H5N1 does not easily infect or spread between humans, and contact with infected birds has caused only a few known human cases. Like other flu viruses, however, H5N1 constantly mutates and could undergo genetic changes that make it more transmissible between humans.[14]

In 2011 two groups of researchers, in the United States and the Netherlands, genetically altered H5N1 to render the virus transmissible between ferrets, a well-recognized model for human influenza transmission. The researchers wanted to increase the understanding of viral host adaption to better prevent and control naturally occurring outbreaks. However, misuse of these results could lead to a global pandemic. This research sparked considerable controversy among scientists and regulators.[15]

Beyond creating more infectious or lethal agents, biosafety risks from GOF research and other forms of synthetic biology include introducing novel pathogens or reintroducing previously eradicated pathogens for which humans have little to no immunity. WHO, for example, declared wild smallpox eradicated in 1980, but the virus's entire genetic sequence has been published, creating the possibility that some actor could reintroduce the virus into society.

## Protecting People and the Environment, Inside and Outside the Laboratory

As science accelerates, so does the complexity of maintaining adequate safeguards to protect humans and the environment from potentially dangerous pathogens and genetically modified organisms. Laboratory workers and their surroundings are the primary consideration in failures in biosafety, but biosafety cannot start and stop at the laboratory door. Contagious pathogens do not respect the walls of a laboratory or the borders of a nation, so a single laboratory acquired infection (LAI) or release outside the laboratory could result in a regional or global health emergency. While not reaching that scale, the risk was made clear in the years following the 2003 SARS epidemic, when multiple laboratory-acquired SARS infections were reported in the Asia-Pacific region;[16] some of these were caused by accidentally spilled waste.[17]

But imagine this risk on an even greater scale, if research involving a highly deadly and infectious pathogen, such as smallpox, resulted in a human LAI. Early detection would be critical to preventing its spread, but symptoms might take days or even weeks to manifest. If laboratory workers cannot immediately identify and report the infection, governments will be unable to respond. Laboratory workers might also lack incentives to report the incident, deterred by the prospect of major fines, reputational risks, or loss of grant funding. In the meantime the virus could rapidly spread from one person to the next, claiming more lives and resources with each passing moment.

Thankfully, a bio-incident of such scale has yet to occur, but human error has led to mishaps that could have been disastrous. In 2014, vials of live smallpox virus were discovered at the US Food and Drug Administration (FDA) that should have been disposed of or transferred decades earlier.[18] In 2015 a top-secret biological and chemical military testing facility in Utah mistakenly shipped vials of live anthrax spores to facilities worldwide that were not authorized to work with these materials. Many of the eighty-six initial recipients shared their samples with other laboratories, resulting in nearly a hundred additional sites having contact with the live specimens. Fortunately no one was infected in this "inexcusable institutional failure."[19] What is most concerning is that these events took place at sites that have high safety standards. Imagine how much greater the risk would be if amateur scientists in makeshift laboratories were handling hazardous biological materials.

Laboratory failures pose risks to the practice of science itself. Safety lapses can damage reputations and create distrust among laboratory workers and scientists. Research involving highly transmissible pathogens, such as novel influenza strains, arouses fear among experts and the public alike. The open science movement has added to the risk by increasing the potential for high-consequence research to be replicated by less experienced scientists—or worse, by those with malevolent intentions. These growing risks fuel arguments against open publication. In the United States, the National Science Advisory Board for Biosecurity (NSABB) asked the H5N1 researchers who genetically altered H5N1 to make the virus transmissible between ferrets to delay publishing their research. In 2014 these same biosafety concerns led, in part, to the government placing a moratorium (later lifted) on federal funding for GOF research involving influenza, MERS, and SARS viruses. Science and innovation stalled while regulators grappled with bringing safety up to speed.

Biosafety risks also arise outside the traditional laboratory setting, when altered organisms are deliberately released outside laboratories for the purpose of bringing a desired change to a natural setting. As discussed in Chapter 3, scientists have used CRISPR to create a gene drive designed to limit the reproductive capacity of disease-carrying mosquitoes, and explored the possibility of releasing these genetically engineered mosquitoes into the wild. And in 2006 researchers treated Crohn's disease patients through topical delivery of living, genetically modified bacteria.[20]

### Biosafety Standards, Controls, and Shortcomings

A bio-incident involving a highly lethal or contagious pathogen, such as H5N1 or smallpox, could have lasting consequences that extend beyond the confines of a laboratory to jeopardize communities, nations, and the practice of science itself. Despite global risks, biosafety has largely been considered a localized concern, with the focus on scientists and laboratories as the first line of defense. Laboratories and institutions worldwide need to follow rigorous safety procedures, either voluntarily or as mandated by national governments. National and institutional standards exist for classifying pathogens for human lethality, with safety and containment requirements set accordingly. Institutional biosafety committees review registrations for clinical trials and work involving recombinant DNA or highly infectious agents. Biosafety officers are often charged with reviewing institutional risks, enforcing biosafety protocols, and monitoring researchers' compliance.

Biosafety procedures are often mandated by national governments, particularly when research involves highly lethal pathogens or is government sponsored (see Table 4.1 for a discussion of US regulatory sources).[21] Yet in an assessment of ten nations' biosafety systems in 2016, researchers found

**Table 4.1.** Sources of US Biosafety Regulation

| Program / Instrument | Lead Agency | Applicability | Description |
|---|---|---|---|
| Federal Select Agent Program (FSAP)[1] | CDC | Any possession, use, or transfer of biological select agents and toxins designated by the US Department of Health and Human Services (HHS) | Requires all individuals and institutions working with listed agents and toxins to register and follow safety protocols set by HHS and Department of Agriculture |
| Biosafety in Microbial and Biomedical Laboratories (BMBL)[2] | National Institutes of Health (NIH) and CDC | US research facilities | Delineates four biosafety levels (BSL 1–4) for work with biological agents that are harmful to human health, and provides safety standards |
| Guidelines for Research Involving Recombinant or Synthetic Nucleic Acid Molecules[3] | NIH | Institutions that receive NIH funding and conduct recombinant and synthetic nucleic acid research | Establishes biosafety standards to be enforced by institutional biosafety committees |

[1] "Federal Select Agent Program," FSAP, https://www.selectagents.gov/index.html.

[2] NIH and CDC, *Biosafety in Microbiological and Biomedical Laboratories, Fifth Edition* (Bethesda: HHS, 2009), https://www.cdc.gov/labs/pdf/CDC-BiosafetyMicrobiologicalBiomedicalLaboratories-2009-P.PDF.

[3] NIH, *NIH Guidelines for Research Involving Recombinant or Synthetic Nucleic Acid Molecules* (April 2019).

large variations in the quantity and quality of national regulations, as well as in the extent of biosafety resources.[22] Inconsistencies were particularly apparent among national policies governing GOF research: some governments imposed strict standards, whereas others had minimal requirements or restricted applicability. Given inconsistent national mandates, we cannot be certain that laboratories will prevent or mitigate dangerous LAIs before they become major incidents.

Some international organizations aim to standardize best practices and protocols for laboratory workers (see Table 4.2).[23] They set voluntary international norms concerning biosafety that help build confidence that research is being conducted safely. WHO and the World Organisation for Animal Health (OIE) publish technical guidance for laboratories and institutions, often specific to a scientific discipline or field of work.[24] International professional organizations such as the European Biosafety Association and the

**Table 4.2.** International Biosafety Norms[1]

| Instrument | Type | Brief description | Target | Enforcement mechanism |
|---|---|---|---|---|
| WHO Laboratory Biosafety Manual (2004)[2] | Guidance document | Provides practical and technical guidance on containment levels, laboratory techniques, and sterilization procedures | Research scientists and laboratories in WHO's 194 member states | Voluntary self-reporting |
| OIE Biological Threat Reduction Strategy (2015)[3] | Guidance document | Sets standards for detecting and responding to the release of animal pathogens | Research scientists and laboratories in OIE's member states | Voluntary self-reporting |
| WHA Resolution 58.29 (2005)[4] | Resolution (voluntary adoption) | Urges national safety programs consistent with WHO's Biosafety Manual | WHO member states | None |
| International Health Regulations (2005)[5] | Legally binding instrument | Requires states to detect and respond to disease threats, in part by meeting laboratory capacities | 196 state parties | Voluntary self-reporting |
| Global Health Security Agenda (2014)[6] | International partnership | Promotes national biosafety and security systems; sets benchmarks to guide programs and measure success toward meeting IHR core capacities | 60+ state partners | None |
| Cartagena Protocol on Biosafety (2003)[7] | International agreement | Provides framework using precautionary principle for using and transporting living modified organisms and assessing risks | 173 state parties[8] | None |
| CEN Workshop Agreement 15793 (2008)[9] | International agreement | Provides framework for laboratory biorisk management | 24 participant nations | None |

[1] UPMC Center for Health Security, "Synopsis of Biological Safety and Security Arrangements," July 2015.

[2] WHO, *Laboratory Biosafety Manual, Third Edition* (Geneva: WHO, 2004).

[3] OIE, *Biological Threat Reduction Strategy: Strengthening Global Biological Security* (Paris: OIE, 2015).

[4] WHA, "Enhancement of Laboratory Biosafety" (Fifth-Eighth World Health Assembly, Ninth Plenary Meeting, May 25, 2005—Committee A, Seventh Report).

[5] WHO, *International Health Regulations, Second Edition* (Geneva: WHO, 2005).

[6] "Global Health Security Agenda," GHSA, https://ghsagenda.org/.

[7] *Cartagena Protocol on Biosafety to the Convention on Biological Diversity* (Montreal: Secretariat of the Convention on Biological Diversity, 2000). The Protocol was adopted on January 29, 2000, as a supplementary agreement to the Convention on Biological Diversity, and entered into force on September 11, 2003.

[8] "The Cartagena Protocol on Biosafety," Convention on Biological Diversity, https://bch.cbd.int/protocol/.

[9] CEN, "Laboratory Biorisk Management" (CWA 15793, A CEN Workshop Agreement, February 2008).

Asia-Pacific Biosafety Association facilitate information sharing, biosafety trainings, and stakeholder collaboration.

Although they are helpful, technical guidance and sharing of information do not ensure uniform implementation of the systems and resources needed for safe and secure laboratory conditions and practices. It would take only one incident involving a highly transmissible pathogen to ignite a global emergency. The 2005 World Health Assembly (WHA) Resolution 58.29 on Enhancement of Biosafety urges WHO member states to implement national programs consistent with WHO's laboratory biosafety manual and asks the director-general of WHO to work with governments to improve laboratory safety.[25] Yet the WHA resolution is voluntary with no compliance-enhancing incentives, and WHO does not systematically assess national compliance.

The International Health Regulations (IHR) (2005) (see Chapter 7) require states to meet core health system capacities, including "reliable and timely laboratory identification of infectious agents and other hazards."[26] However, the laboratories contemplated by the IHR are mostly medical and public health, with a focus on disease surveillance and diagnosis. Research laboratories are not explicitly included, despite their major role in handling highly infectious agents whose escape could cause the type of global emergency that the IHR aim to prevent. And the IHR, like WHA Resolution 58.29, lack compliance-enhancing mechanisms. The US-initiated Global Health Security Agenda (GHSA) was specifically designed to improve national biosafety systems through risk evaluation, oversight, and emergency response.[27] However, GHSA has limited funding, and after an initial allocation of nearly $1 billion during the Obama administration, the US financial commitment has been less robust.[28]

In short, standards need to be more consistent and comprehensive, and there is an extreme lack of governance to ensure compliance. Yet every country has an interest in shoring up biosafety before the release of a novel pathogen becomes a global pandemic.

## Weaponization

Perhaps an even greater threat than an accidental biohazard release is the possibility of nefarious actors weaponizing biology, with catastrophic consequences. Modern biotechnology is not needed to weaponize biology. Naturally occurring, dangerous pathogens can be the starting point of a major biological attack. Consider the anthrax used in the 2001 attacks, which had been first harvested from an infected cow in Texas decades earlier. Such contagious and deadly pathogens could be the ultimate weapon, spreading from person to person and then exponentially. New technologies are making dangerous pathogens faster, easier, and cheaper to make. Yet governments are unprepared for the dangers of bioterrorism, with the potential for acts of bioterrorism to quickly evolve into mass-casualty events. Biosecurity requires standards and processes that are carefully designed to prevent the harmful use of information and technologies of biological research while allowing for legitimate uses—a difficult yet necessary balance—along with rigorous enforcement.

The weaponization of biology has a long history, with well-documented examples dating to ancient times. In the Middle Ages, bodies of plague victims were launched over protective city walls like bombs. In the 1700s settlers in colonial America infected Native Americans by "gifting" them with blankets previously used by persons infected with smallpox. At the turn of the twentieth century, new microbiological techniques to isolate and culture pathogens brought new bioweapons capabilities. Leading up to and during World War II, many countries conducted bioweapons research. For example, in the early 1940s at Fort Detrick (Maryland) the US military filled more than 5,000 bombs with *Bacillus anthracis* spores.[29]

In 1972 the international community sought to address increasing threats from biological weapons through the Biological Weapons Convention (BWC). The multilateral treaty banned the development, production, and stockpiling of pathogens "in quantities that have no justification for prophylactic, protective or other peaceful purposes."[30] The BWC contains no inspection mechanism, and detecting violations has proven challenging. The Soviet Union (and later Russia), for example, kept secret bioweapons programs that employed at least 25,000 scientists into the 1990s. As revealed after the first Gulf War, Iraq had sponsored extensive research on the offensive use of anthrax, botulinum toxins, and *Clostridium perfringens* (a common cause of food poisoning) in the years before the war.

A 2018 report from the US National Academies of Science and the Department of Defense lists three scenarios in which terrorists could utilize synthetic biology to rapidly cause mass fatalities.[31] First is recreating from scratch dangerous viruses that both science and the human immune system would be unprepared to counter. In 2018, for example, University of Alberta researchers built a horsepox virus that is a close relative of smallpox.[32] The second scenario is making harmful bacteria more deadly by enhancing virulence, transmissibility, or resistance. The third scenario is creating biochemicals via in situ synthesis or modifying common microbes to pro-duce deadly toxins.

As biotechnologies have become more accessible, non-state actors have demonstrated increasing capacity to develop bioweapons. As noted earlier, the 2001 US anthrax attacks that brought biosecurity center stage were ul-timately (though controversially) attributed to a single US government sci-entist. In 2014 a laptop belonging to the Islamic State was found containing information about creating bioweapons with bubonic plague.

Sharing genetic sequencing data, while essential to preparing for natural outbreaks, could also facilitate weapons development. Consider smallpox, which WHO declared eradicated in 1980 following a successful global vac-cination campaign. Smallpox eradication has been one of the greatest public health achievements; during the twentieth century the virus took 300–500 million lives worldwide. Since then, WHO has led a strict regulatory re-gime around research involving the two known smallpox stockpiles—one at a CDC laboratory in Atlanta, Georgia, and the other in Russia. Genetic sequencing of smallpox DNA has been used to study whether other pox vi-ruses, such as monkeypox, could mutate to become more virulent and trans-missible among humans. Now that smallpox can be genetically synthesized from scratch, new questions arise as to whether existing stockpiles should be destroyed.[33] A bad actor could recreate the virus and wreak havoc in a world where the population has little immunity.

Meanwhile, the virus's sequence itself is freely accessible online. In 1994 the complete genetic sequencing of smallpox was published in the journal *Virology,* shocking the scientific world.[34] Simply being able to "read" the virus did not mean scientists could "write" a virus containing over 186,000 DNA base pairs, but we have seen how fragments of the virus's DNA can be or-dered online. A 2010 WHO report concluded that advancements in gene synthesis allow "anyone with an Internet connection and access to a DNA synthesizer" to recreate substantial portions of the smallpox virus.[35] At the crux of biosecurity lies this dilemma: How can we balance crucial research and scientific freedom with protecting against intentional misuse?

## Funding Dangerous Research

Dual-use research of concern (DURC) is defined as life-science research rea-sonably anticipated to provide knowledge, information, products, or technolo-gies that could be directly misapplied to pose a significant threat to public health, agriculture, animals, the environment, and national security.[36] In 2001, for example, Australian scientists seeking to develop a type of vaccine that could make mice infertile, as a form of pest control, genetically modified mousepox, which is similar to smallpox. They discovered that the altered virus was far more deadly, and that the mousepox vaccine was much less effective against it. A similar genetic modification of smallpox could greatly increase its virulence and have a similar devastating effect on smallpox vaccines.[37]

The potential benefits and risks of DURC can pose major dilemmas. A 2004 NAM report, *Biotechnology in an Age of Terrorism,* stressed the "affirmative moral duty" of biological scientists to minimize contributions to advancing bioweapons development.[38] The report listed seven types of experiments that warrant special scrutiny before they are undertaken or their results published. The seven types involved how to render a vaccine ineffective, confer resistance to therapeutically useful antibiotics or antiviral agents, enhance a pathogen's virulence or render a nonpathogen virulent, increase transmissibility, alter a pathogen's host range, enable the evasion of diagnostic/detection modalities, or enable the weaponization of a biological agent or toxin.

Scientific associations have adopted policies in line with the report's guidance on taking precautions for DURC.[39] Yet professional self-regulation is unlikely to stop researchers with nefarious intentions. In 2004 the US Department of Health and Human Services (HHS) established the National Science Advisory Board for Biosecurity (NSABB) to provide oversight of research falling into any of the seven dual-use categories. NSABB reviews any federally funded research involving pathogens included in the Federal Select Agent Program.[40] Still, the criteria for funding DURC, and the entities authorized to make those decisions, have remained contentious.

In October 2014 the US government placed a moratorium on federal funding for GOF research on influenza, MERS, and SARS viruses based on the applicability of the dual-use categories listed above. The moratorium was sparked by public fear that erupted when researchers announced they had mutated the deadly H5N1 virus to enhance its transmissibility. The moratorium was lifted in 2017 after the release of a new framework for funding research of "enhanced potential pandemic pathogens" (ePPP).[41] The framework now requires federal agencies such as the National Institutes of Health (NIH) to first assess whether a study would involve ePPP, and if so, determine whether the potential benefits outweigh the risks. If approved, agencies can set reporting requirements for researchers to notify the agency of certain outcomes (such as a pathogen becoming likely to be highly transmissible among humans). Scientists have questioned the utility of this oversight, worried about conflicts of interest among HHS officials reviewing GOF research that the agency itself funds.[42]

Under the new framework, some of the same GOF H5N1 studies the moratorium postponed were given the green light to resume with federal funding in 2019. The decision was not publicly shared, nor were the reasons disclosed, as HHS officials claimed they could not disclose researchers' proprietary information.[43] Lack of government transparency in approving the studies has added to concerns about whether DURC is appropriately assessed and managed.

The government decided to proceed with high-risk research behind closed doors and without public engagement. When misuse of research can result in global hazards, biosecurity becomes an issue of international concern. To establish international trust and security, governments have a responsibility to engage in a transparent process for containing and managing risks at all stages of the research process.

## Information Sharing

Controversy has also surrounded government bans on the publication or dissemination of DURC studies. In line with the rising open access movement, many scientists believe open and informed discussion of research is vital to better understand potentially dangerous genetic mutations—an understanding that is necessary for detecting pathogen variants and developing countermeasures. Scientific integrity and freedom are in tension with government control of channels of dissemination. But there is another perspective: that more weight should be given to the risk of DURC, which could justify limited dissemination of research findings or even censorship.

As noted earlier, the NSABB asked two groups of researchers to voluntarily delay publishing research on enhanced transmissibility of H5N1, but later withdrew its request. If the publication had been forbidden, it could have violated First Amendment protections against the government compelling researchers to withhold publication through force of law. The US Supreme Court gives special scrutiny to "prior restraints," where the government blocks information in advance of publication.[44] The government can oblige scientists to keep information confidential if it is classified for national security purposes. But even for classified information, there is a stronger judicial presumption against enforcing prior restraints against publishers that lawfully obtained the information.[45]

Contrast the US efforts to delay the H5N1 publication with that of the Netherlands, where similar research was being conducted. By the time the NSABB had reversed its publication request, the Netherlands had determined that publishing the H5N1 paper amounted to the exportation of dangerous information outside the European Union (EU).[46] Since 2009 the EU rules designed to prevent the proliferation of biological, chemical, and nuclear weapons have required a license for exporting certain goods, including physical pathogens and technologies, to outside nations.[47] This marked the first time, however, that a researcher was required to obtain a license to export biological information. Although the Netherlands granted the license, the research center launched a formal objection to the threat of restricting the sharing of basic scientific information that was already in the public domain.[48]

As suggested by the H5N1 example, there are considerable differences in how countries handle the dissemination of sensitive research. In the United States a regulatory oversight system specific to DURC has emerged.[49] Export controls, as in the EU,[50] are another strategy. These controls regulate the shipment or transfer of controlled items, software, technology, or services out of one country and into another. The EU is not alone in establishing an export control regime for dual-use items. Export controls are also part of the strategy that the United States and the broader international community employ. The 2001 Patriot Act and 2002 Bioterrorism Act in the United States restrict transfer of and access to potentially dangerous biological materials. The Australia Group, established in 1985, is an international, multilateral export control regime consisting of forty-three nations that agree to control certain exports in order to prevent the spread of chemical and biological weapons.[51]

The United States, an Australia Group member, proposed new export controls in 2018, largely to prevent China, not a member, from obtaining sensitive technologies through unfair, illegal, or discriminatory practices. The 2018 US Export Control Reform Act requires the US Department of Commerce to regulate "emerging and foundational" technologies that are essential to national security and not otherwise captured under US export controls.[52] However, such efforts to stay ahead in science, technology, and defense could have unintended negative consequences. The rules bar relevant information sharing with foreign nationals even within the United States, meaning that academic institutions could be forced to exclude foreign-born students from laboratories, and businesses could be prevented from sharing data on controlled technologies.

There are other approaches to DURC—including no government action at all. Some countries, like Portugal, take a "bottom up" approach by relying on institutional biosecurity committees to raise awareness on DURC.[53] Other countries have little to no risk management mechanisms at all. In part this may be because these countries, particularly in less developed regions, lack the resources to implement and enforce research oversight systems. On the international scale, nations may fear that strict information controls could preclude the exchange of valuable information for legitimate purposes. Having inconsistent regulatory approaches among countries furthers the possibility of dangerous biological tools and information falling into the wrong hands.

## Standards, Controls, and Shortcomings

DURC may present the largest biosecurity governance gap. There is no single international institution that directly governs DURC, nor is there an international agreement. However, existing international agreements could help manage the funding and transfer of potentially hazardous research.

The BWC built upon the 1925 Geneva Protocol that prohibited the first use of bioweapons in armed conflict.[54] Half a century later the BWC prohibited developing and stockpiling biological weapons and their means of delivery.[55] Upon request by a state party, the UN secretary-general can investigate an alleged BWC violation and issue a report.[56] However, the treaty lacks a formal enforcement mechanism to ensure that states parties have disarmed or discontinued prohibited activities. Countries are supposed to voluntarily report their research activities, but many view disclosures as contrary to their national interests.[57] In 2016, negotiations to enforce the BWC broke down amid international disagreement.[58]

Even though the word "research" did not appear in the original BWC agreement, a review conference in 2006 concluded that the BWC *could* consider research.[59] In 2012, following the H5N1 publication controversy, states parties including the United States, Russia, China, and Australia identified scientific research that might be prohibited by the BWC.[60] However, subsequent BWC review conferences (including the most recent in 2016) did not address these concerns, missing the opportunity to establish international dialogue surrounding DURC.

In 2004 the United Nations Security Council adopted Resolution 1540 to address enforcement gaps of the BWC.[61] Resolution 1540 requires states parties to establish and enforce regulatory measures against the development of chemical, biological, radiological, and nuclear weapons, as well as their spread to non-state actors. The 1540 Committee oversees implementation through state reporting, but no onsite inspections are performed. Conceivably the committee could address DURC, as it is a biosecurity issue, but the committee has yet to do so.[62] In 2016 the Security Council adopted Resolution 2325 to strengthen enforcement of 1540. The 2016 resolution "encourages states, as appropriate, to control access to intangible transfers of technology and to information that could be used for weapons of mass destruction and their means of delivery."[63] It comes closer than any other international instrument to addressing research as a biosecurity threat, but lacks binding obligations.

More than the UN Security Council, WHO has taken steps to serve as the international platform for establishing norms around biosecurity and research. In 2010 WHO released a guidance document that provides a tool for researchers and laboratories to voluntarily self-assess their oversight of DURC.[64] Then, during the H5N1 controversy in 2012, WHO held an informal consultation, which recommended that the H5N1 research be published.[65] Many have criticized this recommendation as furthering WHO's own interests, because a recommendation against information sharing could have undermined the role of the Pandemic Influenza Preparedness framework established one year earlier (see Chapter 8).

Among the mechanisms to address biosecurity (see Table 4.3), there has been dysfunction and timidity in adequately regulating DURC, both nationally and globally. In 2013 WHO merely identified well-known DURC issues, including management, regulation, and publication.[66] WHO acknowledged inconsistencies on DURC oversight, largely because many countries lack the capacity to develop risk management mechanisms. Yet WHO member states concluded that international agreement on DURC to create a uniform regulatory system and build capacity would be expensive and slow. And WHO has not held any consultations on DURC since 2013.

## From Complacency to Action

Now that US-funded H5N1 and other high-consequence GOF research is set to resume, there is a growing urgency to prioritize the prevention and management of scientific misuse, whether accidental or intentional, that

**Table 4.3.** International Biosecurity Norms

| Instrument / Forum | Type | Brief description | Target | Enforcement mechanism |
|---|---|---|---|---|
| Geneva Protocol (1925)[1] | International agreement | Prohibits the first use of chemical or biological weapons in armed conflict | 140 state parties | None |
| Biological Weapons Convention (1975)[2] | International agreement | Prohibits the development, production, and stockpiling of biological and toxic weapons | 183 state parties | None |
| UN Security Council Resolution 1540 (2004)[3] | Resolution (mandatory adoption) | Requires member states to adopt and enforce measures against the proliferation of biological weapons, and to prevent their spread to non-state actors | UN member states | Monitoring system based on states' reporting |
| UN Security Council Resolution 2325 (2016)[4] | Resolution | Requests that member states take voluntary measures to prevent the proliferation of biological weapons, including through controls on information sharing | UN member states | None |
| WHO Responsible Life Sciences Research for Global Health Security (2010)[5] | Guidance document | Informs member states on the risks posed by accidental or deliberate misuse of biological sciences and proposes measures to reduce risks | WHO member states | None |
| The Australia Group (1985)[6] | Informal forum of countries | Establishes common export controls for select chemical and biological materials | 43 member states | None |

[1] *Protocol for the Prohibition of the Use in War of Asphyxiating, Poisonous or Other Gases, and of Bacteriological Methods of Warfare (Geneva Protocol)*, signed at Geneva, June 17, 1925; "Geneva Protocol," U.S. Department of State, https://2009-2017.state.gov/t/isn/4784.htm.

[2] *Convention on the Prohibition of the Development, Production and Stockpiling of Bacteriological (Biological) and Toxin Weapons and on Their Destruction*, entered into force, March 26, 1975; "Biological Weapons," UN, https://www.un.org /disarmament/wmd/bio/; UPMC Center for Health Security, "Synopsis of Biological Safety and Security Arrangements," July 2015.

[3] *Non-Proliferation of Weapons of Mass Destruction (Resolution 1540)*, adopted by the Security Council at its 4956th meeting, April 28, 2004; "UN Security Council Resolution 1540 (2004)," UN, https://www.un.org/disarmament /wmd/sc1540/; UPMC Center for Health Security, "Synopsis of Biological Safety and Security Arrangements," July 2015.

[4] *Non-Proliferation of Weapons of Mass Destruction (Resolution 2325)*, adopted by the Security Council at its 7837th meeting, December 15, 2016; UN, "Security Council Adopts Resolution 2325 (2016), Calling for Framework to Keep Terrorists, Other Non-State Actors from Acquiring Weapons of Mass Destruction," Meetings Coverage, December 15, 2016.

[5] WHO, *Responsible Life Sciences Research for Global Health Security: A Guidance Document* (Geneva: WHO, 2010); "Responsible Life Sciences Research for Global Health Security," WHO, https://www.who.int/csr/bioriskreduction /lifesciences_research/Responsible_lifescience_project_Keyactivities/en/.

[6] "AG Objectives," The Australia Group, https://www.dfat.gov.au/publications/minisite/theaustraliagroupnet/site/en /objectives.html; "AG Participarts," The Australia Group, https://www.dfat.gov.au/publications/minisite /theaustraliagroupnet/site/en/participants.html; UPMC Center for Health Security, "Synopsis of Biological Safety and Security Arrangements," July 2015.

could foreseeably result in global catastrophe. National and international regulatory systems must be strengthened to prevent the release of a dangerous pathogen; at the very least, we need systems in place to quickly detect and contain such a release. What is the pathway toward effective action on biosafety and biosecurity? The answer spans development and enforcement of rigorous regulatory standards (both nationally and globally) to capacity building for surveillance and response.

*Rigorous regulation of biosafety and biosecurity.* As we have seen, governments have a hodgepodge of rules to govern biosafety and biosecurity. In an interdependent world, a single weak link could trigger a global health emergency. Thus, uniformly high-level standards and processes in place at the national level are needed to help prevent, detect, and respond to an accidental or intentional release of a novel or highly contagious pathogen. Regulatory standards need to be comprehensive and include rules to maintain secure laboratories, high-quality surveillance systems, and well-rehearsed protocols for rapid detection and containment of biohazard threats. It is also important to fairly govern DURC and open access of potentially sensitive research.

*Building capacities for biosafety and biosecurity.* Having laws and regulations in place will not be effective if the country lacks the capacity to fully implement them. WHO and higher-income countries must devote considerably more resources and technical assistance to help nations build and implement strong biosafety and biosecurity regulatory systems, particularly in less-developed nations. Currently Resolution 58.29 and the GHSA aim to strengthen national systems for biosafety, while Resolutions 1540 and 2325 address biosecurity.

However, dedicated funds and capacity fall far short of meeting overwhelming global need. Additional resources could be used to provide practical guidance and technical assistance for nations to implement effective regulatory, oversight, and incident-reporting systems. Further, with more resources, gaps in DURC oversight and management could be addressed by the 1540 Committee or another designated entity.

*Global coordination and oversight.* National preparedness is vital, but so is global cooperation and oversight. Because biological threats go well beyond state borders, international action must complement state-level regulatory structures. International organizations should lead on governing emerging biosafety and biosecurity threats. An international forum, such as the BWC quinquennial review conferences, could foster dialogue and consensus on DURC-related threats, challenges, and management options. This could set a global norm that rejects the type of secrecy and nondisclosure that the United States has demonstrated. It could foster trust among nations that responsible decisions will be made in allowing sensitive research to proceed, and would encourage sharing findings within and among nations. In addition, WHO, given its hand in the 2011–2012 H5N1 controversy, has an obligation to continue to find solutions relating to the safety and security of GOF research—especially now that studies on enhanced H5N1 transmissibility are set to resume in the United States. A broad mandate from the WHA will be necessary to reignite WHO's efforts in facilitating discussions on the implications of GOF research with diverse international stakeholders.

*Compliance with international norms.* Even if strong global rules were in place, finding solutions to states' failure to comply remains a pressing need. Current agreements, including the IHR, BWC, and relevant UN resolutions, rely heavily on state self-reporting and assessments and lack mechanisms for transparent reporting of biological incidents. These shortcomings have undermined the utility of international controls to manage dangerous pathogens. Reliable systems for monitoring compliance—including verification mechanisms like onsite inspections—are needed. Governments, researchers, and companies must be held accountable for meeting biosafety and biosecurity obligations.

Along with enforcement, a system for reporting biological incidents within and among countries is needed. Failure to promptly communicate a pathogen's release could be the difference between several LAIs and a global pandemic. A transparent reporting system could improve biosurveillance and countermeasures for impending risks. The information provided by full, transparent reporting can also enhance the knowledge base regarding which incidents are likely to be serious and to require a national or even international response to contain them, and which can be handled locally. A better understanding of the nature and extent of biological incidents could also provide lessons that enable evidence-informed, and thus more effective, standards, processes, and training, helping to prevent incidents from happening in the first place.

Existing international structures for biosafety and biosecurity provide a foundation upon which to construct viable solutions to prevent global catastrophe. Global stakeholders, including scientists, national governments, and international organizations, must engage to create a far more rigorous approach to managing emerging biological threats. Only through international cooperation and shared responsibility can the next major biological incident be detected and its consequences mitigated—if not altogether prevented.

# CHAPTER 5

# Antimicrobial Resistance

## Superbugs and the Imperative to Stop Them

**Imagine if we lived in a world** where once fully treatable infections became life-threatening, and routine surgeries posed lethal risks. Mass killers such as AIDS, tuberculosis, and malaria would surge. A century of progress would be reversed, with disastrous consequences. There would be millions of excess deaths every year, with huge economic and social costs.

Few health risks pose as grave a danger as antimicrobial resistance (AMR)—the ability of bacteria, viruses, and other microscopic organisms to change and adapt, rendering standard treatments ineffective. Most health threats are embedded into the twenty-first-century human ecosystem (hyper-urbanization, intense human–animal interchange, and vast travel networks). But the proliferation of antimicrobial-resistant organisms is the result of discrete and destructive ways in which we have developed, or not, our health systems and farms—indiscriminate prophylactic antibiotic use in farmed animals, careless medical prescribing, and poor hospital infection control. The illicit global market in substandard and falsified medications helps fuel this growing danger. In other words, human behavior enables pathogens that have become resistant to many of the antimicrobials we have in our medical arsenal, "superbugs," to develop and thrive. It is, therefore, human behavior that must change to avert a potentially catastrophic health crisis.

Antimicrobial resistance does not discriminate. It plagues the poor and wealthy alike. AMR outbreaks have occurred in world-class health facilities, such as the 2011 outbreak of *Klebsiella pneumoniae,* a bacterium that is multidrug-resistant (resistant to more than one drug), at the National Institutes of Health, causing six deaths.[1] Four years later, Chinese and Danish researchers discovered a gene that renders a whole class of bacteria, including *Klebsiella* and *E. coli*, resistant to antibiotics of last resort (polymyxins). "The last drug has fallen," the press reported.[2] It was a *Klebsiella* infection, too, that proved fatal to a Nevada woman in 2016 when doctors were unable to find *any* antibiotic that would cure her infection. The deadly strain had become resistant to twenty-six drugs.[3]

Absent major changes in human behavior and new discoveries, the future portends far worse, with more microbes evolving to evade our most powerful medicines. Along with vaccination, antimicrobial medication is the most important public health achievement of the twentieth century. Is it possible that infections that today are easily treatable will eventually become lethal?

Today, even while we are all at risk, the world's most disadvantaged people face the highest burden from hard-to-treat infections. Several hundred thousand people die every year of drug-resistant TB,[4] one of humankind's oldest microbial nemeses. Most of these deaths occur in sub-Saharan Africa and South Asia. If the problem worsens significantly, AMR deaths in these regions could climb into the millions every year.[5] But the entire globe faces this frightening future, and mass travel and migration all but ensure that wherever it originates, resistance will spread far and wide. The health of each of us depends on curtailing AMR wherever it is found.

How have we come to this? The answer spans from factory farms to doctors' offices, clinics, and hospitals, and extends to pharmaceutical companies' research priorities. Overuse and misuse of antimicrobials in treating human infections enables resistant bacteria and viruses to multiply, causing harder-to-treat infections and accelerating the spread of genes that cultivate resistance. Heavy antibiotic use in livestock animals to promote growth and prevent infection similarly enables resistant bacteria to flourish. They then enter the food chain and the environment and infect people.[6]

Even as humans are enabling microbes to adapt and evolve, business models are discouraging investment into new antimicrobial medications, leading to a dearth of treatments. Pharmaceutical companies often do not perceive novel antibiotics as profitable. New antibiotics may be short-lived as pathogens develop resistance, even as they need to be conserved to forestall this resistance. Even as the threat grows and grabs the public's attention, the march toward AMR is relentless.

The solutions need to be socially and institutionally embedded: clinical and patient education to prevent indiscriminate prescribing; health systems implementing rigorous infection control and routine testing for resistance; and humane food production, without intense factory farming requiring antibiotic prophylaxis. We also need strategic investments in, and new incentives for, research and development to restock the antimicrobial pipeline.

Fortunately, AMR is now on the political agenda of world leaders, generating national strategies and global initiatives. Public/private partnerships and new incentive structures could encourage badly needed investments in R&D, enabling humanity to succeed in the historic contest between scientific ingenuity and evolutionary microbial adaptation.

## How AMR Arises and Spreads

Good policy is informed by good science. Understanding the scientific underpinnings of antimicrobial resistance is the foundation for stemming this grave threat.

Antimicrobial resistance is the ability of microscopic organisms—bacteria, viruses, fungi, and parasites—to survive the medicines developed to combat them. Viruses are limited in the ways they can develop resistance, due to their simplicity—they are little more than genetic material surrounded by a protein coat and sometimes a lipid membrane, and they replicate by using the machinery within host cells. Yet when mutations do cause resistance, such as with HIV, viruses' high rate of reproduction promotes the rapid spread of genes conferring resistance. Further, viral outbreaks are often tied to increased use of antibiotics. The COVID-19 pandemic, though not treatable with antibiotics, brought a surge in antibiotic use as health care workers sought to avoid secondary infections of bacterial pneumonia among patients with severe respiratory symptoms.[7]

The biggest threat comes from bacteria's resistance to antibiotics because of the extensive use, and overuse, of antibiotics, and our reliance on them.[8] These simple single-cell organisms, with their DNA contained in a circular chromosome, and without a nuclear membrane or other cell parts like the energy-generating mitochondria, also generate rapidly, adding to their threat.

Malaria, which is perhaps one of the best-known antimicrobial resistance threats, comes from the *Plasmodium* protozoa. Protozoa are one type of parasite. Parasites are a diverse set of organisms characterized by their relationship with a host organism, with the parasite dependent on the host for survival.

Protozoa are single-cell organisms with animal-like characteristics. Parasites also include worms, multicellular animals that live inside various organisms, such as *Schistosoma* (blood flukes). While worms may be visible to the unaided eye, and thus are not actually microbes, they can similarly develop drug resistance, as *Schistosoma* have.

Finally, even though fungi constitute only a small portion of the antimicrobial resistance threat, they can cause infections and develop resistance. Fungi share a mix of properties of animal and plant cells, and can be single-celled (e.g., yeast) or multicellular (e.g., mushrooms).

For any of these microbes, antimicrobial resistance can occur naturally. Microbes may have intrinsic resistance, meaning that the microbe's cell structure or natural functions thwart drugs from working. For example, the microbe might have a cell membrane the drug cannot penetrate, or the microbe might efficiently expel the drug before it suffers damage from it. Alternatively, the microbe might not have the enzyme the drug targets, or it might produce an enzyme that degrades the drug.[9] Gram-negative bacteria are a class of bacteria that have an additional outer cellular membrane that gram-positive bacteria lack, making it more difficult to develop drugs to combat them.

A second route to drug resistance, involving random mutations and selective pressure, is where human responsibility comes in. Random mutations will always occur, but our widespread misuse and overuse of antimicrobials accelerates selective pressure and requires policy intervention.

If a mutation enables a pathogen to survive an antimicrobial drug, the pathogen can replicate and pass its altered genetic code on to its progeny. Under "selective pressure"—linked to the basic evolutionary principle of survival of the fittest—resistant microbes are more likely to survive and replicate because they are "fitter" than other microbes in the presence of antimicrobials. These microbes become increasingly prevalent, threatening public health. Preventing unnecessary and inappropriate use of antimicrobials in animals and humans reduces selective pressure, curtailing spread of resistance.

To understand just how mutations enable microbes to survive antimicrobials, we need to understand how these drugs work. Antimicrobials work by killing microbes or preventing them from reproducing. Some, for example, block DNA replication; these include ciprofloxacin (Cipro), which is used to treat infectious diarrhea and anthrax. Others target enzymes that have critical functions within the microbe. Sulfonamides, for example, target an enzyme needed to produce folic acid, which is critical for cellular processes including DNA and RNA synthesis. Sulfonamides treat *Streptococcus* infections, which now pose a major hazard in hospital settings.

Microbes, in turn, can develop a range of mechanisms to block antimicrobials. These mechanisms may lead the antimicrobial to be wholly ineffective (complete resistance) or less effective, but not entirely ineffective (partial resistance). A mutation might enable the microbe to deactivate the drug or cause an enzyme that the antimicrobial targets to change shape, preventing the drug from binding to it. If the microbe has a cell wall (viruses do not), the mutation could affect the wall's properties in ways that impede the drug from entering or improve the cell's ability to expel the drug.

When a microbe becomes resistant, scientists can often develop another antimicrobial drug that remains effective, targeting the pathogen using a different mechanism. Yet the current pipeline of drugs is limited. The more forms of resistance a microbe acquires, the more difficult it becomes to find an effective drug. And because some drugs work through the same mechanism, microbes may become cross-resistant, meaning that when a microbe develops resistance to one drug, it becomes resistant to others as well.[10] Eventually, and without new classes of antibiotics—antibiotics that differ in their structures and chemical properties—the possibilities run out and could precipitate a public health crisis. The need to develop new classes of antibiotics grows ever greater.[11]

Once resistant, microbes spread resistant genes through replication, with viruses and bacteria spreading most rapidly. Microbes, especially bacteria, can also swap genetic material, and even share it with other species, amplifying the dangers.[12] With respect to antimicrobial resistance, gene transfer is most important among bacteria, although there is a growing body of evidence that genes can be passed between fungi, and from bacteria to fungi.[13] Parasitic protozoa have also acquired genes from other microorganisms and from their hosts.[14]

## The Staggering Cost of AMR

Already, at least 700,000 lives are lost to AMR every year.[15] A landmark study, envisioning a future with complete failure of first-line or even all antimicrobial drugs for three major public health threats (HIV, TB, and malaria) and three bacteria that already have concerning levels of resistance (*Klebsiella pneumoniae, Staphylococcus aureus,* and *E. coli*) foresaw the possibility of millions of deaths annually and an immense economic cost. If resistance rates increased 40 percent and infection rates doubled, 10 million people could die from antimicrobial resistance every year by 2050.[16] Excluding COVID-19, that staggering figure exceeds total deaths from all infectious diseases (nearly 9 million) today.[17] The burden would be most heavily felt in poorer countries, with nearly 90 percent of the deaths occurring in Africa and Asia. Yet no country would be spared. The 700,000 drug-resistant deaths that could occur in Europe and North America would be approximately ten times today's total in Europe and the United States.[18]

While AMR's potential toll on human lives is most alarming, its economic cost stands to also be immense, potentially running into the tens of trillions of dollars cumulatively by 2050 in lost economic productivity—plus massive health care costs. That would far exceed the National Academy of Sciences' Pre-COVID-19 projected cost to the global economy of novel infectious diseases for the entire twenty-first century. The economic impact of hospital-acquired infections and reduced utility of key medical interventions could cost many trillions of dollars more.[19]

This crisis is marked not only by the sheer number of people that drug-resistant microbes could directly kill, but also by its threat to modern medicine. Most invasive surgeries that pose low risks do so not only because of skilled health professionals, but also because of antibiotics, as prophylactic use prevents infections, and antibiotics are available for patients who become infected. Without effective antibiotics, caesarean sections could become too dangerous to perform. So might hip replacements.[20] If antibiotics ceased to be effective, postoperative infections from hip replacement surgery could kill about one in every eight patients, or more.[21]

The dangers to modern medicine extend beyond surgery. Chemotherapy would become far more dangerous for immunocompromised cancer patients. Similarly, organ transplants require immunosuppression therapy to prevent patients' immune systems from rejecting the foreign organ, but without effective antibiotics this would greatly increase the risk of infections we could no longer treat. Many intensive care patients require trachea tubes to keep their airways open or to administer drugs, and these tubes pose considerable risk for infections such as pneumonia. Patients on ventilators for respiratory ailments like COVID-19 would face significant risk as well. Without effective antibiotics, many would die.[22] Sepsis—where the body's immune system overreacts to infection, causing inflammation that can lead to organ failure and death—will become harder to treat. An estimated 19 million to

32 million episodes of sepsis are already causing more than 5 million deaths annually.[23] The death toll could grow by millions if antibiotics became ineffective.

Hospitals are a primary locus of risk from drug-resistant infections. Many hospitalized patients have weakened immune systems, making them susceptible to infections a healthy person could easily defeat. The risk is amplified by the concentration of unhealthy patients, especially if health workers fail to adopt rigorous infection control. Health care–associated infections resistant to treatment instill fear, with high-profile cases such as methicillin-resistant *Staphylococcus aureus* (MRSA) and carbapenem-resistant *Enterobacteriaceae* (CRE) (see below).

### Modern Threats: Tuberculosis, Malaria, HIV / AIDS, and Beyond

The "big three"—HIV, tuberculosis, and malaria—all have some level of resistance, which is a threat to any continued progress in the struggles against these diseases, none more so than with the spread of multidrug-resistant TB (MDR-TB).

*Tuberculosis.* MDR-TB (resistant to at least two first-line drugs, isoniazid and rifampicin) is the most lethal of all antimicrobial-resistant infections. In 2018 it infected nearly half a million people worldwide and killed 214,000.[24] Half of drug-resistant TB cases are in India, China, and Russia,[25] though drug resistance is global, and growing. By 2040, one in three TB cases in Russia could be drug-resistant.[26]

The world is now experiencing an even more frightening type of MDR-TB—extensively drug-resistant TB (XDR-TB), whose resistance extends to fluoroquinolone and injectable second-line drugs. By 2018, XDR-TB had been detected in 131 countries, with 6 percent of MDR-TB cases exhibiting this advanced level of resistance.[27] Globally, MDR-TB treatment is successful in only about half of all cases (56 percent in 2016), although with significant variation by country.[28] Success rates can be considerably higher when patients receive a high standard of care, even in impoverished settings.[29] For XDR-TB cases, treatment succeeds in about one-third of cases.[30]

Despite TB's toll, for decades TB research had all but ground to a halt. Then, spurred on by the UN Millennium Development Goals, R&D funding nearly doubled from 2005 to 2009, reaching $637 million, but then plateaued. The Stop TB Partnership calls for triple that amount, about $2 billion per year.[31] In 2014, WHO issued guidance for bedaquiline and delamanid, two new medications to treat MDR-TB and XDR-TB.[32] As of 2017, less than 5 percent of patients in need received these drugs.[33] Recently, a patient developed resistance to both drugs, serving as a warning.[34] There is some promise, though: In "groundbreaking" preliminary results reported in 2019, a new three-drug regimen in a small trial in South Africa cured 90 percent of XDR-TB patients.[35]

Even though recent studies indicate that MDR-TB treatment can be highly successful with a nine- to twelve-month treatment regimen, now endorsed by WHO,[36] for most people treatment remains an arduous, two-year ordeal. Patients endure a complex regimen, totaling 14,000 pills along with six months of daily injections.[37] The drugs are toxic with serious side effects, including nausea, hearing loss, kidney impairment, hepatitis, and even psychosis.[38] The sheer length of treatment, the extreme side effects, and the astronomical costs (twenty times more than treatment for ordinary TB) makes patient adherence exceptionally difficult.[39] Treating XDR-TB in the United States costs well over $400,000.[40] One survivor describes his experience:

> Those that do survive will have likely lost much of their eyesight, hearing, or liver functions from the drug toxicity, and the disease itself will eat away the lungs, leaving dozens of holes and serious pulmonary deficits for the rest of their lives. Few survivors can ever resume physical labors even if declared "cured." Without adequate air supply, muscles stop working and atrophy. Also, as the disease makes holes or caverns in the lungs, they are a great place for clever TB bacteria, among other microbes and fungi, to hide out dormant, waiting to spring back into action when the person is weakened, malnourished, or ill with another sickness.
>
> I have also survived two bad cases of acute Invasive Aspergillosis, a deadly fungus whose treatment is almost as bad as for XDR and MDR. People that survive [drug-resistant] TB are prone to catch aspergillosis—taking a simply breath can be dangerous without an immune system—and it is often fatal. Over the last 15 years, I've cashed-in about half of my nine lives due to nasty bacteria and fungi. Before that, I had already used up most of the rest, so I try now to look out for microscopic airborne killers in my vicinity.[41]

MDR-TB stands out for its devastating impact on poor and marginalized communities, who tend to subsist in a lethal mix of malnutrition that weakens the immune system, crowded housing that propels transmission, and substandard health care.

*Malaria.* In the mid-twentieth century, WHO and partners launched a campaign to eradicate malaria. The campaign failed in its global ambition, but eliminated the disease in Europe, North America, and parts of Latin America.[42] Today successful malaria control strategies have given new life to the quest for eradication. Yet all these advances must contend with the second chapter of drug resistance of *Plasmodium falciparum,* by far the most lethal of the four parasites that cause malaria (see Chapter 2).

The drug chloroquine, along with insecticides, particularly DDT, was a key element of the first eradication effort. Yet by the late 1950s, first in Southeast Asia, strains of *P. falciparum* emerged that were resistant to chloroquine.[43] Resistance quickly spread around the world, causing a steady rise in malaria deaths, from 1 million in 1980 to a peak of 1.8 million in 2004.[44] New medication brought new hope and, combined with successful prevention and funding, helped drive malaria deaths down to 405,000 in 2018.[45] Artemisinin, extracted from a traditional Chinese medical herb, first saw clinical use in 1987,[46] and has become the gold standard for treatment.

To protect against artemisinin resistance, WHO recommended using artemisinin-based combination therapy in 2001,[47] where a fast-acting artemisinin-derived compound is combined with another antimalarial to eliminate the parasite even if it develops resistance to the artemisinin derivative.[48] Nonetheless, resistance was detected at the Thailand–Cambodia border in the early 2000s, leading to concern that there would be worldwide spread of resistance. To avoid a repeat of the chloroquine experience, WHO quickly mobilized, developing a global strategy to contain, and if possible eliminate, the resistant parasite.[49] Yet in a "sinister development," a malaria parasite lineage in Cambodia that was already resistant to artemisinin developed resistance to another drug, piperaquine, and by 2017 the multidrug-resistant parasite had spread into Thailand, Laos, and Vietnam.[50] A 2019 study found that this resistant strain had become dominant in Laos, Vietnam, and northeastern Thailand, creating "the terrifying prospect that it could spread to Africa."[51] The number of malaria cases has, nonetheless, continued to fall in the region.[52] Will progress to reduce and eliminate malaria from the region by 2030 succeed before the multidrug-resistant parasite becomes a global danger?

Overuse of malaria medication is accelerating the spread of resistance. In many African countries and parts of Asia, where malaria is common and health systems are under-resourced, overburdened health workers prescribe antimalarial medication without testing to confirm that the ailment is malaria. Fearing misdiagnosis, some health workers prescribe antimalarials even if tests come back negative.[53] Counterintuitively, prescribing antimalarials to people who do not have malaria can contribute to resistance to longer-lasting malaria medications, if the people subsequently become infected with malaria. If the antimalarials are not yet fully eliminated from the body, the subtherapeutic levels of the drugs that remain are not enough to successfully combat the infection. The drugs create selective pressure that favors the survival of any resistant parasites, as they can outcompete nonresistant parasites.[54]

The problem is exacerbated by the prevalence of substandard and falsified medicines, which often contain subtherapeutic doses, which are a central driver of resistance. A WHO study in twenty-one sub-Saharan African countries found that 35 percent of antimalarial drugs failed chemical analysis;[55] studies suggest that most were substandard.[56]

Along with resistance to medicines, resistance to insecticides is increasing. Seventy-three of eighty-one countries that provided data to WHO during 2010–2018 detected such resistance at least once. And the number of people protected by indoor residual spraying (see Chapter 3) fell by nearly half from 2010 to 2018, from 180 million to 93 million, partly because countries were forced to switch to more expensive insecticides as resistance to the main class of insecticide used (pyrethroids) grew.[57]

Since 2016 the fall in the malaria death rate has slowed. Will it continue to slow—or will the number of cases and deaths begin to rise—as drug resistance increases?

*HIV/AIDS.* Unlike malaria and TB, HIV has been well funded and there has been considerable research into new medications. Many HIV/AIDS drugs with multiple mechanisms are on the market, and the vast majority of HIV strains are treatable. Yet HIV quickly mutates, and therefore many people will develop resistance to initial treatments over time, or if their adherence to their medication regime is poor. Resistant strains can be directly transmitted person-to-person. Thus, many living with HIV will eventually need to transition to more expensive second-line, and even third-line, therapies. The longer that resistance can be delayed, with treatment adherence, the better.

In recent years an important new antiretroviral drug has become available. Dolutegravir (DTG) is used as part of combination antiretroviral therapy in place of older drugs. DTG has faster viral suppression, and resistance to this drug is rare. In 2016 WHO recommended DTG as a first-line therapy to consider, except for pregnant women due to concerns about the risk of neural tube defects, based on limited data from Botswana.[58] Further studies, though, showed a much lower risk of neural tube defects, and in 2019 WHO recommended DTG as a first-line and second-line therapy for all populations.[59]

Still, the need to continue to develop a pipeline of antiretroviral medications is essential. In 2013 a patient in Uganda, who did not survive, was identified as having a strain of HIV that was resistant to all second-line HIV drugs.[60] We have been warned.

*WHO and CDC priorities.* Looking beyond these three diseases, WHO (2017) and the CDC (2019) issued lists of the most serious antimicrobial resistance threats.[61] The WHO list covers twelve bacteria, whereas the CDC list includes sixteen bacteria and two fungi (see Table 5.1). Both lists also include *Salmonella* serotype Typhi (causes food poisoning) and *Neisseria gonorrhoeae* (causes gonorrhea). The infections cause life-threatening diarrhea, pneumonia, bloodstream infections, meningitis, and sepsis. The WHO list highlights the threat of gram-negative bacteria and aims to spur research. The three bacteria it identifies as the most urgent threats share a common feature: resistance to a last-resort antibiotic.

### Four Major Antibiotics Threatened by Resistant Bacteria

*Carbapenem-resistant Enterobacteriaceae (CRE).* In the same class of antibiotics as penicillin (beta-lactam antibiotics), which inhibit bacterial cell wall synthesis, the carbapenems stand out for their effectiveness against a broad spectrum of bacteria. They are particularly valuable against multidrug-resistant bacteria, and are often "antibiotics of last resort." It is of grave concern, then, that bacterial resistance to carbapenems has been detected—and is increasing.[62] CRE, a family of gram-negative bacteria that includes *K. pneumonia* and *E. coli,* poses special concern. CRE is a major risk in health care settings, especially for patients using ventilators and catheters, with mortality rates as high as 50 percent.[63] Former CDC director Tom Friedan called CRE "nightmare bacteria"[64]—a nightmare being dreamed frequently in Greece, where two-thirds of *K. pneumonia* cases are resistant to carbapenems. In the United States, patients with CRE were present in

**Table 5.1** CDC's Top 18 Drug-Resistant Threats Categorized on Level of Hazard (2019)

| Urgent Threats | Serious Threats | Concerning Threats |
|---|---|---|
| Public health threats that require urgent and aggressive action | Public health threats that require prompt and sustained action | Public health threats that require monitoring and prevention action |
| **Carbapenem-resistant** *Acinetobacter* **bacteria** <br> Infections: 8,500 <br> Deaths: 700 | **Drug-resistant** *Campylobacter* **bacteria** <br> Infections: 448,400 <br> Deaths: 70 | **Erythromycin-resistant group A** *streptococcus (GAS)* **bacteria** <br> Infections: 5,400 <br> Deaths: 450 |
| *Candida auris* <br><br> Infections: 323 | **Drug-resistant** *Candida* <br><br> Infections: 34,800 <br> Deaths: 1,700 | **Erythromycin-resistant group B** *Streptococcus* **bacteria** <br> Infections: 13,000 <br> Deaths: 720 |
| *Clostridioides difficile* <br> Infections: 223,900 <br> Deaths: 12,800 | **ESBL-producing Enterobacteriaceae** <br> Infections: 197,400 <br> Deaths: 9,100 | |
| **Carbapenem-resistant Enterobacteriaceae** <br> Infections: 13,100 <br> Deaths: 1,100 | **Vancomycin-resistant** *Enterococci* <br><br> Infections: 54,500 <br> Deaths: 5,400 | |
| **Drug-resistant** *Neisseria gonorrhoeae* <br> Infections: 550,000 | **Multidrug-resistant** *Pseudomonas aeruginosa* <br> Infections: 32,600 <br> Deaths: 2,700 | |
| | **Drug-resistant nontyphoidal** *Salmonella* <br> Infections: 212,500 <br> Deaths: 70 | |
| | **Drug-resistant** *Salmonella* **serotype Typhi** <br> Infections: 4,100 <br> Deaths: (less than) 5 | |
| | **Drug-resistant** *Shigella* <br> Infections: 77,000 <br> Deaths: 5 | |
| | **Methicillin-resistant** *Staphylococcus aureus* <br> Infections: 323,700 <br> Deaths: 10,600 | |
| | **Drug-resistant** *Streptococcus pneumoniae* <br> Infections: 900,000 <br> Deaths: 3,600 | |
| | **Drug-resistant tuberculosis** <br> Infections: 847 <br> Deaths: 62 | |

*Note:* Infection and death figures are for 2016 or 2017.
*Data Source:* CDC, *Antibiotic Resistance Threats in the United States 2019* (Atlanta, GA: CDC, 2019)

4 percent of hospitals and 18 percent of long-term care facilities during the first half of 2012.[65]

*Clostridium difficile (CDIFF).* Responsible for more than 200,000 health care–associated infections per year in the United States, CDIFF, like CRE, is one of the CDC's five most urgent threats. The most common health care–related infection in the United States, CDIFF causes life-threatening diarrhea and is responsible for about 13,000 deaths annually in the United States, mostly among the elderly. Unlike other microbes on the CDC's list of pathogens posing the greatest threats, the CDIFF deaths and infections are not primarily associated with antimicrobial resistance. Rather, they are associated with antimicrobial drugs in another way: these infections typically occur in patients who have taken antibiotics. Patients on broad-spectrum antibiotics, in particular, are at high risk, because the drugs kill protective bacteria in the human microbiome.[66] Such antibiotics (e.g., amoxicillin, Cipro) are useful to combat infections when the bacteria is unknown but treatment needs to begin quickly; when narrow-spectrum drugs (effective against only a small set of bacteria) fail; and prophylactically, before surgery. More discriminant use of antibiotics would significantly reduction CDIFF infections.[67]

CDIFF antibiotic resistance, meanwhile, has been growing.[68] Multidrug-resistant CDIFF is already common in Europe, where some strains are resistant to four or five drugs.[69]

*Vancomycin-resistant Enterococci (VRE).* Both WHO and the CDC identify VRE as a serious threat. *Enterococci* are commonly found in health care settings, and caused about 55,000 infections in the United States in 2017, nearly one-third of which were resistant to vancomycin.[70] VRE is now global, and people with HIV are especially vulnerable.[71] *Enterococci* possess "remarkable genome plasticity," making them "incredibly efficient at attaining antimicrobial resistance."[72]

*Methicillin-resistant Staphylococcus aureus (MRSA).* Perhaps the best known of health care–related infections, MRSA is a major risk in health care settings and, increasingly, in community settings.[73] It was responsible for more than 300,000 infections in 2017 in the United States. Untreated MRSA infections can lead to sepsis.[74] These bacteria are resistant not only to methicillin but also to other antibiotics. MRSA has become common in other regions, including Asia and Europe.[75] Attention surrounding MRSA led to concerted control measures, including rigorous hospital infection control, resulting in significant declines in MRSA infections in the United States. While both community- and health care–associated MRSA rates have fallen significantly, progress in reducing MRSA in health facilities has stalled since 2013.[76] Scientists are researching new drugs to target MRSA, with one possibility yielding great promise in clinical trials in mice.[77]

## Three Roads to AMR

Resistance is an inevitable result of microbial defense mechanisms, but its rapid growth is of our own making: A patient insists on a prescription for antibiotics even though the infection is viral. The doctor complies even though the antibiotic will be useless. A mother in a lower-income country brings her feverish child to a health facility. Her child tests negative for malaria, but not trusting the results, the nurse prescribes antimalarial medication. A person with TB feels better after several weeks and stops taking her pills, never having been informed of the need to finish the full course. A farmer routinely adds antibiotics to his pigs' feed, even if they aren't sick. Another farmer puts low doses of antibiotics in the cows' drinking water.

These actions all factor into the rapid rise of AMR, with poorly functioning health systems and industrial agriculture underlying individual actions. And along with the overuse and misuse of antimicrobials, pharmaceutical incentives to develop new drugs are misaligned, despite the urgent need. With low investment in new drugs, our defenses are failing to keep up. Stemming the spread of antimicrobial resistance will require tackling deep structural barriers.

### How Human Behavior Is Accelerating AMR

The more often germs are exposed to antimicrobials, the more likely they are to develop resistance. Yet health systems provide patients antimicrobials, especially antibiotics, far more often than needed. Up to 50 percent of antibiotic use in the United States is entirely unnecessary or inappropriate, with incorrect selection, dosing, or duration of the antibiotic.[78] Similar levels of misuse are found elsewhere.[79] Globally, antibiotic use is soaring, driven by sharp rises in low- and middle-income countries (LMICs); while antibiotic use in LMICs increased 65 percent from 2000 through 2015, it declined by 4 percent in high-income countries.[80] A 2019 study of eight LMICs (Haiti, Nepal, and six African countries) found that, on average, children in those countries received nearly twenty-five antibiotic prescriptions by the time they were five years old—a level of exposure the study's authors deemed "remarkable," estimating that 49 to 81 percent of the prescriptions were "probably unnecessary."[81] Immense disparities across countries exist in antibiotic use. In 2015 the average Mongolian used sixteen times more antibiotics than the average person in Burundi and about three-and-a-half times the European average—indicating significant overuse in many countries, even as in other countries people lack sufficient access.[82] The average child under five in Uganda receives nearly twelve antibiotic prescriptions per year, compared to little more than one for a child in Senegal.

Some diseases stand out. One-third of antibiotic prescriptions for respiratory infections in the United States are entirely unnecessary, as viruses cause most of these infections. These unnecessary prescriptions add up to 27 million doses of antibiotics annually.[83] Again, the United States is emblematic, not exceptional; the vast majority of patients in China and Indonesia with lung infections take antibiotics.[84]

The dire effects of unnecessary use of antibiotics may be counterintuitive. How can bacteria become resistant when someone who does not have a bacterial infection takes an antibiotic? The answer to this paradox is that each of us plays host to almost innumerable bacteria; a startling 40 trillion bacteria reside in a single human.[85] The selective pressure of antibiotics on these populations enable resistant bacteria in our microbiome to proliferate.[86] Resistant bacteria that are latent may later become active and cause infection. One-quarter of the world's population, for example, has latent tuberculosis.[87] And even if drug-resistant bacteria do not directly cause infection, they can transmit their resistant genes to other bacteria.

Why do doctors frequently prescribe antibiotics unnecessarily or inappropriately?[88] Perhaps they have inadequate training, or prescribe by habit rather than following clinical guidelines, or guidelines are not available. Most health workers prescribe antibiotics based on "their expertise, intuition and professional judgment."[89] Health workers might not fully understand their patients' condition, whether because they have too little time for consultations, patient follow-up is insufficient, or clinical testing capacity to identify the infectious agent is lacking. The proper medication might be unavailable. And in some countries, doctors' payments are linked to the volume of prescribed drugs, a perverse incentive, or they may receive biased information from pharmaceutical companies.

Further, patients might be too ill or unwilling to wait for results, which frequently take hours or days. They might insist on leaving the doctor's office with medicine, and health workers often accede, responding not only on a human level but also with an eye to patient satisfaction as a metric by which the quality of health care is assessed.[90] Patients might also have a poor understanding of when antibiotics might help. A 2010 pan-European survey found that about half of Europeans believe antibiotics kill viruses (53 percent) and can cure colds and influenza (47 percent).[91] Globally, nearly two-thirds (64 percent) of people share the latter belief.[92] In Syria, war resulted in destroyed public health infrastructure, the exodus of health workers, a lack of reliable supplies of antibiotics, and grievous war wounds—conditions that are ripe for the development of AMR to develop—and many view antibiotics as "cure-alls with no side effects."[93]

Not only do many people mistakenly believe that antibiotics might help when these drugs cannot cure them, but they may be able to get antibiotics themselves. Patients can legally purchase antibiotics over the counter in many countries—including in nineteen countries in WHO's European Region as of 2014.[94] Some pharmacies, including 45 percent of pharmacies in a 2008 study in Spain's Catalonia region, sell antibiotics without a prescription even where doing so is illegal.[95] Importantly, India, Brazil, and China have banned over-the-counter sale of antibiotics, but enforcement remains weak, especially outside major cities.[96]

Many people who feel sick believe they know just the antibiotic to take. A quarter of respondents in WHO's twelve-country survey thought that getting antibiotics from a friend or family member was acceptable.[97] Self-medication is common.[98] A survey in Italy in 2012 found that half of respondents had self-medicated in the past year.[99]

Unnecessary and inappropriate use of powerful, often broad-spectrum, antibiotics is especially problematic. In the United Kingdom, 70 to 80 percent of patients with gonorrhea could be treated with older medication, yet almost all receive instead a newer, "last line" treatment.[100]

Patients may believe that they can stop taking antibiotics if they feel better. That was the case for 32 percent of respondents—and more than half in Sudan, Egypt, and China—of the WHO twelve-country survey.[101] The cost of the drug or associated costs, such as transportation to health facilities, may prevent patients from adhering to the full course of the drug, or they might be unable to refill prescriptions because of weak supply chains.[102] Side effects are a frequent source of nonadherence, particularly if patients are not supported. People might stop taking drugs if they are not feeling better, thinking the medicine isn't helping; or they might skip doses simply because they forget or are too busy.[103]

A very different reason patients might receive subtherapeutic doses is criminal activity. A shocking number of drugs are not what they purport to be. They may be substandard, failing to meet national quality standards; perhaps diluted, containing too little of the active ingredient; or falsified, misrepresenting the product's identity, and possibly not medicine at all, but little more than chalk or corn starch.[104] Substandard and falsified drugs are cheap to produce, but ineffective or dangerous, and pose serious risks of creating antimicrobial resistance when sold with subtherapeutic doses of the active pharmacological ingredient. The trade in falsified and substandard drugs is transnational, lucrative, and extensive; the UN Office on Drugs and Crime estimates the value of the illegal antimalarial drug market in West Africa alone exceeds $400 million.[105]

Falsified and substandard drugs are produced by both large-scale operations and "small back street operators." These "drugs" pose dangers everywhere, but poorer countries suffer most, due to weak health care and regulatory systems.[106] WHO estimates that one in ten drugs in LMICs is fake or substandard.[107] As the major producers of active ingredients, China and India are the origins for the lion's share of substandard drugs.[108] WHO estimates that 20 percent of drugs produced in India are fake.[109]

While the prevalence of falsified and substandard drugs varies considerably, a few snapshots reveal the magnitude. Consider antimalarial drugs. They are widely needed and often bought at street markets, making them a prime target for criminal networks. Studies in Southeast Asia and sub-Saharan Africa found that 36 percent and 20 percent of samples, respectively, were falsified. Even this underestimates the threat, because the studies focused on pharmacies rather than unofficial vendors. A study of unlicensed vendors in Guyana and Suriname found 58 percent of antimalarial drug samples to be falsified or substandard; in Burkina Faso, 90 percent were substandard.[110] The consequences could hardly be more devastating. More than 122,000 children in sub-Saharan Africa died from malaria in 2013 due to falsified and substandard drugs.[111]

Drugs may also contain subtherapeutic levels of the active ingredient not out of malevolent intent, but because a manufacturing plants has inadequate quality controls or poor storage that allows active ingredients to degrade. And regulatory capacities can be very low: as of 2014, India's Central Drugs Standard Control Organization had 323 staff, only 2 percent that of the US FDA.[112]

Poor health care practices also contribute to antimicrobial resistance. Weak infection control—health workers failing to wash their hands, equipment not sterilized, aseptic procedures not followed during surgery—enable drug-resistant microbes to flourish.[113] Antimicrobial soaps and handwash that contain the antibiotic triclosan may contribute to resistance.[114]

As extensive as antibiotic use is in people, it is dwarfed by use in livestock, especially in industrial farming. Nearly 80 percent of antibiotics use in the United States is in livestock.[115] Globally, perhaps two-thirds of global antibiotic use is in animals grown for food, primarily chicken, pigs, cows, and sheep.[116] Overall, more than 131,000 tons of antibiotics are used in animals each year, and this is expected to increase to 200,000 tons per year by 2030 if current trends continue.[117]

Increasing meat consumption in developing countries is driving the growth, as more people can afford meat and industrialized farming becomes widespread. China has the highest level of antibiotic use in farm animals.[118] And in India, to promote growth, two-thirds of poultry farms commonly used antibiotics in animal feed—primarily tetracyclines and fluoroquinolones, which are commonly used to treat human infections. Indian farmers also used antibiotics to prevent disease in chickens packed tight in unsanitary conditions and without proper nutrition.[119] Antibiotic use in animals in India will grow by 82 percent by 2030 on current trends.[120] The Asian giants are hardly alone, though. In Rwanda, a 2017 study reported that 44 percent of farmers used antibiotics in animals to prevent disease and 27 percent to promote animal growth.[121]

The use of antibiotics in humans is primarily to treat those who are sick, but their use in animals is most often to treat those that are healthy. Shortly after World War I, scientists discovered that subtherapeutic doses of antibiotics promote animal growth. As the human population expanded and farmland decreased due to urbanization, farmers turned to antibiotics as an inexpensive way to increase meat production.[122] They were hooked. If scientists today could identify inexpensive alternative ways to increase animal growth (e.g., the use of probiotics), farmers might be persuaded to discontinue the prophylactic use of antibiotics.[123]

The desire for cheap food also drove fundamental transformation of the 10,000-year-old human endeavor of agriculture, with the rise of the factory farm. Shortly after World War II,[124] storybook images of cow barns, chicken coops, and pigs slurping their food would be transformed into intense industrial farming and agribusiness in the United States and, increasingly, elsewhere.[125] Packing animals tightly together is a recipe for disease transmission, and antibiotics came to be used not only to promote growth but also to prevent and treat disease.

The resultant emergence of drug-resistant bacteria in farm animals leads to drug-resistance in humans. One means for this is direct contact: exposure of animal handlers to drug-resistant bacteria, people eating meat that contains drug-resistant bacteria, or people drinking water contaminated with drug-resistant bacteria originating from animals. Another pathway is the transfer of genetic material from antibiotic-resistant bacteria in animals to human pathogens.[126] And even if an antibiotic fed to animals is not used in people, genetic alterations to bacteria that become resistant to that antibiotic could confer resistance to similar antibiotics that people do use.

In a world where farm animals and people are in close proximity, it is unsurprising that resistance in farm animals contributes to resistance in people; like other emerging infections, antibiotic resistance often has zoonotic origins.[127] As early as the 1960s experts warned about antibiotic use in animals, though confirmatory research lagged and was limited.[128] But it is coming. In 2004 the US Government Accountability Office concluded that "there is a preponderance of evidence that the use of antimicrobials in food-producing animals has adverse human consequences," with "little evidence to the contrary."[129] Various strands of evidence make the danger clear:

- High levels of vancomycin-resistant bacteria were found in people near turkey farms in the Netherlands; a European ban on avoparcin sharply reduced resistance in humans.[130]
- In the United States, in meat tested in 2011, antibiotic-resistant bacteria were found in much store-bought meat: 81 percent of turkey, 69 percent of pork, 55 percent of ground beef, and 39 percent of raw chicken.[131]
- Genetic strains of antibiotic-resistant *Campylobacter* and *Salmonella* bacteria in infected people were "indistinguishable" from those found in animals.[132]
- An eleven-country study found a high correlation between antibiotic-resistant *E. coli* in people and the prevalence of antibiotic-resistant *E. coli* in pigs and poultry.[133]

## Narrowing Antibiotic Pipeline

The heyday of antibiotic discovery came early. From the introduction of sulfonamides in 1937 and then penicillin, scientists developed new antibiotic classes at a prodigious pace, nearly one a year, with twenty classes by 1962.

Yet the next half century saw only four new classes, two in 2014 and 2015, and two more in 2018.[134] Yet none of these has yet been developed into drugs that have proven effectiveness in people.

There are now more than a hundred known antibiotics,[135] but these are primarily analogues of existing drugs—drugs sharing similar structure and chemical properties, tweaks rather than fundamental changes in chemical structure or mechanisms of action. Analogues are less risky to develop—less likely to fail or to have toxic side effects.[136] Even here, development has slowed. From 1983 to 1993, the US FDA registered thirty new antibiotics, three per year. From 2003 to early 2011, new registration dropped to seven, not even one per year.[137]

The early proliferation of antibiotics resulted in scientific overconfidence, with scant ongoing investment in new discoveries.[138] Researchers also faced difficulties in identifying new metabolic targets and developing broad-spectrum antibiotics.[139] Genetic sequencing to predict new enzyme pathways proved unsuccessful, and economic incentives were badly misaligned.[140] Unlike antibiotics—most of which are given in over a short period of time—pharmaceuticals are most profitable when targeted at long-term use to treat chronic diseases, such as high cholesterol, hypertension, and diabetes. Indeed, new antibiotics are intended for use only if older ones fail.

Consequently, pharmaceutical companies have largely gotten out of the business of antimicrobial R&D. And without good prospects for making a profit on new antibiotics, and given the high costs of developing them, investors are turning elsewhere. Several antibiotic start-ups filed for bankruptcy in 2019, as others struggled to stay afloat.[141]

There is also an urgent need for new, inexpensive diagnostic tools so doctors can prescribe more accurately. Innovation here, too, is slow, and health care providers are not even buying diagnostics that are ready for the market. Diagnostics are often expensive, whereas antibiotics are cheap. Furthermore, accurate diagnoses take valuable health worker and laboratory time.[142]

## Global Response to AMR

The global response to AMR requires a concerted strategy that is multisectoral—including governments, health systems, farms, and research laboratories. A concerted global strategy has four elements: (1) health systems that carefully steward the current supply of antimicrobials; (2) limiting of antibiotic use in animals to treatment only; (3) regulation to ensure high-quality drugs along with law enforcement to curtail substandard and falsi-fied medicines; and (4) funding of research and development. Cutting across all areas is the need for equity.

## Health System Stewardship

Health system stewardship of effective antimicrobials requires rigorous in-fection control, accurate prescribing, conservation of newer broad-spectrum antibiotics, and oversight and education to ensure that patients take the full course of their medications. First and foremost, health facilities should be places of safety and healing—not hazardous environments. Health facilities can ensure safety through basic infection control, including hygiene (e.g., handwashing), sanitary conditions, sterile medical equipment, personal pro-tective equipment, and surveillance of health care–associated infections.

Antimicrobial stewardship requires informed patients. Every patient should understand when antibiotics are needed and, if they are, the need to take the full course of their medications.

Health workers, in turn, require training on accurate prescribing, infec-tion control, and proper use of personal protective equipment—and the time to educate patients. Health worker practices can be vastly improved by means of a few simple strategies, such as peer comparison of antibiotic prescribing rates, or electronic medical records that ask physicians to justify prescrip-tions if the diagnosis does not indicate a need for antibiotics.[143] Such inno-vative approaches are critical; a study in 2011–2015 of antibiotic prescrip-tions for older Americans found high rates of inappropriate prescriptions and only minimal reductions over the four years of the study, despite guidelines and exhortations.[144] Appropriate prescribing will be of limited efficacy if patients can purchase antibiotics without a prescription. Bans on the over-the-counter sale of antibiotics must be universal and rigorously enforced. Health workers also need effective tools, such as rapid diagnostic tests; it is vital for doctors to know what infection the patient has and whether it is drug-resistant.

Audits and surveillance systems can monitor health facility safety prac-tices and antibiotic use, and rapidly identify health care–associated infec-tions. Health agencies need to know whether antimicrobial resistance is rising or falling, what practices make a difference, and where to target in-terventions. Real-time monitoring can quickly identify drug-resistant infec-tions and minimize spread.

## Farms

The strategy to minimize AMR in farm animals is straightforward: antibiotics should be used only to treat sick animals, not for disease prevention or animal growth. Sick animals should be tested so farmers can use antibiotics that have the fewest negative consequences for human health.[145] This approach requires veterinary prescriptions and avoiding antibiotics in animal feed or drinking water. Surveillance of antibiotic use in animals and routine inspections can ensure compliance. Eliminating highly industrialized farming, where animals are crowded together in unhygienic conditions, reduces the need for antibiotics and limits animal-to-animal transmission. Healthy living conditions rather than mass medication should become the basis of disease prevention.

Ending antibiotic use in animals is especially challenging in lower-income countries, where the demands for meat and agribusiness are rising. Governments need to support small-scale and family farmers by promoting their access to seeds, farming technology, and markets. Expanding the number of women in agriculture and increased technology could increase farm yields in Africa by 20 to 30 percent.[146] Lower-income countries also need to build regulatory and surveillance capacities.

## Substandard and Falsified Medications

Combating substandard and falsified medicines requires strengthened national regulatory agencies, rigorous inspections, and postmarketing surveillance. Law enforcement needs to be stepped up. There should be serious criminal penalties for manufacturing or knowingly selling fake and substandard drugs. The National Academy of Medicine proposed the following comprehensive strategy to stem the trade in substandard and falsified medicines:[147]

- *Pharmacovigilance:* Governments should monitor substandard and falsified medicines, integrating pharmacovigilance into routine national surveillance. WHO has a pilot scheme to train regulators for drug quality surveillance. Quality surveillance would improve understanding of compromised products and the extent of the trade.
- *Track and trace:* A porous global supply chain allows poor-quality medicines to be diverted to the legal market. Securing chains of custody would protect the drug supply.

- *Quality manufacturing:* Drug production depends on good manufacturing practices and quality control. Small drug companies in LMICs lack the infrastructure, equipment, and staff necessary to meet international standards.
- *Drug retail:* Poor people often have no choice but to buy drugs from unlicensed shops or open-air markets. Regulatory agencies should ensure that pharmaceuticals are sold only in licensed pharmacies with quality control.
- *International code of practice:* WHO should adopt a code of practice to set standards and coordinate regulatory systems, customs, and law enforcement. A code would catalyze action against criminal syndicates that poison the world's medicine supply.

### Research and Development

Even vigorous efforts to conserve antimicrobials can only slow the spread of resistance. A constant pipeline of new drugs and diagnostics is essential. Yet as we have seen, investment is low and incentives are misaligned. This trend must be reversed. The pace of antibiotic production needs to accelerate, regarding both new analogues—fifteen new analogues per decade is a good target, according to a landmark UK review—and new classes of antibiotics, both broad- and narrow-spectrum.[148] The first twenty antibiotic classes, along with their analogues, served us well for sixty years. We should aim for another twenty classes in the next several decades.[149]

Governments need to prioritize antimicrobial R&D, with funding aligned to global priorities. Special funds and incentives could be developed, including prize money for innovative new drugs, advanced market commitments (guaranteed purchase of a given volume of drug at a predetermined price), tax incentives linked to early-stage research, and paying companies to hold drugs in strategic reserve.[150]

Realigning incentives could accelerate R&D. The current patent system rewards companies with time-limited monopolies, irrespective of the drug's benefit to humankind. Finding alternatives to intellectual property will be hard. The Agreement on Trade-Related Aspects of Intellectual Property Rights (TRIPS), an international legal agreement between World Trade Organization member states, requires that intellectual property rights be protected. One alternative would be global funding for innovative antimicrobials based on well-defined criteria, such as expected number of lives saved.

A new global body could secure intellectual property rights while sufficiently reimbursing the developer for R&D costs and investment risk, and require countries accessing the antimicrobials to implement strict regulations to ensure their conservation, affordability, and accessibility. Another alternative would be for the firm to retain the rights to sell the drug, while being provided international financing attached to conditions requiring marketing restrictions and affordable prices.[151] Indeed, any public funding should be conditioned on stewardship to conserve new antimicrobials.[152]

A Global Innovation Fund for AMR, as proposed by the UK Review of Antimicrobial Resistance, could incentivize early-stage research, including proper dosing, drug combinations to overcome resistance, and stimulating the body's immune system. Furthermore, the UK Review asked the World Bank and high-income countries to establish "Diagnostic Market Stimulus Pots" to subsidize diagnostic tools. Companies that develop new tests and meet criteria (such as affordable pricing) would be eligible. This would encourage the private sector to bring diagnostics to the market quickly and to match marketplace needs, such as the need for very rapid and accurate tests.[153]

Diagnostics also need to be suitable for lower-income countries, where transportation may be difficult and electricity spotty. A new TB diagnostic, Gene Xpert, can detect resistance to first-line rifampin, giving results in two hours. But it is expensive and requires stable electricity supplies.[154]

Scientific innovation requires researchers to possess full information produced in clinical trials. If research produces disappointing results, it might not be published, but negative findings can reveal important information. All clinical trials should be registered and publicly disclosed.[155]

## Global and National Responses to AMR

Governments and international institutions are now seized with the dire threat posed by AMR and are beginning to respond. Will global frameworks and commitments turn into leadership and action in time? Or will actions that require higher levels of funding or overcoming organized resistance (e.g., from farmers) need to wait until new, ever more frightening superbugs emerge?

Global institutions and forums have begun to act, with WHO leadership. In 2015 WHO developed the Global Action Plan on Antimicrobial Resistance.[156] The plan proposes that governments report biannually on implementation, creating new monitoring and accountability. In 2017, WHO advised states to permit antibiotic use in animals only for treatment, based on clinical testing, while allowing prophylactic use only with a veterinarian's assessment that animals are at high risk of infectious diseases based on infections in the same flock or herd. Further, WHO recommended no longer using antibiotics in animals that were medically important for people.[157] WHO has also developed a Global Antibiotic Surveillance System to standardize collecting and sharing data on AMR, building a vital information platform. A network of researchers developed the Global Point Prevalence Survey, a standardized approach to data collection on antibiotic prescribing and resistance in LMICs.[158]

WHO alone cannot adequately respond to AMR. Tackling AMR requires a well-coordinated triple track, comprising human health, animal health, and food production—the "One Health" paradigm. WHO, having long neglected critical interlinkages, has now forged a collaboration with the Food and Agricultural Organization (FAO). The WHO/FAO Codex Alimentarius, although nonbinding, sets two major standards on AMR: (1) a code of practice (2005) setting norms for regulatory agencies, pharmaceutical companies, and veterinarians;[159] and (2) guidelines creating a framework for analyzing risks to human health posed by resistant microbes transmitted through animal feed or food production.[160] The World Organisation for Animal Health (OIE) similarly developed a strategy in 2016 to foster awareness of AMR risks, surveillance and research, good governance, capacity building, and enforcement of international standards.[161]

Political will is indispensible to translate global standards and plans into action, yet heads of state rarely convene to discuss global health issues. Before 2016, the UN hosted high-level summits on three health issues: HIV/AIDS, noncommunicable diseases, and Ebola. However, in September 2016, the UN hosted a High-Level Meeting on Antimicrobial Resistance. Its political declaration put the weight of the world's presidents and prime ministers behind WHO's Global Action Plan. The declaration called on global agencies (e.g., FAO, OIE, and the World Bank) to support national action plans.[162]

In 2017 the UN secretary-general established an interagency coordination group to guide global action on AMR. Spurring multisector collaboration, the group comprises twelve global agencies as diverse as the Global Fund, the World Trade Organization, UNICEF, and OIE.[163] Its recommendations, delivered in 2019, largely covered familiar ground, such as equitable access and prudent use of antibiotics, and greater collaboration and increased investments. The UN group also urged governments, development banks, and private investors to consider AMR risks in their investments, and recommended creating several new international entities. A One Health Global Leadership Group on Antimicrobial Resistance would be managed by WHO, FAO, and OIE, and help maintain momentum, advocate for action, and monitor progress. And an Independent Panel on Evidence for Action against Antimicrobial Resistance would assess relevant evidence and make recommendations on mitigating and adapting to AMR.[164]

Meanwhile, the G7 summits in 2015 and 2016 pledged support for the WHO Global Action Plan. To facilitate new medical countermeasures, G7 nations promised to fund R&D, harmonize global clinical trials, and promote regulatory cooperation. State commitments regarding antimicrobial use in animals were weak, though, saying the G7 aims to "phase out" AMR in animal growth, while emphasizing therapeutic use in people and animals.[165]

The Global Health Security Agenda (GHSA), launched by the Obama administration in 2014, is the most significant multilateral action on global health security outside of WHO. The GHSA—designed to build national capacities for rapid detection and response—has expanded into an international collaboration among well over sixty countries.[166] The GHSA has eleven "action packages," with targets, indicators, monitoring, and evaluation, backed by financing and technical support.[167] The package on antimicrobial resistance supports national plans, laboratory capacity, and surveillance. GHSA works with partner states to conserve existing antimicrobials and develop new antibiotics and other medical technologies.[168]

Well before the Obama administration and GHSA, national leadership could be found in Europe, particularly several countries in Europe's north. Sweden was the first of the northern lights, banning antibiotic use for growth promotion in animals in 1986. Other European countries followed, with an EU-wide ban in 2006. Compliance has been imperfect, though, with farmers using antibiotics for growth promotion, masked as prevention or therapy.[169]

Denmark was another leader. In 1999, when it was the world's top exporter of pork, Denmark banned all nontherapeutic uses of antibiotics in pigs. Data demonstrated the policy's effectiveness and built support within the agricultural community. Dutch farmers took a humane approach, allowing piglets to spend more time with their mothers, enabling the pigs to build their immune systems, which reduced disease without the use of antibiotics. Farming practice reforms increased the cost of raising pigs only very modestly, about 1 euro per pig.[170]

The Netherlands adopted perhaps the most comprehensive strategy to AMR, making it a national priority and setting measurable targets to drive change. By 2015 the government had set a target of reducing antibiotic use in animals by 70 percent. To meet this and earlier targets, Parliament required veterinarians to register all prescriptions for antibiotics, while strictly regulating veterinary use of antibiotics that were the most important for human health.[171] The Netherlands also set targets for antibiotic use in people, aiming to achieve 50 percent reductions in health care–associated infections. The strategy included health communication campaigns, infection prevention, health worker training, and guidelines for hospitals and nursing homes, with periodic facility inspections for antibiotic stewardship.[172]

## Scientific Advances

Another way to tackle this growing threat is to realize the promise of science. Conserving existing antimicrobials will slow the spread of resistance but will not stop it. New therapeutic tools are badly needed, and we have arrived at a time of great hope for discovering new antimicrobials. For example, the natural world—the source of the majority of today's antibiotics—is teeming with possibility, from the soil to plants, mammals, and reptiles.[173] CRISPER can unleash one of humankind's most powerful scientific tools, gene editing, against an ancient foe. What kinds of discoveries might we see if only scientists had the resources to fully pursue novel ideas?

Nature itself holds great potential. *Actinobacteria*, which often live in soil, have been a major source of antibiotics[174] but they are difficult to culture in the laboratory and therefore only 1 percent have been investigated. Exploring the rest would open up a new universe of possibilities. Novel techniques have transformed the research environment. The isolation chip (iChip), for example, is a method of culturing bacteria. Using regular methods, 99 percent of bacterial species cannot be cultured because they don't grow in laboratory conditions. iChip instead cultures bacterial species within the soil environment. iChip, which enabled the groundbreaking discovery in 2015 of a new class of antibiotics (teixobactin), could work for nearly 50 percent of *Actinobacteria*, an enormous advance.[175] Scientists have figured out how to isolate and cultivate slow-growing bacteria.[176] And scientists can now extract DNA directly from the soil, an approach that is already yielding new antibiotics.[177]

Other unexplored habitats, like the deep sea and desert, could produce antibiotic substances.[178] So might plants and animals. Certain reptiles can survive serious wounds, even the loss of a limb, without becoming infected. Komodo dragon blood, for example, contains a chemical that can kill two types of bacteria, with dozens more substances still to be explored.[179] Several essential oils (plant extracts) combined with an extant antibiotic killed drug-resistant *E. coli*, and lemongrass oil has shown promise against MRSA. The secret of the oils? Their chemicals weaken bacteria's cell walls, enabling antibiotics to enter.[180]

New technologies hold further promise for discovering new antimicrobials. Supercomputers can analyze vast genetic databases to predict which protein compounds have antibiotic potential. Scientists discovered oxadiazoles, a new class of antibiotics, by screening 1.2 million compounds for those that could inhibit an enzyme responsible for MRSA's resistance.[181] Screening 6 million compounds led scientists to identify twenty compounds with clear potential for binding to a key protein involved in resistance to ethionamide-based second-line TB drugs, and thus worthy of further exploration for helping overcome that resistance.[182]

Nanotechnology offers another pathway to innovation. Nanoparticles, which have dimensions of 100 billionths of a meter or less, can disrupt the internal chemistry of bacteria when illuminated with light of a certain frequency. This technique could significantly enhance certain resistant bacteria's sensitivity to antibiotics.[183]

Then there is synthetic biology, which involves building new biological systems. For years scientists have modified erythromycin, a commonly used antibiotic, to create analogues to circumvent resistance. Running out of options for chemical modifications, researchers created hundreds of variants of erythromycin from scratch. Most of the molecules that scientists screened were active against *Streptococcus pneumoniae*.[184]

Scientists are also having a fresh look at infection-fighting techniques used before the advent of antibiotics. Ancient remedies—wine, garlic, onions—used to treat eye infections a thousand years ago hold promise in treating MRSA today. An international "ancient biotics team" is reviewing a fifteenth-century text for ingredients commonly used to treat infections.[185]

Bacteriophages, viruses that kill bacteria, are another turn to the past. During the Cold War, limited access to Western antibiotics led Soviet scientists to use these viruses. American and European researchers are giving bacteriophages another look, building libraries of phages. Already certain phages are being used to successfully treat drug-resistant bacteria.[186]

Combining past and future discoveries, the revolutionary gene-editing tool CRISPR could utilize bacteriophages as a delivery system to excise resistance-causing genes. CRISPR enables scientists to alter the genome with great precision. Modified bacteriophages could deliver CRISPR systems to destroy genes responsible for resistance.[187] Early studies focused on destroying antibiotic-resistant *E. coli* and *Staphylococcus aureus*.[188]

## Incentivizing AMR R&D

How can we align incentives and ensure sustainable financing to spur scientific discoveries? Pharmaceutical companies draw economic incentives from the patent system. The law allows companies to hold a monopoly for a novel drug for a period of time, typically twenty years. Yet potential markets for antimicrobials often are unpredictable and short-lived. If microbes gain resistance, the profitable life of a patented medicine can be quite short. New antibiotics also compete with inexpensive generic drugs and should, in any case, be conserved. Finally, recouping high development costs can be difficult when many patients are poor. All in all, incentives are badly aligned with the high social need for new antimicrobials. Bridging the gap requires public financing, new incentives, and antimicrobial stewardship.

Historically, funders have invested primarily in high-profile diseases such as HIV / AIDS, cancer, and heart disease. Yet with the horrifying prospect of losing generations of antibiotics, in 2015 the UK and China established the Global Antimicrobial Resistance Research Innovation Fund, with the goal of investing £1 billion.[189] The following year the United States launched the Combating Antibiotic Resistant Bacteria Biopharmaceutical Accelerator to move drugs from proof of concept to preclinical development.[190] WHO established the Global Antibiotic R&D Partnership, setting research priorities for new antimicrobial research.[191] More is needed. The UK's Antimicrobial Review proposed a Global Innovation Fund, initially resourced at $2 billion.[192]

Public financing is also needed to make antimicrobial R&D a commercially winning proposition. The Antimicrobial Review proposed "market entry rewards," which would require up to $1.3 billion per new antibiotic. Incentivizing a robust pipeline—including about fifteen new antibiotics per decade, a mix of broad- and narrow-spectrum drugs, and some with novel mechanisms of action—could cost $16 billion over ten years.[193]

Governments can take other steps as well. The tax system could create market incentives. The US Reinvigorating Antibiotic and Diagnostic Innovation (READI) Act, if enacted, would offer a 50 percent clinical trial tax credit for antimicrobials and rapid diagnostics.[194] Clinical trials account for two-thirds of the cost of bringing an antibiotic to market.[195] With greater potential still, the proposed Re-Valuing Anti-Microbial Products (REVAMP) Act would provide an extra twelve months of market exclusivity for developers of high-priority antimicrobials. The market exclusivity would be applied not to the antimicrobial, but instead to another the drug of the company's choice. The company could also sell this market exclusivity to another company to apply to one of its products. This incentive is likely worth over $1 billion.[196]

Funding and incentives should be conditioned on stewardship, with strict conditions on drug conservation and ensuring global access. Manufacturers, for example, could agree not to market a drug, or to restrict access, unless no viable alternative treatment exists, and to provide the drug at a locally affordable price. WHO would set research priorities, coordinate, and monitor compliance.[197]

## A Race against Time

We are left, then, with a race against time. Already, antimicrobial resistance takes more lives every week than the West African Ebola epidemic took in over two years. The world has been slow to act. Yet we know what needs to be done.

WHO's Global Action Plan laid out a path to help stem this threat. Political leaders have asserted their commitment. And we have seen true leadership in countries that have taken strong measures. The Netherlands set aggressive targets accompanied by comprehensive strategies for reducing antibiotic use in both people and animals. Denmark prohibited nontherapeutic use of antibiotics in pigs more than two decades ago. Countries including the United States and the United Kingdom have created new, if insufficient, funding streams for antibiotic R&D, while legislation has been proposed in the United States that would offer incentives that could spur private companies to develop new antimicrobials. And there is more. In Israel, for example, rigorous hospital oversight, including reporting and site visits, contained a CRE outbreak within a year.[198] To combat fake and substandard medicine, Nigeria took measures including increased penalties, import controls, pharmacist education, and new technology.[199]

Much hinges now on at least four factors. (1) Will national leadership become the rule rather than notable exceptions in prevention efforts, especially in countries like China, where antibiotic use is widespread in people and rapidly escalating in animals? (2) Can incentives and public funding reverse the drought in new classes of antibiotics, with sustained production instead? (3) Will the promises of new scientific technologies for developing new antibiotics, like CRISPR and new methods of antibiotic discovery, and rediscovered old tools, primarily bacteriophages, bear out? (4) Even if funding and scientific advances turn into new classes of antibiotics, will countries have health systems that are capable of delivering affordable drugs to the people who need them—and not providing them to people who do not need them?

The oft-cited figure of 10 million deaths annually from antimicrobial resistance by 2050 is far from destiny. It is a possibility that looms if some of the most significant antimicrobial-resistant infections double and the level of resistance becomes considerably higher.[200] It is still well within our power to create a very different future.

# CHAPTER 6

# The Climate Crisis

**For all of human history,** natural climatic shifts have impacted the planet, human health, and society. Consider the change between the Roman Warm Period, which contributed to the Roman Empire's expansion, and the cold darkness of Charles Dickens's London during the Little Ice Age. Natural changes in climate have both enhanced human flourishing and inflicted great hardship. Now, however, the Earth faces a calamitous climatic crisis, one that is unprecedented and far from natural. In response, nature is setting off "a deafening, piercing smoke alarm."[1]

One climate scientist put it this way: "When something happens—a cold-snap, wild fire, a hurricane, any of those things—we need to assume it will be worse than anything we've ever seen."[2] In the summer of 2018, Kerala, India, experienced the worst flooding in a century, causing 400 deaths and displacing one million people. During the following summer of 2019, India experienced an alarming water crisis. Piped water ran dry in Chennai, while twenty-one other Indian cities faced the specter of "Day Zero," a point at which municipal water sources can no longer meet demand.[3] India is one of seventeen countries—collectively including one-quarter of the world's population—with "extremely high" water stress, meaning that they are already using more than 80 percent of available water. This makes them particularly vulnerable to droughts, especially as the population grows and water demand increases.[4] Scientists forecast that more Day Zeroes are on the horizon.

Climate change is already contributing to food shortages, as drought and other extreme weather events degrade land and soil, higher carbon dioxide concentrations in the atmosphere reduce food's nutritional quality, and rising temperatures reduce crop yields and hurt livestock. Global warming that exceeds preindustrial levels by 2°C (3.6 °F) could increase the number of people at risk of hunger by at least 100 million.[5]

Climate change creates massive swings in weather patterns and temperature. In 2018 a British heat wave broke all records. Forests in California burned more ferociously than ever before. North of the Arctic Circle, Swedish temperatures soared while record wildfires raged. Japan's rainfall was the heaviest ever, followed by record-setting heat (41°C / 106°F). Death Valley reached 52°C (127°F). Eastern Australia was parched by the worst drought in living memory. By 2020 the World Wide Fund for Nature declared Australian wildfires the "worst wildlife disasters in modern history." More than 46 million acres were scorched, affecting 1.25 billion animals. That same year, the largest wildfire season in California's history covered more than 4 percent of the state's land. Intense summer heat is a "silent killer," and if humankind remains on the same path, extreme heat could become quite literally unbearable.[6]

In 2020, Earth's average surface temperature tied with that of 2016 to constitute the warmest year on record in nearly 140 years of record keeping, even despite global shutdowns due to the COVID-19 pandemic.[7] The five warmest years in recorded history have been the last five, and eighteen of the nineteen warmest years have occurred since 2001.[8] Meanwhile, the first month of 2019 saw thirty-five all-time record high temperatures in the Southern Hemisphere, reported by weather stations from Australia to Chile to Namibia. Port Augusta, Australia, experienced a temperature of 49.5°C (121°F).[9] When summer came to the Northern Hemisphere in 2019, cities in California and Alaska were among those experiencing all-time highs.[10] France recorded its highest-ever recorded temperature, 45.9°C (115°F).[11] June 2019 clocked in as the hottest June ever. Scientists have concluded that the climate crisis has made summer heat waves five times more likely and significantly more intense.[12]

As summer wanes, hurricane season arrives. The 2017 Atlantic season was among the most catastrophic. Hurricane Irma's maximum sustained winds (298 kph / 185 mph) were unprecedented. Hurricane Maria caused approximately 3,000 deaths in Puerto Rico in September 2017, leaving the island without electricity.[13] Eight months later, when tens of thousands still had no power, Puerto Rico's official hurricane season began. In October 2018, Hurricane Michael made landfall off the US Gulf Coast, becoming the most ferocious hurricane in Florida's history. The brutal 2020 Atlantic hurricane season generated an extraordinary thirty named storms, the highest on record.

Then comes winter, bringing bone-jarring cold. In early January 2019, Chicago officials warned residents of the risk of almost instant frostbite on perhaps the coldest day on record. That was a continuation of the 2017–2018 North American cold snap, which broke low temperature records and generated severe blizzards.

Dramatic weather events garner the most attention, but chronic harms caused and accelerated by climate change take an even greater toll. The Lancet Commission on Pollution and Health estimated that pollution causes 9 million premature deaths worldwide every year—16 percent of global deaths.[14] Most pollution-related deaths are caused by the air we breathe. WHO estimates that more than 90 percent of the world's population live in neighborhoods with polluted air.[15] Climate change will only exacerbate this air pollution, increasing ground-level ozone and particulate matter.[16] Food production is dramatically altered as temperatures unnaturally rise or fall, or conditions become unusually more wet or dry, resulting in long-term food insecurity and water scarcity. Further impacts are mediated through human social systems, including mass human displacement as those most vulnerable flee from monsoon rains, droughts, and wildfires.

This chapter explores why anthropogenic climate change brings life-defining hazards, endangering the planet and human survival, while accelerating the spread of pathogens.

## Scenarios of Global Disaster

The Earth's climate is determined by a system of interactions between the atmosphere, oceans, land, and polar surfaces. While weather comprises short-term shifts in temperature, rain, clouds, and wind, the term "climate" refers to the typical weather of a region, such as average temperatures or rainfall in a season. Changes in regional, or even planetary, climate significantly impact life on Earth.

Multiple data sources, collected independently, have observed Earth's average surface temperature rising precipitously.[17] Between 1880 and 2012, the Earth's average land and ocean surface temperatures increased by 0.85°C

(1.53°F).[18] From 2014 to 2016, the global average land and ocean tempera-ture record was broken *each* successive year, with 2016 recording an average temperature of 0.94°C (1.69°F) higher than the twentieth-century average.[19] With an average global land and ocean surface temperature increase of 0.84°C (1.51°F), 2017 was the third-warmest year on record.[20] The most recent data indicate that human activity has caused approximately 1°C of global warming above preindustrial average temperatures (between 1850 to 1900).[21]

Over our planet's 4.5-billion-year history, the Earth's climate has under-gone profound changes, causing life to blossom and expire through natural changes such as volcanic and ocean activity, solar shifts, and changes in the Earth's orbit. These warmer and cooler periods lasted millennia, affecting not only surface temperatures, but also the ocean, rainfall, and wind. Now the overwhelming scientific consensus is that severe warming can no longer be explained by natural events. Instead, this new phenomenon has been caused by human activity since the Industrial Revolution.[22]

The most concerning human activity is burning fossil fuels such as coal, oil, and natural gas. This results in greenhouse gas emissions, including carbon dioxide and methane, at unsustainable levels.[23] Greenhouse gas emissions trap excess heat within the Earth's atmosphere, leading to major changes in the global climate.[24] Given the impact of anthropogenic greenhouse gases, reducing emissions is at the center of climate change treaties. International agreements, which we will examine below, seek to limit greenhouse gas emis-sions to prevent perilous disruptions to the global climate system.

The most comprehensive understanding of what our climate change future will hold comes from the UN Intergovernmental Panel on Climate Change (IPCC), which provides consensus on scientific conclusions on anthropolog-ical influence and climate change. Through the IPCC, thousands of global experts synthesize climate science. They have concluded that human activity has caused virtually all the warming observed since 1950.

The IPCC examined four emission concentration scenarios to estimate their impact on future climate change: one scenario involving stringent emis-sions mitigation, two intermediate emissions scenarios, and one scenario with very high greenhouse gas emissions.[25] Current emission rates are on track to fall at the higher end of these scenarios.[26] Under every emissions scenario, Earth's mean surface temperature would rise by at least 0.3°C to 0.7°C (0.54°F to 1.26°F) over the next two decades.[27]

In 2017 experts projected that global surface temperatures will rise 2.0°C to 4.9°C (3.6°F to 8.8°F) by 2100.[28] The Paris Agreement aims to keep global temperature increases below 2°C, while hoping to meet a more demanding goal of no more than a 1.5°C increase.[29] In 2018 the IPCC released a special report on the feasibility of limiting global warming to 1.5°C, noting that significant harms caused by climate change could be avoided by achieving this more stringent target. Based on current warming rates, the world will experience human-induced global warming of 1.5°C by 2040.[30] Limiting warming to 1.5°C will require unprecedented, immediate, determined, well-enforced, international collective action.

The consequences of a 2°C rise would be devastating. The IPCC states that it is a virtual certainty that the globe will experience more catastrophic events, including enduring heat waves and periodic extreme cold.[31] Global sea levels will likely continue to rise as a result of increasing ocean temperatures, along with melting glaciers and polar ice sheets.[32] Between 1901 and 2010, global average sea levels rose by 19 centimeters.[33] Between 1993 and 2010, global sea levels rose at an average rate of 3.2 millimeters per year.[34] The IPCC estimates that by 2100, based on intermediate emissions scenarios, sea levels will rise 0.32 to 0.63 meters. Under the highest emission scenarios, they will rise 0.45 to 0.82 meters. In 2019 scientists found that the world's oceans are warming 40 percent faster than predicted by the IPCC, with dire implications for climate change because almost all excess heat absorbed by the planet ends up stored in the oceans.[35]

Given the distribution of heat in the ocean, sea levels will continue to rise for thousands of years even if global temperatures are stabilized.[36] This will increase extreme sea surges and massive flooding.[37] Hurricane activity in the North Atlantic[38] and typhoons across Asia Pacific have intensified.[39] Climate change will also result in global shifts in rainfall intensity and frequency.[40] If emissions reach the highest levels of the IPCC scenarios, we will see intense and prolonged periods of drought.[41] This has the potential to cause irreversible human and social devastation.

### It's Already Happening

Humanity is already experiencing the profound harms of climate change. After Hurricane Maria ravaged the Caribbean in 2017, Dominica's prime minister Roosevelt Skerrit told the United Nations, "To deny climate change . . . is to deny a truth that we have just lived."[42] And still, the familiar refrain following extreme weather events is that it is impossible to say whether climate change caused it. This disregards and undermines the severity of the longer-term degradation of the planet. Instead, there should be two clear responses. First, even though it is difficult to establish that any single event has been caused by climate change, the cumulative impact of severe events makes the association evident. Second, climate scientists are devising methods to assess whether single events are exacerbated by major climate shifts. Singular, extreme weather events rightfully capture the public's attention. The lesser-acknowledged fact is that changes to the global climate system will wreak havoc in virtually every sphere of human life.

The IPCC classifies climate change's health impacts based on direct and indirect impacts. Direct impacts include injury, disease, and death from heat waves, fires, and floods.[43] Storms and floods—the most common natural disasters—cause drowning, injuries, and outbreaks of waterborne diseases such as cholera (see Chapter 2).[44] Heat waves disproportionately affect the poor, sick, elderly, and children. Climate change indirectly affects human health by altering ecosystems, which determine how pathogens emerge and proliferate. Pathogens, and their hosts, are embedded in the environment; climate change affects how vectors breed, flourish, and bite. Climate change also impacts human activities, such as food production. Agriculture—essential for nutrition and food security—depends on soil, temperature, and water. When a hostile climate places extreme social and economic pressure on families and communities (such as worries about food security and potable water), it fuels conflicts, violence, and mass migration. Ultimately, hostile climates further destabilize communities that are already on the edge, sometimes to the point of collapse.[45]

The effects of climate change extend beyond destruction of the planet's natural beauty and the built environment. Consider its profound impacts on mental health as a result of disaster-related trauma, chronic psychological distress, and grieving.[46] Climate change threatens human health and well-being, with the heaviest burdens borne by the poor and disadvantaged.

Although climate change is a global issue that poses a risk to everyone on the planet, it does not affect everyone equally. Rather, it exacerbates existing health inequalities. Populations that are already vulnerable are particularly susceptible to the effects of climate change, and are also the least equipped to adapt. Age, gender, socioeconomic status, and health status affect one's vulnerability to climate change. Children, for example, are more vulnerable than adults to infectious diseases, undernutrition, and heat-related illness and stress, whereas the elderly are often less mobile and able to seek help.[47] People with chronic diseases, such as diabetes and obesity, are especially prone to the potentially fatal effects of intense heat.[48] Location also plays a role. Those who live on small islands or in coastal regions, megacities, and mountainous and polar regions face heightened risks.

One of the most visible, dramatic consequences of climate change is the mass migration of people within countries and across borders. António Guterres, UN secretary-general and previous high commissioner for refugees, noted in 2015 that the world is sliding "into an era in which the scale of global forced displacement, as well as the response required, is now clearly dwarfing anything seen before."[49]

Conflict, food shortages, and economic and humanitarian crises had forcibly displaced 70.8 million people worldwide by the end of 2018.[50] Disasters— most of them weather-related, including hurricanes, floods, and droughts— internally displaced 18.8 million people in 2018. Climate change often plays a role, compounding the effects of these immediate drivers of forced displacement.[51] In Somalia, for example, food insecurity brought on by extreme drought, coupled with ongoing internal conflict, has displaced millions, within Somalia and as refugees.

The effects of climate change can dramatically worsen conditions for those who are forcibly displaced for other reasons, especially those who live in overcrowded refugee camps. In late 2017 WHO reported a major diphtheria outbreak in Kutupalong as a result of monsoon rains, overcrowding, and inadequate vaccination. That same year the Somali refugee camp in Dadaab, Kenya, experienced cholera caused by lack of clean water and poor sanitation. Many millions more internally displaced persons live in similarly precarious circumstances.

## The Threat to Global Health Security

Climactic factors influence the growth and life cycle of pathogens, the habitat of zoonotic hosts and vectors, and vector biology and biting behavior. Complex biological, social, and ecological systems, in turn, determine the likelihood of outbreaks, epidemics, and endemic disease. Thus, fighting climate change is a crucial aspect of strengthening our defenses against fast-moving microbes. The solutions include decelerating the rise in global temperature, while adapting to infectious disease threats by building and maintaining robust public health systems. Public health systems (e.g., sanitation, clean water, access to vaccines and medicines) play a crucial role in preventing, detecting, and responding to infectious diseases.

As described in Chapters 1–4, infectious diseases spread through multiple pathways: from zoonotic sources, making the leap from animal to human; from the bite of a vector that carries the pathogen, such as mosquitoes and ticks; and from the environment, such as waterborne or foodborne diseases. For this reason, animals, vectors, and water are the primary interfaces between climate change and global health security.

## Animals

Between 60 and 80 percent of newly emerging infectious diseases are zoonotic, making the leap from animals to humans, sometimes with the help of a vector.[52] Many factors underpin this zoonotic leap, one of which is a pathogen's genes. Genetic mutations in the influenza virus, for example, result in certain strains that are more easily transmissible among humans. As discussed in Chapter 5, travel, migration, and trade, as well as the misuse of antibiotics, can propel drug-resistant zoonotic infections. Here, we consider what occurs when climate change further complicates these scenarios. Crucially, alterations in ecosystems, weather, and climate provide the environment in which microbes can flourish.[53]

The impacts of climate change on zoonotic diseases are largely indirect and part of complex, multifactorial systems. Recent emerging infectious diseases are believed to have arisen from close contact between animals and humans; these include severe acute respiratory syndrome (SARS), coronavirus disease 2019 (COVID-19), Middle East respiratory syndrome (MERS), Nipah virus, Ebola, and multiple influenzas, such as H5N1 and H7N9. Climate change may have unexpected outcomes, such as reducing the risk of certain zoonotic viruses that favor colder climates, while amplifying risks of others as shifting geographic habitats create more adaptable, or altogether new, pathogens. The latter has been the case with influenza and Ebola.

Rising global temperatures may increase the risk of pandemic influenza. Temperature and climate have major effects on the migratory patterns of birds: the hosts for avian influenza viruses. With near certainty, climate change will alter bird migration, influencing the transmission cycle of avian influenza viruses, and impacting the survival of avian viruses in the environment.[54] Although influenza typically is associated with the colder, drier air of the winter season, it is a highly adaptable virus. WHO reports that more-recent H5N1 influenza strains survived longer in warmer temperatures than previous viruses, possibly explaining viral reemergence during summer months.[55] This is only one example, but it reveals the potential for zoonotic viruses to deftly adapt to the environmental pressures of climate change.

As we saw in Chapter 2, the West African Ebola epidemic originated when a two-year-old boy in the remote village of Meliandou, Guinea, came into contact with a fruit bat and contracted the virus. How did that child come into contact with an infected fruit bat? One likely explanation is that the distance between human settlements and the habitat of fruit bats has become ever smaller.[56] Deforestation has been associated with Ebola outbreaks in Central and West Africa, resulting in increased contact between animals and humans.[57] Similarly, the COVID-19 pandemic originated in bats and, through another animal, crossed into humans at a live animal market in Wuhan, China, where humans and diverse animal species mingle. Such species interactions, which would never happen in the wild, create ideal conditions for viral evolution. As humankind exploits natural resources through mining, illegal logging, animal trade, and agriculture, climate change is accelerated. These activities contribute to more greenhouse gases than produced by motor vehicles worldwide.[58] Preventing deforestation and preserving natural habitats therefore benefit both the climate and human health.

Climate change also destroys ecosystems, through forest fires, strong winds, drought, and flooding. This reduces biodiversity, habitat suitability, and food availability, forcing animals into areas where they are in closer contact with humans.

## Vectors

Vector-borne diseases are viruses, bacteria, or other pathogens that are transmitted to humans by another organism—a "vector." Common vectors include mosquitoes, sandflies, snails, blackflies, triatomic bugs, ticks, and fleas. We saw in Chapter 3 the harm that mosquito-borne diseases cause. Ticks cause over half a million cases of Borreliosis—or Lyme disease—each year, along with the highly lethal Crimean-Congo hemorrhagic fever and severe fever with thrombocytopenia syndrome, caused by a virus only discovered in 2009. Snails transmit schistosomiasis, which infects an estimated 207 million people each year.[59]

Vector-borne diseases already pose a major threat to global health security, causing more than 700,000 deaths annually. More than 80 percent of the world's population live in a region at risk of at least one vector-borne disease. Most vector-borne diseases currently occur in tropical and subtropical areas. However, changing climatic conditions provide fertile ground for disease vectors to alter or expand their geographic range to include more temperate climates.[60] This, combined with other factors such as increased deforestation, brings vectors into increasing contact with humans.[61] The incidence and intensity of vector-borne pathogens such as malaria, dengue, and Zika virus is therefore likely to rise. Worst-case scenarios predict that as many as one billion people will be newly exposed to vector-borne diseases by 2080 (see Chapter 3).[62] Climate change is already altering the constant evolutionary battle between humans and vector-borne pathogens in profound ways.

The IPCC notes that vector-borne diseases are "some of the best studied diseases associated with climate change" as a result of their global prevalence and sensitivity to changes in the climate.[63] Vector survival, reproduction, and biting rates depend on climatic conditions, which include rainfall, temperature, and relative humidity.

One of the diseases most studied for the potential impact of climate change is malaria (see Chapter 3). After years of falling numbers of cases worldwide, case numbers began edging upward in 2014.[64] Along with antimicrobial resistance (see Chapter 5), climate change may be playing a role.

Kenyan tea plantations have served as the scientific battleground for studies examining the impacts of climate change on malaria. Since 2002, warming temperatures (compared to the three prior decades) have increased malaria incidence.[65] This relationship is nonlinear due to the role of the vector in the malaria parasite's life cycle, requiring vectors to be active and biting when the parasite is at the appropriate stage of maturity.[66] Rising temperatures promote malaria transmission to a certain extent; once temperatures rise above the malaria parasite and mosquito vector's maximum temperature, transmission is reduced.[67] If temperatures in tropical climates rise to levels that are too hot for sustained transmission, it is likely that the disease burden will shift to other regions, such as Europe, where increasing temperatures and shifts in rainfall are creating conditions more favorable to the *Anopheles* mosquito and certain malaria parasites.

Widespread vector control is vital for controlling malaria. However, countries that are not currently experiencing the effects of high malaria burdens are less inclined to prioritize the public health measures needed to control its spread. In the last decade Europe has reported locally transmitted malaria. Greece reported more than sixty cases of locally acquired *Plasmodium vivax* malaria infections from 2009 to 2012, in part caused by the economic crisis and austerity measures that cut public health funding.[68]

Climate change will affect the range of another disease transmitted by mosquitoes, dengue. Dengue is the viral infection transmitted through the bite of infected *Aedes* mosquitoes, predominantly the *Aedes aegypti* (see Chapter 3). Nearly 40 percent of the world's population live in areas at risk of dengue infection (see Figure 6.1). Both of the main dengue vectors, *Aedes aegypti* and *Aedes albopictus* mosquitoes, are climate sensitive. Dengue transmission is dependent on the season, occurring predominantly in months with higher rainfall.

Modeling shows that predicted changes in the climate will shift the habitable range of the *Aedes aegypti* mosquito. In certain dengue-endemic areas, the presence of the *Aedes aegypti* vector will likely be reduced. However, in other areas, where climate change is causing rainfall and temperature increases, the suitability for *Aedes aegypti* mosquitoes will increase.[69] Meanwhile, the geographical range of the *Aedes albopictus* mosquito in Europe has shifted northward, as northern regions become warmer and wetter and southern regions becomes drier, with warmer summers.[70] One study has found that under the most severe scenarios, an additional 900 million people may be exposed for the first time to the *Aedes aegypti* mosquito, while nearly 600 million people could be newly exposed to another deadly species, *Aedes albopictus*, under more moderate temperature increases.[71] In 2012, Madeira, Portugal, experienced the first sustained transmission of dengue in Europe since the 1920s.[72] In 2017, dengue emergencies were reported in Sri Lanka,[73] Burkina Faso,[74] and Côte d'Ivoire.[75]

The increasing impact of dengue globally, especially with the shifting habitable range of *Aedes aegypti* mosquitoes, has increased awareness of the impact of dengue on global health security. Improving surveillance and diagnostics may help minimize the impacts of outbreaks. The potential emergence of dengue in new regions, such as Europe, should be monitored as climatic conditions shift.[76]

Ensuring global health security in the face of climate change requires improving the surveillance of both vector and disease, coupled with rigorous control programs. These climate change adaptation strategies, along with mitigation strategies that reduce the impact of climate change on the *Aedes* mosquito, are critical for ensuring global health security over the next century.

## Water

Diarrheal diseases are one of the leading health risks of climate change.[77] More than 1.57 million people died from diarrheal diseases in 2017; of these,

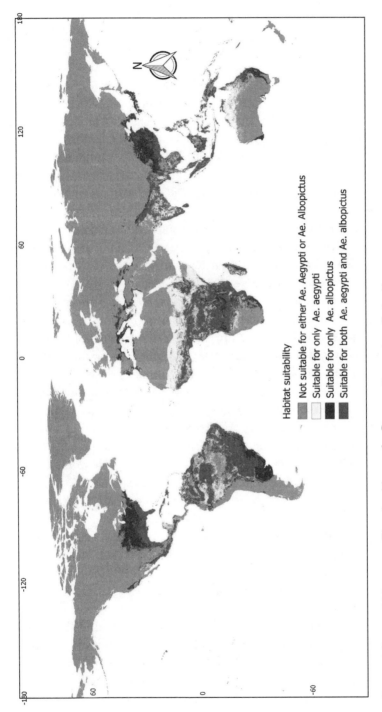

**Figure 6.1** Range of Mosquitoes That Are Vectors for Dengue. Samson Leta, Tariku Jibat Beyene, Eva M. De Clercq, Kebede Amenu, Moritz U.G. Kraemer, Crawford W. Revie. "Global Risk Mapping for Major Diseases Transmitted by *Aedes aegypti* and *Aedes albopictus*," *International Journal of Infectious Diseases* 67 (2018): 25–35, Figure 1. ©2017 The Authors. CC BY-NC-ND.

34 percent were children under the age of five.[78] And even though such deaths have dropped by 36 percent since 2000,[79] diarrheal diseases (such as cholera, rotavirus, and *Escherichia coli*) were still the seventh leading cause of death globally in 2016. Long-term meteorological data show a strong relationship between diarrheal diseases and increased land temperatures, heavy rainfall, and flooding.[80] Based on historical data, scientists predict that global climate change—in particular, rising sea levels and temperatures—will increase diarrheal diseases globally.[81] Climate change will not only exacerbate the conditions for the spread of waterborne diseases, but will also disrupt sanitation and clean water systems, reversing advances in public health and global development.

One devastating disease that often accompanies inadequate sanitation and clean water systems is cholera. This was the case in Haiti, where a cholera epidemic broke out following the 2010 earthquake (see Chapter 2). Throughout the nineteenth century, successive cholera outbreaks served as the impetus for European states to engage in international diplomacy to protect national health security. Beginning in Paris in 1851, Europe hosted a series of International Sanitary Conferences, culminating in the International Sanitary Convention. The Convention would later form the basis for the main piece of international law that governs global health security today: the International Health Regulations (IHR).[82] Despite two centuries of efforts to control cholera, major outbreaks continue. Every year there are 1.3 million to 4 million cases of cholera.[83] The IHR recognize that cholera has a serious public health impact, with the potential for international spread. In 2017, Yemen—torn by war and civil unrest—experienced the worst cholera outbreak in history, surpassing more than 1 million cases.[84]

Cholera is an acute diarrheal disease caused by the bacteria *Vibrio cholerae* and is transmitted mainly through drinking contaminated water or eating food such as shellfish or produce contaminated from the water. Environmental factors such as temperature, precipitation, and changes in water salinity all contribute to the risk of infection.[85] Because cholera is a climate-sensitive disease, rising temperatures could increase cholera infections worldwide.[86]

The strong relationship between cholera and environmental changes means that monitoring plankton blooms can help predict potential outbreaks.[87] With early surveillance, governments can prepare for a potential outbreak, reducing infections through health information campaigns to boil or avoid contaminated water, providing safe drinking water, and marshaling public health resources, such sufficient supplies of oral rehydration solutions. Climate change could also alter the geographic patterns of cholera, requiring countries with little experience of the disease to actively prepare.[88] In addition to the impact of increased ocean temperatures on algae blooms that facilitate cholera, increased flooding from rising sea levels and extreme weather events will disrupt and intermingle clean water and waste systems, which can lead to outbreaks.[89]

Ensuring global health security by preventing waterborne diseases will require various climate change adaptation measures. These might include strengthening surveillance systems, investing in public education, improving access to vaccines and medical equipment, and maintaining water and sanitation infrastructure sufficient to withstand rising temperatures, rainfall, sea levels, and extreme weather events. Governments can also mitigate harms by improving socioeconomic conditions (e.g., housing, air conditioning, and health services) and by building flood barriers.

As the cases of malaria and dengue demonstrate, climate change has the potential to profoundly impact global health security through multiple pathways. Climate change should be understood as a force multiplier and paradigm shift to global health security, bringing with it many unknowns. As an unprecedented anthropogenic phenomenon, there is an inherent scarcity of data. We can predict, based on the evolution of pathogens and their ability to adapt, that humanity may face a whole raft of unknown novel diseases as a result of warming oceans, melting ice sheets, and closer contact between animals, vectors, and humans. However, humanity has the ingenuity to adapt. To do so we must harness the potential of international law and collective action to mitigate, and adapt to, climate change.

### International Law and Collective Action on Global Climate Change

The scientific consensus on climate change is well established. Since the late twentieth century, scientists working in the fields of geophysical science, meteorology, volcanography, and oceanography have regularly met to discuss research. In 1980 the World Meteorological Organization, the UN Environment Programme, and the International Council of Scientific Unions sponsored such a conference in Villach, Austria.[90] In 1985, at the fifth Villach conference, scientists concluded that greenhouse gases could cause several degrees Celsius of global warming.[91] The conference called for prioritizing climate science as a matter of global concern, noting that "the rate and degree of future warming could be profoundly affected by governmental poli-cies."[92] This finding spurred international cooperation, leading the World Meteorological Organization and the UN Environment Programme to form the IPCC in 1988 to evaluate extant scientific evidence and the potential for mitigation and adaptation.[93]

The IPCC's First Assessment Report in 1990 called for negotiations of an international agreement to take urgent action to arrest global warming. At the 1992 Earth Summit, the UN Framework Convention on Climate Change (UNFCCC) opened for signature; the convention took effect in 1994. The UNFCCC has 197 states parties, including all UN member states. The UNFCCC's objective is to stabilize atmospheric greenhouse gas con-centrations at a level that prevents dangerous interference with the climate system.[94] The UNFCCC parties agreed to take precautionary measures to anticipate, prevent, or minimize the adverse effects of climate change, rec-ognizing that "lack of full scientific certainty should not be used as a reason for postponing measures," as the world faced serious and irreversible harms.[95]

As a framework convention, the UNFCCC relies on a series of specific additional international agreements, known as protocols, that set out legally binding measures to address climate change, such as limits on greenhouse gas emissions. UNFCCC parties meet annually at the Conference of Par-ties to assess their progress in addressing climate change. In 1997, at the third Conference of Parties, the first UNFCCC protocol, the Kyoto Protocol, was opened for signature; it entered into force in 2005. The Kyoto Protocol es-tablished legally binding emissions reduction targets over a five-year period (2008–2012) for six greenhouse gases (including carbon dioxide and methane) for thirty-six developed and transitional economy countries. However, under the Kyoto Protocol regime, low-income developing countries were not sub-ject to binding emissions reduction or emissions targets. The Kyoto Protocol urged additional market-based mechanisms, such as emissions-trading schemes, to reduce global greenhouse gas emissions and enable sustainable development that prioritizes poverty alleviation and access to health care.

In 2015 the Conference of Parties adopted a second UNFCCC protocol, the Paris Agreement, which entered into force in 2016. Under the Paris Agreement, parties expressly acknowledge that climate change is a common concern of humankind and that states parties should "respect, promote and consider their respective obligations on human rights, the right to health, the rights of indigenous peoples, local communities, migrants, children, per-sons with disabilities and people in vulnerable situations and the right to development, as well as gender equality, empowerment of women and intergenerational equity."[96]

As their core Paris Agreement obligation, parties committed to keeping global average temperature increases below 2°C from preindustrial levels and to pursue efforts to limit warming to 1.5°C,[97] as noted earlier. Limiting warming to between 1.5°C and 2°C will still result in significant threats to global health. The strictest IPCC emissions reduction scenario—representative of an emissions scenario associated with 2°C warming—suggests that the associated temperate increases would expand the habitat range of *Aedes aegypti* mosquitoes to many parts of France.[98] Limiting warming to 1.5°C would decrease the risk of the impacts of global warming on global health, such as reducing the risk of vector-borne diseases,[99] deaths and illness from heat waves and water stress, and the negative impact on food production.[100] It would likely also avoid catastrophic climate change scenarios, including the complete loss of certain island nations and coastal cities. With very few exceptions and subject to regional variation, global warming of 2°C poses more risks to human health than a warming of 1.5°C.[101]

Rather than setting specific, legally binding emissions targets, the Paris Agreement requires that all parties self-determine and report on the steps they are taking to progressively mitigate and limit global warming—known as nationally determined contributions (NDCs).[102] In setting their NDCs, parties should commit to rapid reductions to achieve net-zero greenhouse gas emissions by 2050.[103] This will require a significant shift in current government commitments, with a requisite net emissions reduction of about 45 percent from 2010 levels by 2030, and net zero emissions by 2052.[104] The sooner net-zero global anthropogenic $CO_2$ emissions are achieved, the greater the chance that humanity will be able to limit global warming to 1.5°C.[105]

The divide between middle-income and high-income countries has posed a political challenge to collective action by states parties. High-income countries have disproportionally contributed to global greenhouse emissions, and lower-income countries have been disproportionately burdened by their impacts. With economic development, middle-income countries such as China and India are now producing larger amounts of greenhouse gas emissions. Despite these political challenges, the UNFCCC protocols illustrate how the world has recently coalesced around addressing climate change. The adoption of long-term mitigation measures, like the Paris Agreement, has been a major advance in international climate politics. Still, NDCs are voluntary and the Paris Agreement contains no enforcement mechanisms, such as penalties. Based on initial NDC commitments, the world will fail to limit warming to 2°C, resulting in a global temperature increase of 3°C by 2100.[106]

Even more recently another political threat has emerged. Populist governments, especially in high-income countries like the United States (particularly during the Trump administration), have begun to place their own perceived economic interests above the collective response to a global threat. Populist leaders, who express discontent with collective action and disavow even the *fact* of climate change, threaten the Paris Agreement's potential. On November 4, 2019, President Trump filed his intent to withdraw the United States from the Paris Agreement, which took effect a year later. President Biden quickly rejoined the Agreement, promising an administration that would lead on the climate crisis. The Trump administration unraveled President Obama's rules limiting greenhouse gases in such areas as vehicle emissions, coal, and methane emissions; President Biden promised to restore those rules.

## Our Planetary Home

The planet's future and the population's health are at stake. The devastating impacts of climate change that are already occurring show how humanity has been actively destroying its only home. The consequences of a shifting climate for global human health are profound and will disproportionately burden the world's most disadvantaged people. While the twentieth century saw the deep impacts of globalization, international travel, and trade on global health security, climate change will surely be the twenty-first century's most profound challenge. Key advancements in global health and development over the past decades could easily be reversed as temperatures rise, rainfall patterns shift, and we experience more frequent extreme weather events. As sea levels rise, entire nations will be displaced. Droughts may turn arable land that once sustained populations into deserts. The real risk of increased conflict, malnutrition, mental illness, and human suffering extend beyond the issue of global health security.

There *are* solutions. Clean power—for homes, vehicles, and industry—could stem the relentless rise in climate extremes, making us all healthier and safer. Reliable storage of renewable energy would enable societies to avoid the variability of wind, wave, and solar energy. Forest sequestration and other technologies could capture carbon dioxide from the atmosphere, bringing humanity back from the brink of catastrophic disaster. Individuals' adopting more plant-based diets would reduce the agricultural emissions that result from diets centered on meat. But achieving the drastic reductions required in emissions must go far beyond relying on individual food choices—government action must be massively scaled up.[107]

Indeed, international legal action, such as the Paris Agreement, reflects a global political will to address climate change. However, this will may be subject to trends in nationalism and climate change denialism. These beliefs will not stop the impact of greenhouse gas emissions on the climate.

Global collective action is the only solution. This includes mutually agreed-upon mitigation measures that focus on reducing emissions, developing carbon-capture technologies, and sharing technology and best practices between nations for the benefit of humanity. Because progress has thus far been limited, adaptation strategies will also be needed. As the historic contributors to greenhouse gas emissions, wealthy countries have a particular duty to alleviate the burden climate change will have on poorer countries, providing them with financial and technical support to sustainably develop while adapting to a changing climate. Human health and equity demand nothing less.

# PART II

# FROM RISK TO ACTION

# CHAPTER 7

# Governing Global Health Security

On April 14, 2020, US president Trump announced the suspension of US funding for the World Health Organization for sixty to ninety days while his administration investigated WHO's response to the COVID-19 pandemic.[1] The president criticized WHO for its "China-centric" response. He alleged that the outbreak became a pandemic because WHO declined to recommend travel restrictions from China, was slow to declare a global health emergency, and failed to detect and report human-to-human transmission of SARS-CoV-2 in early January 2020. On July 7, 2020, the Trump administration sent formal notice of US withdrawal from WHO to UN secretary-general António Guterres, effective a year later on July 6, 2021, which President Biden reversed upon taking office in January 2021.[2]

Even though WHO has acted in accordance with its authority under the International Health Regulations (IHR) in responding to COVID-19, its constrained response, and the ability of WHO's largest donor to pull funding and support during a global pandemic, highlight the urgent need to reform the agency's governance structure, increase its capacity to control an outbreak, and ensure political support for the agency and its leadership. The COVID-19 outbreak is not the first time that such governance pitfalls have been revealed; it must become the last.

The 2014–2015 West African Ebola epidemic had already exposed major gaps in global governance for health. Global institutions were underprepared and underfunded, failing to stem the outbreak before it spun out of control.

WHO was slow to act, as its leaders—at headquarters and the regional office—fought for control. Funding for direly needed personnel and resources relied on countries' inconsistent donations. Around the world, there was little political will or willingness to assume responsibility, as evidenced by this account of one doctor on the ground:

> The most discouraging thing was to be sitting in [Liberia's capital] Monrovia, asking teams to step forward and for the world to remain silent. To have nobody, I mean nobody, answering. That was truly awful. Then to have to . . . phone the ministry in Sierra Leone and say, "I'm sorry, nobody wants to come, nobody is capable of coming forward."[3]

Ultimately, over 11,000 people in the world's poorest region died in this preventable epidemic.

As this chapter discusses, WHO instituted reforms to close these gaps in global governance for health. Still, major new governance problems emerged in a subsequent Ebola epidemic in the Democratic Republic of Congo (DRC) beginning in August 2018. This time WHO responded faster, utilizing a new Ebola vaccine effectively. Yet political violence and deep community distrust stymied WHO and DRC government responses to a complex humanitarian crisis. Ebola treatment centers were bombed and safe burial teams were attacked.[4] Fear of travel and trade restrictions added to the complexity. The DRC did not declare the end of that epidemic until June 25, 2020.[5]

In our globalized world, recent COVID-19 and Ebola epidemics demonstrate that the tension between state sovereignty and international obligation persists. Infectious diseases rapidly transcend borders, and therefore no state acting alone can secure the public's health. International institutions are vital to establishing a healthier and more secure world. They provide the norms, technical assistance, and resources needed to prevent, detect, and respond to outbreaks. Without robust international institutions to promote cross-border cooperation, information sharing and collective action prove challenging.

These institutions must be backed by the rule of law. Among the other features essential for effective governance—transparency, inclusive participation, performance effectiveness, leadership, and accountability—the rule of law is supreme. Without it, the other aspects of effective governance have little chance of taking hold. The rule of law is the ideal that law is consistent with and promotes human rights and public good. Further, all individuals and institutions are equally accountable to the law, however powerful they may be. All government officials and institutions must abide by and promote principles of good governance, honesty, and integrity. On a global scale, the rule of law promotes accountability and helps ensure that states will coordinate and cooperate to achieve global health objectives.[6]

Today a multitude of diverse actors inhabit the global health landscape: from the old guard—intergovernmental institutions and other multilateral organizations like WHO and the World Bank—to "new governance" actors ranging from civil society and philanthropists to corporations (such as pharmaceutical companies). Major philanthropies, such as the Gates Foundation and Rockefeller Foundation, spark innovation and offer vast resources for global health. Civil society organizations, such as Médecins Sans Frontières and Partners In Health, can be catalysts for reform while also providing humanitarian assistance in health emergencies.

Meanwhile, global public-private partnerships have innovative governance models that can be nimbler. Some focus on specific diseases, like the Global Fund to Fight AIDS, Tuberculosis and Malaria. Other partnerships focus on high-impact preventive strategies, such as Gavi, the Vaccine Alliance (Gavi), or mobilize funding for developing vaccines against high-risk pathogens, such as the Coalition for Epidemic Preparedness Innovations (CEPI). Sometimes diverse governance institutions partner together to tackle momentous global health threats. During the COVID-19 pandemic, WHO, Gavi, and CEPI spearheaded the COVAX facility designed to deliver affordable vaccines, especially to low-income countries.

The proliferation of global health actors has increased funding, governance, and social mobilization. Still, the global landscape is plagued by failures of leadership, coordination, and accountability. Vital institutions are chronically starved of funding and struggle to compete. States often disregard global norms and evidence-based recommendations.

This chapter offers ideas for empowered global health institutions, ranging from sustainable financing models to strategies for leadership and good governance. There are more than 200 international health agencies and initiatives. This chapter focuses on the ones that play the largest roles in ensuring global health security.[7] The central question for this chapter: How can we harness the power of robust international institutions to achieve global health security?[8]

## Reforms and Lasting Shortfalls

Agreements for international cooperation to prevent the spread of infectious diseases predate the COVID-19 and Ebola epidemics by more than a century.

In 1907, following a series of International Sanitary Conferences in Paris, European nations formed the Office International d'Hygiène Publique (OIHP) to collect data on quarantinable diseases and share it with member states—a narrow, noninterventionist agenda. At the turn of the twentieth century, European states adopted the International Sanitary Regulations (ISR), the world's first health treaty. These early agreements were of limited scope and minimal force, but they marked an initial step away from a purely national approach to health security, favoring shared responsibility for global health security.

### The Institutional Apex: The World Health Organization

In the aftermath of World War II, the United Nations was created to promote international cooperation and maintain peace. Health and human rights were integral to its mission. In 1945 the UN approved the creation of WHO as its first specialized agency. WHO's constitution was adopted the following year and came into force in 1948. It enshrined health as a global public good and human right, and empowers WHO to act as "the directing and coordinating authority on international health work" and to effectively collaborate with other UN agencies, including the UN Global Health Cluster (see Table 7.1).[9]

Today, virtually all countries are WHO members, giving it unrivaled global influence, normative authority, and political legitimacy. Every country has an equal voice, with each member state having one vote in WHO's top governing body, the World Health Assembly (WHA), which convenes annually. Along with its headquarters in Geneva, WHO has six regional offices as well as country offices in 150 countries, territories, and other areas.[10] WHO seeks to achieve its mission through guidelines and technical assistance, advocacy and political dialogues, norm-setting and law. WHO's constitution empowers the organization to develop binding law, both international regulations and conventions.

WHO's constitutional mandate includes stemming infectious diseases that pose an international threat, furnishing technical assistance and necessary aid during emergencies, and working toward eradicating epidemics and endemic diseases. This mandate is consistent with its origins, with the OIHP as a predecessor agency along with the short-lived League of Nations Health Organization. Throughout WHO's more than seven decades, infectious disease control has been a mainstay of its work and the source of both its crowning achievement and one of its most notable failures.

**Table 7.1.** Key International Governance Structures for Global Health

| Organization / Institution (year founded) | Type of global health power | Mission / description | Participation | Funding source |
|---|---|---|---|---|
| World Health Organization (1946)[1] | Specialized UN agency with explicit health mandate | Directs and coordinates international health work within the UN system | 194 member states | Mandatory and voluntary annual contributions by member states plus voluntary contributions by non-state actors |
| UN Global Health Cluster (2005)[2] | Collection of organizations, led by WHO, under the UN Interagency Standing Committee with explicit health mandate | One of 11 UN clusters for coordinating responses to humanitarian disasters and emergencies; provides tools and guidance, helping ensure surge capacity and expertise, and developing national capacities for humanitarian health action | More than 50 partner organizations and agencies engaged at the global level, and more than 900 partners at country level | WHO and partner organizations and agencies funded through own budgets |
| UN Security Council (1946)[3] | UN organ with indirect health mandate | Aims to ensure international peace and security, including health security | 15 member states | UN member states |
| World Organisation for Animal Health (1924)[4] | Organization under the World Assembly of Delegates with indirect human health mandate | Fights animal diseases and improves animal health worldwide; requires states to report animal diseases and publishes standards for sharing animal products | 182 member states | Mandatory and voluntary annual contributions by member states |
| Food and Agricultural Organization (1945)[5] | UN agency with indirect health mandate | Leads international efforts to defeat hunger; adopted frameworks in food-related health emergencies | 194 member states | Mandatory and voluntary annual contributions by member states |

*(Continued)*

**Table 7.1.** (continued)

| Organization / Institution (year founded) | Type of global health power | Mission / description | Participation | Funding source |
|---|---|---|---|---|
| World Bank (1944)[6] | Multilateral organization with direct and indirect health impacts | Aims to reduce poverty and promote shared prosperity globally through financing, technical support, and partnerships with governments and the private sectors | 189 member states | Diverse sources including return on investments, funding from member states, and private investments |
| World Trade Organization (1995)[7] | Multilateral organization with indirect health impact | Aims to facilitate global movement of goods and services by promoting free trade | 164 member states | Member contributions based on share of international trade |
| Global Fund to Fight AIDS, Tuberculosis and Malaria (2002)[8] | Public-private partnership with direct health impact | Raises, manages, and invests funds in three of the deadliest infectious diseases in the world | Governments and civil society, foundations, and private sector partners | Donations, primarily from governments, as well as funding from foundations, the private sector, and innovative financing initiatives |
| Global Alliance for Vaccines and Immunizations (Gavi) (2000)[9] | Public-private partnership with direct health impact | Aims to expand vaccine coverage by funding vaccines and strengthening health systems for vaccine sustainability and equity | Governments and civil society, foundations, and private sector partners | Government donors, Gates Foundation, and innovative financing mechanisms |
| UNITAID (2006)[10] | Public-private partnership with direct health impact | Aims to increase access to HIV, TB, and malaria medications by through its purchasing and negotiation power | Governments, civil society, Gates Foundation, WHO, technical partners, and private sector partners | Government donors, Gates Foundation, and airline tax |
| Coalition for Epidemic Preparedness Innovations (2017)[11] | Public-private partnership with direct health impact | Aims to prevent and control emerging infectious diseases by funding and coordinating rapid vaccine development | Governments, civil society, technical partners, and private sector partners | Government investments / donations, Gates Foundation, and Wellcome Trust |

| | | | | |
|---|---|---|---|---|
| G7 (1975)[12] | Political network with indirect health impacts | Discusses priorities among the world's advanced economies, and provides support for select initiatives, including in global health | 7 member states | Member contributions |
| G20 (1999)[13] | Political network with indirect health impacts | Discusses policies for the promotion of international financial stability, and provides support for select initiatives, including in global health | 19 member states plus the European Union | Member contributions |

1  "History of WHO," WHO, https://www.who.int/about/who-we-are/history; "WHO Brochure," WHO, https://www.who.int/about/what-we-do/who-brochure/; "How WHO Is Funded," WHO, https://www.who.int/about/planning-finance-and-accountability/how-who-is-funded.

2  "The Cluster System," Health Cluster, https://www.who.int/health-cluster/about/cluster-system/en/; "About Us," Health Cluster, https://www.who.int/health-cluster/about/en/.

3  "What Is the Security Council?," UN Security Council, https://www.un.org/securitycouncil/content/what-security-council; "Current Members," UN Security Council, https://www.un.org/securitycouncil/content/current-members.

4  "About Us," OIE, https://www.oie.int/about-us/; "Our Missions," OIE, https://www.oie.int/about-us/our-missions/.

5  FAO, One Health: Food and Agriculture of the United Nations Strategic Action Plan (Rome: FAO, 2011); "About FAO," FAO, http://www.fao.org/about/en/.

6  "Who We Are," World Bank, https://www.worldbank.org/en/who-we-are; Jennifer Prah Ruger, "The Changing Role of the World Bank in Global Health," American Journal of Public Health 95 (2005): 60–70; UK House of Commons, International Development Committee, International Development Committee—Fourth Report: The World Bank (London: House of Commons, 2011).

7  "What Is the WTO?," WTO, https://www.wto.org/english/thewto_e/whatis_e/whatis_e.htm; "Budget," WTO, https://www.wto.org/english/thewto_e/secre_e/budget_e.htm; WTO & WHO, WTO Agreements & Public Health: A Joint Study by the WHO and the WTO Secretariat (Geneva: WTO / WHO, 2002).

8  "Global Fund Overview," Global Fund, https://www.theglobalfund.org/en/overview/; "Resource Mobilization," Global Fund, https://www.theglobalfund.org/en/replenishment/.

9  "Our Alliance," Gavi, https://www.gavi.org/our-alliance. "Gavi—The Global Alliance for Vaccines and Immunizations," WHO, https://www.who.int/workforcealliance/members_partners /member_list/gavi/en/; "Cash Received by Gavi," Gavi, https://www.gavi.org/news/document-library/cash-receipts-31-december-2019.

10  "About Us," Unitaid, https://unitaid.org/about-us/#en; Unitaid, UNITAID at Accelerating Innovation in Global Health (Vernier: Unitaid Secretariat, 2016); Rachel Silverman, "UNITAID (Value for Money Working Group Background Paper)," Center for Global Development, October 2012 (revised April 2013).

11  "Mission," CEPI, https://cepi.net/about/whyweexist/; "Funding and Expenditure (December 2018)," CEPI, https://cepi.net/wp-content/uploads/2019/03/050319-Funding-and-Expenditure -Final_V3.pdf.

12  "What Are the G7 and G8?," G7 Research Group, http://www.g7.utoronto.ca/what_is_g8.html; Brian Lucas, "G7 and G20 Commitments on Health," K4D, September 27, 2019; "G7 Leaders' "Vision for Global Health," GLOPID-R, February 6, 2016.

13  "What Is the G20?," G20, https://g20.org/en/about/Pages/whatis.aspx; "G20 Participants," G20, https://g20.org/en/about/Pages/Participants.aspx; David Branigan, "G20 Leaders Declare General Commitment to Advance Global Health," Health Policy Watch, July 1, 2019.

In its early years the organization focused on tuberculosis, malaria, smallpox, and yaws. WHO's smallpox eradication campaign was a singular achievement: In 1980, twenty-one years after the campaign began to eradicate a disease that took millions of lives per year, the 33rd WHA declared, "The world and all its peoples have won freedom from smallpox."[11]

Polio was WHO's next target; in 1988 the WHA set the goal to eradicate polio by 2000.[12] While eradication has not been achieved as of 2021, the disease is now confined to Afghanistan and Pakistan, with only thirty-three cases of wild-type polio in 2018, before an increase in 2019. The COVID-19 pandemic further imperiled efforts to eradicate polio.[13]

Elsewhere, WHO's record is mixed. Its Global Program for Malaria Eradication, launched in 1955, achieved significant gains but was ultimately unsuccessful (see Chapter 3). Concern over WHO's response to AIDS contributed to the formation of UNAIDS in 1996. WHO's "3 by 5" campaign to enable 3 million people in low- and middle-income countries to receive AIDS treatment by 2005 fell short of its target, but it did help accelerate treatment and pave the way, years later, for the goal of universal access.[14]

Since WHO's early days, influenza has been a top infectious disease focus. WHO's surveillance network and partner laboratories have been foundational to global preparedness and vaccine creation (see Chapter 8). More recently, emerging and infectious diseases, like Ebola and COVID-19, have commanded WHO's attention.

The 2014–2016 West Africa Ebola epidemic was a low point for WHO, forcing reform (see below). WHO had cut its emergency response units and budget to help address a budget shortfall, leaving it particularly unprepared. WHO waited more than four months after Ebola was detected to declare a public health emergency, letting states' economic and political considerations interfere with its judgment, while local and regional WHO officials underperformed.[15] In defending the organization's response, Director-General Margaret Chan called WHO a "technical agency," asserting that "we are not the first responder."[16]

Infectious diseases command the lion's share of WHO's budget, but WHO works in all other health areas—including injuries, mental and physical disabilities, health systems, the social determinants of health, and noncommunicable diseases. Along with smallpox eradication, two other top achievements for WHO are the adoption of the Framework Convention on Tobacco Control and the International Health Regulations (see below). The tobacco convention has catalyzed a raft of tobacco control measures at the national level, like smoking bans in public places, graphic warning labels, and advertising bans.[17]

Along with health emergencies, universal health coverage has returned as a top WHO priority, decades after WHO turned away from its 1978 Alma-Ata Declaration to achieve health for all by 2000 and instead adopted a more selective—and cheaper—approach to primary health care, focusing on a narrower set of cost-effective interventions.[18]

## The International Health Regulations

At its formation in 1948, WHO adopted the International Sanitary Regulations, later named the International Health Regulations (IHR). In 2005, following the SARS epidemic, WHO fundamentally revised the IHR, which are binding on all 196 states parties. The IHR (2005) gave WHO new authority and expanded state obligations to assist in achieving health security. At their core, the regulations demand respect for human rights in carrying out public health measures.[19]

The IHR created a global preparedness framework to protect against the international spread of disease. This framework is not limited to specific diseases, as earlier versions of the IHR had been. Rather, the IHR give the WHO director-general (DG) power to declare a public health emergency of international concern (PHEIC) in response to any "extraordinary event" that poses a risk of international spread and requires a coordinated international response. To date, the DG has declared six PHEICs: influenza (H1N1) (2009), polio (2014), Ebola (2014), Zika (2016), Ebola (2019), and COVID-19 (2020). The IHR states parties must use a "decision tree" in Annex 2 to quickly report all events that may become a PHEIC (see Figure 7.1). The DG may use unofficial information sources in determining whether to declare a PHEIC, rather than only official data from governments. However, WHO must attempt to collaborate with the state party, and may share unofficial information with other states only if the government refuses collaboration. The DG may also make nonbinding recommendations to states parties based on scientific evidence, in an effort to balance health security, human rights, trade, and travel.

The IHR require states to develop and maintain core health system capacities to prevent, detect, and respond to outbreaks. These capacities include (1) national legislation, policy, and financing, (2) national focal points, (3) notification (reporting), (4) planning and risk communication, and (5) public health infrastructure. The IHR require countries to self-report the status of

# ANNEX 2
## DECISION INSTRUMENT FOR THE ASSESSMENT AND NOTIFICATION OF EVENTS THAT MAY CONSTITUTE A PUBLIC HEALTH EMERGENCY OF INTERNATIONAL CONCERN

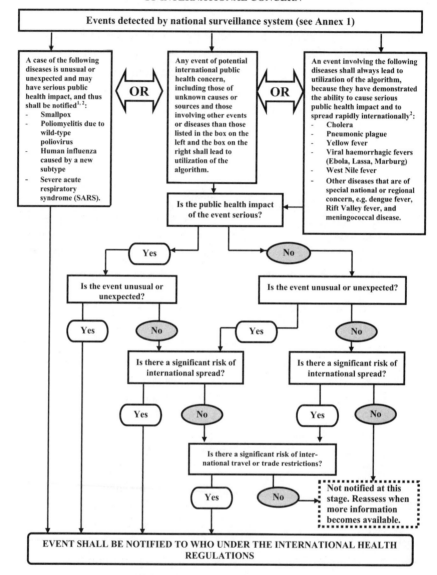

[1] As per WHO case definitions.
[2] The disease list shall be used only for the purposes of these Regulations.

**Figure 7.1** International Health Regulations Decision Tree. Decision instrument for the assessment and notification of events that may constitute a public health emergency of international concern. *International Health Regulations (2005) Third Edition,* Annex 2. Geneva: World Health Organization; 2016. CC BY-NC-SA 3.0 IGO.

their core capacities, leaving WHO with little power to monitor state compliance, impose sanctions, or provide incentives.[20]

The IHR also require governments to provide resources to build and maintain national health system capacities. Many states have failed to meet these obligations.[21] Article 44 of the IHR requires collaboration and assistance between states parties and WHO to create and implement core capacities, but it lacks specificity and compliance-enhancing incentives.

In 2016 WHO announced a new framework to monitor IHR core capacities: the Joint External Evaluation (JEE).[22] The JEE systematically evaluates a country's preparedness capabilities and infrastructure, identifying gaps and areas for improvement. JEEs are voluntary, but an increasing number of states have completed them.[23] Funding for the JEE is far from secure. In 2015 the Global Health Security Agenda (GHSA), which has supported the JEE, under the Obama administration allocated $1 billion to support pandemic preparedness. Yet as of 2020 the US Congress had not allocated additional major funding for the GHSA.[24]

## WHO Reforms

The IHR proved inadequate in the face of the West African Ebola epidemic, which highlighted weaknesses in WHO's emergency preparedness and response capabilities. This followed years of eroding confidence in WHO. Member states have been steadfastly refusing to increase WHO's budget and instead have moved their attention to public-private partnerships, such as the Global Fund, Gavi, and CEPI.

Following the West Africa Ebola epidemic, WHO underwent several major reforms. In 2015, even before WHO officially declared the West African Ebola emergency, the agency created a Contingency Fund for Emergencies to rapidly mobilize funds in the face of a crisis.[25] Financed by voluntary contributions, the fund has a target capitalization of $100 million, far short of the billions needed for global preparedness.[26] Initial contributions to the fund were limited, totaling approximately $45 million by the end of 2017. More funding followed, with about $81 million in contributions in 2018–2019. As 2019 ended, the fund had allocated $68 billion, more than 80 percent of which went to the DRC. Initial funding in 2020 continued to focus on the DRC, along with COVID-19, particularly to support critical health supplies, notably personal protective equipment.[27] Overall, the allocations have covered a range of natural disasters, epidemics, and even conflicts, and spanned the globe. In its first two years, allocations covered twenty-one emergencies.[28] Among the activities the Contingency Fund supported were:

- Health care in Ethiopia to respond to the hunger and disease resulting from El Niño-driven drought and floods in 2015.
- Medical supplies and personnel to help Fiji in the immediate aftermath of Cyclone Winston.
- Technical assistance and response preparedness (e.g., strengthening hospital surveillance) in response to the Zika epidemic beginning in 2016.
- Emergency health kits, community health worker training, and measles vaccination for the crisis in northeastern Nigeria resulting from the Boko Haram insurgency.
- Vaccination, disease surveillance, clinical management, and risk communication to respond to a yellow fever outbreak in Angola and in Kinshasa, DRC.

In a second major reform, in March 2016 WHO launched the Health Emergencies Programme to create a streamlined emergency response through one line of authority, one workforce, one budget, one set of rules and processes, and one set of performance metrics, aimed at delivering rapid support to countries facing or recovering from emergencies.[29] The Programme, with independent oversight and monitoring, combines expertise and resources by partnering with UN agencies, states, and nongovernmental organizations (NGOs), such as Médecins Sans Frontières.[30]

As part of the Health Emergencies Programme, WHO developed a Global Health Emergency Workforce (GHEW) to address the paucity of trained health workers and poor global coordination.[31] The GHEW includes national and international responders from partnerships including the Global Outbreak Alert and Response Network (GOARN) and the UN Inter-Agency Standing Committee.[32] Central to GHEW are Emergency Medical Teams, drawn from governments and civil society on standby to join first responders.[33] There are barriers to deploying GHEW, such as the slow processes for obtaining visas and permits for foreign personnel, and the difficulty of moving medical supplies, humanitarian equipment, and personal protective equipment to areas in need.[34]

Despite these two major reforms to WHO, serious structural weaknesses remain. As a largely donor-driven organization (with mandatory assessments constituting only 20 percent of its budget), WHO continues to face financial shortfalls.[35] Its 2018–2019 budget of $4.42 billion was just over one-fourth of that of the US Centers for Disease Control and Prevention, and less than that of a large US hospital.[36] Without a commensurate budget, how can WHO possibly be expected to meet global health needs worldwide? A significant portion of WHO's budget is earmarked, leaving some priority areas without funding. WHO projected that its Health Emergencies Programme, for example, would receive only 85 percent of needed funds in 2018–2019.[37] When the organization falls short due to constraints, donors further lose confidence and seek out other institutions to support.

Aside from financial struggles, WHO suffers from lack of coordination between its headquarters, six regional offices, and country officials. Regional offices are uniquely independent within the UN system, with little oversight, control, or budgetary constraints from WHO headquarters. During the West Africa Ebola epidemic, the challenges posed by this decentralized structure became clear as WHO DG Margaret Chan and the Regional Office for Africa (AFRO) argued over control and deflected responsibility.[38]

WHO provides little room for non-state actors to support its mission.[39] Non-state actors play no formal role in WHO governing structures, and strict criteria prevent most NGOs from participating in governance meetings.[40] NGOs must gain "official relations status" and have two years of informal relations prior to applying to participate.[41] Domestic, poorly funded, and small NGOs have little chance of being considered. WHO must make it simpler for stakeholders to participate by allowing extemporaneous statements, and by directly including civil society organizations in its governing bodies.

Due to WHO's shortcomings, other organizations have stepped into the field of global governance for health, gaining recognition as key players in the changing landscape.

## The Rise of New Powers

In the decades following its creation in 1948, WHO was the primary, if not the sole, global health institution. Today it operates in a sea of powerful actors with diverse aims. From other UN agencies and organs, to international institutions, to public-private partnerships, a range of powers have played an increasingly important role in responding to global health security threats. These rising powers bring along the benefits of stronger enforcement mechanisms, systems for coordinated information sharing, and expertise in critical areas. They are also working with countries to meet the UN Sustainable Development Goals (SDGs), "a shared blueprint for peace and prosperity, from now into the future," which all UN member states adopted in 2015 as part of the 2030 Agenda for Sustainable Development.[42] Achieving the seventeen goals requires coordinated, global action across both developed and developing nations. The SDGs recognize that efforts to end poverty must coincide with efforts to improve health and education, address inequalities, spur economic growth, and tackle climate change, among other objectives.[43]

### The UN System

While WHO leads the UN's health promotion efforts, various other UN agencies also address global health-related matters (see Figure 7.2). In contrast to WHO's largely voluntary measures, the UN Security Council has the authority to make binding resolutions on member states and the secretary-general to mobilize coordinated, UN system-wide responses.[44] In May 2020 the Security Council considered a resolution calling for a global ceasefire during the COVID-19 pandemic.[45] However, the United States blocked a vote on the resolution because it called for WHO support. In September 2014 the Security Council adopted a resolution declaring the West Africa Ebola epidemic a threat to international peace and security, and called on member states to respond urgently.[46] UN secretary-general Ban Ki-Moon established the UN's first-ever emergency health mission, the UN Mission for Ebola Emergency Response (UNMEER) to coordinate efforts among UN agencies. UNMEER improved cross-border coordination, information sharing, and monitoring of viral transmission. In 2018 the Security Council adopted another resolution in response to Ebola in the DRC, condemning attacks on humanitarian responders and civilians by armed groups.[47] The following year the UN secretary-general appointed an Emergency Ebola Response Coordinator to lead a UN-wide response.

The World Organisation for Animal Health (OIE) (which is outside the UN system) and the Food and Agriculture Organization (FAO) also promote global health security. The "One Health" approach, which acknowledges the interconnectedness between human health, animals, and the environment, underscores the importance of their mandate. These agencies protect against infectious disease threats through standard-setting, information sharing, and, in the case of the OIE, mandated reporting of events. Both the OIE and FAO have established international trade standards to avoid spreading dan-

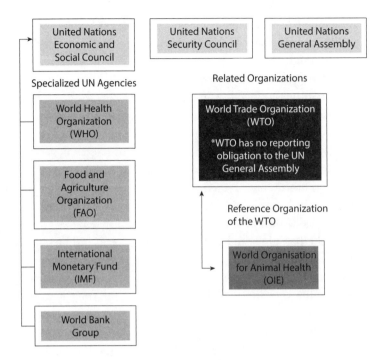

**Figure 7.2** The UN System and Global Health Security Governance.
*Data source:* "The United Nations System," United Nations Department of Global Communications, 19-000073, July 2019. © 2019 United Nations.

gerous pathogens and pests. The Codex Alimentarius, for example, is a collection of international food safety standards developed as a joint initiative between WHO and the FAO. These evidence-based standards may help prevent the next infectious outbreak. They can also protect against harmful trade practices during emergencies, given that the World Trade Organization (WTO), which renders and monitors binding decisions through its dispute settlement body, relies on these types of standards to counter unfair and unfounded trade practices.[48] If wielded smartly, this authority could prove critical in outbreaks like the West African Ebola outbreak, where trade restrictions (implemented against WHO's recommendations) hurt the local economy and complicated health workers' efforts.[49]

Analogous to the requirement to notify WHO of a possible PHEIC, OIE requires member states to notify the organization of a "relevant epidemiological event" regarding animal health. This information is collected and shared through the World Animal Health Information System (WAHIS).[50] Unlike any WHO database, WAHIS provides internet users easy access to transparent, real-time data on potential outbreaks. Further, in October 2006 FAO opened the Crisis Management Center–Animal Health in collaboration with the OIE[51] to assess, diagnose, and field rapid responses to epidemiologic situations.[52] The center continually monitors and updates disease information, and dispatches experts to respond to potential emergencies—ideally, to suppress an outbreak before it becomes an epidemic or pandemic.[53]

Other multilateral groups like the World Bank, whose mission is seemingly adjacent to health, have brought financing and expertise to global governance for health.[54] Since the 1960s the World Bank has offered technical guidance in global health financing, in some ways usurping WHO.[55] From 2000 to 2016 the Bank invested $35 billion to support health, nutrition, and resilient health systems.[56] Recently, pandemic preparedness, including surveillance and stronger laboratory networks, has become a Bank priority.[57] With great fanfare in 2016, then Bank president Jim Yong Kim launched the Pandemic Emergency Financing Facility (PEF), an innovative fund to rapidly fund lower-income countries that are facing major outbreaks.[58]

The PEF is the first insurance market for pandemics. It is capable of rapidly disbursing financial resources for pandemic outbreaks, with an "insurance window" funded by a private insurance market and a "cash window" funded by donors. In 2017 the World Bank issued $425 million in pandemic bonds, which were quickly bought by investors, while Germany provided an initial 50 million euros for the cash window. The bonds cover six viruses likely to spark outbreaks: new influenza viruses, coronaviruses (like SARS, MERS, and COVID-19), filoviruses (like Ebola), Lassa fever, Rift Valley fever, and Crimean Congo fever. The cash window may be used to cover diseases not eligible for insurance window financing.[59]

PEF funds were used during the Ebola epidemic in the DRC in 2018–2019, including $80 million approved by February 2019.[60] When the Ebola response was stalled by escalating violence, however, the PEF was criticized for being too inflexible and unresponsive. In April 2020 the PEF allotted $196 million to assist countries with reported cases of COVID-19, intended to supplement the World Bank Group's initial $160 billion commitment to COVID-19 response (though it was unclear how much of the $160 commitment, most of which would be loans, was an increase in overall Bank lending).[61] The PEF funding came almost three months after WHO declared COVID-19 a PHEIC, since the trigger criteria set by the Bank in consultation with WHO (relating to outbreak size, growth, and spread) were not met until March 31, 2020. As with Ebola, this delay suggests that the usefulness of PEF funding is constrained by the requirement that payouts be released to support emergency response operations only once a pandemic is spreading rapidly. This policy is inconsistent with the goal of prevention, and it disadvantages countries that are unable to rapidly track and report cases and deaths to demonstrate that the criteria for funding have been met.

To improve its role in global governance for health, moving forward, the World Bank could include meeting or progress toward meeting IHR obligations in its criteria for PEF disbursements, and consider modifying the payout trigger requirements so that recipient countries receive funds without delay.[62]

Multilateral institutions do not invariably contribute to global health security. The mission of the International Monetary Fund (IMF) is to protect the international monetary system's stability, which it does through lending and capacity development of member countries. The IMF has long been criticized for imposing conditions on countries that receive funds to combat financial crises; these conditions often include budget austerity requirements such as wage bill caps that constrain health spending and undermine the public health workforce.[63] Despite recent policy changes, evidence suggests that "unhealthy conditionality" continues to undermine health services and the health workforce.[64] With further changes, however, the IMF could contribute to global health security. If it were to incorporate core health system capacities into its evaluations of macroeconomic stability, it could incentivize nations to invest in pandemic preparedness. The IMF assessments could be powerful incentives because they affect governments' ability to access capital. The IMF has played a helpful role during COVID-19, calling for debt suspension and doubling its emergency lending capacity.[65]

Like the IMF, the WTO—which aims to facilitate global movement of goods and services by promoting free trade—has the potential to both harm and support health security. Under its Trade-Related Intellectual Property Rights (TRIPS) agreement, WTO member states must commit to strong protection for intellectual property, which can limit generic production and increase the cost of essential medicines.[66] By contrast, the WTO's Sanitary and Phytosanitary (SPS) Agreement safeguards governments' ability to establish measures that protect human, plant, and animal health.[67] The SPS Agreement encourages members to base these measures on standards set by authoritative bodies, including the OIE and the Codex Alimentarius Commission;

this promotes harmonization, but it limits states' ability to take more protective measures.

The WTO could act as a greater ally to WHO by calling out unfair trade practices when governments erect trade restrictions in response to health emergencies. During the 2009 H1N1 influenza pandemic, for instance, twenty countries banned pork imports from Mexico, Canada, and the United States, despite WHO recommendations against travel and trade restrictions.[68] Although such restrictions violate the SPS Agreement, the WTO was slow to respond. It waited eight days to issue a joint statement with the FAO, OIE, and WHO that properly handled pork products were not a source of infection. Because no formal notification or complaints from WTO members had been received, the director-general's ability to respond during the health emergency was constrained.[69] If the WTO were able to address unjustified trade restrictions during disease outbreaks, even in the absence of notifications from member states, it could serve a powerful function.

The WTO's dispute settlement body, with its authority to require compensation and permit retaliatory measures, would be an enforcement mechanism, and would create a strong incentive to comply with WHO recommendations. WHO and the WTO could also create a joint committee during public health emergencies, combining WHO expertise and WTO enforcement powers, to assess and more rapidly adjudicate trade-related disputes.[70]

Yet the WTO is often slow to act for the global public good. In December 2020 India and South Africa asked WTO member states to waive certain intellectual property rights for the development of COVID diagnostics, treatments, and vaccines. The idea was to sweep aside some of proprietary interests to speed development of lifesaving medical resources. The United States, European states, and other high-income countries blocked the resolution.

### Public-Private Partnerships

Public-private partnerships—where private entities contribute vital resources and shared governance to an organization that enjoys some of the legitimacy of a public body—have also emerged as powerful global health leaders. Where public bodies bring together their expertise and resources, partnerships attract donors by giving them flexibility that is not always available through intergovernmental institutions. These partnerships often include entities such as corporations and foundations, as well as civil society organizations, embodying multi-stakeholder governance in a way that WHO does not.

High-profile public-private partnerships focus their strategic efforts—and donors' attention—on the deadliest infectious diseases the world has ever known. Between its founding in 2002 and early 2019, the Global Fund to Fight AIDS, Tuberculosis and Malaria disbursed over $41 billion to fighting these diseases, with impressive results.[71] The Fund's groundbreaking governance remains a model for international organizations. Its board and country coordinating mechanisms (CCMs) include civil society and affected communities as full participants. Without the constraints of traditional governance, such as with the World Bank's PEF, the Global Fund uses innovative funding criteria that incorporate a country's economic capacity as well as disease burden. This brings much needed resources to middle-income countries, hard hit by these diseases, which would likely otherwise be excluded from aid determinations based strongly on national income.[72] Meanwhile, in several otherwise ineligible countries, NGO recipients can seek funding to support marginalized populations.

The Global Fund has demonstrated its flexibility in response to the COVID-19 pandemic by allowing countries to repurpose and reprogram underused funding from existing grants to fight COVID-19. In addition, it has allocated $500 million to its COVID-19 Response Mechanism, which uses CCMs to direct funding toward programming that supports COVID-19 responses and mitigates the impacts of COVID-19 on existing HIV, tuberculosis, and malaria efforts.[73]

Other global public-private partnerships focus on high-impact, preventative strategies for global health. Gavi uses innovative financing strategies to support vaccines, vaccine equipment, and strengthened health systems in low-income countries.[74] Like the Global Fund, Gavi has a diverse board, composed of governments, civil society, the vaccine industry, health researchers, and others who lend fundraising skills and independent perspectives. Its funding comes primarily from donations, but also from innovative financing mechanisms, including an Advanced Market Commitment for pneumococcal vaccines. This mechanism incentivizes manufacturers to invest in producing vaccines for unstable markets by committing to purchase an agreed amount at a set price, enabling manufacturers to profit while ensuring an affordable price in developing countries.[75] In 2020 Gavi proposed a new Advance Market Commitment for COVID-19 vaccines, agreeing to buy large quantities of vaccines at established prices to incentivize manufacturers to invest in and rapidly scale up manufacturing (see Chapter 10).[76] Another of Gavi's innovating financing instruments, the International Finance Facility for Immunisation (IFFIm), seeks to stabilize vaccine demand by selling bonds on capital markets backed by long-term donors.[77] In December 2020, it was estimated that over a quarter of Gavi's funding needs to purchase and distribute COVID-19 vaccines to low-income countries would be met through IFFIm bonds.[78]

Along with the Advance Market Commitment and IFFIm, Gavi features three other innovative financing mechanisms. First, it has a straightforward matching fund, which encourages private sector contributions to Gavi. By promising matching donor funds, it incentivizes businesses, employees, and customers to donate to Gavi.[79] Second, Gavi's loan buydown facility, established in 2016 in partnership with the Gates Foundation and the French Development Agency, enables Gavi to access low-interest loans to improve vaccine coverage in Africa's Sahel region.[80] And third, a panel of experts, INFUSE (Innovation for Uptake, Scale and Equity in Immunisation), launched in 2016, identifies promising technologies to improve the uptake and scale of immunizations. The initiative connects "INFUSE Pacesetters" to Gavi partners to bring them to scale.[81]

Innovative financing is central to another public-private partnership, Unitaid, which France, Brazil, Chile, Norway, and the United Kingdom created in 2006 as an international drug-purchasing institution focused on HIV, tuberculosis, and malaria. It has since expanded to cover drugs for HIV opportunistic infections (infections in persons with weakened immune systems), such as hepatitis C and human papillomavirus (HPV).[82] Unitaid uses its purchasing and negotiating power to sustainably reduce drug prices, with a focus on low-income countries.[83]

Unitaid's innovative financing model is an airline tax added to plane tickets in participating countries, with revenue earmarked for Unitaid. While countries as diverse as France, Cameroon, Niger, Chile, and South Korea have implemented the airline tax, the United States and Europe (apart from France) have not.[84]

Another Unitaid innovation is the Medicines Patent Pool (see Chapter 10). Through negotiations with the patent pool, pharmaceutical companies issue voluntary licenses for generic production. From the patent pool's beginning in 2010 through to 2017, nine patent-holding companies entered into licensing agreements involving thirteen antiretroviral drugs, two hepatitis C drugs, a tuberculosis treatment, and an HIV technology platform. The Medicines Patent Pool, in turn, has sub-licensed these to at least twenty-five generic companies. This initiative led to cumulative price reductions of more than $300 million through 2017 for the HIV medications alone.[85]

Beyond increasing access to existing countermeasures, public-private partnerships may prove to be game changers in the development of new vaccines. With high uncertainty regarding what the next epidemic will be, how do we incentivize investments in vaccines for which there is little to no commercial market? CEPI aims to tackle this problem by coordinating stakeholders and building capacity, including regulatory, to develop and deploy vaccines to prevent outbreaks. It is committed to equitable access to vaccines, so that price is not a barrier to countries and populations in need.[86] The coalition initially focused on five known diseases (MERS-CoV, Nipah virus, Lassa virus, Rift Valley fever, and chikungunya viruses). CEPI now also prioritizes a sixth disease—Disease X—pathogens not yet known to cause human diseases but that one day might cause an epidemic. Here, the goal is to develop rapid-response platforms.[87]

CEPI's mandate was recently put to the test by the COVID-19 pandemic (see Chapter 10). It began actively working to finance the development and manufacturing of a COVID-19 vaccine, launching a campaign in March 2020 to raise $2 billion. CEPI invested in 11 COVID-19 vaccine candidates; seven of these candidates were in clinical trials as of March 2021.[88] It focused on funding vaccine programs with the potential to be manufactured on a global scale.[89] It also monitored the global landscape of COVID-19 vaccine development so that global resources could be coordinated accordingly.

As demonstrated by the above examples, today's understanding of global governance for health embraces actors well beyond WHO. Other UN agencies as well as intergovernmental institutions and public-private partnerships have stepped into governance roles that WHO has not or could not fill. Meanwhile, political networks like the Group of 7 (G7) and Group of 20 (G20)—groupings of seven major industrialized countries and twenty of the world's largest economic powers—seek to boost political engagement, signal political priorities, and catalyze funding and health security-enhancing policies.

The benefits and opportunities from the rise of new powers in global health security are undeniable. They have increased stakeholder engagement, tailored missions capable of taking quick action, introduced innovative funding and financing strategies, and created new mechanisms for keeping actors accountable. Yet the increasingly disjointed nature of the global health security landscape raises concerns about duplication of effort and unaddressed gaps in emergency preparedness. While WHO remains the de facto coordinating authority, the proliferation of global health organizations makes it more difficult for individual actors, especially those that are not tethered to the UN system, to participate in a unified system of governance.

Many international organizations have acknowledged this fragmentation and committed to collaboration. Eleven heads of the world's leading health and development organizations—including Gavi, the Global Fund, UNAIDS, the World Bank, and WHO—joined together to form the Global Action Plan for Healthy Lives and Well-Being for All.[90] Their goal is to coordinate efforts toward achieving health-related SDGs, which is closely linked with achieving global health security, and directly incorporates the need to increase national capacity to address national and global health risks. There is also bilateral cooperation between international institutions. The WTO and the OIE, for example, entered into a formal agreement in 1998 to collaborate on questions of mutual interest, notably the application of the SPS Agreement.[91] The two organizations exchange information and technical documents and are invited to participate in each other's relevant committee meetings.

Yet behind the haze of multilayered institutions lies a troubling reality. Without strong global governance, it becomes less clear which voices are most actively shaping the agenda, whether the global burden of financing emergency preparedness is being borne equitably, and whether reliable systems are in place to track and respond to biological threats. As our once-centralized governance structure becomes increasingly disintegrated, we must examine the challenges and threats this poses to global health security.

## Challenges to Sound Global Governance for Health

With new institutions entering the global governance for health arena, there is a risk that WHO's authority will be undermined and its power usurped. Funders could take their money elsewhere. Institutions focused on immunizations or other areas could establish policies that conflict with rather than reinforce WHO norms, or set their own priorities. For example, they might promote the safety of therapies that WHO has not yet recommended, or their research priorities might differ with those of WHO. A fragmented governance system, with a multitude of powers taking the lead on divergent missions, presents challenges that could ultimately threaten global health and make the world less safe.

In contrast to WHO's direct, comprehensive health mission, other governance sources are often charged with alternative priorities, like economics or trade, with health only at the periphery. In other cases, primarily with public-private partnerships, organizations are directly concerned with global health, but hold a more narrow agenda, focusing on just a few diseases, or even a single disease.[92] And to maintain donors' interests, organizations may seek the type of action that will produce quick results, without addressing longer-term health security needs. In a system that promotes operating under a narrow and short-term agenda, root causes that demand system-wide change—such as poverty and access to basic necessities like clean water—could be neglected.

Because a large part of funding for global health is donation-based, it has been primarily a zero-sum game. Outside of innovative financing mechanisms, directing money toward one objective often means taking funds away from another. So how do organizations make funding decisions?

Unlike WHO's one-country-one-vote policy, not all stakeholders hold an equal voice in public-private partnerships. Despite having governance structures that incorporate civil society, formal participation does not mean equal voice, and marginalized populations could remain marginalized even when nominally included.[93] More generous donors—both public donors, like the United States, and private donors, like the Gates Foundation—generally have a larger say in how their monies are spent. They may have motivations or priorities apart from the public good, such as geostrategic interests or seeking to enhance their reputation. Donors may be more interested in funding "hot topics" that are highly visible and garner media attention. Meanwhile, other conditions like neglected tropical diseases, which affect over a billion largely impoverished people each year, receive research funding equivalent to less than 10 percent of funds directed to malaria, tuberculosis, and HIV / AIDS.[94] By ignoring a wide subset of the global disease burden during nonemergency times, organizations that supposedly are primarily geared toward health solutions in lower-income countries could lose communities' trust.

On top of challenges from rising global health powers outside WHO, the US notice of withdrawal from and suspension of funding to WHO during COVID-19 demonstrates how fragile the agency, and its capacity to respond to a pandemic, truly are. Responding to WHO's shortcomings by pulling funding and political support can only weaken the agency at a time when defeating the virus required global strength and unity.

## A Path toward Sound Governance

It is imperative that we fix our fragmented system of global governance for health. Global coordination is key, and WHO remains uniquely important for global health security. Its legitimacy stems from the participation and at least nominally equal voice of all governments, and from the agency's normative powers, scientific authority, scope, and global reach. It is essential that WHO remain a leader in global governance for health. The COVID-19 pandemic has brought heightened attention to the role of WHO in maintaining health security, and offers an unprecedented opportunity to reform the agency to give it the funding and authority necessary to protect the world from major health threats.

WHO must reestablish its legitimacy as the guardian of global health through reform and embodiment of the principles of good governance. In part this requires structural changes in WHO itself to address the underlying reasons its authority began to erode in the first place. As an integral part of its reform, WHO must open avenues to harness the capabilities of the various global health organizations described above through strategic partnerships, while leading coordinated efforts to meet global health priorities.

*Building a more robust World Health Organization.* Currently WHO's meager annual budget is perhaps its most limiting factor in fulfilling its role as a leader in global health. WHO's budget has remained largely static over the years despite the agency taking on a greater scope of responsibility and more complex challenges, like novel and emerging infectious diseases, antimicrobial resistance, noncommunicable diseases, and climate change. With its funding already stretched thin, WHO is forced to rely on unpredictable donations to achieve the objectives set out in its constitution, such as helping governments strengthen their health systems and providing technical assistance and aid during emergencies. Member states must become genuine shareholders in WHO by raising contributions to cover a needs-based budget. In 2018 WHO estimated it needed $14.1 billion from 2019 through 2023.[95] Mandatory dues should constitute at least 50 percent of WHO's budget—a historic benchmark. As discussed in the Introduction, a "peace" or "security" dividend to ramp up global preparedness and prevention would produce dividends for public health, avoiding incalculable human suffering and economic loss caused by failures in pandemic preparedness. Further, WHO headquarters should exercise more oversight over regional personnel and decision making. WHO should fully disclose the funds held by each regional office and how regions meet health objectives, with monitoring and benchmarks of success. If decentralized decision making remains the norm, WHO should apply the same yardstick across regions to assess efficiency.

*Gaining public trust through transparent decision making.* WHO must be a global model for transparent decision making in global governance for health. The COVID-19 pandemic demonstrated how WHO can get caught in the crossfires of countries' geopolitical disputes, as the United States accused WHO of promoting China's interests ahead of global health in its COVID-19 response. Such accusations hurt WHO, especially when they lead states parties to pull voluntary funding and support, or even exit WHO entirely. The 2018–2020 DRC Ebola epidemic further demonstrated that deep-rooted governmental mistrust, which extends to international humanitarian organizations, can result in the rejection of lifesaving treatment, prevention, and information during emergencies.[96] Transparency in the processes of governance, including decisions on initiatives to fund, leaders to elect or appoint, or strategies to implement, would help counter these sentiments. While maintaining good working relationships with national governments, WHO must be viewed as an independent resource with an unquestionable objective of promoting health and human rights. And WHO must go one step further to promote the same type of transparency among other key actors, whether public or private, in global governance for health. This includes working to ensure that developing countries are not overshadowed by higher-income nations and entities, but also have a strong voice in decisions that will impact the health of their people.

*Harnessing global expertise through collaboration.* WHO must identify and open avenues for more inclusive participation by civil society and other global health partners. Otherwise WHO could be left behind as rising institutions carve out new and divergent governance paths. With WHO as a centralized leader, agencies and partnerships should explore new ways to innovate and collaborate to strengthen global health security, such as by collaborating with the IMF and World Bank to use the IMF's macroeconomic stability evaluations and the World Bank's PEF to incentivize meeting IHR obligations. Collaboration, instead of competition, should be encouraged under a comprehensive perspective of global health promotion.

While WHO remains at the core of global health, its mission hinges critically on willingness, accountability, and coordinated action by other institutions. Navigating narrow political agendas and power dynamics is no easy task. But WHO must prove its capacity to lead cohesive international efforts on building health systems, creating and enforcing norms, and, when defenses fail, rapidly mobilizing an international response. Only then, through sound governance, will a healthier and more secure world be achieved.

# CHAPTER 8

# International Pathogen Sharing and Global Health Equity

**In principle**, there is wide international agreement on two fundamental pillars of global health security: sharing and fairness. Governments agree that virus samples and their derivative genetic sequencing data should be responsibly shared to foster vital R&D of vaccines and pharmaceuticals against pandemic threats. The first phase 1 clinical trial of a COVID-19 vaccine candidate was initiated less than ten weeks after China released the genomic sequence of SARS-CoV-2 (see Chapter 10). Governments similarly accept the value of global equity, so that the benefits of R&D are shared equitably among nations, rich and poor.

In realpolitik, however, that global consensus breaks down sharply, particularly between high-income countries and low- and middle-income countries (LMICs). For the world's rich, rapid sharing of biosamples to advance science is of primary importance. For less well-off nations, attaining equitable benefits is a precondition to sharing. In other words, withholding samples is a form of leverage to gain affordable access to scientific discoveries.

For each value, there is an international legal agreement that is salient. WHO's Pandemic Influenza Preparedness (PIP) Framework explicitly links sharing and benefits, but its primary purpose is to encourage global cooperation to advance R&D. Importantly, the PIP Framework covers only pandemic influenza strains and not any other biological materials—such as SARS-CoV-2 and other coronaviruses. The PIP Framework also does not explicitly cover genetic sequencing data (GSD). The Nagoya Protocol on

Access and Benefit Sharing, a 2010 supplementary agreement to the 1992 Convention on Biological Diversity (CBD), primarily advances an equity agenda. It views pathogens as a genetic resource owned by the country in which they are found. That is, a country in which a wild virus is circulating can lay a sovereign claim to a pathogen isolated in its territory and can therefore refuse to share it with WHO Collaborating Center laboratories.

While these two international agreements are in tension, WHO and the parties to the Nagoya Protocol are in active discussions about reconciling the two instruments. Is there a clear pathway to affirm the values of both pathogen sharing and global health equity? Enhancing research cooperation and advancing equity are both vital global public goods. Each idea deserves careful attention without pitting one against the other.

How did the tension between sharing biological samples and equitable access to benefits arise? In December 2006 Indonesia refused to share samples of avian influenza A (H5N1), which laid bare a widening divide in the international community. The minister of health, Siti Fadila Supari, shocked the world by announcing that Indonesia would not share samples of a pandemic flu virus with WHO's Global Influenza Surveillance Network.[1] Indonesia staked its claim on the CBD's Nagoya Protocol, claiming it prevents exploitation of countries' biological and genetic resources.[2] Indonesia's insistence on equitable access to therapeutic products is widely shared among LMICs. Research with these viruses can translate into essential vaccines and pharmaceuticals, which are then often unaffordable in lower-income countries. Consequently, Indonesia invoked sovereign ownership of the virus unless and until a fairer system could be developed.[3] This episode highlighted the deep tension between two imperatives: the need for research to rapidly develop medical countermeasures for pandemic threats versus the ethical claim for equitable access to the fruits of research.[4]

WHO stressed that mitigating the impact of a highly lethal influenza pandemic requires close international cooperation. For five arduous years it worked to broker a compromise that would address the equity concerns raised by LMICs but also ensure that countries would expeditiously share samples with the global surveillance network. That work culminated in the World Health Assembly's adoption in 2011 of WHO's PIP Framework for the Sharing of Influenza Viruses and Access to Vaccines and Other Benefits,[5] a novel agreement for sharing access to virus samples and the benefits derived from them.

Well-functioning global cooperation to combat pandemic influenza and other viral threats is vital. However, signs of cracks in the PIP Framework are emerging. In 2018 China reportedly failed to share a novel influenza virus (H7N9 avian flu) with the US Centers for Disease Control and Prevention (CDC), a WHO Collaborating Center laboratory. The reasons were never fully revealed, but observers postulated mistrust that had little to do with sharing benefits: the samples may have become caught up in a trade dispute between the two countries.[6] In early 2020, scientists in China released the genetic sequence of SARS-CoV-2 little more than ten days after initial cases were reported.[7] Though WHO publicly praised China for timely sharing the sequence, it had pressed China to do so for several days prior.[8] But with the PIP Framework not covering viruses other than pandemic influenza strains, its deficiencies were also vividly highlighted by the Democratic Republic of Congo's (DRC) failure to share samples from four recent Ebola outbreaks—in 2014, 2016, and two in 2018, the second of which became the second worst Ebola outbreak in history. It is unclear why the DRC has not been cooperatively sharing, though a CDC scientist speculated that logistical challenges may have played a role.[9]

As we will see, there is no settled resolution about the scope of the Nagoya Protocol or how it conforms to legal and ethical duties to safeguard the public's health embodied in the PIP Framework. Even more importantly, the PIP Framework was premised on sharing biological samples, but today it is possible to genetically sequence viruses, so there may be no need to possess the actual virus. Will the PIP Framework's basic bargain survive when freely available genetic sequences for viruses become all that is required? Beyond that knotty problem is also the concern that the PIP Framework covers only pandemic strains of influenza—and not seasonal flu viruses or other pathogens with pandemic potential such as Ebola, Zika, SARS, MERS, or COVID-19. All of that needs to be urgently resolved among WHO member states. The stakes are high, both because of the potential human toll of a pandemic and because if the PIP Framework functions well, it could be a model of equity for other global health problems.

### Leveraging Virus Samples to Reshuffle Pandemic Preparedness

The import of Indonesia's refusal, and its effect on the subsequent development and implementation of the PIP Framework, is best understood in the specific context of influenza and global preparedness dynamics. Influenza viruses possess unique characteristics that heighten their risks to global health. Even seasonal influenza, which traverses the globe in waves, kills

250,000 to 500,000 every year.[10] In its highly pathogenic form, pandemic influenza is an ever-present threat to cause a catastrophic event.

Why are influenza viruses so special in their form and consequence? First, flu viruses mutate prodigiously and are in a constant state of flux. New strains emerge either incrementally or as abrupt transformations.[11] Through a process known as "reassortment," influenza viruses swap gene segments. The viral diversity generated through natural reassortment is vast and plays an important role in the evolution of influenza viruses. The constant viral shifting means that exposure to any given strain does not confer effective immunity to the next strain. Second, influenza is a zoonotic virus, meaning that it can be transmitted between, or shared by, both animals and humans. Animals that host influenza viruses, such as birds and pigs, are often in close proximity to humans, so the virus can "jump" species, infecting people. Third, many influenza strains are highly transmissible human-to-human.[12] Thus, once infection takes hold in a population, it can spread uncontrollably. During the 2009 H1N1 pandemic, the virus traversed the world in a matter of only months. Finally, developing a flu vaccine normally takes more than six months, and the vaccine then must be affordably distributed to large populations across regions.[13] This confluence of characteristics poses a unique threat requiring resources and global cooperation.

Long before the PIP Framework, WHO sought to foster collaboration, publishing an influenza pandemic preparedness plan in 1999 (updated in 2005 and 2009).[14] But even nominal steps toward preparedness have been halting, with many national influenza strategies failing to reflect WHO best practices.[15] WHO's Global Action Plan (GAP) for Pandemic Influenza Vaccines, issued in 2006, promotes seasonal vaccines, aiming to raise production capacity, and urging R&D.[16] In 2012, WHO issued a second plan, GAP II, which also encompassed surveillance and regulation. GAP III in 2016 highlighted ongoing challenges.[17] Yet implementation is badly hampered by insufficient funding and generalized pandemic fatigue.

WHO has coordinated influenza surveillance through a semi-informal network since 1952. The Global Influenza Surveillance Network, later renamed the Global Influenza Surveillance and Response System (GISRS), comprises affiliated laboratories in 114 countries, along with collaborating vaccine manufacturers, regulatory agencies, research centers, and veterinary institutions.[18] The GISRS conducts an important screening function, receiving a million or more influenza virus samples per year and determining whether any strain has pandemic potential.[19] Based on this information, the

GISRS refines its risk assessment and issues recommendations for prophylactic measures. The GISRS also helps ensure that samples are available for rapid and efficient sharing.[20]

Despite its cooperative nature, the GISRS's development and distribution of vaccines raise acute equity issues. LMICs are often at the forefront of the surveillance needed to develop seasonal influenza vaccines, but higher-income countries maintain the lion's share of vaccines.[21] To some extent this inequity is due to considerably lower demand for seasonal influenza vaccines in LMICs, although this is beginning to change.

The reduced demand often reflects the vaccines' costs and the need to balance immunization with other pressing national health priorities.[22] During an influenza pandemic, all nations would demand equitable access. If two doses of the vaccine were required, and people everywhere were vulnerable, demand would rapidly exceed current manufacturing capacity.[23] This extreme inequity is further complicated because manufacturing capacity, along with wealth, is concentrated in higher-income countries.[24] This creates a significant likelihood—clear from past experience—that high-income countries will gain priority during periods of vaccine scarcity.[25] LMICs also often have weak health systems, impeding rapid vaccination of the population. If vaccines are needed in remote areas, the unreliability of transport routes and electricity supplies for cold storage can make delivery extraordinarily challenging.

Indonesia's 2006 refusal to share biological material highlighted global tensions, reaching the level of "high" politics. Indonesia's firm position upended traditional power dynamics.[26] Further complicating matters, Indonesia entered into successful, unilateral negotiations with a pharmaceutical company, Baxter Healthcare, exchanging access to virus samples with rights to vaccines derived from them.[27] Thus, WHO was left to remedy the unfair status quo faced by LMICs. The agency also needed to deter unilateral action that could undermine global cooperation. Brokering a compromise proved no easy task, but a novel agreement emerged.

## The PIP Framework

Born of the tension between access and equity, the PIP Framework embodies a series of critical compromises, creating responsibilities for governments, national laboratories, vaccine manufacturers, and WHO.[28] It establishes a key example of WHO's effective use of its normative powers as the global focal point for global health (see Chapter 7). The PIP Framework tries to align two primary goals (Article 2): (1) to encourage international virus sample sharing, and (2) to foster equitable access to vaccines and other benefits. To these ends, the PIP Framework has two parts: (1) the main body, which creates nonbinding commitments for WHO member states and directions to WHO; and (2) the annexes, which incorporate Standard Material Transfer Agreements (Annexes 1, 2), terms of reference for an Advisory Group (Annex 3) and for WHO Collaborating Centers (Annex 5), and principles for future terms of reference for GISRS laboratories (Annex 4).

*The virus-sharing system (Article 5).* Member states agree to provide "PIP biological materials from all cases of influenza viruses with human pandemic potential" to WHO Collaborating Centers on Influenza. By providing virus samples, their genetic material, and human specimens (e.g., blood used for diagnosing and detecting pathogens), states also consent to later transfers and uses, subject to Standard Material Transfer Agreements (SMTAs). States may opt to share materials bilaterally, provided they also share materials with WHO Collaborating Centers as a priority. Article 5 also promotes sharing GSD with the originating state and GISRS laboratories. However, how to handle GSD more broadly remains controversial and unresolved. Consequently, the director-general is tasked with consulting with an advisory group to resolve GSD issues as well as developing an electronic system for tracking the movement of PIP biological materials into, within, and out of GISRS.

*Benefits-sharing system (Article 6).* The benefits sharing system creates largely aspirational responsibilities for WHO and member states concerning risk assessment and surveillance, capacity building, equitable distribution of antivirals and vaccines, and building technical capacities within countries. These responsibilities include coordinating influenza preparedness and response, providing candidate vaccine viruses upon request to influenza vaccine manufacturers and laboratories that meet biosafety guidelines, capacity building in member states (e.g., laboratory, surveillance, and regulatory capacities), stockpiling antivirals and vaccines, access to vaccines in interpandemic and pandemic periods, tiered pricing whereby manufacturers consider a country's income level to negotiate a price, technology transfer to increase vaccine supplies, and sustainable and innovative financing.

## Standard Material Transfer Agreements (SMTAs)

The PIP Framework is not a binding international treaty, but it establishes an innovative mechanism for legally binding private sector responsibilities.

The private sector is a crucial player in vaccine and antiviral R&D, but typical international agreements encompass the responsibilities of governments, not industry. WHO's solution to this paradox was SMTAs, which serve as contracts with pre-negotiated terms that govern virus transfers within the GISRS laboratory network (SMTA1, Annex 1) and to entities outside of that network (SMTA2, Annex 2).

In particular, SMTA2 presents an important opportunity to advance equity.[29] Through the SMTA2, private entities that receive PIP biological materials, including vaccine manufacturers, provide certain benefits. The exact commitment is negotiated between the company and WHO based on a series of "benefit sharing options," found in Table 8.1. The vaccine or antiviral manufacturer is required to settle on two of six benefits in exchange for the virus samples. This could entail, for example, donating or affordably pricing a percentage of real-time vaccine or antiviral production to WHO; licensing technology, know-how, processes, or products needed to develop influenza vaccines, antivirals, or adjuvants (ingredients in vaccines that enhance their effectiveness) to developing-country manufacturers on mutually agreed terms; and royalty-free licenses to developing-country manufacturers or WHO to produce influenza vaccines, antivirals, or adjuvants.[30] Manufacturers of other relevant products, such as diagnostics, must agree to only one of a series of six benefits, such as donating a certain number of diagnostic kits, strengthening influenza-specific laboratory and surveillance capacity in developing countries, or granting royalty-free licenses to developing-country manufacturers or WHO. Agreed-to benefits are provided before or during a pandemic, depending on the terms of the SMTA2. For example, some benefits, like technology transfer, could be provided soon after signing the SMTA2, whereas others, like pandemic vaccines, could be provided only after a pandemic emerges.

By mid-2019 thirteen companies had entered into SMTA2s with WHO, each selecting a range of benefit-sharing options.[31] WHO has been able to generate private sector interest in large part because of its global surveillance system. The system and its samples are necessary to produce seasonal vaccines, and these vaccines generate consistent profits.

Equity concerns nonetheless persist. For instance, no manufacturer has selected technology transfer to developing countries or WHO.[32] Further, although the PIP Framework is nonbinding, SMTAs, when signed, are legally enforceable private contracts between WHO and virus sample recipients. Yet they assume the cooperation of member states and their court systems to enforce these contracts—a problematic assumption, given political pressures on governments to make scarce vaccines available to their residents during a pandemic.

**Table 8.1.** Summary of PIP Framework SMTA2 Benefit-Sharing Options

Manufacturers of influenza vaccines and antivirals must commit to at least two benefit-sharing options from Category A, while manufacturers of other relevant products must commit to one benefit from Category B. All manufacturers entering into SMTA2 agreements are encouraged to also contribute to benefits in Category C.

| | Category A (Select 2 of 6) | Category B (Select 1 of 6) | Category C (Consider) |
|---|---|---|---|
| 1 | Donate % of real-time vaccine production to WHO | Donate diagnostic kits to WHO | Consider contributing to the measures listed |
| 2 | Reserve % of real-time vaccine production at affordable pricing to WHO | Reserve diagnostic kits at affordable pricing to WHO | below, as appropriate:<br>• Donations of vaccines<br>• Donations of pre- |
| 3 | Donate antivirals to WHO | Support laboratory and surveillance capacity strengthening | pandemic vaccines<br>• Donations of antivirals<br>• Donations of medical |
| 4 | Reserve antivirals at affordable pricing to WHO | Support transfer of technology, know-how, and / or processes | devices<br>• Donations of diagnostic kits |
| 5 | License on technology, know-how, processes, or products needed for the production of influenza vaccines, antivirals, or adjuvants to developing country manufacturers, on mutually-agreed fair terms | License on technology, know-how, processes, or products needed for the production of influenza vaccines, antivirals, or adjuvants to developing country manufacturers, on mutually-agreed fair terms | • Affordable pricing of pandemic products<br>• Transfer of technology and processes<br>• Granting of sublicenses to WHO<br>• Laboratory and surveillance capacity |
| 6 | Royalty-free license to developing country manufacturers or WHO for production of influenza vaccines, antivirals, or adjuvants | Royalty-free license to developing country manufacturers or WHO for production of influenza vaccines, antivirals, or adjuvants | building |

*Source:* World Health Organization, "Summary of Benefit Sharing Options," 2016, https://www.who.int/influenza/pip/benefit_sharing/SMTA2BenefitSharingOptions.pdf.

## Gaps in the PIP Framework

As technology surges ahead, the PIP Framework's focus on the transfer of biological material as the trigger for benefits poses a major obstacle for keeping to the PIP Framework's essential bargain. The PIP Framework's benefit-sharing scheme specifically contemplates the exchange of "biological material." The PIP Framework, however, defines "biological materials" as influenza viruses with human pandemic potential, including extracted RNA and cDNA. This definition appears to exclude GSD.

The march of technology suggests that in the future, GSD could virtually replace the need for holding actual viral samples. In 2013 scientists demonstrated that GSD alone could be used to rapidly develop synthetic viruses for product development.[33] If manufacturers did not require access to biological materials to develop products, private sector cooperation could decline, undermining SMTA2s, the PIP Framework's most powerful mechanism. Because SMTA2s contemplate the exchange of biological materials as the primary incentive for industry cooperation, a shift toward leveraging GSD to reach the same result could reduce or eliminate that incentive. Could WHO continue to recruit vaccine manufacturers to sign SMTA2s absent a clear incentive? What if manufacturers choose to avoid benefit sharing by developing their products from GSD, not biological materials? Enforcing SMTAs could prove even more difficult in a pandemic if countries refuse to mandate compliance with SMTA2s on emergency grounds.

One mitigating factor is the critical mass of manufacturers that have already signed SMTA2s.[34] WHO could negotiate for manufacturers to agree to interpret existing SMTA2 obligations as applying to vaccines synthesized using GSD data, though contractual enforcement of SMTA2s could still be jeopardized.[35] In addition, as of 2019, US and European regulatory agencies have not granted approval for any vaccine produced solely from a synthesized virus.[36] Therefore, GSD has not yet eroded the PIP Framework's benefit-sharing scheme.

GSD also raises another long-term issue of concern. Genetic sequencing contains digitized data that can readily be shared through open access. The benefits of open access to GSD are that scientists across the globe would be empowered to engage in vital research. Yet open access also can be hazardous, because unsecure laboratories and even rogue actors could have access to data needed to manipulate dangerous pathogens (see Chapter 4).

### Tension between PIP Framework and Nagoya Protocol

The 1992 CBD is a multilateral treaty with three primary goals: conserving biological diversity (biodiversity), sustainable use of its components, and the fair and equitable sharing of benefits arising from genetic resources.[37] Building upon this last aim, the Nagoya Protocol was adopted in 2010 (entering into force in 2014) as a supplemental agreement to clarify rights and obligations in accessing and sharing benefits related to genetic resources.[38] The basic principle expressed in both the CBD and the Nagoya Protocol is that genetic resources, like other natural resources, are subject to sovereign determinations of conditions for access.[39] This norm formed the basis of Indonesia's refusal to share influenza virus samples.

A critical question is whether pathogens are "genetic resources." After all, pathogens move freely beyond national borders. The fact that one country might isolate the virus in its territory doesn't mean that it has a sovereign claim to "own" the virus. (That same virus might well be circulating in other states.) The issue arose during negotiations over the Nagoya Protocol, with sharp differences of opinion. As a compromise, neither course was pursued. Instead, the protocol directs states parties to pay special attention to health emergencies.[40]

In 2016 WHO undertook a study of the Nagoya Protocol's implementation, paying particular attention to pathogens. The study concluded that the protocol had the potential to strengthen GISRS and the PIP Framework by raising awareness of its core principles of equity. WHO similarly concluded that the Nagoya Protocol could promote trust among countries, encouraging them to share seasonal influenza viruses. However, the protocol does pose major challenges to the influenza virus sharing system. The ongoing lack of clarity leaves significant discretion to the protocol's states parties, making it crucial to find clarity. It is entirely possible that differing interpretations could render access to viruses more complex, thus compromising risk assessment, research, and product development. Finally, given the large volume of viruses shared through GISRS, bilateral negotiations for each virus would be resource- and time-intensive, a threat to the timely and coordinated global surveillance and response that underpins the multilateral PIP Framework.[41] The threat from the bilateral arrangements under the Nagoya Protocol is even more concerning because the protocol, unlike the PIP Framework, is a binding treaty. Countries might consider their rights under the Nagoya Protocol as taking precedence over the PIP Framework.

Article 4(4) of the protocol, however, provides a pathway toward reducing this tension.

Article 4(4) recognizes separate multilateral access and benefit-sharing mechanisms for particular kinds of genetic resources. Such exceptions to the protocol can arise where there is a specialized international instrument that is intended to manage access and benefit sharing of a peculiar set of genetic resources for a given purpose, and where the instrument is not contrary to the objectives of either the convention or protocol. In such circumstances, the specialized instrument, rather than the protocol, would apply to parties to that instrument.[42]

The extent to which the PIP Framework comes within this exception is hotly debated. The PIP Framework clearly is intended to manage access and benefit sharing, with clearly defined genetic resources and with a clear purpose. Yet is the PIP Framework the type of international instrument that the Nagoya Protocol encompasses? During the protocol negotiations, states parties deleted a provision explicitly declaring the PIP Framework a "specialized instrument" under the protocol.[43] Moreover, the term "specialized instrument" is neither defined within the protocol nor, as of yet, fleshed out through states party agreement or definitive state practice.[44]

Some progress on this vital issue shows promise. A 2018 study offered criteria for what qualifies as a specialized instrument. Later that year states parties agreed to offer views on the study's proposed criteria, which would serve as a basis for final criteria.[45] A CBD-commissioned review concluded that because Article 4(4) refers to "instruments" rather than "treaties," it covers treaties as well as other, formally non-legally-binding intergovernmental agreements "approved in the context of a treaty framework."[46]

A further question is whether the PIP Framework is consistent with the CBD's objectives. The 2018 study suggested that there is consistency of objectives. A specialized instrument should support equity in sharing benefits, which is a core aim of the PIP Framework. A specialized instrument should also contribute to sustainable development; the PIP Framework contributes to the Sustainable Development Goals, which encompass managing health risks.[47] Moreover, in 2014 the European Union recognized the PIP Framework as a specialized instrument for the purposes of Article 4(4).[48] And in 2018, Nagoya Protocol states parties agreed that if they also participated in another specialized agreement, the parties should implement both in a mutually supportive manner.[49]

## The Future of the PIP Framework

A PIP paradox has emerged: the PIP Framework is a highly innovative modern international agreement, but already seems behind the times. At its core the PIP Framework is about sharing physical biological specimens, yet increasingly, genetic data are all that is needed. The PIP Framework isn't a formal treaty, but since it was adopted, the Nagoya Protocol, a binding treaty, has added a layer of uncertainty. How can the international community resolve the PIP paradox? And can PIP serve as a benefit-sharing model for non-influenza pathogens, such as SARS-CoV-2, with pandemic potential? WHO developed a six-point action plan to resolve this paradox and to expand benefit-sharing among nations:

1)    *Ensure SMTA2s expressly include GSD.* SMTA2s are the lynchpin of the PIP Framework's benefit-sharing scheme. Using contract law as a means of compliance is highly innovative, perhaps unique, in international law. However, unless all parties accept GSD as part of the benefit-sharing bargain, the PIP Framework could lose the crucial incentive needed for global cooperation. WHO and partners could clarify SMTA2 contracts to clearly encompass GSD. The agency should assess existing SMTA2 agreements to determine whether they cover products derived solely from GSD. WHO should then renegotiate contracts that do not expressly include genetic sequencing, while specifically including GSD in all future SMTA2 agreements. To better understand the evolving use of GSD in science and to ensure accountability, WHO should develop a searchable database able to identify vaccines and therapies developed using GSD.[50]

2)    *Build LMICs' self-sufficiency for development of medical countermeasures.* The most important means to promote health equity is to build LMIC capacity in R&D of vaccines and antiviral treatments. This requires not only financial resources but also genuine partnerships and technology transfer. As of 2019 no company has agreed to technology transfer as an SMTA2 benefit. Without self-sufficiency, LMICs will remain vulnerable during a pandemic, especially if higher-income countries refuse to rigorously enforce SMTA2 contracts. It is essential to shift toward more durable, long-term benefits to ensure pandemic preparedness.

3)    *Reconciling PIP with the Nagoya Protocol.* The two instruments must be clarified to operate synergistically. This requires a consensus among Nagoya Protocol states parties to include PIP as a "specialized international instrument" within the protocol's Article 4. Otherwise countries claiming sovereign ownership of biological or genetic materials and refusing to share them could jeopardize the pandemic influenza system.

4)   *Expand PIP to include seasonal influenza.* The PIP Framework was designed specifically to provide benefit sharing for pandemic influenza. To be sure, pandemic influenza poses a distinct threat, given the viruses' genetic variability and potential for rapid international spread. The most modest reform would extend the PIP Framework to seasonal influenza, which already kills hundreds of thousands every year. This reform could increase seasonal vaccine accessibility in lower-income countries, saving lives. Yet WHO member states' support for reforming PIP appears low, and WHO expresses concern that extension to seasonal flu could overburden GISRS.[51]

5)   *Expand PIP or negotiate a new international agreement to include all pathogens of international concern.* The UN secretary-general's report in the aftermath of the West African Ebola epidemic recommended renegotiating the PIP Framework to encompass all pathogens of international concern.[52] (The report also recommended upgrading the PIP Framework to a binding international treaty.) If WHO members are reluctant to include seasonal influenza, it would surely be politically difficult to expand the PIP Framework to pathogens like Ebola, MERS, SARS, and SARS-CoV-2. And WHO understandably is reluctant to reopen the PIP Framework to negotiation, because member states might water it down. Still, non-influenza pathogens pose a significant risk of a major epidemic or pandemic, evidenced by the world's lack of preparedness in dealing with COVID-19.[53] Consider that since the PIP Framework was agreed, WHO has already declared two Ebola epidemics and COVID-19 to be public health emergencies of international concern. Even if the PIP Framework is not the ideal instrument to promote benefit sharing of non-influenza pathogens, the need for global cooperation is just as great.

6)   *Use the PIP Framework as a model for other international agreements.* The PIP Framework is a highly innovative international agreement, both with its binding element and with its scope beyond states parties. Global health law often suffers due to its near-exclusive application to states parties. Using contract law, it could create legal obligations on purely private actors. Thus, if the PIP Framework were to prove itself as a robust agreement, it could be used as an effective model to develop other international health law frameworks, including those for dealing with other pathogens of international health importance, like novel coronaviruses.

Concerns about whether diagnostics, therapies, and vaccines for COVID-19 will be equitably shared became very real as vaccine candidates proceeded through human trials and gained emergency approval. Indeed, the world's response to distribution of personal protective equipment and other medical supplies and equipment—including tests—needed for COVID-19 has been entirely uncoordinated, based on ability to pay, not equity and need.[54] Raising similar equity concerns, higher-income countries are expected to fully vaccinate their populations by the end of 2021, whereas lower-income countries may not achieve the same until 2024.

This is a pivotal moment for global health security and equity. Global cooperation and rapid development of medical countermeasures have never been more important. Yet lower-income countries feel aggrieved at the unfairness of the global system. They understand full well that when a pandemic strikes, they will be most vulnerable.

Imagine this scenario. The vaccine and effective therapeutics for COVID-19, or even the next pandemic, become available, but only rich nations have access and can safeguard their people, while millions continue to die in LMICs. This is the likely scenario as the world is racing to vaccinate populations against COVID-19. As French president Emmanuel Macron stated, we are seeing a "two-speed world," one for high-income nations and quite another for lower-income nations. As rich countries bring COVID-19 under control and recover economically, poorer countries will be left largely unvaccinated and deeply vulnerable. This kind of outcome would unravel trust among nations and international cooperation, ranging from diplomacy and peace to travel and trade. It is in everyone's best interests to have highly effective international agreements that achieve the dual imperatives of scientific research and fair access to essential vaccines and medicines.

# CHAPTER 9

# Universal Health Coverage

**What if you had** to choose between being treated for a novel infectious disease during a major outbreak such as the COVID-19 pandemic, or receiving care for a preexisting health condition? What if you had to choose between purchasing groceries or paying for medications? Would you travel long distances to a well-equipped hospital, or see a community health worker nearby? In many countries, all but the most privileged are forced to make these types of decisions during their lifetimes. Millions lack access to basic health services, and health systems are too weak to meet everyday health needs. And when an epidemic strikes, there is no surge capacity to respond—no stockpile of vaccines, antibiotics, or ventilators. The universal yearning for affordable access to quality health care becomes more pressing in the face of an emergency.

In 2011, Aliyatu Alola, a young expectant mother from a rural village in Malawi, developed a severe fever and had to travel twenty-five miles to the nearest clinic. She waited eight hours only to learn that the clinic lacked the necessary medications to treat her. When she returned to the clinic days later, she was given aspirin, which failed to abate her dangerously high fever. Aliyatu's distraught husband then carried his semiconscious wife for an hour until they reached Lake Malawi. After traveling six hours by boat across the lake, Aliyatu arrived at the maternity ward. Her lifeless body was still warm, and pale with anemia. Doctors could not find her stillborn child's heartbeat.[1]

With twenty-first century medicine, Aliyatu's experience should not have happened. Yet for the world's poor, her story remains common. Worldwide, health systems suffer from crumbling infrastructure, untrained workforces, insufficient financing, and weak regulation. Aliyatu and her baby would have survived if well-trained maternity services and basic medications were within reach. But instead her family, and so many more families around the globe, have their own tragic stories to tell.

Robust health systems are critically important to patients, families, and the community. They are also essential for health security. A robust health system not only encompasses all aspects of primary health care delivery, but also crucial public health infrastructure, including, for example, surveillance systems and research laboratories. In regions where the baseline for adequate health care is low during nonemergency times, outbreaks can cripple health systems. We do not yet know the full impacts that the COVID-19 pandemic will have on poor countries with fragile health systems—how they could deal with reoccurring surges in the need for hospital care for COVID-19, as we have seen in places like Italy and New York, and the effects on other health conditions as health resources are redirected to COVID-19. The possibilities are terrifying.

We know that fast-moving infectious diseases can occur without warning, but still we do not prepare. Even before the 2014–2015 West African Ebola epidemic, Liberia, Sierra Leone, and Guinea had some of the world's weakest national health systems.[2] A complete breakdown of their vulnerable systems led to rapid spread of the Ebola virus. With disruptions to regular health services, even more people died from everyday health concerns, ranging from childbirth to malaria, tuberculosis, and chronic diseases. Health systems collapsed at every turn—from untrained workers, poor infection control and drug shortages, to surveillance and isolation. Ill-prepared hospitals shut down to prevent in-hospital viral transmission. Emergency obstetric care decreased dramatically, leaving pregnant women to die needlessly.[3] The West African Ebola outbreak made one thing clear: The international community cannot ignore the vital need for sustainable health systems and expect a deadly outbreak to be quickly contained. The COVID-19 pandemic has reinforced that lesson. Universal health coverage (UHC) is the foundation on which global health security rests.

In 2017 WHO director-general Tedros Adhanom aptly said, "All roads lead to universal health coverage."[4] If security is only as strong as the weakest link, then the world is at considerable risk. Many health systems are fragile, unable to rapidly detect and respond to outbreaks, enabling pathogens to spill over borders and spread regionally and globally. And even where health systems are strong, inequities within nations often leave many outside or at the margins of accessible care.

Governments have a legal duty to build and maintain strong, all-inclusive health systems. The right to health is entrenched in international law and incorporated into many countries' constitutions, but cannot be realized within the confines of a failing health system. Achieving UHC is at the heart of the UN Sustainable Development Goals (SDGs),[5] but many countries are far from hitting that target. WHO's International Health Regulations (IHR) require states parties to develop "core" health system capacities. Without these essential capabilities, such as surveillance and labs, countries simply cannot detect, report, and respond to novel infections.

Health systems must be a shared responsibility, a key underpinning of global solidarity. The international community should create norms, build incentives, and close financing gaps, while national and local governments should invest in strong health systems. The UN and WHO must partner with countries to set technical guidelines, mobilize funding, and support monitoring and evaluation to attain UHC. Robust national health systems will protect not only the inhabitants of that particular country, but the entire globe. They will help ensure that the next story that begins like Aliyatu's ends differently.

## The Critical Importance of Robust Health Systems

West Africa had yet to fully recover from the 2014–2015 Ebola epidemic when the Democratic Republic of Congo (DRC) reported a new outbreak in 2017. The first case in the DRC was a thirty-nine-year-old man experiencing fever, vomiting, and bleeding who died in transit to a hospital. His transporter and caretaker died a few days later. Shortly thereafter, dozens of cases appeared in a remote northeastern area of the Congo.[6] This time WHO reacted rapidly, mobilizing the new Health Emergencies Programme and deploying a "ring" vaccination strategy. Two more Ebola outbreaks would strike the DRC in 2018, and another would strike in early 2021.

The timing and location of novel infections are unpredictable, underscoring the importance of universal epidemic preparedness. The continuance of one deadly outbreak does not preclude another outbreak, as demonstrated by the emergence of COVID-19 while Ebola stubbornly persisted in the DRC. Another novel outbreak could emerge before the COVID-19 pandemic ends. Preparedness begins with health systems. Rapid response will never suffice without the foundation of a strong health system upon which that response can build.

A strong health system functions like a well-oiled machine. Each component operates effectively and complements all other parts of a larger network. Health facilities must be located within reasonable traveling distance of those in need, and those facilities must be well stocked with medical equipment, personal protective equipment, and essential vaccines and medicines. Facilities must be clean and hygienic. Health workers must be well trained, of sufficient number to serve the population, and equitably distributed. In short, health systems require universal access, affordability, and quality.

The IHR mandate that all countries possess core public health capacities to detect, report, and respond to novel infections (see Chapter 7). Governments must plan, fund, and operate a health system commensurate to the needs of their entire population. Only then can the system protect peoples' day-to-day health while mitigating the impact of a disease outbreak. And yet, despite what we know about building a well-functioning health system, and how imperative this is in responding to disease outbreaks, health systems around the globe are broken.

Prevention, preparedness, and mitigation all serve critical functions in the health system "machine." There is no surrogate for prevention, the most cost-effective component.[7] With stable, secure financing, health systems are able to protect the population day in and day out. When individuals cannot access or afford vaccinations, it is impossible to achieve "herd" or "community" immunity (when a sufficiently high proportion of the population is immune).[8] If, for example, people cannot access influenza vaccines, they remain vulnerable to a virulent flu virus that can spread rapidly from person to person and across borders.

A strong health system reduces disease susceptibility, as it ensures that anyone can readily access high-quality care. It prevents the spread of disease by using effective communication channels to educate communities on protecting themselves. It protects health workers and promotes worker retention by prioritizing a healthy and sustainable workforce. Robust health systems have endless preventative, positive impacts on the health and security of a country and its inhabitants—and ultimately the world.

Outbreaks may be inevitable, but strong health systems can rapidly bring them under control. Under the IHR, preparedness includes well-designed plans and protocols, laboratories and surveillance systems, and "surge" capacity such as stockpiling vaccines and antimicrobial drugs.[9] If a health system functions effectively on a day-to-day basis, it has a foundation for its operations to enter overdrive when disaster strikes. Without planning and preparedness, policymakers and professionals waste valuable time and are unable to focus on the critical task of executing an already devised plan, which enables the pathogen to continue to spread. States with robust health systems are empowered to mitigate the impact of fast-moving diseases. Surveillance can rapidly detect an outbreak, giving decision makers time to assess the risk and respond efficiently.[10] Laboratories can quickly identify the responsible pathogen, and information systems can tell communities what preventive measures to take. Cultural competency within health systems helps maintain the trust of communities, effectively reaching people of diverse religions, ethnicities, and languages.

Leadership is another touchstone of resilient health systems. Strong leaders can effectively coordinate responses at the regional, national, and even global level. Weak leadership has consequences even for countries that take pride in having high-quality health systems. Consider major outbreaks of SARS in Canada (2003) and MERS in the Republic of Korea (2015), as well as the nurse in Dallas, Texas, who contracted Ebola in 2014 due to inadequate infection control.

## Stronger Health Systems

The suffering and loss of life from disease outbreaks and epidemics justifies building resilient health systems. Beyond this clear humanitarian rationale, international law establishes the obligation to be prepared. Governments have committed to prioritizing high-quality health systems through international instruments such as the SDGs, the IHR, the International Covenant of Social and Economic Rights (ICESCR), the Alma-Ata Declaration—and the list goes on.[11] Even though the SDGs are not backed by force of law, they hold high normative value and prioritize UHC. Every WHO member state has ratified at least one treaty that upholds the right to health.[12] Further, the IHR legally bind all 196 WHO member states to meeting core public health capacities.[13]

### Universal Health Coverage

In 2015 the 193 UN member states adopted the SDGs, the successor to the Millennium Development Goals. The SDGs embody a "one-health" strategy—healthy people living on a habitable planet. The seventeen goals and 169 targets span social development, the environment, economic progress, and good governance. Goal 3 commits member states to ensuring healthy lives and promoting well-being, with one of thirteen targets being UHC.[14] This target is perhaps the most transformative. It directs member states to promote quality health services; guarantee access to safe, effective, and affordable medicines and vaccines; and protect their populations from financial hardship. WHO and the World Bank explain well UHC's full scope:

> Broadly defined, UHC means all people receiving the health services they need, including health initiatives designed to promote better health (such as anti-tobacco policies), prevent illness (such as vaccinations), and to provide treatment, rehabilitation, and palliative care (such as end-of-life care) of sufficient quality to be effective while at the same time ensuring that the use of these services does not expose the user to financial hardship. Thus UHC comprises two main components: quality, essential health service coverage and financial coverage—both extended to the whole population.[15]

In line with the SDGs, both WHO and the World Bank prioritize attaining UHC.[16] WHO has identified three dimensions of UHC: the proportion of the population covered, the level of services provided, and the proportion of costs covered (see Figure 9.1). In 2018, forty years after the Declaration of Alma-Ata, the global community recommitted to primary health care as "a cornerstone of a sustainable health system for universal health coverage" in its Declaration of Astana.[17]

The political fuel for UHC reached its height in September 2019 when the UN General Assembly held a high-level summit on universal health coverage. The assembly adopted a political declaration that pledged UN member states to ensure UHC. What is needed now, however, is funding, political will, and accountability—especially at the national level, and by higher-income states to support countries that have insufficient resources.

Most countries are far from realizing UHC for their entire population. Financing is deeply inadequate, and it can be genuinely difficult to achieve UHC, requiring overcoming such obstacles as remote populations, severe health worker shortages, and even entrenched corruption. Meanwhile, governments may have little will to ensure health for marginalized populations, like undocumented immigrants.

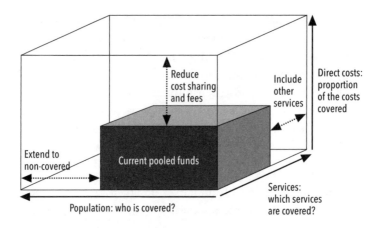

**Figure 9.1** The Three Dimensions of Universal Health Coverage.
*The World Health Report 2010: Health System Financing: The Path to Universal Health Coverage*, Fig. 1. Geneva: World Health Organization; 2010. CC BY-NC-SA 3.0 IGO.

WHO estimated that as of 2017 less than half of the world's population—33 to 49 percent of people—had access to essential health services.[18] This puts population health and global health security at risk. Consider the myriad of reforms needed in the Malawian health system, for example, to prevent another maternal death like Aliyatu's. Then consider how much more tragic the story may have been if her village had also been ravaged by an epidemic at the time her fever took hold. That is the scenario that took place with Ebola in West Africa, to a lesser degree with Zika in Latin America and the Caribbean, and has unfolded with COVID-19.[19]

Even when people are able to access care, it is often poor quality. The consequences of poor-quality health care can hardly be overstated. A 2018 Lancet Commission review found that the majority of deaths from treatable causes in low- and middle-income countries—5.0 million out of 8.6 million deaths—were due to low-quality care.[20]

### The Right to Health

Following World War II, the international community recognized health as a global public good. On December 10, 1948, the UN General Assembly adopted the Universal Declaration of Human Rights as a common standard for universal respect for human rights, including the right to health.[21] In the ensuing years, states have negotiated human rights treaties, enshrining a raft of legally binding health rights, including the rights to life, nondiscrimination, a safe environment, and freedom from inhumane treatment.

Virtually all states have ratified at least one of two foundational human rights treaties—the ICESCR and the International Covenant on Civil and Political Rights.[22] The ICESCR enunciates the definitive formulation of the right to health: "the right of everyone to the enjoyment of the highest attainable standard of physical and mental health." It also captures key social determinants of health: the right to "an adequate standard of living . . . including adequate food, clothing and housing, and to the continuous improvement of living conditions."

In 2000 the UN Committee on Economic, Social and Cultural Rights (CESCR) issued General Comment 14, providing a definitive—though not legally binding—interpretation of the right to health.[23] It identifies four "interrelated and essential elements," encompassing health care, public health, and underlying social determinants. Health goods, services, and facilities must be (1) *available* in sufficient quantity; (2) *accessible* to everyone without discrimination, including financially affordable and geographically accessible; (3) *acceptable*—ethically, culturally, and with respect for privacy; and (4) of *good quality* and scientific appropriateness.

At the domestic level, more than a hundred national constitutions—representing over 50 percent of UN states parties, from Asia and Africa to Europe and Latin America—enshrine the right to health.

These constitutions guarantee or aim to protect health rights generally, a right to public or preventive health, and in some cases, a right to medical services.[24] For example, Brazil's constitution mandates that "health is the right of all and a duty of the State and shall be guaranteed by . . . universal access to all activities and services for its promotion, protection, and recovery."[25] Haiti's constitution recognizes the state's "absolute obligation to guarantee the right to life, health, and respect of the human person."[26] Many states also incorporate the right to health in domestic statutes, rendering it potentially enforceable through the courts. In many Latin American countries, for example, citizens may file "writs of protection" to safeguard these rights.[27]

The days when a government could argue that the right to health was simply aspirational and unenforceable seem distant. Increasingly, courts and constitutional assemblies invoke the right to health as a tool for achieving a more just society. Court decisions based on the right to health are burgeoning. Social movements are beginning to advocate for the right to health. This right is not a magic bullet for attaining health security and equity, though. Accountability for compliance is weak. Human rights abuses remain common. Socioeconomic rights are hedged by broad stipulations, such as allowing for progressive realization within "maximum available . . . resources."[28]

### International Health Regulations (2005)

More concrete than the right to health, the origins of the IHR can be traced to a series of European sanitary conferences held from 1851 to 1926, ultimately resulting in the International Sanitary Regulations (ISR). WHO adopted the ISR at its founding in 1948; the World Health Assembly amended the sanitary regulations several times, renaming the treaty the IHR in 1969. In the aftermath of SARS in 2005, WHO adopted fundamentally revised regulations (see Chapter 7).

The 2005 revision ushered in transformational reforms, including an "all-hazards" (biological, chemical, radiological, and nuclear) strategy, use of unofficial (non-state) data sources, and building health system capacities to prevent, detect, and respond to health emergencies. The IHR empower WHO to protect the public's health, while balancing health with trade and human rights. Yet the gap between the IHR's norms and its real-world impact is cavernous, as the West African and DRC Ebola epidemics and the COVID-19 pandemic have revealed.[29]

Under the IHR, states have a legal duty to develop core health system capacities, such as laboratories, surveillance, risk communication, and human resources (see Figure 9.2). As we saw in Chapter 7, though, most countries have not met these legal obligations. Furthermore, the IHR are not well understood outside health ministries, and governments have not integrated IHR capacities into UHC. Consequently, the IHR and UHC operate in siloes. Perhaps most limiting, there is no mechanism for ensuring uniform and rigorous observance of international law, impeding the power of the IHR, the right to health, and other legal frameworks.

### The Need for Enforcement Mechanisms

Compliance is essential for a treaty's effectiveness, but WHO has few enforcement tools to hold states accountable for inadequate public health capacities. National capacities to detect, report, and respond to novel infections are foundational for preparedness, but WHO has routinely allowed

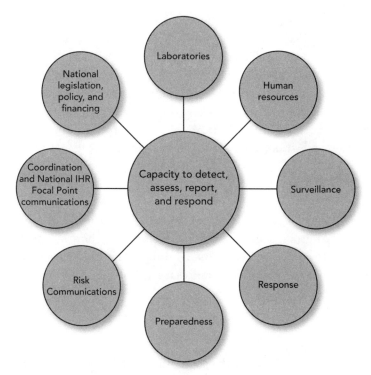

**Figure 9.2** International Health Regulations Core Capacities.
*Data source: Joint External Evaluation Tool, International Health Regulations (2005), Second Edition, Appendix 2.* Geneva: World Health Organization; 2018. CC BY-NC-SA 3.0 IGO.

states to delay fulfilling their responsibilities. In 2014 sixty-four countries (30 percent) reportedly met IHR core capacities, while forty-eight failed even to provide WHO information.[30] The actual compliance rate was likely lower, given that states self-evaluated.[31] Governments have few geopolitical incentives to build core capacities, and many have not devoted the necessary resources.[32] The IHR require states to provide technical and financial assistance to the extent possible, but sustainable financing has lagged.

In 2016 WHO announced a new framework—the Joint External Evaluation (JEE)—to monitor IHR core capacities.[33] The JEE relies on independent experts working alongside national health officials, with transparent disclosure of outcomes.[34] The JEE systematically evaluates a country's preparedness capabilities and infrastructure across nineteen domains, identifying gaps and areas for improvement. The JEE is voluntary, but by mid-2019 more than eighty states had completed an evaluation.[35] The five-year interval between JEE evaluations, however, is too long, given the need for up-to-date capacities, and its funding is insecure (see Chapter 7). WHO also encourages states to conduct in-country simulations of public health emergencies. These kinds of "tabletop" exercises are vital to test capabilities and coordination in the event a real-life crisis occurs (see the Appendix for model tabletop exercises). Countries are expected to develop national action plans to address gaps and weaknesses, but few lower-income countries have done so.

## A Global Plight

Despite the importance—and legal imperative—of robust health systems, a review of the current state of the world demonstrates how far many countries remain from achieving UHC. Multilevel, multidimensional health system reform is needed, which requires recognizing pervasive inadequacies and inequities around the world.

### Access to Care

Accessing heath care involves the ability to afford and physically access appropriate health resources and services. Across the globe, individuals struggle to find an entry point into the health system, leaving them vulnerable to disease threats. Sick individuals without adequate access to care may stay home, exposing their families and communities to infection. A 2013 review found that a quarter of Ugandans did not live within five kilometers of a health facility.[36] A health facility may be particularly distant in remote, rural areas.

In one striking example of physical inaccessibility, Dr. Thembinkosi Motlhabane stood in the parking lot of his small hospital in South Africa's poor, rural Oliver Tambo District, awaiting the ambulance he had called. His dying HIV-infected patient needed a better-equipped hospital, but the nearest was sixty miles away. He knew the ambulance could take a half-day to arrive—and his patient did not have that kind of time—but he was at the mercy of the country's fractured health system.[37] These stories of barriers to access define health experiences around the world. Unreasonable travel distances, along with long waiting times, overcrowded facilities, and inopportune hours, can make access to treatment difficult at best, and impossible at worst.

Poor health care access takes an abysmal toll on health outcomes. The trickle-down effects are far reaching, impacting everything from immunization rates to availability of clean water and sanitation, to outbreak prevention and response. In rural Burkina Faso, long distances to health facilities contribute to high child mortality rates.[38] Put simply, the inaccessibility of health services is quite literally killing our children—and adults are no better off.

Accessibility of health services varies dramatically between urban and rural populations, and gaping disparities exist across racial, ethnic, and economic lines.[39] These differences are hardly unique to lower-income countries. Middle- and high-income countries, too, typically parse out health coverage based on wealth and geography—the United States being a prime example.[40] During the COVID-19 pandemic, in April 2020, the death rate in rural, high-poverty Franklin County, Massachusetts (35 per 100,000 people), was nearly triple that of the state's more urban counties that experienced higher caseloads.[41] Ease of access can also depend on the season. Especially where roads are unpaved and terrain is rough, travel time to health facilities increases significantly during the wet season. For example, 39 percent of Niger's population is within an hour's walking distance of a health facility during the dry season, but this drops to only 24 percent during the wet season.[42]

When the decision to seek treatment is a multiday endeavor, many forego care, unable to take time away from work and family. Such was the decision made by Savita Das, a mother of five in Mumbai, India. When her daughter fell into dirty floodwaters, Savita knew she needed a hospital. But because Savita was a widow with five children and no one to look after them, she was forced to let her young daughter die—a heartrending choice.[43]

If care is inaccessible in normal times, imagine the difficulties during a health crisis. During the West African Ebola outbreak, poor road systems and inadequate transportation hindered patients traveling to treatment centers and blood samples traveling to laboratories,[44] imposing harmful—and sometimes fatal—delays. Not only were Ebola-stricken patients less likely to access care, but so were those needing more routine services. In-hospital emergency obstetric care decreased dramatically, with a steep rise in maternal mortality.[45] By the end of the outbreak an estimated 1,091 additional people died of HIV, 2,714 of tuberculosis, and 6,818 of malaria. Treatment services for these conditions were cut in half in Guinea, Liberia, and Sierra Leone.[46] More recently, the COVID-19 pandemic interfered with global efforts to eradicate other infectious diseases such as AIDS, tuberculosis, and cholera.

In India the country's lockdown prevented patients from collecting government-supplied anti-HIV medication, while patients in South Korea were unable to access tuberculosis treatment.[47] The sad truth is that when epidemics strike, many untreated illnesses and deaths come from other diseases, including cancer, diabetes, and heart disease.

So long as physical and economic barriers to health services persist, health security remains in peril. Access to health care depends heavily on the equitable and adequate distribution of facilities to ensure that the entire population is served. Access also depends on nonhealth sectors: affordable, safe transportation to reach a facility; roads fit for purpose; and childcare to enable individuals to leave their children at home when seeking care. Electricity and other aspects of infrastructure are vital to refrigerate vaccines, operate medical equipment, and turn on hospital lights.

## Equity

Life expectancies of residents living in neighborhoods only miles apart can differ by twenty years or more. Vulnerable populations, such as indigenous peoples, ethnic minorities, people with disabilities, and people who are homeless and living in poverty, may have far less opportunity to live long and healthy lives. In a health emergency, the most disadvantaged people suffer most and perish first. Thus, national health preparedness plans should include dedicated, sustained, and prioritized efforts to address health inequities. In planning for an emergency, the needs of society's most vulnerable should be proactively anticipated, and carefully considered. It is not enough to generally serve the population in a crisis without giving particular attention to children, the elderly, persons with disabilities, the poor, and those living in under-served locations.

Equity is a global, as well as national, concern. When a novel infection becomes a pandemic, richer countries will usually fare best. They can afford new drugs and vaccines, and their health systems are far more resilient. Consider the race to develop a vaccine for COVID-19 (see Chapter 10). If richer countries access scarce vaccine supplies and their citizens live, while people in lower-income countries perish, global solidarity—even basic trust—will evaporate. The same applies to efforts to gather essential medical supplies. During COVID-19, global demand for supplies such as masks and ventilators soared, such that poorer countries—often those already lacking necessary equipment—were unable to compete with wealthier nations in a bidding war for scarce resources.[48] To protect against this outcome, international strategies for equity must be a vital part of pandemic preparedness.

WHO's PIP Framework requires equitable sharing of the benefits of research such as vaccines. In essence, pharmaceutical companies and researchers contract with WHO. In exchange for access to samples of novel influenza viruses, they agree to offer certain benefits, such as a percentage of vaccines produced or financial payments. But the framework has cavernous gaps. PIP applies only to pandemic influenza; governments do not undertake to share vaccine supplies; and participation is voluntary (see Chapter 8).

## Health Infrastructure

During the West African Ebola epidemic, many hospitals shut down or decreased functioning to prevent hospital-acquired infections, as health facilities became a hotbed for viral spread.[49] People avoided hospitals for fear of infection. Others were frightened that they would be quarantined or separated from their families. During COVID-19 many hospitals canceled or postponed elective procedures to reserve capacity for COVID-19 patients and also prevent hospital-acquired infections. A novel virus can grind an already weak health system practically to a halt.

A health system requires the infrastructure and capacity to provide individual care and ensure population-level protection, with the wherewithal to withstand a health emergency. Yet many countries fail to secure either. Crumbling infrastructure (e.g., surveillance, laboratories, and human resources) leaves states vulnerable to novel infections. Many lower-income countries lack the diagnostic, tracking, and reporting tools necessary for surveillance, leaving disease incidence woefully misunderstood and underreported.[50] Failures in communication between government, health workers, patients, and the community undermine timely, transparent, and accurate information during an infectious outbreak. Ultimately, public trust deteriorates in the face of poor health care infrastructure.

An example from Ghana demonstrates how treatment suffers when health infrastructure is weak. Referring to the 2014 Ebola outbreak, a district director of health services noted, "We did not even have infra-red thermometers at the peak of the [Ebola] epidemic and we still have gaps in personal protective equipment; the waiting centre at the border is a small room with no fence and there are only two beds in that isolation centre."[51] A municipal disease control officer observed, "If Ebola happens in Ghana, we will not survive it."[52] Bordering on the Gulf of Guinea, Ghana was lucky to escape Ebola.

Other countries are bereft of the basic resources to treat sick patients. India can offer only half a hospital bed for every 1,000 members of its population; Colombia and Mexico can offer one and a half. Compare those numbers to more than thirteen hospital beds per 1,000 inhabitants in Japan.[53] Several African countries (Central African Republic, Liberia, and South Sudan) have only three or four ventilators for the whole nation.[54] Somalia has only fifteen ICU beds; the DRC has only two dozen. These African countries and their hospitals became quickly overwhelmed during the peak of their COVID-19 epidemics.

Dilapidated facilities, outdated or unsafe medical supplies, and failing health infrastructure expose patients to infection and poor outcomes. In Uganda, Carol Atuhirwe was diagnosed with throat cancer and suffered through thirty-six surgeries and multiple rounds of treatment at the country's only cancer facility. She often left those sessions with burnt skin, as the facility used a radiotherapy machine that should have been decommissioned years earlier. But because it was the nation's only machine at the time, doctors had no choice. Carol needed reconstructive surgery for severe radiation burns.[55]

## Health Workforce

Health workers can only provide quality care and respond effectively to a disease outbreak if they are well trained. Every day the poor training of health professionals leads to avoidable harm. In an overburdened clinic or hospital, health workers are forced to perform duties well beyond the scope of their skill sets, resulting in mistakes—and sometimes fatal errors. Dr. Carolyn Nduhiu, an obstetrician at Nairobi's MSI Eastleigh Clinic, relays how abortions performed by untrained personnel can be lethal. In one case, a sixteen-year-old girl arrived in the operating room with her intestines exposed through her vagina; the untrained abortion-provider had accidentally perforated the girl's uterus and extracted her insides. Surgery could not save her life.[56]

Little is more tragic than a woman dying during childbirth. In West and Central Africa, less than 60 percent of all deliveries have a skilled birth attendant present.[57] Approximately 90 percent of maternal deaths and 80 percent of stillbirths take place in fifty-eight countries with severe deficits in trained midwives.[58] And when either deliveries or abortions go terribly wrong, there are too few skilled surgeons like Dr. Nduhiu to pick up the pieces.

In 2013 WHO reported a deficit of 7.9 million health workers; that number is expected to increase to 18 million by 2030, primarily affecting low- and middle-income countries (see Table 9.1).[59] The problem is exacerbated by low-quality or insufficient medical training and a failure to retain professionals, who are drawn to wealthier countries by the lure of higher pay. Only 168 medical schools operate across all forty-seven countries in WHO's African Region; eleven countries have no medical schools, and twenty-eight have only one.[60] All too often, those who receive medical training leave the country or prefer to work in urban areas, leaving rural communities vastly underserved.

Health worker retention is essential, yet across the world, shortages and limitations abound. Wealthier countries poaching graduates from abroad have a knock-on effect on weaker health systems. In May 2010 WHO adopted the Global Code of Practice on the International Recruitment of Health Personnel, but its impact has been limited. We see a continuing migration of health workers from low- to middle-income countries, and from middle-income to high-income countries. At the bottom of that pecking order lie the world's poorest countries with the most fragile health systems.

The shortcomings of the health workforce become particularly apparent during public health emergencies. Without well-trained epidemiologists and laboratory workers, novel outbreaks cannot be detected or confirmed. If doctors and nurses lack infection control training, much less protective gear, they are at risk along with their patients. Facilities that suffer from staff shortages cannot admit or adequately treat patients. In the West African Ebola epidemic, 881 doctors, nurses, and midwives contracted the virus, killing 513 of them.[61] This further depleted an already bare-bones workforce. Many ancillary workers, ranging from security guards, to burial teams, to community-based volunteers, also died. Even countries with relatively strong health systems may struggle to support an overburdened health workforce during a disease outbreak. In Italy COVID-19 infected 10,000 hospital workers and killed seventy-four doctors by April 2020.[62] Without better preparation, training, and tools, the health workforce remains unequipped to soften the impact of infectious disease outbreaks.

### Essential Vaccines and Medicines

Vaccinations and medicines prevent and treat infections, serving critical aspects of public health. Every two years WHO publishes an updated model list of essential medicines, including core pharmaceuticals for meeting

**Table 9.1.** Median Density of Health Workforce (per 10,000 population) among the Top Five Cadres, by WHO Region, 2000–2013

| Region | Physicians | Nursing and midwifery | Dentistry | Pharmaceutical |
|---|---|---|---|---|
| Africa | 2.4 | 10.7 | 0.5 | 1.0 |
| Americas | 20.0 | 24.1 | 4.1 | 3.2 |
| Southeast Asia | 6.1 | 9.0 | 1.0 | 3.9 |
| Europe | 32.3 | 41.7 | 5.6 | 8.6 |
| Eastern Mediterranean | 10.3 | 10.7 | 1.5 | 5.6 |
| Western Pacific | 13.5 | 24.1 | 0.2 | 3.5 |
| Global | 12.3 | 17.6 | 0.8 | 3.6 |

*Data source:* WHO, *World Health Statistics 2016: Monitoring Health for the SDGs* (Geneva: WHO, 2016).

population-level needs, as well as complementary medicines targeted to priority diseases.[63] These essential medicines address priority health care needs, and are "selected with due regard to public health relevance, evidence on efficacy and safety, and comparative cost-effectiveness." As essential medicines, they should always be available in adequate amounts, their quality assured, their dosage appropriate, and their prices affordable.[64]

Essential medicines include antibiotics and antivirals, which are especially important in curtailing outbreaks. Having a wide range of antimicrobials is vital, as pathogens become resistant to standard treatments (see Chapter 5). Yet 60 percent of WHO-listed medications may be unavailable to patients in Africa, Southeast Asia, and the Western Pacific for two critical (though not exclusive) reasons.[65]

First, many lower-income countries can only produce less-expensive medications, like analgesics, in-country. As a result they must import essential, and expensive, drugs such as those for HIV and tuberculosis. Imported medicines are often branded, so the population cannot benefit from less-expensive generic alternatives. Even when pharmaceutical companies offer lower prices for developing countries (as with antiretroviral medications), the prices are still generally higher than those of generics.

Second, poor supply-chain management often leaves medications understocked or poorly handled, threatening the products' integrity. Many health facilities lack the capacity to store essential vaccines at adequately cold temperatures, and as a result those medicines may spoil before reaching their desired location. In late 2018 UNICEF used commercial drones to distribute vaccines to children on Vanuatu, the Pacific nation consisting of eighty islands, where nurses transported ice boxes across rivers, mountains, and rocky ledges. In Mali, long walks with donkey carts remain the order of the day. Preserving the integrity of vaccinations through that amount of travel is no small feat.[66]

### Financing

From funding the health system to paying for individualized care, what is the price tag, and who pays? That individuals with the lowest income pay the highest percentage out of pocket for health care is deeply incongruous, but remains the reality in many low- and middle-income countries. In some of the poorest regions of the world, individuals are forced to pay upward of 45 percent out of pocket to meet their health needs (see Figure 9.3). This starkly contrasts with states' human rights commitments.

Public health emergencies exacerbate inequities when low-income persons can ill afford to seek diagnosis and care. When poor individuals stay away from health services due to the cost, they risk spreading their infection to family members and to the wider community. Thus, affordable access to care is not only equitable, but also vital in bringing outbreaks under control. Leaving the impoverished effectively outside the health system will almost certainly result in ongoing spread of infectious diseases.

The World Bank's Health Security Financing Assessment Tool supports governments in translating costed and prioritized plans into detailed financing solutions. All countries must mobilize the resources and adequately fund their health system, including through fair, participatory, and transparent taxation. The International Monetary Fund has identified more effective taxation as an important means of generating revenue, while potentially earmarking funds for health systems.[67] Private sector support can also be leveraged by highlighting corporate social responsibility and the economic impacts that affordable—or unaffordable—health care could have on businesses.

When governments fail to adequately fund health services, out-of-pocket expenditures rise and people's access to care falls. International donors must provide additional development assistance for health (DAH), both (1) compensating for insufficient national financing, and (2) supporting low-income countries that would have insufficient finances even with considerable resource mobilization. With increased economic development, government

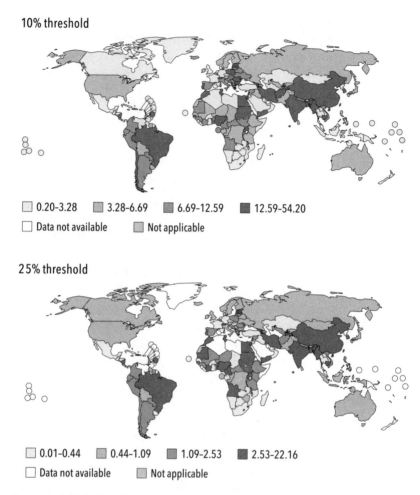

**10% threshold**

☐ 0.20-3.28    ▨ 3.28-6.69    ▨ 6.69-12.59    ▧ 12.59-54.20
☐ Data not available    ▨ Not applicable

**25% threshold**

☐ 0.01-0.44    ▨ 0.44-1.09    ▨ 1.09-2.53    ▧ 2.53-22.16
☐ Data not available    ▨ Not applicable

**Figure 9.3** Percentage of Population with Out-of-Pocket Heath Spending Exceeding 10% or 25% of Household Budget (most recent data available as of 2019). Reformatted from *Primary Health Care on the Road to Universal Health Coverage: 2019 Monitoring Report*, Figure 2.2. Geneva: World Health Organization; 2019. CC BY-NC-SA 3.0 IGO.

health spending grows significantly; as government spending grows, DAH drops off.

Lower-income countries will need DAH for the foreseeable future, but they should maximize domestic resources and avoid relying too heavily on external aid. Governments and nonprofits often have their own priorities, which might not align with areas of greatest need in the host country.

Commitments and disbursements of aid can vary, creating fluctuations in contributions and an unpredictable stream of funding.[68] Further, DAH should not be a substitute for a government's own investment in its health system. Too often DAH encourages governments to reduce their health care spending.[69] A well-functioning health system requires sustainable, consistent financing, which DAH does not necessarily support. Meanwhile, governments will see significant economic benefits from investing in UHC, with $1.40 in economic returns for each $1 invested.[70]

By failing to prioritize funding for epidemic preparedness, countries leave themselves dangerously vulnerable. Time and again, countries' populations succumb to highly preventable diseases because their health systems are too weak. And the effects are felt far beyond a single country. Failure to contain a virulent pathogen risks rapid viral spread through mass travel and migration. When national health systems fail to detect and respond to a novel infection, emergency response can require extraordinary financial and technical support from the international community. The lessons are made clear with each emerging infectious disease: robust health systems not only fulfill everyday health needs, but also enable countries to detect, report, and respond to novel infectious diseases. This benefits every person, business, and government worldwide. Health systems are a shared responsibility, offering mutual benefits—not only for health but also for political stability, economic prosperity, and human flourishing.

# CHAPTER 10

# Global Medical War Chest

**China's release of genomic sequencing data** for SARS-CoV-2 on January 11, 2020, was the start of a race to develop vaccines and other medical countermeasures for COVID-19. The Coalition for Epidemic Preparedness Innovations (CEPI) (see Chapter 7) quickly contacted its partners developing novel platforms that could be adapted to new pathogens and offered financial support to direct their efforts to SARS-CoV-2.[1] Less than ten weeks later, on March 16, Moderna's vaccine candidate entered a phase 1 clinical trial, and on July 27 it entered phase 3.[2] The vaccine candidate—a novel messenger RNA (mRNA) vaccine—was based on a similar vaccine Moderna had been developing for MERS. Biotech companies from around the globe also launched clinical trials of SARS-CoV-2 vaccine candidates. China and Russia began deploying their vaccines for selected populations even before phase 3 trials were completed. By December 2 the United Kingdom granted approval for another mRNA vaccine manufactured by Pfizer/BioNTech, with US approval for both mRNA vaccines following closely behind.[3] By December 29 the UK approved yet another vaccine developed by AstraZeneca/Oxford. In just one year, scientists from around the world had developed safe and effective vaccines against COVID-19, a triumph unprecedented in human history.

How was it possible to develop COVID-19 vaccines at "pandemic" speed? Scientific understanding and technologies for genomics and structural biology have exploded. High-income countries and biotech companies also had clear incentives to invest substantially in COVID-19 vaccine development, given the virus's global spread and massive health, economic, and social impacts.

The COVID-19 pandemic overwhelmed the world's capacity to respond effectively. Nontherapeutic interventions (e.g., masks, distancing, and stay-at-home orders) failed to keep the virus under control in most countries. Vaccines became the only way to return to a semblance of normalcy, with schools and businesses fully open, people socializing, and travel resuming.

Previous Ebola outbreaks demonstrated the difference that a timely vaccine can make in confronting a deadly threat—and the factors that contribute to costly vaccine development delays.

The Ebola epidemic in the DRC began on August 1, 2018, and ended two years later on Jun 25, 2020. The epidemic was particularly challenging because it took place in an active conflict zone.[4] Were it not for the deployment of a promising vaccine, rVSV-ZEBOV, the death toll would have been far higher.[5] The vaccine was administered in rings to high-risk individuals who were geographically or socially connected to patients: contacts, contacts of contacts, and front-line responders. The vaccine proved effective, building on evidence gathered from Guinea in 2015. In both outbreaks, researchers found that vaccinated individuals did not contract Ebola virus disease.[6]

The rVSV-ZEBOV vaccine was not new. The Public Health Agency of Canada applied for a patent on the vaccine in 2003.[7] But the first human clinical trial didn't begin until over a decade later when the West African Ebola crisis finally spurred action. NewLink Genetics commenced a phase 1 clinical trial in 2014, supported by the National Institutes of Health and US Department of Defense.[8] NewLink then licensed vaccine rights to Merck Pharmaceuticals, which pushed the vaccine into additional clinical trials. In late 2019 the vaccine would ultimately become the first Ebola vaccine to be approved by regulators in Europe and the US FDA.[9]

Why did such a promising vaccine with the potential to save thousands of lives languish for years? The intellectual property system does not generally incentivize companies to produce vaccines or medicines intended for small or uncertain markets. It costs millions of dollars to bring a vaccine to the market, and pharmaceutical companies, largely located in high-income countries, hesitate to invest in vaccine candidates intended primarily for low-income countries or sporadic outbreak diseases.[10]

The devastating West African Ebola epidemic galvanized political will and funding for Ebola R&D, which more than tripled from 2014 to 2015.[11]

While the US government provided the majority of resources for Ebola and other viral hemorrhagic fevers, funding from private industry increased sevenfold.[12] Merck donated vaccine doses, while Gavi, the Vaccine Alliance, provided $1 million for operational costs.[13] The DRC, supported by WHO, Médecins Sans Frontières (MSF), and UNICEF, implemented ring vaccinations. Governments, international organizations, public-private partnerships, and NGOs offered additional support.[14]

Vaccines and medicines are essential components of our medical war chest. The Ebola vaccine development highlights the fact that promising technologies can languish due to lack of funding and political attention. But it also demonstrates how we can overcome market disincentives through targeted financing and partnerships to harness varied expertise. The COVID-19 pandemic was a game changer, demonstrating scientific prowess beyond what would have seemed possible.

This chapter explores the gap between technology's promise and our ability to realize the global public goods of vaccines and medicines. This gap stems from significant market disincentives in the R&D process, along with clinical trial challenges and regulatory hurdles. Yet a range of innovative financing strategies to delink R&D costs from vaccine and drug prices, along with well-designed and ethically run clinical trials, can fill this gap, facilitating the development of urgently needed medical countermeasures.

## Why Outbreak Disease Research Can Falter and Fail

In 2018 WHO identified eight priority diseases (including Ebola virus disease, SARS, and Zika) that warranted accelerated research and development, given their potential to cause epidemics and the absence of efficacious medical countermeasures.[15] In many cases, development of countermeasures for these diseases has stalled at the clinical testing phase.[16]

Given that billions of dollars are spent on pharmaceutical research each year, what explains the lack of medical countermeasures for outbreak diseases? At its core, it's a question of market incentives: R&D is expensive, and the market for technologies to fight infectious diseases with epidemic potential is often small and uncertain. Even with a predictable market of consumers in high-income countries, the process of bringing a new health product to market is expensive and time-consuming. Including out-of-pocket expenses and opportunity costs, bringing a new drug to market in the United States costs roughly $2.6 billion by one calculation, and takes over a decade.[17]

And successful regulatory approval is not guaranteed. Most new drugs that enter clinical trials fail; the rate of successful FDA approval is estimated at only 11 to 14 percent.[18]

For outbreak disease countermeasures, the lack of a clearly defined market exacerbates the costs and risks. Outbreaks, by definition, are sporadic and unpredictable. It is nearly impossible to know precisely which pathogens will cause health emergencies, or when. And even identifying high-risk pathogens is only a first step, as pathogens mutate over time. Pharmaceutical companies also cannot predict the number of doses needed to contain an outbreak, which might be quite small. And low- and middle-income countries are often hit hardest by novel pathogens. Consequently, industry lacks financial incentives to develop products for many novel diseases.

Each stage in the medical countermeasure development process highlights the deficiency of existing market incentives to stimulate innovations.

Most drug and vaccine development originates with basic scientific research, most often conducted by government-funded academic researchers.[19] Traditionally governments fund research for diseases that cause the most illness and death in their populations, such as cancer, diabetes, or cardiovascular disease. This is beginning to change. The United States, for example, has classified Ebola as a bioterrorism threat and a "category A priority pathogen." But the NIH has not prioritized other novel pathogens, and thus extant pipelines reflect fewer drug candidates.[20]

The second step in the process is product development, where researchers translate basic scientific findings into a drug or vaccine candidate. This resource- and time-intensive process involves identifying a candidate, optimizing it to lessen unintended interactions, and testing it for toxicity. If successful in animal models, the drug or vaccine undergoes three phases of clinical trials, using increasing numbers of patients, to gather evidence about the candidate's safety and efficacy. Clinical trials are challenging under the best conditions, but when the study timeline must be compressed to fit within an outbreak, a trial's chance of success can be crippled by lengthy regulatory review, dosage shortages, low participation, and poor trial design.[21]

In some cases a medical countermeasure can gain emergency use authorization (EUA) before completing the entire clinical trial process. For example, in May 2020 the FDA authorized the emergency use of the drug remdesivir to treat COVID-19 patients hospitalized with severe respiratory symptoms.[22] The FDA's decision followed two clinical trials demonstrating efficacy in COVID-19 recovery. The pharmaceutical company Gilead originally developed remdesivir to treat Ebola, but it had been found ineffective for that purpose.

EUA can be controversial precisely because phase 3 clinical trials often have yet to be completed. For example, on August 23 the FDA issued an EUA for investigational convalescent plasma for the treatment of COVID-19 in hospitalized patients.[23] The EUA coincided with warnings from senior National Institute of Health officials that the data were not sufficient for such authorization.[24]

If a product successfully completes clinical trials, its sponsor must obtain regulatory approval from each country in which the product will be marketed and distributed. Countries usually have their own national regulatory agencies, and the rigor of agency reviews are highly variable. For countermeasures primarily used in lower-income countries, drug sponsors must navigate regulatory regimes that often lack capacity to conduct robust and independent reviews. Thus, sponsors often also seek approval from a more stringent regulatory agency, such as those in the United States, European Union, or Japan, and also seek prequalification from WHO, which is frequently viewed by low-income countries as a prerequisite for national approval.

Finally, after receiving regulatory approval, the product must be manufactured at scale and introduced into the country, raising a new set of logistical and operational challenges. Manufacturing capabilities in lower-income countries are often weak. Successful product introduction requires effective distribution channels, ensuring sufficient supply and procurement. Health providers must be made aware of the new product, and, if necessary, trained in its use.

## Overcoming R&D Obstacles

Scientific understanding and technologies for developing medical countermeasures have exploded in recent years. Advancements in genetics allow for early pathogen sequencing, helping to identify the proteins needed for vaccine design. Two technologies have especially catapulted vaccine development: synthetic vaccinology and platform technologies. In synthetic vaccinology, sequencing data are digitally communicated—from scientist to scientist and from country to country—without the need to transfer biological samples.

With platform technologies, instead of "one bug, one drug," the idea is to support the development of multiple vaccines or drugs that share one or more components.[25] As demonstrated by COVID-19 vaccine development, platform technologies can speed up and simplify vaccine production, enabling the rapid development of "plug and play" vaccines where multiple different vaccines can be developed using the same system. Platform technologies can also reduce the need for cold storage, easing the burdens on stockpiling and distribution.

While the science behind developing countermeasures has progressed rapidly, the incentives and regulatory processes for translating scientific research into safe and effective products with market approval have lagged behind. The COVID-19 pandemic has compelled the investment and regulatory systems that govern R&D to "catch up" to the science, with reforms to overcome many of barriers in the R&D process. Yet challenges remain.

## Coordinating Research and Development

The 2014–2016 West African Ebola epidemic highlighted major gaps in R&D coordination between stakeholders: confusion and poor organization led to delays in affected countries receiving funds, equipment, medical countermeasures, and personnel.[26] In the wake of the outbreak, global commissions examined the international response and identified the importance of cooperation and coordination.

Coordination of stakeholders' R&D activities helps ensure efficient use of scarce resources, prioritize work on the most worrying diseases and most promising technologies, reduce duplicative activities, and marshal technical expertise. With COVID-19 vaccine development proceeding at record pace, coordination has proven critical on other grounds: both ensuring sufficient global supply of the safest and most efficacious COVID-19 vaccines and equitably distributing those vaccines among the world's population.

In April 2020 WHO launched the Access to COVID-19 Tools (ACT) Accelerator, supported by public and private actors including the European Commission, the Bill and Melinda Gates Foundation, CEPI, Gavi, the Global Fund, Unitaid, and the Wellcome Trust.[27] The ACT Accelerator aims to align global efforts for equitable access to new COVID-19 diagnostics, therapeutics, and vaccines. WHO, given its technical expertise and unique legitimacy for global leadership, has developed global policy recommendations on the use of COVID-19 vaccines though its Strategic Advisory Group of Experts (SAGE) on Immunisation.

Equitable and timely access to COVID-19 vaccines simply cannot be achieved, though, without reaching the scale of vaccine production necessary to meet vast global need. For manufacturers, the idea of expanding production for vaccines that are still being developed, and may never get approved, presents enormous financial risk. Many countries and groups of countries, including Canada, China, the United States, and the European Union, have addressed this challenge through bilateral agreements with vaccine manufacturers to meet their own COVID-19 needs—a troubling development that coined the term "vaccine nationalism," the hording of vaccines by governments to meet their populations' needs.[28]

On May 15, 2020, the Trump administration launched Operation Warp Speed, which had the goal of delivering 300 million COVID-19 vaccine doses across the United States, with initial supplies by January 2021.[29] A key element was to manufacture vaccines at industrial scale while they were simultaneously undergoing clinical trials. Normally vaccines are not manufactured at scale until after regulatory approval. As only 11 to 14 percent of countermeasures typically become approved, waiting for approval before large-scale manufacture reduces the possibility of wasted investments.

However, in Operation Warp Speed the US government took on the financial risk, allowing vaccine developers to expedite production of the most promising vaccine candidates. In July 2020 the US government announced a $2.1 billion deal with vaccine makers Sanofi and GlaxoSmithKline to develop their COVID-19 vaccine candidate and produce 100 million doses by 2021—bringing the list of US-supported COVID-19 vaccine candidates to six.[30] Operation Warp Speed's overall budget is $10 billion, with $6.5 billion directed toward countermeasure development, and the remainder for NIH research.

Other high-income countries, along with some middle-income countries, have undertaken similar efforts to rapidly develop and produce COVID-19 vaccines. France, Italy, Germany, and the Netherlands formed the Inclusive Vaccine Alliance, with a deal to purchase 400 million doses of AstraZeneca's vaccine for European Union member states.[31] The United Kingdom signed its own deals with AstraZeneca and other companies as well. All told, high-income countries had agreements covering more than 4.5 billion doses by early 2021, while middle-income countries had agreements for well over 2 billion doses. These agreements threatened the ability of low- and many middle-income countries to procure a share of global vaccine supplies.[32] Meanwhile, China and Russia developed their own COVID-19 vaccines, and through a mix of purchase agreements and donations, shared them with numerous countries in Latin America, Africa, Asia, and the Mideast.[33] The Serum Institute of India produced 50 million doses of the AstraZeneca vaccine even before the UK and India granted regulatory approval, and as the Serum Institute produced more of the vaccine, India sold or donated doses to dozens of countries.[34]

Beyond the enormous financial risks governments take by investing in the large-scale production of still-unapproved vaccines, this siloed, country-by-country, approach is concerning for two major reasons. First, competition among vaccine candidates could lead countries to "panic buy"—creating a bidding war and driving up prices on the global market. Second, given that many vaccine candidates will fail, access to successful candidates may become limited to the few privileged countries that selected them. Lower-income countries, lacking the ability to take financial risks and enter advance supply agreements, would be left especially defenseless.

To avoid this dire outcome, the COVID-19 Vaccine Global Access (COVAX) Facility was assembled by CEPI and Gavi, working under WHO's leadership.[35] Founded in 2017, CEPI's mission is to engage governments and the commercial sector to improve public health preparedness—which proved critical during the COVID-19 pandemic. Gavi was founded in 2000 to expand childhood vaccine campaigns in the world's poorest countries, but has since expanded its charge to procure COVID-19 vaccines globally. The COVAX Facility is a financing a procurement mechanism that pools countries' demand and resources for COVID-19 vaccines. By inviting all countries to join, COVAX takes a collective approach, allowing for a much larger portfolio of vaccine candidates than countries can achieve on their own, thus reducing the risk that countries will fail to secure access to successful vaccines. For manufacturers, it reduces the risks that major production investments could result in no or low demand.

Costing an estimated $11.7 billion for 2020–21, COVAX aimed to deliver 2 billion doses of safe and effective COVID-19 vaccines, ones that have passed regulatory approval or WHO prequalification, by the end of 2021.[36] Vaccines were to be distributed to all participating countries equally, proportional to population size, initially prioritizing health care workers and then expanding to cover the most vulnerable 20 percent of every participating country. As of December 2020, 190 countries had agreed to participate in COVAX—though not the United States or Russia. The United States finally joined COVAX in January 2021 when President Biden took office. Wealthier nations would self-finance their vaccines from their own public budgets, and partner with ninety-two low- and lower-middle income countries that are supported through voluntary donations.

Global public-private partnerships, such as CEPI and Gavi, have been highly effective at bringing rapid funding and expertise to thorny health problems like COVID-19. They have demonstrated the ability to bring governments together to increase the purchasing power of lower-income countries, while also benefiting higher-income countries that can expand their portfolio of vaccine candidates during an outbreak. But while funding was slow in coming, billions of dollars in pledges from the G7 in February 2021, led by pledges from the Biden administration, put COVAX on firmer footing, even creating the potential that it would exceed its target of vaccinating 20 percent of all participating countries.[37] Yet the vaccination effort—including procurement, R&D, and country readiness—still required more than $3 billion as of March 2021.[38] Just how many doses COVAX would deliver remained uncertain. In rich countries, national leaders have poured resources into their own vaccine development and purchasing, taking care of their own citizens first—while also taking up large portions of the global manufacturing capacity, jeopardizing the possibility of low-income nations having access to COVID-19 vaccines.

But the reality must not be ignored: without investments in equitable vaccine distribution, COVID-19 will continue to circulate among poor, unvaccinated populations. As the virus mutates, it could increase in virulence and transmissibility, and spread throughout the world, infecting even vaccinated populations. Strategies for financing the development and distribution of outbreak countermeasures are discussed below.

### Financing Innovative R&D

Whether R&D is coordinated by WHO, governments, partnerships, or private entities, its acceleration requires sustainable funding. Traditionally governments have offered most R&D funding, supplemented by philanthropy and private industry. In 2015 governments funded 63 percent of neglected-disease R&D. Philanthropies, mainly the Gates Foundation and the Wellcome Trust, contributed 21 percent of global funding, and the pharmaceutical industry contributed the remaining 17 percent.[39] In 2015 industry increased Ebola R&D sevenfold over the previous year, becoming the second largest funder of Ebola R&D and other African viral hemorrhagic fevers, behind only the NIH.[40]

In 2016 the Commission on a Global Health Risk Framework for the Future recommended a global commitment of an incremental increase of $1 billion per year to accelerate R&D of drugs, vaccines, personal protective equipment, and medical devices.[41] Yet much more is needed. Developing COVID-19 countermeasures has demanded multibillion-dollar investments in R&D, and has stimulated the use of financing mechanisms to secure funding.

### Funding and Financing Mechanisms

Funds can be used to stimulate R&D and overcome market failures, but the question remains how best to channel resources to maximize results. "Delinking" R&D costs from the price of health products is an important concept. The current intellectual property (IP) system encourages companies to recoup development costs by charging high prices, which can make drugs and vaccines unaffordable. The IP system also protects companies from competition by providing patents, exclusive licenses, and regulatory exclusivities—driving up the costs of drugs and vaccines even further. This system can cause two major problems: first, companies may simply avoid developing products needed in uncertain or unlucrative markets; and second, high prices can put essential medicines out of reach of the world's poorest. Imagine if a vaccine for COVID-19 were finally developed, but was cost-prohibitive to all but the wealthiest societies and individuals.

By delinking R&D costs from product prices, financing mechanisms aim to encourage innovation without prohibitively expensive prices. Delinkage includes mechanisms to offset development costs through upfront payments or back-end rewards, or through the strategic softening of intellectual property protections. Governments and partnerships have relied on these mechanisms to stimulate the development of COVID-19 vaccines and ultimately ensure their affordability.

### Offsetting R&D Costs: Push and Pull Mechanisms

Financing to offset development costs can either provide funding upfront (called a push) or offer a financial reward once a product has been developed (called a pull).[42]

Push mechanisms include upfront payments such as grants and innovation funds, and are highly effective in spurring R&D for neglected diseases. In 2016, for example, USAID issued a challenge called "Combating Zika and Future Threats." Parties from academia and industry submitted proposals to combat Zika, and USAID awarded $15 million in grants for projects that ranged from insecticide-treated sandals to mosquitoes infected with bacteria that prevent the spread of disease to humans.[43]

Although push financing mechanisms are popular, funding is not contingent upon the recipient successfully furthering R&D. Pull mechanisms, alternatively, reward successful innovation with financing. Pull mechanisms come in a variety of forms, including prizes, transferable vouchers, and advance market commitments. For example, the FDA Priority Review Voucher program awards a transferable voucher to the sponsor of a new drug to treat delineated tropical diseases, such as Ebola, Zika, and Lassa fever. The holder of the voucher can redeem it for expedited review of a new drug or can sell it to another company. For example, a voucher awarded to Knight Therapeutics in 2014 for its leishmaniasis drug was sold to Gilead Sciences for $125 million. Gilead used the voucher for accelerated review of its HIV drug Odefsey.[44]

The race for COVID-19 vaccines has been financed through both push and pull mechanisms. As part of Operation Warp Speed in the United States, the Biomedical Advanced Research and Medical Authority (BARDA) had a budget of $6.5 billion to push the development, manufacture, and distribution of promising COVID-19 vaccine candidates.[45] BARDA formed agreements to provide millions and even billions to vaccine companies (including Pfizer, AstraZeneca, Moderna, Johnson & Johnson, Novavax, Sanofi, and GlaxoSmithKline) to cover the costs of testing, commercialization, and manufacturing. BARDA has also partnered with manufacturers and producers of supplies such as vials, syringes, and plastic containers. By securing the financing upfront, companies can focus on rapid vaccine development without incurring much financial risk.

Similar to BARDA, CEPI's role in the COVAX Facility is to push the development of COVID-19 vaccines by signing contracts with developers of promising candidates to help fund research, clinical trials, and manufacturing capacity.[46] CEPI initiated partnerships with twelve vaccine companies to finance the development of their COVID-19 vaccine candidates.

Concurrent with CEPI's push mechanisms within COVAX, Gavi is employing a pull mechanism: advance market commitments (AMCs).[47] The goal of AMCs is to counter market forces that push down drug prices by ensuring a stable market for a product once it is developed. Many factors can drive down drug prices, including the absence of a lucrative market in low-income countries, and the practice of bulk-purchasing vaccines. Under bulk purchases, health ministries purchase most vaccines, using their buying power to negotiate lower prices. From the country's perspective, this is a wise use of limited resources, but by driving vaccine company profits even lower, bulk purchasing can disincentivize vaccine development targeted at low-income countries.[48] With AMCs a purchaser promises vaccine developers that it will buy a certain number of doses, at a predetermined price, if the developers can clear the necessary regulatory hurdles.

In 2010 Gavi successfully piloted an AMC for pneumococcal vaccines.[49] Donors committed $1.5 billion to the World Bank to guarantee the price of pneumococcal vaccines once developed, and suppliers agreed to provide vaccine doses at a determined price. In return, each manufacturer received its proportional share of the committed funds.[50] It has been estimated that this financing program has funded the vaccination of 225 million children across sixty low- and low-middle-income countries within a decade of the program's launch.[51]

Within COVAX, Gavi is working with participating countries and donors to assemble the funding to enter into AMCs with CEPI's COVID-19 vaccine development partners.[52] As with the pneumococcal vaccine program, the AMCs will help ensure that the funding of vaccines for low-income countries remains stable, thus incentivizing their development and manufacture. Gavi estimated that $2 billion is needed to provide 1 billion doses to ninety-two low-income countries through AMCs. By the end of October 2020, Gavi had successfully raised these funds from participating countries (including Italy, the United Kingdom, Canada, and Norway) and the private sector. Yet as 2020 drew to a close, the COVAX AMC still needed nearly $5 billion, and more than $2 billion was still required for country readiness and late-stage clinical trials.[53]

As demonstrated by COVAX, push and pull mechanisms can work in concert: initial financing agreements reduce the risks of product development, whereas purchase agreements contingent on product approval help ensure a stable market in low-income countries.

## Decreasing R&D Costs: More Flexible IP Protections

The push and pull mechanisms discussed above all involved funding to offset R&D costs, lessening the need for companies to set high drug or vaccine prices to recoup costs, while leaving IP protections intact. But problems remain. Successful COVID-19 vaccines developed in rich countries, outside of COVAX's AMCs or other agreements, could be unaffordable for poorer persons in all other countries. Decreasing IP protections in defined scenarios, such as patent pools, licensing agreements, and open source approaches to R&D, is thus essential to global access.

Patents raise drug prices by providing companies an exclusive right to use, make, or sell their inventions for a defined period of time, blocking competition for the length of the patent period. Without competition, the patent holder can charge high prices even for essential drugs.

Patent pools aim to lower IP barriers to competition and affordable pricing. The Medicines Patent Pool is an existing UN-backed entity that pools patents for HIV, hepatitis C, and tuberculosis medicines. During the COVID-19 pandemic, the pool's scope was expanded to cover COVID-related medical products. Under the pool's model, patent holders voluntarily license patented products to the pool, which then sublicenses them to generic manufacturers. The voluntary licenses are generally restricted geographically to low- and middle-income countries so that the patent holder retains exclusive rights in lucrative markets. Royalties (albeit low) are paid to patent holders upon sale of the resulting products.

In May 2020 WHO and Costa Rica launched the Solidarity Call to Action as a complement to the WHO's ACT Accelerator.[54] The Solidarity Call asks countries to ensure that all COVID-19 publicly funded and donor-funded research outcomes are made affordable, accessible, and available on a global scale through provisions in funding agreements (e.g., nonexclusive voluntary licensing), as well as national legal and policy measures to lower barriers like intellectual property rights. In an open source approach, the Solidarity Call encourages publishing research outcomes with no restrictions, and collaborative efforts in pre-competitive drug discovery. By December 2020 about forty countries had endorsed the Solidarity Call, but notably the United States, China, the United Kingdom, and other countries with high vaccine development capacity had not.[55]

Not surprisingly, the pharmaceutical industry strongly opposed the Solidarity Call.[56] Companies that are investing billions in developing COVID-19 countermeasures could lose their incentive to innovate if they perceive that their intellectual property rights could be jeopardized. Industry has similarly opposed countries' efforts to lay the legal groundwork for issuing compulsory licensing agreements for COVID-19 countermeasures if necessary. Under compulsory licensing, which the 2001 Doha Declaration allows under extraordinary circumstances to protect public health, governments can grant a license to a public agency or generic drug maker to copy a patented medicine without the patent owner's consent.[57] To avoid this, companies have voluntarily entered into licensing agreements to supply COVID-19 countermeasures to low-income countries. For example, AstraZeneca reached an agreement with the Serum Institute of India to supply one billion doses of its COVID-19 vaccine candidate, once approved, to low- and middle-income countries, including India.[58]

The coming together of individual countries and industry stakeholders to overcome IP barriers is important. But as long as these efforts remain disjointed, equitable access to outbreak countermeasures among the world's poorest remains at stake. Global solidarity in efforts like the Medicines Patent Pool and Solidarity Call to Action may be the only true solution to ensuring affordable countermeasures universally.

## Facilitating Product Approval

Even with good coordination and adequate funding, many promising medical countermeasures fail during clinical trials or are delayed due to the product approval process. Under an accelerated timeline, the Ebola vaccine did not receive full regulatory approval until five years after it entered clinical testing. Clinical trials and regulatory approval are both vital to ensure safety and effectiveness, and yet research and regulatory processes could be far more efficient.

### Resolving Clinical Trial Design Conflicts

The challenges of designing and conducting clinical trials for outbreak diseases slows or stops promising products from advancing. Clinical research often can only be conducted during a major outbreak, when there are sufficient numbers of patients to support well-designed trials. In fact, the WHO Ethics Working Group has stated that only by conducting clinical trials in outbreak settings could clinicians be assured that scarce resources were being put to their best use.[59] Developing a clinical trial for implementation during an epidemic is especially complex. Authorities must determine which products are sufficiently promising to be tested during the compressed timeline of an outbreak.[60] In designing the trials, researchers must consider factors such as relevant clinical end points, the study size, the effect of herd immunity, and whether to include vulnerable populations like pregnant women and children. Prior to approval, products typically undergo three phases of clinical testing, a process that can take a decade.

Development of the Ebola vaccine from 2014–2019 yielded several lessons on expediting vaccine development.[61] Researchers were given more flexibility in conducting clinical trials. Regulatory agencies from the United States, Canada, and Europe collaborated closely with each other and with national regulatory authorities of the impacted West African countries, sharing information on vaccine candidates and testing protocols.[62] Regulatory agencies also consulted with researchers on the safety and efficacy thresholds required for vaccine approval.

These lessons have facilitated COVID-19 vaccine development: researchers were authorized to conduct combined phase 1/2 and phase 2/3 trials—simultaneously testing safety and efficacy to cut months off the clinical trial process.[63] Companies like Pfizer were authorized to design trials where multiple vaccine candidates were tested in parallel.[64] Both WHO and the FDA have advised on clinical trial study design, outlining that vaccines must prevent infections or reduce the severity of COVID-19 cases by at least 50 percent to be approved. The FDA's Fast Track designation allows drug sponsors to interact with the FDA review team about clinical trial concerns such as study design, safety data, dosing, and biomarker use. In the FDA's guidance for COVID-19 Fast Track review, the agency emphasized the need for including diverse populations in clinical testing, using sufficiently large populations to detect safety or efficacy issues, and conducting postmarket studies to continue evaluating safety and efficacy even after approval.[65]

The 2014–2016 Ebola epidemic also revealed an R&D pitfall: stakeholders had no clear agreement on what epidemiological and research data to share and how to do it. This slowed experts' understanding of the outbreak and hindered the response.[66] The lack of a sharing platform led to post-outbreak calls for developing better incentives and mechanisms for sharing data. It also incentivized the WHO's ACT Accelerator for sharing COVID-19 data, as discussed previously. But sharing data remains difficult. Intellectual property and ownership claims arise, such as who owns submitted data, and who has the right to access and benefit from its eventual commercialization. Questions arise on patients' privacy and consent—what aspects of patients' personal information should be protected when their data is shared. Researchers bear uncertainty about their rights to publish previously submitted data, and they face potential reputational damage if early research findings are later undermined. Despite these concerns, it remains essential that information on drug and vaccine efficacy, as well as adverse events, are shared quickly and openly to ensure rapid development of safe and effective outbreak countermeasures.

Steps taken before an outbreak occurs can facilitate the rapid development of countermeasures. It is important, for example, to identify promising products during inter-epidemic periods. Identification by WHO of technical specifications for drugs and vaccines for priority pathogens can reduce the time spent evaluating products. And work by CEPI to advance vaccine candidates and platform technologies should make it simpler to identify products for clinical trials.

In addition, using inter-epidemic periods to manage regulatory and administrative tasks can facilitate a more rapid response. For example, developing generic clinical trial designs for likely outbreak scenarios and getting buy-in from stakeholders such as ethics boards and communities will provide affected parties with an advanced starting point for discussions when an outbreak occurs. Similarly, protocols and platforms for sharing outbreak and countermeasure data should be established far in advance of an outbreak, with regulatory guidelines on protecting intellectual property and patients' privacy.

## Reforming Product Registration

Once a product is developed, regulatory approvals are needed prior to marketing a drug or vaccine in a country.[67] Products must be registered with a country's national regulatory agency before they may be sold in the country, ensuring that the products are safe, effective, and meet quality manufacturing standards. Regulatory hurdles can delay the time for products, which are typically developed in higher-income countries, to be distributed in the lower-income countries where they are often needed most.

Products registered in low- and middle-income countries tend to follow a three-step registration process. First, products are registered in the country where they are manufactured. This initial registration often occurs under "stringent regulatory authority," adhering to the International Conference on Harmonisation of Technical Requirements for Registration of Pharmaceuticals for Human Use (ICH). ICH is a collaboration, begun in 1990, between the United States, the European Union, and Japan to harmonize the scientific and technical aspects of drug registration. An increasing number of generic products, however, are first registered by other national regulatory authorities, such as those of India and China.[68]

After initial product registration, the manufacturer can apply to WHO for prequalification, which typically is a prerequisite for international aid agencies, such as Gavi, UNICEF, or the Global Fund, to purchase a product for distribution. For example, WHO prequalification is a prerequisite for COVID-19 vaccine developers participating in COVAX's AMCs.[69] WHO assesses the product's performance, its risk-to-benefit ratio for the intended population, and whether the product is suitable for the proposed use.[70] Lastly, the product is registered with the national regulatory agencies in the low- to middle-income countries where the product will be sold and used. These authorities work to ensure the safety, efficacy, and quality of the products as applied to the health needs of their citizens.

A 2016 study on product registration in sub-Saharan Africa found that the time between a product's first regulatory submission and its approval ranged from four to seven years.[71] This lag—where the drug has been approved by a stringent regulatory authority but is not accessible to vulnerable populations in low-income countries—has led to calls for reform.

Proposed reforms to improve efficiency can improve the clinical trial and product approval processes. Agencies can avoid duplicative review by leveraging stringent regulatory assessments. Instead of repeating steps, such as inspections of manufacturing facilities, subsequent assessments could focus on activities that fill key gaps. Eliminating duplication could shorten registration time. Countries can also standardize registration requirements among regional or global partners. For example, technical registration requirements differ among African countries, but efforts to develop uniform standards are occurring. In 2012, regulatory agencies in Burundi, Kenya, Rwanda, Tanzania, Uganda, and Zanzibar launched the African Medicine Regulatory Harmonisation program, which strives to encourage regional collaboration and harmonization of regulatory standards.[72]

Just as with clinical testing of outbreak countermeasures, costly delays could be avoided if efforts to reform the product registration process are initiated well ahead of an outbreak.

## Safety and Ethical Considerations

Reforms to facilitate the testing and approval of outbreak countermeasures could provide drugs and vaccines to at-risk populations sooner—saving countless lives during future epidemics. In some cases, however, expediting countermeasure development raises safety and ethical considerations that, if ignored, could result in harm to individuals and societies, and destroy trust between authorities, researchers, and communities. Concerns about cutting ethical or scientific corners are especially acute when there is political pressure to bring drugs and vaccines to the market before completion of clinical trials.

The Declaration of Helsinki requires independent ethics review of human participant research. Even in a health emergency, ethical values are vital.[73] At its core, a clinical trial must have sufficient scientific and social value to justify its risks and burdens, and be designed to create quality data to guide regulatory agencies and clinicians. Respect for the participants and community is another core requirement, including participants' rights to informed consent and privacy. Communities should be meaningfully engaged, respecting values, cultures, and traditions, with host countries and local researchers treated as equal partners. Trials should be conducted to ensure that benefits and burdens are distributed equitably. Vulnerable populations should be identified and protected. Once the trial is complete, the community and participants should be informed of the trial results, and have access to successful medical countermeasures.

Even with seemingly straightforward ethics principles, ethically appropriate decisions can be complicated, especially during health emergencies. In some settings, trials might exclude pregnant women and children to avoid health risks. But in other settings, such as when pregnant women are especially vulnerable to a disease like Zika virus, it may be preferable to include them in clinical trials. Early phase 3 clinical trials of COVID-19 vaccines, for example, excluded children, thus creating uncertainty as to the vaccines' safety and effectiveness in this population. The policy implications are huge, as it will take longer to determine whether children could be vaccinated to enable schools to safely open.

During the 2014 West African Ebola outbreak, an ethical debate raged on the use of randomized controlled trials (RCTs)—typically the gold standard for clinical trials—for Ebola vaccine candidates.[74] In most RCTs one group receives an experimental intervention while the other group receives a placebo or the conventional care. Even though RCTs may be the fastest way to generate high-quality data about efficacy and safety, RCTs are not ethical when conventional care means a high probability of death, as with Ebola.[75] Withholding promising interventions under these circumstances also creates distrust and animosity among communities and researchers. For these reasons, a number of leading voices argued against RCTs in the context of the deadly Ebola epidemic.[76] A US National Academies of Sciences committee tasked with reviewing the Ebola vaccine clinical trials acknowledged that uncontrolled trials may be warranted under certain circumstances, such as the unavailability of another treatment as a control and certainty that patients who don't receive an intervention will have a poor prognosis.[77]

As recognized in the National Academies of Sciences report, the safety and ethics considerations behind clinical trials are highly contextual to the condition being studied. Consider vaccine development for COVID-19, a disease with a far lower death rate than Ebola. As the race for the vaccine progressed, many scientists voiced concerns that skipping steps to vaccinate more persons sooner could do more harm than good. In 2017 a dengue vaccine was pulled from the market in the Philippines after the under-studied vaccine was discovered to cause severe cases of dengue.[78]

Similar outcomes could result from COVID-19 vaccines hurried to the markets. In June 2020 China approved the use of an experimental vaccine, manufactured by the company CanSino, for the country's military. Phase 1 and 2 trials of CanSino's vaccine had demonstrated largely mild adverse reactions in some patients, though 9 percent of overall patients had severe side effects that "prevented activity."[79] In August 2020 Russia's Ministry of Health approved a COVID-19 vaccine that had been tested in just seventy-six people by the Gamaleya Research Institute.[80] The vaccine had undergone phase 1 testing on volunteers from Russia's military—whose ability to render informed consent is highly questionable. Dubbed "Sputnik V", scientists around the world denounced the approval as premature and inappropriate, because the vaccine had not yet been proven safe and effective for a large group of people.[81]

In the United States, the FDA by law can approve only those vaccine candidates that have been proven safe and effective in phase 3 trials. Vaccine candidates in phase 3 are tested on tens of thousands of people with diverse health circumstances from across the country; thus phase 3 is critical to determining safety and efficacy in a real-world setting.[82] If the FDA determines that a vaccine is safe and effective, the agency can approve the vaccine through an emergency use authorization prior to the trial's completion. Yet the US regulatory system was put under pressure by the Trump administration and Operation Warp Speed. Many experts worried that the FDA would succumb to pressure to approve a COVID-19 vaccine prior to the presidential election in November 2020.[83] Unlike in Russia, the FDA has an independent advisory committee that reviews approval applications. Still, concerns arose when the FDA issued and later revoked emergency approval for hydroxy-chloroquine to treat COVID-19 patients. The drug, which had been praised by President Trump, was found to be ineffective at treating COVID-19 and to be associated with severely adverse cardiac events.[84] Fortunately the FDA ultimately performed admirably in granting emergency use authorization for COVID-19 vaccines. The agency used its scientific advisory committee, disclosed all data transparently, and granted authorization only after all the processes were completed.

Unproven countermeasures come with enormous safety risks, underscoring the need for fully informed consent for participation in clinical trials. Candidates for COVID-19 countermeasures could cause serious adverse reactions, or even make COVID-19 infections more lethal—inducing thousands of needless hospitalizations and deaths. Aside from these immediate harms, approving unproven countermeasures contributes to distrust of science when those countermeasures are found to be unsafe or ineffective at preventing disease in a population. Vaccine hesitancy has been a major challenge globally, resulting in a resurgence of measles and other childhood diseases.[85] In a poll from August 2020, one-third of Americans, and more than 40 percent of nonwhite Americans, said they would not get a COVID-19 vaccine if it were available.[86] Such high levels of refusal would jeopardize immunity, particularly among populations that suffered a history of medical inequities. A rigorous scientific process for putting new countermeasures on the market is absolutely critical to countering public distrust of science and political leaders.

Rigorous scientific process must go hand in hand with transparency from decision makers at every stage of the R&D process. Transparency helps win public trust and encourages people to comply with public health recommendations. Operation Warp Speed was criticized when scientists involved with the program disclosed that they were excluded from decisions to select the vaccine candidates to receive funding for rapid testing and manufacture.[87] In a letter signed by over 400 experts in infectious diseases, vaccines, and other medical specialties, the group implored FDA commissioner Stephen Hahn to disclose the agency's deliberations on whether to approve a COVID-19 vaccine.[88] Access to this information would enable scientists and health professionals to independently assess and, ideally, promote a safe and effective COVID-19 vaccine to the American people. On a global scale, WHO must be provided full access to robust information on countermeasure approval decisions. With trusted and informed gatekeepers in place from multiple governance realms, the world can maximize the use of safe and effective countermeasures, with a defense against potentially harmful ones.

## Enabling Scientific Innovation

Modern medical tools are essential to combat ongoing threats to global health. Technology offers a way to stock our medical war chest before the next outbreak, whether epidemic or pandemic. Vaccines are among the greatest public health achievements in the modern era. Discovering and deploying vaccines against outbreak diseases would be a sound investment in national and global security. Therapeutic agents such as drugs and biologics would reduce suffering and death worldwide. Improvements in diagnostic devices, surveillance, and data-sharing platforms could enable faster and more efficient detection and response to outbreak pathogens and reduce mortality and morbidity.

Science has the potential for major innovation, which often is our last defense against the catastrophic consequences of pandemic disease. But the financing, law, and ethics must be in place—not just when an outbreak strikes, but more importantly during periods of calm. Lurching from complacency to crisis, and back, will never reduce global vulnerabilities. Collectively, policies and processes that support all the building blocks of research and development can save millions of lives. It is wise to remember that there is an ongoing struggle between pathogens with vast power to mutate and to kill, and science with its capacity to prevent and treat disease. For science to enable humanity to prevail over nature, we need to invest and prepare, building scientific and manufacturing capacity well before the next pandemic strikes.

# In and beyond the Age of COVID-19

## What Does the Future Hold?

**It is one thing to warn leaders** of the dangers of complacency and the inevitability of novel infectious diseases. It is another thing altogether to live through the profound consequences of a world, and a country, deeply unprepared to face a pandemic. COVID-19 changed the world in so many ways.

It is one thing to predict that a future pandemic will take millions of lives, and another to have watched every day as death tolls rose by the thousands, to watch memorial concerts online with names of just the smallest fraction of COVID-19 deaths scrolling on-screen. And we know that for every person whose name we read or heard, so many more also perished. Patients in their final weeks and days could not have family by their side in an era of social distancing. Hospital nurses and doctors were utterly shattered by the workload.

And we know that so many other people died, not because they contracted SARS-CoV-2, but because "elective" yet critical care was postponed, doctor visits canceled, and people afraid to go to hospitals. Still others died in their homes and in shelters, nursing homes, and prisons. They died not only from COVID-19, but also from suicide, drug overdoses, and partner abuse. And the incalculable economic hardships imposed by the pandemic, along with the lockdowns, diminished both quality of life and longevity.

We saw long-standing inequities amplified in this global health crisis. We have long known that the poor and people of color have less access to health care, as well as to underlying determinants of health, including clean air, secure housing, and nutritious food, as well as social protections like sick leave and unemployment insurance. But during the pandemic these inequities manifested in far higher rates of infection and death among the most disadvantaged. The vulnerable suffered most—the elderly, homeless, prisoners, residents of group homes for people with developmental disabilities.[1] From lack of protection for farmworkers living in crowded trailers in upstate New York to outbreaks among migrant workers living in crowded dormitories in Singapore, people already at the very margins of society saw their margins reinforced, with lethal consequences.[2] Tragically, inexcusably, the people society never seemed to care for before never got the resources they so desperately needed.

And the role of racial injustice in American society came to the fore. Blacks, Native Americans, and other minorities suffered up to four times the rates of COVID-19 hospitalizations and deaths. Protests against racial injustice literally exploded onto city streets. The killing of George Floyd by a Minneapolis police officer in May 2020 sparked civil unrest and protests throughout America and in much of the world—a true summer of discontent. These two defining events—health disparities in a pandemic and police brutality—were deeply intertwined.

Some of what we have witnessed was expected—cavernous inequities, rapid global spread in an interconnected world, surges in hospitalization, health systems stretched to their limits. And we have also seen confirmation of the thesis that preparation matters. Hong Kong, Taiwan, and South Korea, having experienced SARS, responded quickly and aggressively to COVID-19, including with mass testing and extensive contact tracing, isolation, and quarantine, and kept their rates of infection and death low. Although each of these nations experienced second COVID-19 surges, overall their people lived relatively normal lives, protected by governments that followed the science.

But much less expected was the failure of political leadership and the breakdown of global solidarity. A product of a nationalistic age, and despite all of the warnings and simulations that made the risks clear, the US led a delayed and bungled response. And globally, when a coordinated international response might have saved countless lives, we instead witnessed an "every nation for itself" scramble for diagnostic tests, personal protective equipment, ventilators, and vaccines, along with insufficient funding to support lower-income countries. Whatever COVID-19's ultimate death toll, the effects on life-threatening poverty and hunger will be similarly devastating. Sadly, WHO found itself caught in the middle of a war of words among hypernationalist leaders, politically distracting the agency when we needed it most.

And even though economic harm was predictable, the level of that harm was not—how quickly we lost jobs in the United States, with unemployment moving in only two months from a fifty-year low to levels not seen since the Great Depression. Similar economic hardship was evident the world over. In India, 140 million lost work during the first month and a half of the national lockdown, and South Africa's unemployment rate reached nearly 40 percent.[3] Countries that could do so poured hundreds of billions, even trillions, of dollars into economic rescue packages, and even that was not enough. Lockdowns caused whole sectors, like travel and hospitality, to shut down almost entirely, with small businesses like restaurants quickly going out of business.

Lockdowns were the hallmark of the pandemic, and had not been seen since the Great Influenza Pandemic of 1918. Along with the economic consequences were the health consequences of staying at home. Domestic violence was on the rise, as people, especially women, subject to abuse were locked in with their abusers.[4] Two-thirds of Americans reported feeling more depressed and anxious, as they suffered economic distress and uncertainty.[5] Alcohol and drug use skyrocketed. So many people felt alone, fearful, lonely.

Even as many governments have displayed their worst instincts—nationalism, underfunding, incompetence, denial, disparaging science—the COVID-19 pandemic also brought out the best in us. Sometimes the best came from national leaders, in countries like New Zealand and Finland, where leaders followed the science, mixing aggressive measures with compassion. In the words of New Zealand's prime minister, Jacinda Ardern, these countries responded "with unity, with fast support, by looking after each other."[6] In the United States, some governors acted recklessly—politicizing masks, refusing to take aggressive measures, and even easing restrictions as cases rose. Yet most gained public trust, working closely with the health and scientific communities.

The scientific community was the greatest bright spot. In earlier chapters (see Chapters 5 and 10) we saw scientific ingenuity, whether in the promises of CRISPR-enabled genetic engineering or in using big data and artificial intelligence to scan millions of molecules for promising therapies. During the pandemic, scientists around the world were hard at work searching for vaccines and therapies, identifying promising therapies, and moving vaccine candidates into human trials only months after the virus's genetic code became available. While many governments hoarded and competed, scientists largely shared data and worked together.

Neighbors looked out for each other. People sheltering in place applauded health workers as they changed shifts, going to and returning from the hospital every day, many with their wards filled with COVID-19 patients. Around the world, health workers put themselves at risk, sometimes sleeping in their garages to protect their families so they could treat others. Tens of thousands of health workers died in almost all countries, their names often going unrecorded.[7] They worked tirelessly and committed to saving the lives of their patients, even as governments failed to keep their end of the social contract by keeping them as safe as possible with personal protective equipment.

Meanwhile, grocery store workers, sanitation workers, drivers delivering packages, and other essential workers kept society functioning and enabled us to meet our basic needs. Many left their loved ones each morning with a prayer that they would come back healthy that night.

## Our Choice: Lurching from Complacency to Panic—or Transformation

We all saw how life can be so hard, without schools, restaurants, travel, and entertainment. But with vaccines, COVID-19's tight grip on our daily reality gradually eased, at least in higher-income countries.

What happens next? What path will the United States and other countries forge? Will we put this nightmare behind us, and go back to life more or less as normal? That choice would suggest that it is acceptable to underinvest in robust health systems and biomedical research. That new habits of personal hygiene will wane. That chronic health inequalities can continue as they did before. That it's acceptable to leave the vulnerable behind. In other words, back to normal means we can leave preparation for the next pandemic to the future. Perhaps we will act surprised all over again when the next biological threat strikes.

It seems unlikely that we will take that path, but it is possible. History teaches that that is exactly what could happen. After the terrorist attacks of September 11, 2001, we believed that everything would be different. And for the sliver of the population that were part of the military, and their families, everything was different. And other segments of society, particularly Muslims, have felt the discriminatory aftermath of September 11 linger to this day.

But for the most part, with trivial exceptions like the routine of removing our shoes in airport security lines, life resumed more or less as normal. We say now, as then, that the world will change after COVID-19, our lives will never be the same. But that is not inevitable.

To take the path of pre-COVID-19 normality would be to court disaster. The next once-in-a-hundred-years pandemic could happen next year, even next week. And all the drivers of novel and emerging infections that I have discussed in this book—megacities and slums, mass travel, human/animal interchange, the climate crisis, fragile states, a weak WHO—remain and, even with some COVID-19-related pauses, accelerate. Bioterrorism and failures of biosecurity are ongoing threats, and antimicrobial resistance expands every year. All the forces of modern society amplify disease threats. What used to be once-in-a-century could occur with regularity, a new normal. Without preparation, we will experience more novel epidemics, more avoidable death and disease, hospitals overrun, more economic and social deprivation.

There is only one path we can responsibly take, and that is transformation. COVID-19 should mark the end of the cycle of complacency and panic, launching a new era of deliberate, systematic, and well-resourced preparation, extending from health systems to One Health, and reaching into our political, social, and economic systems.

We must prepare for all risks. We need to be ready for the next corona, influenza, or Ebola virus. Learning hard lessons from a devastating epidemic disease can prepare use to do better in the future, as we have seen in the responses to COVID-19 among countries that had experienced SARS.

But the next big threat—or simultaneous threats—may well require other, or additional, strategies. The next headline-catching health security threat might come from an outbreak in a conflict zone, or a superbug, or a mosquito, or bioterrorism. Then there will be the threats that might not make the headlines, such as the slow but certain growth in antimicrobial resistance, or a cholera outbreak in a distant part of the world—little threat to most but causing a terrible toll among refugees, perhaps. And for all of these, we must not wait to respond, but take a comprehensive set of actions to prepare, prevent, and mitigate the risk.

## Robust, Equitable, and Universal Public Health Systems

Here is a short list of high-priority actions the United States and the world must take now.

### Universal Health Coverage

A transformation in global health security begins at the core—in robust public health systems. Universal health coverage (UHC) is a must. Health is a human right grounded in the WHO constitution and numerous treaties. Beyond a right, UHC is vital for health security. Through universal access, everyone can come into contact with the health system, improving early diagnosis and surveillance. Novel infections can be detected more rapidly. Infectious individuals can be isolated, and their contacts traced. Health access can also prevent and manage chronic diseases; as we have seen with COVID-19, underlying conditions exacerbate the effects of infectious diseases.

Health systems must provide quality care for all. This requires not only well-equipped health facilities, but also major investments in health workforces to overcome shortages in health personnel. Health workers must be well educated, including on proper antibiotic use—an area where patient education also is critical.

Health systems should be community-oriented, including being staffed by community health workers. Such orientation can help build trust, effectively disseminate critical public health information during an outbreak, improve surveillance, and enable large-scale contact tracing. We have seen how hard it is to control outbreaks when the community lacks trust, such as during the Ebola epidemics in West Africa and the Democratic Republic of Congo. Even in the United States, during the COVID-19 pandemic many people distrusted science and public health agencies.

Strong health systems include effective legal and policy frameworks—to regulate the safety and efficacy of new drugs, for example, and to curtail the importation and sale of fake and substandard medicines, which not only fail to heal the sick but contribute to the spread of antimicrobial resistance.

As we have seen, the COVID-19 pandemic revealed deep health inequities. UHC, therefore, must meet the needs of marginalized populations. No one should avoid seeing a doctor because they are worried that they might not be able to afford it or, like undocumented immigrants, that they may be reported to law enforcement. Health equity is not only a human value in and of itself. Disease detection and response require giving everyone access to high-quality services. If individuals stay away from the health system, they cannot be tested, their contacts cannot be traced, and they will continue to spread infection in the community.

COVID-19 has also taught us that keeping health workers and patients safe is one of the highest priorities. Having ample supplies of personal protective equipment and ensuring rigorous infection control can keep health professionals in the workplace and encourage patients to access care when they are symptomatic.

For a major epidemic, like COVID-19, even all of this is insufficient. Health systems must also have surge capacity, the ability to rapidly scale up services in a health emergency. This requires investing in stockpiles of PPE, essential vaccines and medicines, and medical equipment like ventilators. Plans should be in place to support a surge in health personnel, such as by calling retired health workers back into service or calling on medical and nursing students in their final year of schooling. Investing in local manufacturing capacity can protect against global supply chain disruptions and, by increasing overall global manufacturing capacity, help prevent the global scramble for medical resources, with poorer countries being left behind.

## Core Public Health Capacities

The International Health Regulations (IHR) require all countries to develop core public health capacities, including laboratories, surveillance, and rapid notification and response. Developing laboratory capacities must also include biosafety, from frameworks on risk classification to containment and other safety measures.

Health security extends well beyond health care. Public health services are crucial for disease detection and response, health education, and even the efficient rollout of vaccines. We have seen how contaminated water, poor hygiene, and insects can amplify disease spread. Many people in lower-income countries lack clean water and soap, making it almost impossible for them to practice good hygiene. Poor sanitation fuels waterborne diseases like cholera. Controlling vectors—above all, mosquitoes—is central to health security, and all necessary controls should be pursued, from draining swamps to indoor residual spraying to new biotechnologies. Routine vaccinations protect people from a wide range of infectious diseases. We need to invest in a vaccination infrastructure, ranging from research and innovative technologies to rapid manufacturing.

Food safety, to prevent the spread of foodborne pathogens, ranges from good farming and food-manufacturing processes to testing and protocols for early detection and recall. It includes nutritious food to help prevent non-communicable diseases like diabetes and asthma that may weaken the body's ability to fight infectious diseases. Pollution causes respiratory diseases, which, as COVID-19 teaches, can amplify the harm of infectious diseases. We need to urgently clean the air we breathe.

## Research and Development

COVID-19 highlighted the centrality of research and development. The major scientific achievement of the pandemic was the development of safe and effective vaccines with unprecedented speed. While we cannot prepare a vaccine in advance for every infectious disease—especially for novel viruses like COVID-19—we could do far more to develop the medical technologies to protect us: new antibiotics to slow the spread of resistance, universal flu vaccines, and new technologies and platforms for vaccine discovery. Research for developing vaccines for coronaviruses like SARS and MERS (like Moderna's mRNA-based vaccine candidate; see Chapter 10) provided a crucial head start for developing a COVID-19 vaccine. The transformation in science must now be matched with a transformation in how we expand R&D.

The rapid progress needed for global health security requires scaled-up investments—at the very least, the additional $1 billion per year the Commission on a Global Health Risk Framework for the Future recommended, with more for developing new antibiotics. As COVID-19 reminds us, not being prepared has far greater costs than investing wisely now.

Investments will need to be coupled with smart policies. New antibiotics will need to be conserved. And as a rule, the diagnostics, therapies, and vaccines we need for global health security must be affordable for all, ensured through public funding, advance market commitments, technology transfer, and patent pooling. Governments can offer incentives for R&D where markets may be lacking or limited. And even as scientists develop new medical technologies, policymakers should work with companies to plan how to rapidly scale up manufacturing in the case of a widespread outbreak.

## One Health

One Health, recognizing the integral link between human, animal, and environmental health, will need to be another centerpiece of transformative action. The zoonotic leap of a novel coronavirus spurred a worldwide pandemic. Bird populations carry novel influenzas on migratory flights. Mosquitoes thrive and expand their geographic footprint as the climate warms and becomes wetter.

## Responding to the Climate Crisis and Protecting Biodiversity

Even though reduced economic activity during the COVID-19 pandemic may have paused the rise in greenhouse gas emissions, we emerged with the climate crisis still upon us, expanding the range of vectors, destroying ecosystems, and creating conditions for waterborne infections. Decarbonizing the world's economy requires rapidly scaling up renewable energy and developing technologies for reliable electricity storage. We will need to change other ways of economic life, and even lifestyles—from protecting our forests rather than cutting them down to transitioning to more plant-based diets, along with changes in agricultural policies and food pricing.

Global cooperation, including the Paris Agreement—and well beyond—remain vital, generating global solidarity to solve a crisis that requires collective action.

Preserving biodiversity is necessary not only for its own sake, as part of our global heritage and stewardship, but also for global health security. For this entails preserving habitats, reducing human / animal interchange—a dramatic change for our species, which has been steadily destroying natural habitats. And by slowing, if not ending, the de-speciation of our planet, we will be keeping alive the plants and animals that are a prime source of new antimicrobials and other therapies.

## Understanding and Protecting Animal Health

Factory farms supply us with cheap meat, but they also supply us with antibiotic-resistant bacteria. Farmers seeking higher profits use antibiotics in their animals, which then promote resistance. The inhumane conditions often associated with the cheap-meat industry also can spread disease, as occurred in meatpacking plants during the COVID-19 crisis.[8] We need a new, sustainable, and humane agriculture. This could raise the price of meat, but that would move us toward plant-based diets, which are healthier for people and the planet.

Markets selling live wildlife, with wild animals slaughtered and sold on site, present another danger.[9] Such a market was the source of the first cluster of COVID-19 cases in Wuhan. Selling live wildlife should be banned, and the trade in wildlife curtailed, as China did in February 2020 with respect to nonaquatic wildlife, though with the significant exceptions for trade in fur, medicine, and research.[10] Presently some wildlife trade is banned globally, but much is not. Millions of animals are legally or illegally trafficked each day, and incredibly, the wildlife trade includes one-fifth of the more than 5,000 known vertebrate species.[11]

A ban alone is insufficient. Far more resources are required for enforcement; the illegal trade in wildlife is a multibillion-dollar criminal enterprise.[12] Moreover, sales of domesticated animals for eating require stringent health and safety measures, such as separating live animals and people, as does meat handling more generally, again with strong enforcement.[13]

We will be better prepared to predict and respond to zoonotic diseases, including to develop vaccines and therapies, if we fully understand animal pathogens. We need to invest far more in virus surveillance. Surveillance could help identify and understand animal pathogens, including their movement among species and toward human populations.[14] We can use this information to enhance human disease prevention, as well as to develop vaccines and therapies. Researching animal pathogens must meet biosafety and biosecurity standards to prevent accidental or intentional release of man-made threats (see Chapter 4).

## Equitable Societies

In my earlier book *Global Health Law,* I proposed that the world's vision should be to attain both global health (that is, ever-increasing health outcomes) with justice (that is, equitably sharing health benefits and burdens). In other words, we must strive to achieve good health for everyone, not only in the aggregate, but also distributed fairly across all populations.[15] Likewise, global health security must not be the province only of wealthy nations or privileged populations—only those who can telework, only those who can easily access vaccines and treatments. Security must be for everyone, "health with justice." If any country or population is left out, infections will spread. No one is safe from infectious diseases unless everyone is safe.

In an equitable world, we would transform how we approach health security. We would not accept disparate impacts of AIDS, tuberculosis, malaria, or any disease, on people who are poorer or disadvantaged. We would begin by addressing upstream determinants of health and organize our health systems to offer equal benefit to all. When we discover new vaccines and therapies, they must be affordable and available to people everywhere.[16] We would ensure social safety nets to support the poor and vulnerable, spanning universal paid sick leave, health and hygiene for refugees, and environmental justice. If future epidemics require lockdowns, we would prioritize providing health and economic resources to people with greatest need, like migrants, low-paid workers in essential businesses, and informal laborers who are a day's loss of pay away from hunger.

## Transforming Global Health Governance

The rapid transition of COVID-19 from a local outbreak to a global pandemic reminded us how important it is to have a World Health Organization. But WHO cannot fully meet our expectations unless member states amply fund it, grant it strong powers, and provide political support. Currently WHO is heavily reliant on governments' goodwill, making it easily caught up in political disputes. But the pandemic also presented the opportunity to recreate the global health governance landscape that will keep us safe from the full gamut of diseases and injuries.

Reforms must start with providing WHO with the funds commensurate with its global mandate. As discussed in Chapter 7, member states should significantly increase WHO funding, also giving the agency flexibility to allocate funding toward the most pressing global health issues. With a far larger budget, WHO would be empowered to assist low- and middle-income countries in meeting IHR obligations, increasing their capacity to detect, report, and respond to novel infections. With new funding and powers, WHO could help every country to rapidly respond to health threats, and every person to access essential care.

Further, we cannot continue to rely on member states' voluntary compliance with global health norms. Long predating COVID-19, states have failed to comply with even legally binding IHR norms, much less WHO recommendations on travel, trade, and quarantine. Most states have not built core health system capacities as required by the IHR. Strong enforcement mechanisms must be in place so that WHO's director-general can ensure that member states are prepared to detect and respond to emerging threats. The director-general could publicly "call out" offending member states. To ensure transparency, civil society could provide "shadow reports" on state adherence to their obligations. WHO could also withdraw voting rights from member states that chronically defy legal norms.

Even bolder, WHO could develop an inspection system to ensure IHR compliance, much in the way that nuclear treaties are enforced. If WHO or an independent inspectorate were empowered to enter a sovereign territory, it could independently verify official reports. Notably, WHO was unable to independently verify China's reporting during the early days of the COVID-19 pandemic. WHO tried to send a team to Wuhan, but China denied permission until January 2021, a whole year after the initial outbreak.

Enhanced WHO funding and robust norms could be beneficial in other ways. The agency, for example, could negotiate urgently needed agreements on issues like antimicrobial resistance, and hold countries accountable for nontherapeutic use of antibiotics in animals. WHO could set global norms for dual-use research of concern, ensuring that biological research adheres to high biosafety and biosecurity standards.

WHO also needs to better coordinate with allied agencies, like the World Organisation for Animal Health. Acting as a global health leader, WHO must be able to harness the power and expertise of its diverse global health partners, uniting them in the mission of promoting health security.

Meanwhile, we should look to new approaches to strengthen global governance for health, such as by enhancing the right to health accountability through a new treaty and funding mechanism, as I have detailed elsewhere.[17]

## Remaking Society and Preparing for the Next Pandemic

One day the COVID-19 pandemic will come under control globally, even though SARS-CoV-2 will likely linger in pockets, often as an endemic disease. When that day happens, will the world go back to business as usual, or will we fundamentally change the way we live and our world for the better?

*Healthier and more resilient cities.* COVID-19 is a driving force for reshaping cities for the long term. More than half of the world's population currently lives in urban areas; this is projected to increase to two-thirds by 2050.[18] Densely crowded cities are proven hotspots for contagions like SARS-CoV-2, where the virus easily spreads in densely packed apartment buildings, packed subways and buses, and even on crowded city sidewalks. With constant human-to-human contact, cities amplify pandemic risks. During an outbreak, densely populated places impede our physical distancing, rendering it nearly impossible to maintain safe distancing practices without causing major social and economic disruptions.

COVID-19 forced unprecedented changes in major metropolitan areas. For the first time in its 115 history, New York City shut down its subway system every night for disinfection.[19] Essential workers had to find other ways to get to their jobs. Homeless persons were asked to leave subway cars. This displacement, along with unprecedented unemployment, led to further crowding of homeless shelters. In the future, more green spaces, walking paths, and bike lanes would facilitate safer recreation and travel.

These simple policies would have multiple benefits beyond disease prevention and control. They would make cities cleaner and less polluted, promote emotional well-being, and facilitate healthier behaviors such as physical activity. The post-COVID-19 city could re-emerge as more resilient to threats, healthier both physically and mentally, and more sustainable for the future.

*The future of consumerism.* COVID-19 has also challenged the ways we typically access the things we want and need, from clothing and household items, to food, and even health care. With retail stores shuttered, consumers turned to e-commerce, increasing online purchases by 75 percent.[20] Online grocery shopping has gone mainstream.[21] Restaurants shifted to delivery or take-out. Even health care is often delivered remotely, with 76 percent of US hospitals connecting patients via video, audio, and other telehealth technologies.[22] Now that businesses have altered their practices, it's unlikely they will return to pre-COVID-19 modes of operation.

*Schools and workplaces.* Some of the most drastic—and likely lasting—changes brought by the COVID-19 pandemic are to the settings in which we learn and work. From preschool to universities, education has gone virtual, with teachers delivering lectures via online platforms, and assignments and exams administered remotely. Similarly, where possible, workplaces have shifted to promoting telework. These remote learning and working practices could change the post-COVID-19 world. But we need to better understand whether they improve, or detract from, quality productive learning and working, and the social costs, such as loneliness and isolation. Remote learning and working can also be unfair without equal access to the internet and the technological devices needed to succeed.

*Human and social behaviors.* In the COVID-19 world, once-common behaviors (such as shaking hands, hugging, large gatherings) have nearly vanished, and new habits (e.g., copious hand hygiene, cough etiquette, mask wearing) have emerged. Will they—should they—persist in a post-COVID-19 world? Sanitary behaviors would reduce transmission of a large range of common respiratory diseases like colds and flu. But they would also change human intimacy: limiting our ability to see facial expressions, touch, socialize.

*Travel.* COVID-19 put a rapid halt to travel and tourism, as if the pandemic hit a "reset" button to halt or reverse globalization. In 2018, 1.4 billion passengers traveled to another country, a 56-fold increase from 1950.[23] As air travel has become safer and more affordable, travel and tourism have become social and economic staples. While air travel enriches lives in many ways, it is also a major driver of disease transmission and climate change. Can travel be made safer and more environmentally friendly? Will the public learn to be more content in place, or will the relentless increases in travel continue?

*A stronger safety net and more-equitable societies.* COVID-19 made glaringly obvious what we have already known: The United States and much of the world have deep inequities, with cavernous gaps in the social safety net. Poorer Americans and people of color experienced far more hospitalization and death than others, a pattern also seen in places ranging from Singapore and India to the United Kingdom. COVID-19 creates the opportunity to address structural factors underlying health inequalities, including vastly unequal wealth and political power. Creating a more equitable society would be a fitting legacy to all the vulnerable people who suffered and died from COVID-19.

*A new politics for global health security.* A bold global health security agenda requires transformation in society, economics, and politics. The global cooperation envisioned in this book, from an empowered WHO to new modes of global governance for health, is the polar opposite of the nationalist populism that has taken hold in much of the world. Nationalist leaders who put their country (though not everyone within their country) first, with little concern for the global common good, are not likely to cede authority to, or devote increased funding to, WHO. And nationalist leaders frequently ignore science and undercut experts.

More than any single law or regulation, investment or intervention, national policy or global strategy, global health security requires a new politics. Nationalistic populism must give way to a concern for the common good—for all people within a country, and for people around the world. The new politics will depend not on division and global competition, but instead on national and international unity and inclusion.

For global health security is a common venture. The health of each of us depends on the health of all of us, with threats like climate change, antimicrobial resistance, and zoonotic diseases knowing no borders and demanding collective action.

The choice is ours. If we choose leaders who abide by science and advocate for the common good, we will have a political landscape conducive to global health security. And if we use the catastrophe of COVID-19, knowing it was preventable, to break the cycle of panic and complacency, we will find that solutions exist to create a healthier, safer future for us all. We can, together, achieve global health security, with justice.

# Appendix: Tabletop Exercises to Prepare for the Impact

Preparing for a health emergency requires long-term planning. Investments, institutional capacity-building, innovative thinking and policies, sound legal frameworks—all are needed if we are to achieve genuine, if unavoidably imperfect, global health security. An effective response also requires that the individuals who are responding to a health emergency are able to put all these preparations to good use. Will policymakers, public health authorities, frontline health workers, and others involved in an outbreak response be able to effectively contain an outbreak of a novel or emerging infection and protect their—and the world's—population when an outbreak occurs? Along with the planning, investments, and well-developed policies and frameworks, the best way to ensure that they can quickly bring an outbreak under control is to simulate a crisis—to practice, practice, practice.

WHO recommends that countries undergo simulations to test and validate their IHR capacities.[1] WHO has identified several ways to simulate future health emergencies: drills designed to test responders' abilities to carry out particular interventions; functional exercises, to test multiple parts of a response plan; full-scale exercises, which simulate the real event as closely as possible, including mobilization of emergency personnel and equipment; and tabletop exercises, which entail guided discussions of a hypothetical scenario in a low-stress environment.[2]

Here, we focus on tabletop exercises to aid responders in synthesizing how various elements of a health emergency could interact as a health event unfolds and is ultimately resolved. By using tabletop exercises, key actors will gain a deeper understanding of the most pressing health threats. They will learn about the twists and turns requiring advance preparation. They will understand the art of global health diplomacy and working as a team. With these benefits in mind, I conclude this book with three tabletop exercises for you—whether you are a policymaker, first responder, or someone else who might be involved in an outbreak response, or a student or interested reader. These can help you to practice critical skills, assess how well you grasp key concepts in global health security, and gain a greater understanding of the decisions, competing interests, and other considerations faced by policymakers and others responding to health emergencies.

Tabletop exercises begin with a scenario, and proceed with the gradual unfolding of events, as they might occur in real time. At various points along the way, participants discuss—and actors reflect upon—reasons the situation might have evolved as it has, what actions or capacities might have led to a different result, what actions they (or the relevant actors in a real-life situation) might undertake at that that point and why. Following each exercise comes a debriefing (sometimes called a hot wash), where participants reflect on the scenario's methods and outcomes, and, going forward, on what is needed to create a better outcome.

Following are three tabletop exercises for readers, which you can either work through individually or as part of a team. The first is novel influenza. Even a century after the Spanish influenza, perhaps no global health threat is as terrifying as a highly transmissible, lethal strain of influenza. The second exercise involves bioterrorism. With rapidly advancing genetic technologies and their accessibility, the potential toll of malevolent uses of these technologies only grows. The third exercise involves a scenario around a major waterborne disease, cholera. This is a disease of special concern, not solely for its potential for rapid global spread and millions of deaths, but because it is so easily preventable with basic investments in clean water and sanitation. And cholera brings into sharp relief the inequitable impact of failures in global health security. As I have emphasized throughout this book, we are all at risk—self-interest in the narrowest sense demands action. Yet people who are poor and marginalized face the greatest threats to their health, an unconscionable reality that should also motivate us to act.

## Global Pandemic Influenza Tabletop Exercise

A century ago, the 1918 Spanish influenza devastated the world, claiming 50 million lives from a global population much smaller than today's. Although we now have scientific capabilities far beyond those that existed in the early twentieth century, the emergence of a novel highly pathogenic flu virus today could again ravage the globe.[3]

The risk of a future pandemic is made all the more real given that, on average, every thirty to forty years a major change occurs in the influenza virus as a result of antigenic drift (small cumulative changes) or antigenic shift (a major abrupt change).[4] Each alteration can bring a more virulent—and more dangerous—strain. Because significant genetic change would mean that the virus would be entirely new to humans, no one would have natural immunity. Current vaccines would be ineffective. Further complicating any efforts to get the new virus under control, typical manufacturing times for influenza vaccines stand at more than six months.[5] Further, characteristics of the flu make containing the virus difficult: it spreads by way of respiratory secretions from an infected person; it can be transmitted a day or more before the onset of symptoms and five to seven days after symptoms manifest, with children transmitting the virus for longer than seven days. The onset of symptoms occurs one to four days after infection; and the disease typically lasts five to seven days.[6]

The confluence of complex factors calls for a closer examination of the systems in place to respond to the emergence a novel highly pathogenic flu virus. The scenario below will carefully walk you through events as they could unfold. At each stage, readers will assume a role and be asked to make a series of decisions that carry international consequences. These decisions will require consideration of a particular country's capacity, information available, implications, and the rights and obligations of states toward one another under international law, as well as ethics.

### Scenario Phase I

Sporadic outbreaks of a strain of influenza A(H5N1) have decimated bird flocks in Thailand and neighboring countries in Southeast Asia since 2004. In addition to killing off large numbers of birds, health authorities have reported 25 human cases, with 17 proving fatal. Another highly pathogenic strain, A(H7N9), is also a suspected culprit in the deaths of the birds; samples from Bangkok's poultry market have been sent to WHO collaborating laboratories for testing.

You are the director of Thailand's Ministry of Health. Thailand is in the midst of its annual flu season, and sporadic reports of flu arise consistent with the season. Yet several news outlets are suggesting that some cases are not ordinary flu, but instead are a mysterious respiratory illness. In response, you ask health professionals to report any unusual cases. The head of Thailand's infectious disease department presents the following case reports (see Figure App1):

- Day 1: Malee and Kasem are two poultry farmers who presented at a clinic in a rural village. Both farmers had inflamed eyes and upper respiratory symptoms. Their doctor treated the eye inflammation, diagnosed a mild viral illness, and discharged them.
- Day 5: Amarin is a 48-year-old farmer from the same village who died of pneumonia. More than half of his flock of chickens and ducks had died the previous week.
- Day 8: Malee returns to the clinic with a high-grade fever and pneumonia. Doctors suspect that the pneumonia is secondary to influenza. Malee is hospitalized, started on a course of antibiotics, and then discharged on Day 12.
- Day 10: Anong is a nurse who had treated Malee. The nurse presents with acute respiratory distress and is placed on a ventilator. The nurse has a small flock of chickens and a few pigs in her backyard.
- Day 11: Chakrii, a teacher from the same village, presented to the clinic with upper respiratory symptoms. Chakrii helped care for Amarin.
- Day 14: Chakrii's wife, Prida, develops severe pneumonia and dies four days later. There is no evidence that Prida was in contact with poultry.

It is now Day 19. In light of these reports, you must make critical decisions that could have major implications for the health of the Thai population, the nation's economy, and Thailand's rights and obligations under international law. As minister of health you will need to consider the following questions:

- Is this outbreak a potential Public Health Emergency of International Concern (PHEIC) under the WHO's International Health Regulations (IHR)?

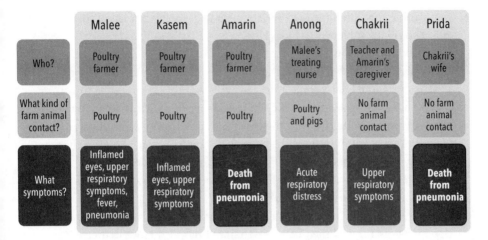

|  | Malee | Kasem | Amarin | Anong | Chakrii | Prida |
|---|---|---|---|---|---|---|
| Who? | Poultry farmer | Poultry farmer | Poultry farmer | Malee's treating nurse | Teacher and Amarin's caregiver | Chakrii's wife |
| What kind of farm animal contact? | Poultry | Poultry | Poultry | Poultry and pigs | No farm animal contact | No farm animal contact |
| What symptoms? | Inflamed eyes, upper respiratory symptoms, fever, pneumonia | Inflamed eyes, upper respiratory symptoms | **Death from pneumonia** | Acute respiratory distress | Upper respiratory symptoms | **Death from pneumonia** |

**Figure App1**  Villagers Who Have Become Ill. © Lawrence O. Gostin.

- To decide this, you will need to take account of the IHR Annex II. See Figure 7.1.
- To whom should you report? And when?

- What steps should you take?

  - What further information do you need to make your decision?
  - Should you request help? If so, from whom? And what kind of help?
  - What preparations will need to be made? For example, for a surge in demand for health care?

- Who should be alerted?

  - How broadly should the alert be disseminated? To health care workers? To your entire population?
  - What consequences flow from dissemination of information or warnings?

- What are Thailand's legal obligations under international law?

*Convene a group of cabinet members and other decision makers to discuss all the ramifications. Come to an informed decision.*

## Scenario Phase II

It is now Day 41, and you are the director-general of WHO. Thailand has notified WHO of a possible PHEIC, and WHO has published a statement confirming that Thailand is experiencing a widespread human outbreak of a novel strain of influenza A(H7N1).

The outbreak, thus far, is localized to Thailand, but the situation is dire and worsening. So far, Thai authorities have reported 1,027 cases, with 55 deaths. As reports of people infected with A(H7N1) continue to roll in, WHO has determined that although initial reports were from rural villages, cases are now coming in from the capital, Bangkok—an ominous sign.

Preliminary laboratory results raise still more concern, showing that the strain possesses characteristics of two influenza viruses, A(H7N9) and A(H1N1). The new strain is highly virulent and easily transmissible among humans. No vaccine is yet available.

WHO and Thailand have urgently requested public health assistance and donations of antiviral medications. Thailand has also requested emergency assistance from the World Bank's Pandemic Emergency Financing Facility Cash Window (PEF). However, the PEF is cash strapped, having only recently been established; it only has $25 million available. The World Bank will defer to WHO regarding eligibility and funding requests.

As the WHO director-general, you must decide:

- Should you convene an Emergency Committee under the IHR to advise whether this a PHEIC? If the Emergency Committee recommends declaring a PHEIC, should you do so? If it does not, should you follow its advice or declare a PHEIC nonetheless? Why or why not? What are the possible immediate and long-term consequences—for health, for travel, for trade? What are the human rights implications?
- Should Thailand's PEF request be granted? To what interventions would the money be directed?
- What national and international public health measures should be implemented?
- What requests should be made of other countries?
- What steps should be taken?

  - Should WHO support isolation and quarantine in Thailand?
  - Should WHO support infection control procedures in Thailand?
  - Should WHO put in place enhanced surveillance measures? In Thailand? In other countries?
  - Should WHO recommend border screening, such as fever monitoring?
  - Should WHO recommend international travel or trade restrictions?

As you make these decisions, you must keep in mind the scarce supply of antivirals, intellectual property restrictions, nationalization of production, and obligations of Thailand and other nations under international law. Bear in mind the powers granted to the director-general under the IHR.

*Convene an appropriate team from WHO headquarters, regional and country offices, and other relevant parties and discuss all the public health, economic, and human rights ramifications. Come to an informed decision.*

## Scenario Phase III

You are the WHO director-general.

Recognizing the importance of moving the world toward an effective vaccine, Thailand has shared samples of the influenza strain with WHO collaborating laboratories under the Pandemic Influenza Preparedness (PIP) Framework. As a result, multiple vaccine manufacturers have received virus samples from WHO under a Standard Material Transfer Agreement that reserves 10 percent of any of the vaccines that they produce for WHO to purchase at reasonable prices and use as WHO sees fit.

As promising work on the vaccine begins, the novel influenza, however, continues to spread. On Day 52, health authorities in Vietnam confirm a severe outbreak of influenza. Foreseeing further spread of the disease to wealthier countries, Thai and Vietnamese officials have lost confidence that they will receive ample supplies of a lifesaving vaccine when it becomes available in four to six months, despite the SMTAs. They worry that political pressures in high-income countries may override legal agreements or ethical considerations of equity.

As Thailand and Vietnam respond to the rise in cases, international interest in the virus has catalyzed research. On Day 53 an explosive revelation arrives in the form of an article in the CDC's journal *Emerging Infectious Diseases.* The article provides the first detailed genetic analysis of the H7N1 virus. The analysis suggests that the virus originated in Vietnam, not Thailand as had been originally reported. The response to the article is equally stunning: Seeking to claim sovereign rights over the virus, and, as a result, claim the right to priority access to any future vaccine, Vietnam invokes the Convention on Biological Diversity on Day 54. At the same time, fearing that it may lose its priority status over vaccines to Vietnam, Thailand makes a similar claim, the *Emerging Infectious Diseases* article notwithstanding. Now there are two nations claiming sovereignty or ownership of a novel virus.

You are the WHO director-general. You must decide:

- What should be done if Thailand and Vietnam follow through on their threats to withhold virus samples?
- What guarantees should you ask other countries, including the United States and other high-income countries, to make regarding access to their future vaccine supplies?
- What further contributions do you think are fair to ask of the private sector?

As you are thinking through these decisions, consider:

- What leverage does each country have?
- What are the benefits or harms from cooperation? What kind of cooperation? How do the benefits and harms compare to those from noncooperation?
- What ethical duties do states have to one another? To their own residents?
- Are there creative alternatives that could satisfy each country's political and health needs?

*Convene an appropriate team from WHO headquarters, regional and country offices, and other relevant parties and discuss all the public health, economic, and international ramifications. Come to an informed decision.*

### Scenario Phase IV

You are the WHO director-general.

Confirmed cases of H7N1 have now emerged in every WHO region. The number of confirmed cases globally has skyrocketed to 20,200. That number, however, is likely a substantial underestimate because countries are confirming only a small percentage of possible cases. Despite the seemingly uncontrollable spread, the case fatality rate remains stable at 2 percent.

An international crisis over travel and trade restrictions emerges. Because of the widespread transmission, WHO does not believe that travel or trade restrictions will significantly alter the spread of the virus. Instead, WHO recommends that individuals with influenza symptoms postpone their travel until their symptoms are gone.

But governments are not heeding WHO recommendations. Instead, many countries are taking measures into their own hands to slow the spread of the virus, signaling to their populations that the situation is under control. Most notably, the United States, Canada, and Vietnam have all begun screening all incoming travelers for influenza. Travelers who have been exposed to possibly infected animals or humans are quarantined. Those who test positive for influenza virus are isolated. Thailand has also ceased importing foreign poultry. Some countries have begun blocking all airline service from highly infected countries; many governments will not issue visas to travelers from Thailand or Vietnam.

In the United States, widespread fear and chaos are emerging. Hospital emergency departments report large increases in patients. Most of the uptick they attribute to "worried well" patients, who do not have the virulent flu but divert resources from true emergency cases. State governors are considering taking actions such as closing schools, canceling sporting events, and restricting public transportation. They are also planning for possible mass quarantines.

As the WHO director-general, you are concerned about the measures states are taking in response to the influenza A(H7N1) pandemic. You must decide what steps WHO should take. In doing so, you should consider these questions:

- What steps do the IHR allow?
- Which, if any, control measures should WHO discourage?

  - Are there any control measures that are supported (or discredited) scientifically?
  - Do they unduly restrict trade or travel?
  - Do they infringe on human rights?

- If WHO chooses to discourage any measure, how should it do so?
- What recourse does WHO have if governments disregard its advice?

*Convene an appropriate team from WHO headquarters, regional and country offices, and other relevant parties and discuss all the public health, economic, and international ramifications. Come to an informed decision.*

## Scenario Hot Wash (Debriefing)

Take a while to reflect on what happened. What went well? What should have been done differently? And what changes are needed to improve future responses?

In answering these questions, consider:

- The role and effectiveness of international frameworks like the IHR and PIP Framework at mitigating the spread of disease, as well as the personal, social, and economic harms of a novel influenza epidemic / pandemic.
- Whether stronger national core public health capacities could mitigate the spread and harms of an influenza outbreak, and the role and effectiveness of the IHR, the Joint External Evaluation, and the Global Health Security Agenda.
- The levels of investment countries are making in research and development in diseases with outbreak potential and in new antibiotics and antivirals.
- The challenges for health systems in many countries to deliver routine health services to their whole populations and their capacity for a surge response during a severe outbreak.
- The added difficulties of responding to the growing threat of health emergencies in countries experiencing complex humanitarian crises, including violence, political instability, and public distrust.
- The role high-income countries, like the United States, can play in ensuring both national and global health security.
- The roles and responsibilities of various stakeholders, including WHO, other UN agencies, governments, the media, the private sector, and the public.

In thinking through the vast implications of a novel influenza pandemic, what can we learn from this simulated exercise? Should all key actors go through similar exercises? How can nations and international organizations better prepare for the next pandemic? What will it take in terms of planning, capacities, and resources? The task seems overwhelming at times. But the alternative to preparedness could be countless lives lost, human suffering, and economic devastation. The stakes are enormously high.

### Bioterrorism Tabletop Exercise

Captain Blaze Spiker is a reserve officer in the Medical Services Corps basic branch located just outside Vacaville, California. In late 2014 Spiker was deployed to Liberia as part of containment and relief operations in response to the West African Ebola crisis. Following his deployment, Spiker returned to the United States and enrolled as a graduate student in molecular biology at the University of Arizona (UA). While at UA, Spiker was influenced by the ideas of a renowned evolutionary ecologist, Professor James Dasher. At the 115th Annual Meeting of the Arizona Academy of Science in 2015, Dr. Dasher asserted that Earth would not survive unless its population was reduced by 90 percent. Following the conference, Spiker became obsessed with the notion of Earth becoming overpopulated and was convinced the population growth rate would eventually cause an environmental catastrophe.

In June 2015 Spiker graduated from UA and became a part-time research associate at the laboratory of the California National Research Center for Zoonotic Disease (CaNRCZD) at the University of California, San Francisco. Having secured a grant from NIH and the Department of Defense, the lab discovered what may be a novel strain of Ebola that, under laboratory conditions, exhibits a shorter incubation period and a faster replication rate, leading to higher viral loads. Because of his background and apparent dedication, Spiker secures greater access at CaNRCZD to the novel Ebola strain, charged with cataloging the total quantity of virus produced.

To help make ends meet, Spiker accepts another part-time job as a technician, working the graveyard shift, at LifeBlood's Donor Testing-Quality Control Laboratory in Oakland, California. The laboratory provides blood to patients who require blood transfusions, often due to traumatic injuries and burns, cancer, blood diseases, and surgery. LifeBlood supplies hospitals across California with blood in emergency situations.

Spiker circumvents protocols from CaNRCZD and steals a 1-milliliter glass ampule containing the highly concentrated Ebola virus, covering his tracks to appear as if the ampule never existed. His goal is to develop a large number of Ebola virus vials and to wage a bioterror attack to decrease the world population. To this end, he runs a makeshift laboratory from his San Francisco apartment. Spiker takes from LifeBlood the supplies he needs to store and replicate Ebola virus. He manufactures more than ten ampules of Ebola virus and infects stolen blood packs from LifeBlood before sending them off for processing and shipment. Spiker wears personal protective equipment (PPE) while handling the ampules of Ebola virus, but not while handling the blood packs, which sometimes leak blood on him while he is injecting them with Ebola virus. LifeBlood begins shipping infected blood packs to California hospitals for transfusions.

At each of the below stages of the scenario, you will be assigned a role and asked to make decisions that will contribute to the response to this bioterror attack. You will need to consider national and global interests and values, the information available to you, competing considerations, potential implications, and international obligations and responsibilities.

## Scenario Phase I: An Outbreak Linked to Blood Transfusions

Day 1: Nora Jefferson, a 28-year-old social worker, suffers substantial blood loss while receiving an emergency pacemaker implant at San Francisco Medical Center (SFMC). Doctors transfuse a substantial amount of blood from a new shipment from LifeBlood during her surgery.

Day 3: Jacob Jones, a 52-year old teacher from Oakland with advanced liver disease, suffers severe, post-transfusion liver failure. Among other things, his skin is turning yellow, his stool is pale, and his bilirubin levels continue to rise. Earlier in the day he had received emergency blood transfusion therapy at Bay Area Hospital (BAH) after presenting to the emergency department in critical condition. The transfused blood came from a new shipment from LifeBlood.

Day 5: The director of blood banking and transfusion at BAH receives a suspicious phone call from someone claiming to be speaking on behalf of LifeBlood's chief medical officer. The caller asks whether the recent shipment was delivered on time, and if any patients had received the blood through a transfusion. The director considers this strange behavior, which also implicates the HIPAA privacy rule. She sends an email to LifeBlood's chief medical officer, asking why she had a low-level technician call to inquire about a recent shipment. Unbeknownst to the director, the chief medical officer is away from work for the next three days.

By 10:00 pm, eleven SFMC patients, including Nora Jefferson, begin to exhibit severe flu-like symptoms. Medical staff suspect illness linked to blood transfusions due to the common trend of transfusion recipients falling ill. SFMC begins testing for pathogens but does not suspect Ebola virus and takes no extra precautions in handling cases or samples. The California Office of Communicable Disease Epidemiology is notified of a possible viral outbreak.

Day 6: Jacob Jones's symptoms continue to worsen. Doctors do not suspect Ebola virus disease (EVD), but they become suspicious when Jones develops a fever of 103°F and severe gastrointestinal discomfort before dying at BAH. The hospital performs an autopsy.

You are the governor of California. You receive the report of the severe flu-like outbreak at two hospitals in California, including the suspicious death at BAH.

- What measures do you take to identify and contain the potential flu-like outbreak?
  - Enhanced surveillance?
  - Isolation and quarantine?
  - Contact tracing?
- Is there any reason to believe that the source of infection is the result of a bioterror attack at this point? What more information would you need to make this determination?
- What information, if any, will be released to the public through the media regarding the potential viral outbreak?
- Do you declare a statewide emergency? Why or why not?
- Do you notify national authorities? Which ones? Thinking ahead, what type of federal resources may be necessary to prevent or contain the spread of infectious disease?

### Scenario Phase II: The Outbreak Spreads in North America

Day 7: Spiker develops a headache, sore throat, runny nose, and gastrointestinal discomfort. He tests himself using a stolen rapid antigen test, and his results indicate that he likely contracted EVD. Knowing that his time is limited, Spiker decides to wage another bioterror attack, this time in Toronto, Canada. Spiker uses his credit card to purchase a one-way plane ticket from San Francisco to Toronto and sends the following manifesto to local news organizations, demanding that they air it:

> *My name is Captain Blaze Spiker. By the time you read this, I will likely be dead, bringing the cure to our world. I first found the light in Arizona, listening to a brave man talk about overpopulation and how it is dooming this planet. And so, through blood, I have brought the salvation, and my virus will make everything right. My work in microbiology and my service to our country in infectious diseases led me to realize that I could bring healing to our planet. From the tracks to the sky, San Francisco will see this virus spread <u>everywhere across the globe</u>. Many will perish from this disease, but I had to do this so that some may live. Please forgive me for the pain but know that I HAD TO DO IT!!*

Spiker leaves his apartment with a brown leather fanny pack containing Ebola virus ampules and an anonymous handwritten note: "There is nothing you can do now because the END is here! The Virus is upon your city! I am saving the planet!" Spiker leaves the fanny pack on the metro, arrives at San Francisco International Airport, and departs for Toronto as scheduled. He resolves to become a vector himself, using his own blood and bodily fluids. He boards the Union Pearson Express Train en route to Union Station in downtown Toronto. Spiker emerges from Union Station, making a purchase at the Star Coffee in the train station. He then shops at the Toronto Centre Shopping Mall and dines at the Maple Leaf Cafe. Later that night he checks into a room on the fifth floor of the Kazelton Hotel Toronto. His reservation is for four nights.

Day 8: The San Francisco County sheriff's office and transit police find the fanny pack. It is wet and found to contain broken glass ampules and a blood-stained note. There is no telling how many people may have come into contact with the fanny pack or when the ampules broke or how. Initially, the sheriff's office suspects HIV or an STI and begin testing.

Day 9: Eighteen patients who received blood transfusions at SFMC in the last week are in critical condition. More than twenty health care workers begin manifesting flu-like symptoms. Laboratory tests are returned positive for EVD.

You are the secretary of the US Department of Health and Human Services. You have been notified of the growing number of positive EVD tests among hospital patients and staff in California.

- Do you recommend that a national emergency be declared? Why or why not?
- What type of measures may be necessary to contain the spread of EVD?

  - Closing borders?
  - Issuing travel restrictions?
  - Identifying potentially exposed persons?

- What national or international authorities do you notify? Is there enough information to involve:

  - Ministry of Health Canada?
  - US Departments of State or Homeland Security?
  - WHO or the UN Security Council?

- How should response efforts be coordinated across the US-Canada border?
- Under the IHR, what obligations exist at this stage? Reporting? Surveillance?

## Scenario Phase III: Time to Declare a Global Health Emergency?

Day 11: On the day of Spiker's checkout, a Kazelton Hotel Toronto housekeeper discovers Spiker's deceased body in his fifth-floor suite. The body looks horrible. Spiker is in bed, wrapped in sheets covered in bloody diarrhea. She promptly notifies her manager, who calls the Toronto Police Department (TPD). The housekeeper and manager both disturb the sheets and touch the body to see whether Spiker is alive.

TPD arrive and do a preliminary room search, touching the body (although wearing gloves). TPD searches the room and finds Spiker's passport, wallet (with credit cards that can be used for contact tracing and investigation into his travel), the document containing Spiker's final manifesto, and vials of liquid. TPD initially suspects overdose. TPD calls in the Ontario Coroner's Service (OCS).

OCS arrives on scene. Upon viewing the body and hearing of the victim's state of origin (California), the manifesto, and the vials of liquid, the coroner calls the local Ministry of Health office, which contacts the Ontario public health officer with concerns that this might be linked to the EVD outbreak in California. The public health officer immediately gives the order to place the body in a body bag and cordon the scene. The public health officer also orders witnesses to be quarantined on site.

Day 13: Dozens more people in California and surrounding US states are experiencing flu-like symptoms and testing positive for EVD. Several deaths have been reported. Many cases of EVD have been reported in Canada as well.

You are the WHO director-general. You are concerned about the growing number of EVD cases and now international spread across North America. It is only matter of time before the virus spreads across continents. You are aware that there is a limited supply of an EVD vaccine stockpile with unknown effectiveness for this strain.

- Do you declare a Public Health Emergency of International Concern under the IHR? Why or why not?
- Should WHO support the quarantine of witnesses at the site in Toronto?
- What international public health measures should be recommended and implemented to track and contain the spread of EVD?
- Do you allocate funding toward the response in the United States and Canada? Why or why not?

- How should vaccine allocation decisions be made? Who do you prioritize to receive the vaccination? Should any vaccine be kept in reserve (e.g., for health workers) even if the United States and Canada reach a point of unmet need?

## Hot Wash / Debriefing:

Take some time to reflect on what happened and what lessons can be learned from this exercise. What went well? What mistakes were made? What should have been done differently? How can we better prevent or mitigate the impacts of acts of bioterrorism?

In answering these questions, consider:

- How do the culprit's actions relate to dual-use research of concern (see Chapter 4)?
- What factors enabled the culprit to manufacture and release the Ebola virus?
- What policies and procedures could have prevented him from being able to weaponize and spread Ebola virus?

    - At the institutional level?
    - At the national level?
    - At the international level?

- How can policies to prevent scientific misuse be balanced against interests in advancing science and medicine?
- What errors were made in identifying and handling EVD? How did these errors contribute to additional EVD cases?
- When and how should information be communicated to the public during an investigation of a possible act of bioterrorism? What are the dangers of releasing information too early or too late?
- How did this event implicate the Biological Weapons Convention (BWC) (see Chapter 4)? What shortcomings or gaps in the BWC may have contributed to this event? Would you recommend revising the BWC based on this event? If so, how?
- How well do the IHR, BWC, GHSA, or other international instruments enable or hinder international response to events of bioterrorism? How could they be improved?
- What if this event originated in a country other than the United States? In what ways might the scenario unfold differently?

· What ethical implications were raised throughout the process of responding to the event?

  · Vaccine allocation?
  · Quarantine?
  · Travel restrictions?
  · Anything else?

In reflecting on this biosecurity exercise, think about the plausibility of such an event of bioterrorism. Is it plausible that this could happen in real life? Are nations prepared to counter modern bioterrorism threats? Preventing the weaponization of biological tools and materials is extremely challenging, as demonstrated in this exercise and in Chapter 4. But given the severity and magnitude of the threat, it is a challenge that nations must be prepared to meet.

## Cholera Tabletop Exercise

Cholera is an acute diarrheal disease caused by the bacterium *Vibrio cholerae*. In severe cases, it is a frightful disease, with onset in as few as twelve hours (or as long as five days). Untreated, cholera can lead to death from dehydration within hours.[7]

Cholera originated in the Ganges Delta, a region shared by India and Bangladesh. However, it did not remain there. In 1817 cholera emerged from Southeast Asia in full force, becoming a global pandemic. Fear of cholera grew immensely, catalyzing the first International Sanitary Conference in Paris in 1851. The 1817 pandemic would be the first of seven thus far, the most recent of which originated in Indonesia in 1961. This last pandemic ultimately reached Latin America three decades later, and continues into the present day.[8]

Even in today's modern scientific era, cholera can still be lethal, killing 21,000 to 143,000 people every year, out of 1.3 to 4.0 million cases.[9] These data are probably a vast underestimate of cholera's scope, as numerous cases and deaths go unreported. This is due in part to insufficient surveillance, along with government fears of restricting travel and trade, which deter reporting or lead to misclassifying cases as "acute watery diarrhea."[10]

The risk of cholera is closely linked to an area's water and sanitation systems, with contaminated water and food spreading the disease. This makes areas experiencing humanitarian crises of particular concern. For example, migrants often live in overcrowded camps with poor sanitation and a paucity of potable water. Risk conditions can be exacerbated by natural disasters, such as the Haitian earthquake, which resulted in some 800,000 cases and 10,000 deaths over eight years (see Chapter 2).[11] Yemen, in the midst of intense political violence and famine, had more than 1.3 million cases and 2,500 deaths through 2018, following an earlier wave in 2016–2017.[12]

Oral rehydration solutions can successfully treat most cholera cases. Severe disease requires intravenous fluids, aided by antibiotics to lessen the duration of the diarrhea and the amount of fluid required, though antibiotic resistance is a growing threat.[13] Rapid treatment during outbreaks can keep fatality rates below 1 percent. Effective oral vaccines exist, and may be used during humanitarian crises and outbreaks, and in areas at high risk of cholera. Community mobilization is also vital.[14]

## The Scenario

Armed conflicts between the government of Myanmar and ethnic minorities struggling for independence, autonomy, and self-determination have deepened following the military's genocide against the Rohingya. The genocide gave the military confidence that it could perpetrate attacks with relative impunity, and enhanced concerns among Myanmar's minorities that they had no future in their country.

The fighting has forced thousands of people to flee. Most seek safety in internally displaced persons camps, though many also make their way to Bangladesh, which has received over 1 million Rohingya refugees, with smaller numbers crossing to Thailand. Myanmar refuses to allow international aid agencies into the camps or conflict regions more generally, claiming security concerns; NGOs believe that the authorities' true motivation relates to human rights abuses by the Burmese military. The camps, therefore, are sparse, with only the most rudimentary sanitation facilities and insufficient supplies of clean water. People leaving the camp because of intolerable conditions are reporting severe cases of diarrhea, with ongoing deaths. Some return home despite fears for their safety.

Meanwhile, the WHO director-general has recently declared a PHEIC for an influenza outbreak that began in the Americas, where it remains concentrated, though several dozen countries in other regions have confirmed cases.

At each of the below stages of the scenario, you will be assigned a role and asked to make decisions that will contribute to the course the outbreak takes. You will need to consider national and global interests and values, the

information available to you, competing considerations, potential implications, and international obligations and responsibilities.

## Scenario Phase I

Day 1: Local health authorities in one of the conflict regions report several
dozen cases of acute watery diarrhea to the central government health ministry. The health minister coordinates with local authorities for laboratory
testing.

Day 12: After an extended silence, Myanmar's information minister reports a cholera outbreak, stating that there is evidence the disease has arrived with travelers from Bangladesh. Bangladesh and aid agencies along the
Bangladesh / Myanmar border report no cases of cholera. The following day,
Myanmar's health minister officially notifies WHO of the outbreak.

Day 13: Burmese authorities begin testing travelers entering from Bangladesh for cholera. Many who are tested consider it humiliating.[15]

Day 20: Local health authorities have now reported nearly than 300 suspected cases of cholera, including at least a dozen deaths. The conflict is
making it difficult for government health workers to reach towns where
cholera is being reported.

Day 32: You are the WHO director-general (DG).

1. Should you convene an Emergency Committee under the International
   Health Regulations to provide recommendations on whether to declare
   a PHEIC? Should you follow its recommendation, or are there considerations that might make you more or less inclined to declare a PHEIC?

2. How might the fact of simultaneous events (influenza and cholera)
   influence your decision?

3. There is only $6 million in WHO's Contingency Fund for Emergencies;
   most of the fund's money has been used to fight the influenza pandemic.
   Do you release any funds to Myanmar?

## Scenario Phase II

Day 36: The mix of the conflict and the refugee flow lead the Emergency
Committee to recommend a PHEIC. However, in an unprecedented move,
the WHO director-general declines to make such a declaration, citing the

relative paucity of cases. The DG, however, does support the Emergency Committee's recommendation that Myanmar cease testing Bangladeshi travelers; along with lack of evidence that the cholera outbreak originated in Bangladesh, there is little evidence that the testing is effective.

Seasoned WHO observers believe that the DG's decision was motivated by concern about keeping global attention on the influenza pandemic—which had already killed tens of thousands of people—and WHO's relative powerlessness in the face of the cholera outbreak, given that WHO lacks the capacity to address the political conflict in Myanmar that underlies the cholera outbreak.

The director-general does not release any Contingency Fund resources, noting concerns about unethical restrictions on aid organizations. The DG, however, does implore the international community to provide assistance, including supporting refugees in Bangladesh and Thailand.

Day 40: Several of the world's most renowned infectious disease experts publish an op-ed in the *New York Times* criticizing the director-general's decision. They urge the DG to declare a PHEIC, citing the threat cholera poses to migrants crossing into Bangladesh and Thailand. They also cite the humanitarian crisis that hinders the public health response. Less than a week letter, several major newspapers carry an open letter with more than a hundred infectious disease experts and global health luminaries making the case for a PHEIC.

Day 50: The Bangladeshi prime minister makes a televised address, demanding that Myanmar cease screening travelers from Bangladesh into Myanmar, and warning of "severe consequences." Myanmar's foreign minister and state-run media fire off a heated response.

Day 58: The number of cholera cases has reached 4,000, with an unusually high fatality rate of 5 percent—200 deaths already. The high fatality rate appears to have several causes. The conflict has generated deep distrust of anyone associated with the government, including health workers, and has degraded already weak local infrastructure, including water and sanitation systems. As a result, a cholera vaccination campaign the government initiated has had little success, and many people in need of oral rehydration therapy are staying away from treatment centers. Yet even patients taking antibiotics have perished, indicating possible resistance. The government has continued to restrict access of international aid organizations, as well as local organizations perceived to be sympathetic to the country's ethnic minorities. The CDC has offered assistance, but the Myanmar government has refused entry of US personnel. The only hope seems to come from locally driven community mobilization.

Meanwhile, the global influenza pandemic continues to grow, though at a slower rate than before, with new weekly cases beginning to decline modestly.

You are the WHO director-general. What steps do you take now?

- Do you reverse your decision about a PHEIC for the cholera epidemic?
- What can you do to address the security situation?
- What can you do to address other issues related to the conflict and regional tensions, such as the Myanmar government's refusal to permit external assistance, community distrust for health workers, and the growing tensions between Bangladesh and Myanmar?
- Do you need to call for help from the UN Security Council, including UN Peacekeepers?
- Is there any way, whether in the near term or longer-term, to address the antibiotic resistance that is also impeding the response?

### Scenario Phase III

Day 60: The director-general makes a surprise visit to Myanmar, meeting the minister of health. In a joint press conference, the DG announces plans to reconvene the Emergency Committee.

The DG also announces plans to fly to New York to meet with the UN secretary-general and the president of the Security Council to discuss a possible UN response. When asked about any meetings with Myanmar's leader, the director-general states that despite the gravity of the situation, he has declined to do so because of the government's human rights record. Within several hours, the director-general is on a plane to New York.

Meanwhile, the executive director of WHO's Health Emergencies Programme authorizes the release of $200,000 from the Contingency Fund, with the stipulation that it must be used for training and supplies directly delivered to members of affected communities.

Day 61: The Emergency Committee meets, again recommending a PHEIC. The director-general joins the meeting remotely, and as soon as the meeting ends, holds a press conference in New York to declare that the cholera epidemic in Myanmar is a PHEIC.

Day 64: The director-general attends a special session of the UN Security Council, along with the UN secretary-general. In addressing Security Council members, the DG urges a major surge response to fight the growing cholera outbreak. The director-general also urges world leaders to build on their commitments at the 2016 UN High-Level Meeting to mobilize to fight the antimicrobial resistance crisis, noting its role in the high fatality rate in the current cholera epidemic. The Myanmar ambassador welcomes assistance but insists that no military forces or outside observers will be allowed into the country, claiming that this would disrupt military efforts to counter what he calls "terrorist forces" operating in ethnic minority regions.

Day 65: Russian and Chinese delegations are temporarily absent from the Security Council as part of intensive security cooperation discussions. Intense negotiations are under way among the other thirteen Security Council members, who are also consulting the DG and the UN secretary-general.

The risk of international spread is high and growing, as deaths among the Myanmar population, particularly its marginalized ethnic minorities, continue to grow. You are the US ambassador to the United Nations. How do you respond to the director-general's request for action?

- Do you support a UN peacekeeping force? If so, what should be its mandate? Will they need special training?
- How would you work to build community trust in first responders?
- How should the Security Council respond to the growing tension between Myanmar and Bangladesh?
- How should the Security Council respond to the antimicrobial crisis, including its impact on cholera?

## Scenario Phase IV

Day 66: The Security Council passes a powerful resolution, which:

- Demands that the Myanmar government allow international aid agencies to operate freely and without restrictions.
- Demands an end to military operations by all parties and urges dialogue and the resolution of conditions that have led to decades of conflict.
- Establishes the UN Mission on Cholera Response in Myanmar (UNMCRM), authorized at up to 6,000 troops and police, all to be trained in community policing, the history of the conflicts and grievances of Myanmar's ethnic minorities, the recent genocide of the Rohingya and the world's response, cholera, and the importance of their maintaining the highest sanitary standards. The aim of

UNMCRM is to ensure the safety of health and humanitarian workers operating in areas of ongoing conflict. UNMCRM is established under Article VII of the UN Charter, under which the UN Security Council may authorize the use of force.
- Urges Myanmar's government to fully cooperate with UNMCRM.
- Urges Myanmar to stop screening travelers from Bangladesh and warns that the Security Council remains alert of the issue, with sanctions possible.
- Asks the secretary-general, in cooperation with the director-general, to organize a second High-Level Meeting on Antimicrobial Resistance.
- Urges governments to increase funding for antimicrobial resistance research, and for pharmaceutical and biotech companies and university researchers to prioritize research.

Meanwhile, the UN secretary-general appoints a respected former high-level diplomat as a special envoy for peace in Myanmar, charged with negotiating a permanent ceasefire and, ultimately, peaceful resolution to the fighting.

Day 86: Myanmar screening of travelers from Bangladesh has become more sporadic, but has not ended completely. Tensions between the two countries remain high. Fighting within Myanmar continues. The UN special envoy has found it difficult to make progress, as the government considers all members of the armed movements to be terrorists.

Day 108: Several cases of cholera are reported in Yangon, Myanmar's capital. In the days that follow, other case reports start arriving into the Ministry of Health from areas of the country without large ethnic populations.

Day 118: The total number of cholera cases exceeds 10,000. As small increases in aid trickle in, the fatality rate has decreased only slightly to 4 percent. There are reports of some significant decreases in cholera in communities where Contingency Fund resources have supported community action. Several cases of cholera are reported among Myanmar refugees in Bangladesh.

Day 128: The first 600 members of UNMCRM have arrived. However, their initial impact proves limited at best. Myanmar authorities have formally welcomed in international aid agencies, but visa and travel restrictions, registration requirements, and other obstacles have left most international health and humanitarian workers stuck in Yangon. Intimidation campaigns are limiting their ability to deploy their staff.

The US president is committed to exerting global health and moral leadership, and tasks the secretary of state to work with governments and multilateral institutions to try to make progress on an effective response to the cholera epidemic and humanitarian crisis that continues to grow.

You are the US secretary of state.

- What is most needed?

  - Unfettered access for health and humanitarian workers?
  - An end to the fighting?
  - More funding?
  - Community trust?

- Are there countries that could play a constructive role? What could other countries do?
- Does the spread of cholera outside ethnic minority areas present any special challenges or opportunities?
- Are there longer-term actions that could reduce the risk of future cholera outbreaks in the region?

### Scenario Phase V

Day 156: The US secretary of state announces that unless Myanmar permits health and humanitarian workers full access and removes obstacles, the United States will reimpose sanctions that it had lifted in 2016 following the country's partial democratic transition.[16] The announcement comes at a joint press conference with the ministers of foreign affairs of India and Thailand, who also warn of sanctions. With the spread of cholera into Bangladesh, the Indian government considers the cholera epidemic a threat, and Thailand's government fears that with a continued, though smaller, exodus of refugees from Myanmar to Thailand, cholera could enter its country as well. The European Council warns that it might expand the sanctions the European Union ultimately imposed following the Rohingya genocide several years earlier.

Day 158: Myanmar newspapers report rapidly growing public concern about cholera, now that it is no longer contained in internally displaced persons camps and ethnic minority communities.

Day 162: Several thousand people rally in Yangon calling for peace with Myanmar's ethnic minority communities and for the government to bring the cholera epidemic under control. Security forces break up the protests, arresting numerous protesters.

Day 172: Médecins Sans Frontières reports that some of their staff have been permitted to move into heavily affected communities.

Day 184: There is a slowly growing presence of UNMCRM forces, though they report that their activities have been confined by Myanmar's military. It does appear, however, that the level of fighting between the Myanmar military and ethnic minority communities has been falling over the past month, as has the number of newly displaced persons.

Day 202: There are signs that the spread of cholera is slowing. The fatality rate over the past month has been 2 percent, as more NGOs are able to respond, focusing on improving sanitation in internally displaced persons camps, community mobilization, oral rehydration therapy, and vaccinations.

Meanwhile an effective vaccine has now been developed for the strain of influenza causing the current influenza epidemic, leading to hopes that, along with ongoing infection prevention and control measures and a change in seasons, the epidemic will soon be "well under control."

### Scenario Hot Wash (Debriefing)

Take a moment to reflect on what happened. What worked and what did not? What could have been done differently, or could have happened earlier? How could the world better prepare for cholera outbreaks in conflict zones? How could we prepare for infectious disease outbreaks amid complex humanitarian crises in the future?

In answering these questions, consider:

- How can the world prepare for multiple serious disease outbreaks simultaneously?
- How can the world prepare for infectious disease outbreaks during armed conflicts or other humanitarian crises?
- What are the potential risks and benefits of declaring a PHEIC sooner rather than later?
- What are the potential risks and benefits of seeking a UN response, especially involving the use of armed force or economic sanctions?
- What is the role of "smart" diplomacy in responding to outbreaks in situations of conflict and in fragile states? What would such diplomacy look like?
- How do civil and political rights, economic and cultural rights, and global health security all interact?

- What are the underlying conditions that enable cholera outbreaks to occur and spread, and how can these conditions be mitigated?
- What is the role of antimicrobial resistance in reducing the fatality rate of cholera epidemics, and what needs to be done to strengthen our current supply of effective antimicrobial medicines?
- What potential is there for US leadership to strengthen the response to epidemics?
- How is the population's trust of authorities related to global health security? What might be done to increase that trust?
- What community assets might be brought to bear against epidemics, including when international assistance cannot be relied upon, and how might these assets be fostered and mobilized?

# Notes

## Introduction

1. WHO, "WHO Timeline—COVID-19," April 27, 2020, https://www.who
.int/news-room/detail/27-04-2020-who-timeline—covid-19.
2. Jun Zheng, "SARS-CoV-2: An Emerging Coronavirus That Causes a
Global Threat," *International Journal of Biological Sciences* 16, no. 10 (2020):
1678–1685, https://www.ncbi.nlm.nih.gov/pmc/articles/PMC7098030/
(March 15, 2020).
3. Jun Zheng, "SARS-CoV-2."
4. CDC, "What You Should Know about COVID-19 to Protect Yourself and
Others," Fact Sheet, April 15, 2020, https://www.cdc.gov/coronavirus/2019
-ncov/downloads/2019-ncov-factsheet.pdf.
5. Ewen Callaway, "The Coronavirus Is Mutating—Does It Matter?," *Nature,*
September 8, 2020, https://www.nature.com/articles/d41586-020-02544-6;
Ed Yong, "Why the Coronavirus Has Been So Successful," *The Atlantic,*
March 20, 2020, https://www.theatlantic.com/science/archive/2020/03
/biography-new-coronavirus/608338/.
6. Derrick Bryson Taylor, "How the Coronavirus Pandemic Unfolded: A
Timeline," *New York Times,* May 12, 2020.
7. David Cyranoski, "What China's Coronavirus Response Can Teach the
Rest of the World," *Nature* 579 (2020): 479–480.
8. Gabriel Crossley, "Wuhan Lockdown 'Unprecedented,' Shows Commitment
to Contain Virus: WHO Representative in China," *Reuters,* January 23,
2020.
9. Priyanka Boghani, "A Timeline of China's Response in the First Days of
COVID-19," *PBS,* February 2, 2021.
10. Helen Davidson, "China's Coronavirus Health Code Apps Raise Concerns
over Privacy," *Guardian,* April 1, 2020.
11. Andrew Green, "Li Wenliang," *Lancet,* February 18, 2020, https://www
.thelancet.com/journals/lancet/article/PIIS0140-6736(20)30382-2/fulltext.
12. Vaishnavi Chandrashekhar, "1.3 Billion People. A 21-Day Lockdown. Can
India Curb the Coronavirus?," *Science,* March 31, 2020.

13. UNESCO, "COVID-19 Educational Disruption and Response," https://en
    .unesco.org/covid19/educationresponse.
14. International Monetary Fund, "A Crisis Like No Other, Uncertain Recovery,"
    World Economic Outlook Update, June 2020, https://www.imf.org/en
    /Publications/WEO/Issues/2020/06/24/WEOUpdateJune2020.
15. Fitch Ratings, "Unparalleled Global Recession Underway," April 22, 2020,
    https://www.fitchratings.com/research/sovereigns/unparalleled-global
    -recession-underway-22-04-2020.
16. Nelson D. Schwartz, Ben Casselman, and Ella Koeze, "How Bad Is
    Unemployment? Literally Off the Charts," *New York Times,* May 8, 2020.
17. Maria Abi-Habib, "Billions Slide Down Ladder That Took Decades to
    Climb," *New York Times,* May 1, 2020.
18. Paul Anthem, "Risk of Hunger Pandemic as COVID-19 Set to Almost
    Double Acute Hunger by End of 2020," *World Food Programme Insight,*
    April 16, 2020, https://insight.wfp.org/covid-19-will-almost-double-people
    -in-acute-hunger-by-end-of-2020-59df0c4a8072.
19. WHO, "Shortage of Personal Protective Equipment Endangering Health
    Workers Worldwide," News Release, March 3, 2020, https://www.who.int
    /news-room/detail/03-03-2020-shortage-of-personal-protective-equipment
    -endangering-health-workers-worldwide.
20. The White House, "President Donald J. Trump Is Demanding Account-
    ability from the World Health Organization," April 8, 2020, https://www
    .whitehouse.gov/briefings-statements/president-donald-j-trump-demanding
    -accountability-world-health-organization/.
21. WHO, "Seventy-Third World Health Assembly," May 18–29, 2020,
    https://www.who.int/about/governance/world-health-assembly/seventy
    -third-world-health-assembly.
22. Patrick Wintour and Julian Borger, "Member States Back WHO after
    Renewed Donald Trump Attack," *Guardian,* May 19, 2020.
23. WHO, "Seventy-Third World Health Assembly," May 18–29, 2020,
    https://www.who.int/about/governance/world-health-assembly/seventy
    -third-world-health-assembly.
24. US Department of Health and Human Services, "Trump Administration
    Announces Framework and Leadership for 'Operation Warp Speed,'" May 15,
    2020, https://www.hhs.gov/about/news/2020/05/15/trump-administration
    -announces-framework-and-leadership-for-operation-warp-speed.html.
25. Raya Jalabi, Ryan Woo, and Andrea Shalal, "G20 Leaders Seek to Help
    Poorest Nations in Post-COVID World," Reuters, November 21, 2020,
    https://www.reuters.com/article/uk-g20-saudi/g20-leaders-seek-to-help
    -poorest-nations-in-post-covid-world-idUSKBN2810JD; Geoffrey York,
    "New Vaccine Deals Seek to Overcome 'Vaccine Apartheid' in Developing
    World," *Globe and Mail,* December 18, 2020, https://www.theglobeandmail
    .com/world/article-new-vaccine-deals-seek-to-overcome-vaccine-apartheid
    -in-developing/.

26. Johns Hopkins Center for Global Health Security, "Global Health Security Index," http://www.centerforhealthsecurity.org/our-work/current-projects /global-health-security-index.html.

27. Harvard Global Health Institute, "Global Monitoring of Disease Outbreak Preparedness," http://globalhealth.harvard.edu/monitoring-disease -preparedness.

28. "$2 Billion Required to Develop a Vaccine against the COVID-19 Virus," CEPI, March 14, 2020, https://cepi.net/news_cepi/2-billion-required-to -develop-a-vaccine-against-the-covid-19-virus-2/.

29. John Luke Gallup and Jeffrey D. Sachs, "The Economic Burden of Malaria," *American Journal of Tropical Medicine and Hygiene* 64, no. 1, suppl. (2001): 85–96.

30. Commission on a Global Health Risk Framework for the Future, "The Neglected Dimension of Global Security: A Framework to Counter Infectious Disease Crises," 2016, https://pubmed.ncbi.nlm.nih.gov/27336117/.

## Chapter 1  ·  The Impending Threat

1. Alexandra L. Phelan, Rebecca Katz, and Lawrence O. Gostin, "The Novel Coronavirus Originating in Wuhan, China: Challenges for Global Health Governance," *JAMA* 323, no. 8 (2020): 709–710; World Health Organization (WHO), "Coronavirus Disease (COVID-19) Outbreak," https://www.who .int/emergencies/diseases/novel-coronavirus-2019.

2. Bill Gates, "Shattuck Lecture: Innovation for Pandemics," *New England Journal of Medicine* 378 (2018): 2057–2060.

3. Lawrence O. Gostin and Lindsay F. Wiley, *Public Health Law: Power, Duty, Restraint* (Oakland: University of California Press, 2016), 416.

4. WHO, "Health Emergencies Represent Some of the Greatest Risks to the Global Economy and Security," July 8, 2017, https://www.who.int/dg /speeches/detail/health-emergencies-represent-some-of-the-greatest-risks-to -the-global-economy-and-security.

5. Valentino M. Gantz, Nijole Jasinskiene, Olga Tatarenkova, et al., "Highly Efficient Cas9-Mediated Gene Drive for Population Modification of the Malaria Vector Mosquito Anopheles Stephensi," *PNAS* 112, no. 49 (2015): E6736–E6743.

6. World Health Assembly (WHA), Resolution WHA 66.12, "World Health Assembly Adopts Resolution on Neglected Tropical Diseases," May 27, 2013, https://www.who.int/neglected_diseases/WHA_66_seventh_day _resolution_adopted/en/.

7. WHO, "Emergencies Preparedness, Response: WHO Recommendations on Pandemic (H1N1) 2009 Vaccines," July 13, 2019, https://www.who.int /csr/disease/swineflu/notes/h1n1_vaccine_20090713/en/.

8. Tung Thanh Le, Zacharias Andreadakis, Arun Kumar, et al., "The COVID-19 Vaccine Development Landscape," *Nature Reviews Drug Discovery* 19 (2020): 305–306.

9. CDC, "CDC Global Rapid Response Team," https://www.cdc.gov /globalhealth/healthprotection/errb/global-rrt.htm.

10. UN Department of Economics and Social Affairs, *World Urbanization Prospects* (New York: United Nations, 2014).

11. K. D. Reed, J. K. Meece, J. S. Henkel, and S. K. Shukla, "Birds, Migration and Emerging Zoonoses: West Nile Virus, Lyme Disease, Influenza A and Enteropathogens," *Journal of Clinical Medicine and Research* 1, no. 1 (January 2003): 5–12.

12. CDC, "One Health: Zoonotic Diseases," https://www.cdc.gov/onehealth /basics/zoonotic-diseases.html.

13. J. J. Muyembe-Tamfum, S. Mulangu, Justin Masumu, et al., "Ebola Virus Outbreaks in Africa: Past and Present," *Onderstepoort Journal of Veterinary Research* 79, no. 2 (2012): art. 451.

14. Patrick J. O'Reilly, Michael O'Connor, Anne Harrington, et al., "Foot and Mouth Disease in Ireland: History, Diagnosis, Eradication and Serosurveillance," *European Commission for the Control of Foot and Mouth Disease* (2002): 46–57.

15. Nick Cumming-Bruce, "Number of People Fleeing Conflict Is Highest since World War II, UN Says," *New York Times,* June 16, 2019.

16. Chris Buckley, Raymond Zhong, Denise Grady, and Roni Caryn Rabin, "Coronavirus Fears Intensify, Effectiveness of Quarantines Is Questioned," *New York Times,* January 26, 2020.

17. CDC, "Zika Virus: Statistics and Maps," https://www.cdc.gov/zika /reporting/.

18. CDC, "Swine Influenza A (H1N1) Infection in Two Children: Southern California, March–April 2009," *Morbidity and Mortality Weekly Report* 58, no. 15 (2009): 400–402.

19. Linda Marsa, "Hot Zone: A Warming Planet's Rising Tide of Disaster," *Discover,* February 4, 2011.

20. Rick Gladstone, "U.N. Brought Cholera to Haiti. Now It Is Fumbling Its Effort to Atone," *New York Times,* June 26, 2017.

21. Jasmin Fox-Skelly, "There Are Diseases Hidden in Ice, and They Are Waking Up," BBC, May 4, 2017.

22. WHO, "Anthrax," https://www.who.int/csr/disease/Anthrax/en/.

23. Ian Johnson, "Smallpox Could Return as Siberia's Melting Permafrost Exposes Ancient Graves," *Independent* (UK), August 16, 2016.

24. Enrico Pavignani and Sandro Colombo, *Analysing Disrupted Health Sectors: A Modular Manual* (Geneva: WHO, 2009), http://www.who.int/hac /techguidance/tools/disrupted_sectors/adhsm_en.pdf.

25. Luma Akil and H. Anwar Ahmad, "The Recent Outbreaks and Reemergence of Poliovirus in War and Conflict-Affected Areas," *International Journal of Infectious Diseases* 49 (2016): 40–46.

26. UN Department of Global Communications, "UN Scaling Up COVID-19 Response to Protect Refugees and Migrants," https://www.un.org/en/un

-coronavirus-communications-team/un-scaling-covid-19-response-protect
-refugees-and-migrants.

27. WHO, *Antimicrobial Resistance: Global Report on Surveillance, 2014* (Geneva: WHO, 2014).

28. UN, *High-Level Meeting on Antimicrobial Resistance*, UN General Assembly, New York, September 21, 2016.

29. The Review on Antimicrobial Resistance, "Tackling Drug-Resistant Infections: Final Report on Recommendations (May 2016)," https://amr -review.org/sites/default/files/160525_Final%20paper_with%20cover.pdf.

30. CDC, "Antibiotic/Antimicrobial Resistance (AR/AMR): Biggest Threats and Data," https://www.cdc.gov/drugresistance/biggest-threats.html.

31. WHO, *The Evolving Threat of Antimicrobial Resistance: Options for Action* (Geneva: WHO, 2012), 38.

32. WHO, "Coronavirus Disease 2019 (COVID-19) Situation Report—98," data as received by April 28, 2020, https://www.who.int/docs/default-source/coronaviruse /situation-reports/20200427-sitrep-98-covid-19.pdf?sfvrsn=90323472_4.

33. James K. Jackson, Martin A. Weiss, Andres B. Shwarzenberg, and Rebecca M. Nelson, "Global Economic Effects of COVID-19," *Congressional Research Service Report*, updated May 1, 2020.

34. Anas El Turabi and Philip Saynisch, "Modeling the Economic Threat of Pandemics" in *The Neglected Dimension of Global Health Security: A Framework to Counter Infectious Disease Crises* (Washington, DC: National Academy of Medicine, 2016), 111.

35. World Bank, "Pandemic Preparedness and Health Systems Strengthening," http://www.worldbank.org/en/topic/pandemics/overview.

36. Victoria Y. Fan, Dean T. Jamison, and Lawrence H. Summers, *The Inclusive Cost of Pandemic Influenza Risk* (Cambridge, MA: National Bureau of Economic Research, 2016).

37. Graeme Wearden and Jasper Jolly, "IMF: Global Economy Faces Worst Recession since the Great Depression—As It Happened," *Guardian* (UK), April 14, 2020.

38. WTO, "Trade Set to Plunge as COVID-19 Pandemic Upends Global Economy," press release, April 8, 2020, https://www.wto.org/english/new_e /pres20_e/pr855_e.pdf.

39. *Emerging Infectious Disease Journal* 23, no. 13, supplement (December 2017).

40. C. H. Cassell, Z. Bambery, K. Roy, et al., "Relevance of Global Health Security to the US Export Economy," *Health Security* 15, no. 6 (2017): 563–568.

41. WHO, *An R&D Blueprint for Action to Prevent Epidemics* (Geneva: WHO, 2016), 5.

42. World Bank, *People, Pathogens and Our Planet: The Economics of One Health* (Washington, DC: World Bank, 2012), xii.

43. Vince Golle and Sarina Yoo, "The Post-Coronavirus Unemployment Crisis Could Last for Years, Economists Say, *Time*, April 10, 2020.

44. Joe Bavier and Giulia Paravicini, "Africa Could Lose 20 Million Jobs Due to Pandemic: AU Study," Reuters, April 5, 2020; Maria Abi-Habib, "Billions Slide Down the Ladder That Took Decades to Climb," *New York Times,* May 1 2020.

45. US Institute of Medicine Forum on Microbial Threats, *Learning from SARS: Preparing for the Next Disease Outbreak: Workshop Summary,* ed. S. Knobler, A. Mahmoud, S. Lemon, et al. (Washington DC: National Academies Press, 2004).

46. Grace C. L. Chien and Rob Law, "The Impact of the Severe Acute Respiratory Syndrome on Hotels: A Case Study of Hong Kong," *International Journal of Hospitality Management* 22, no. 3 (2003): 327–332.

47. Iain Marlow, "What's the Economic Impact of the MERS Outbreak in South Korea?," *Globe and Mail,* June 18, 2015, https://www.theglobeandmail .com/news/british-columbia/whats-the-economic-impact-of-the-mers -outbreak-in-south-korea/article25031999/; Eri Sugiura, "Club Med's Chinese Owner Fosun Bets Billions on Family Fun," *Nikkei Asian Review,* July 5, 2019, https://asia.nikkei.com/Business/Company-in-focus/Club-Med -s-Chinese-owner-Fosun-bets-billions-on-family-fun.

48. Matthew M. Kavanagh, Harsha Thirumurthy, Rebecca L. Katz, et al., "Ending Pandemics: Foreign Policy to Mitigate Today's Major Killers, Tomorrow's Outbreaks, and the Health Impacts of Climate Change," *Journal of International Affairs* 73, no. 1 (2019).

49. CDC, "COVID-19 in Racial & Ethnic Minority Groups," https://www.cdc .gov/coronavirus/2019-ncov/need-extra-precautions/racial-ethnic-minorities .html.

## Chapter 2 · The Human Link

1. John M. Barry, "The Site of Origin of the 1918 Influenza Pandemic and Its Public Health Implications," *Journal of Translational Medicine* 2, no. 3 (2004): 3; John M. Barry, "How the Horrific 1918 Flu Spread across America," *Smithsonian Magazine,* November 2017, https://www.smithsonianmag.com /history/journal-plague-year-180965222/.

2. WHO, "Pneumonia of Unknown Cause—China," Disease Outbreak News, January 5, 2020, https://www.who.int/csr/don/05-january-2020-pneumonia -of-unknown-cause-china/en.

3. WHO, "Novel Coronavirus—China," Disease Outbreak News, January 12, 2020, https://www.who.int/csr/don/12-january-2020-novel-coronavirus -china/en/.

4. Kristian G. Andersen, Andrew Rambaut, W. Ian Lipkin, et al., "The Proximal Origin of SARS-CoV-2," *Nature Medicine* 26 (2020): 450–452.

5. Michael Levenson, "Scale of China's Wuhan Shutdown Is Believed to Be without Precedent," *New York Times,* January 22, 2020.

6. WHO, "Novel Coronavirus—Thailand (ex-China)," Disease Outbreak News, January 14, 2020, https://www.who.int/csr/don/14-january-2020

-novel-coronavirus-thailand/en/; Hillary Leung, "'An Eternal Hero': Whistle-blower Doctor Who Sounded Alarm on Coronavirus Dies in China," *Time,* February 7, 2020.

7. WHO, "Mission Summary: WHO Field Visit to Wuhan, China, 20–21 January 2020," January 22, 2020, https://www.who.int/china/news/detail/22 -01-2020-field-visit-wuhan-china-jan-2020.

8. WHO, "Statement on the Second Meeting of the International Health Regulations (2005) Emergency Committee regarding the Outbreak of Novel Coronavirus (2019-nCov)," January 30, 2020, https://www.who.int /news-room/detail/30-01-2020-statement-on-the-second-meeting-of-the -international-health-regulations-(2005)-emergency-committee-regarding -the-outbreak-of-novel-coronavirus-(2019-ncov).

9. Report of the WHO–China Joint Mission on Coronavirus Disease 2019 (COVID-19), February 28, 2020, https://www.who.int/publications/i /item/report-of-the-who-china-joint-mission-on-coronavirus-disease-2019 -(covid-19).

10. WHO, "WHO Director-General's Opening Remarks at the Media Briefing on 2019 Novel Coronavirus—7 February 2020," February 7, 2020, https://www.who.int/dg/speeches/detail/who-director-general-s-opening -remarks-at-the-media-briefing-on-2019-novel-coronavirus-7-february -2020.

11. Philip Bump, "Trump Again Downplays Coronavirus by Comparing It to the Seasonal Flu: It's Not a Fair Comparison," *Washington Post,* March 24, 2020.

12. WHO, "Coronavirus Disease 2019 (COVID-19) Situation Report—71," https://www.who.int/docs/default-source/coronaviruse/situation-reports /20200331-sitrep-71-covid-19.pdf?sfvrsn=4360e92b_8v.

13. Bill Chappell, "Coronavirus: COVID-19 Is Now Officially a Pandemic, WHO Says," NPR, March 11, 2020.

14. UN Development Programme, "COVID-19: Looming Crisis in Developing Countries Threatens to Devastate Economies and Ramp Up Inequality," March 30, 2020, https://www.undp.org/content/undp/en/home/news-centre /news/2020/COVID19_Crisis_in_developing_countries_threatens_devastate _economies.html.

15. G20 Information Centre, *Extraordinary G20 Leaders' Summit: Statement on COVID-19* (video conference, Riyadh, Saudi Arabia, March 26, 2020), http://www.g20.utoronto.ca/2020/2020-g20-statement-0326.html.

16. WHO, "Coronavirus Disease 2019 (COVID-19) Situation Report—101," https://www.who.int/docs/default-source/coronaviruse/situation-reports /20200430-sitrep-101-covid-19.pdf?sfvrsn=2ba4e093_2.

17. Africa CDC, "Coronavirus Disease 2019 (COVID-19): Latest Updates on the COVID-19 Crisis from Africa CDC," https://africacdc.org/covid-19/.

18. Paul Anthem, "Risk of Hunger Pandemic as COVID-19 Set to Almost Double Acute Hunger by End of 2020," *World Food Programme Insight,* April 16, 2020, https://insight.wfp.org/covid-19-will-almost-double-people -in-acute-hunger-by-end-of-2020-59df0c4a8072.

19. UN Office for the Coordination of Humanitarian Affairs, "UN Issues $6.7 Billion Appeal to Protect Millions of Lives and Stem the Spread of COVID-19 in Fragile Countries," May 7, 2020, https://www.unocha.org /story/un-issues-67-billion-appeal-protect-millions-lives-and-stem-spread -covid-19-fragile-countries.

20. WHO, "Coronavirus Disease 2019 (COVID-19) Situation Report—85," https://www.who.int/docs/default-source/coronaviruse/situation-reports /20200414-sitrep-85-covid-19.pdf?sfvrsn=7b8629bb_4.

21. The White House, "President Donald J. Trump Is Demanding Account-ability from the World Health Organization," Briefings & Statements, April 15, 2020, https://www.whitehouse.gov/briefings-statements/president -donald-j-trump-demanding-accountability-world-health-organization/.

22. WHO, "COVID-19 Virtual Press Conference—8 April, 2020," April 8, 2020, https://www.who.int/docs/default-source/coronaviruse/transcripts /who-audio-emergencies-coronavirus-press-conference-full-08apr2020.pdf ?sfvrsn=267145f5_2.

23. WHO, "Coronavirus Disease (COVID-19) Situation Report—106," https://www.who.int/docs/default-source/coronaviruse/situation-reports /20200505covid-19-sitrep-106.pdf?sfvrsn=47090f63_2.

24. CIDRAP, "COVID-19: The CIDRAP Viewpoint," April 30, 2020, https://www.cidrap.umn.edu/sites/default/files/public/downloads/cidrap -covid19-viewpoint-part1_0.pdf.

25. "Models Project Sharp Rise in Deaths as States Reopen," *New York Times*, Coronavirus Live Updates, May 4, 2020, https://www.nytimes.com/2020 /05/04/us/coronavirus-live-updates.html.

26. WHO, "Weekly Operational Update on COVID-19," December 7, 2020. https://www.who.int/publications/m/item/weekly-operational-update-on -covid-19—7-december-2020.

27. UN Office for the Coordination of Humanitarian Affairs, "Haiti: Cholera Figures, as of 26 December 2018," https://reliefweb.int/sites/reliefweb.int /files/resources/ocha-hti-cholera-figures-2018123_en.pdf.

28. UN Secretary-General, *A New Approach to Cholera in Haiti*, UN Doc. A/71/620/, November 25, 2016, https://undocs.org/A/71/620.

29. Institute for Democracy and Justice in Haiti, "Advocates Denounce UN Breaking Promise of Compensation for Cholera Victims," June 15, 2017, http://www.ijdh.org/2017/06/projects/advocates-denounce-un-breaking -promise-of-compensation-for-cholera-victims/.

30. UN, "Water," https://www.un.org/en/sections/issues-depth/water/.

31. CDC, "Global Diarrhea Burden," www.cdc.gov/healthywater/global /diarrhea-burden.html.

32. Isabel Blackett and Peter Hawkins, "A Tale of Two Cities: How Cities Can Improve Fecal Sludge Management," *World Bank Blogs*, November 8, 2016, http://blogs.worldbank.org/water/tale-two-cities-how-cities-can-improve -fecal-sludge-management.

33. WHO, "Report on the Burden of Endemic Health Care–Associated Infection Worldwide," 2011, https://apps.who.int/iris/bitstream/handle /10665/80135/9789241501507_eng.pdf.

34. Hassan Ahmed Khan, Aftab Ahmad, and Riffat Mehboob, "Nosocomial Infections and Their Control Strategies," *Asian Pacific Journal of Tropical Medicine* 5, no. 7 (July 2015): 509–514.

35. Khan, Ahmad, and Mehboob, "Nosocomial Infections."

36. WHO, "Core Components for Infection Prevention and Control Programmes," 2009, https://apps.who.int/iris/bitstream/handle/10665/69982 /WHO_HSE_EPR_2009.1_eng.pdf.

37. WHO and UNICEF, *Water and Sanitation for Health Facility Improvement Tool (WASH FIT)* (Geneva: WHO, 2017), https://apps.who.int/iris /bitstream/handle/10665/254910/9789241511698-eng.pdf.

38. Neil Genzlinger, "Review: 'Frontline' Looks at Missteps during the Ebola Outbreak," *New York Times,* May 3, 2015.

39. BBC, "Timeline: How We Lost Control of the Ebola Virus in 2014," BBC News, May 9, 2015, https://www.bbc.co.uk/timelines/z9gkj6f.

40. Peter Wonacott, "Africa's Village Healers Complicate Ebola Fight," *Wall Street Journal,* November 7, 2014.

41. Amy Maxmen, "How the Fight against Ebola Tested a Culture's Traditions," *National Geographic,* January 30, 2015.

42. Maxmen, "Fight against Ebola."

43. C. Wejnert, K. L. Hess, H. I. Hall, et al., "Vital Signs: Trends in HIV Diagnoses, Risk Behaviors, and Prevention among Persons Who Inject Drugs—United States," *CDC Morbidity and Mortality Weekly Report* 65, no 47 (December 2016): 1336–1342.

44. CDC, "Access to Clean Syringes," August 5, 2016, https://www.cdc.gov /policy/hst/hi5/cleansyringes/index.html.

45. Austin Frakt, "Politics Are Tricky but Science Is Clear: Needle Exchanges Work," *New York Times,* September 5, 2016.

46. WHO, *Effectiveness of Sterile Needle and Syringe Programming in Reducing HIV/AIDS among Injecting Drug Users* (Geneva: WHO, 2004), https://www .who.int/hiv/pub/prev_care/effectivenesssterileneedle.pdf.

47. Günther Burg, "History of Sexually Transmitted Infections," *Dermatol Venereol* 147, no. 4 (August 2012): 329–340.

48. WHO, "Sexually Transmitted Infections (STIs)," Fact Sheet, February 28, 2019, https://www.who.int/mediacentre/factsheets/fs110/en/.

49. Gaby Gavin, "STDs Combine for Record High in U.S.," *U.S. News and World Report,* October 8, 2019; Ashley Fetters, "Why Are STDs on the Rise if Americans Are Having Less Sex?," *Atlantic,* August 29, 2018; Jacqueline Howard, "3 STDs Reach All-Time Highs in the US, New CDC Report Says," CNN, October 8, 2019.

50. UNAIDS Inter-Agency Task Team on Young People, *WHO Technical Report Series 938: Preventing HIV/AIDS in Young People: A Systematic*

*Review of the Evidence from Developing Countries* (Geneva: WHO, 2006), https://apps.who.int/iris/bitstream/handle/10665/43453/WHO_TRS_938 _eng.pdf.

51. CDC, "Frequently Asked Questions about SARS," April 26, 2004, https://www.cdc.gov/sars/about/faq.html.

52. Jong-Wha Lee and Warwick J. McKibbin, "Estimating the Global Economic Cost of SARS," in *Learning from SARS: Preparing for the Next Disease Outbreak,* ed. Stacey Knobler et al., (Washington, DC: National Academies Press, 2008): 92–109; Alexandra A. Sidorenko and Warwick J. McKibbin, "What a Flu Pandemic Could Cost the World," Brookings Institution, April 28, 2009, https://www.brookings.edu/opinions/what-a-flu-pandemic -could-cost-the-world/.

53. CDC, "CDC Emergency Operations Center," April 10, 2019, https://www .cdc.gov/cpr/eoc.htm.

54. Martin N. Adokiya and John K. Awoonor-Williams, "Ebola Virus Disease Surveillance and Response Preparedness in Northern Ghana," *Global Health Action* 9, no. 1 (2016).

55. Kevin Sack, Sheri Fink, Pam Belluck, and Adam Nossiter, "How Ebola Roared Back," *New York Times,* December 29, 2014.

## Chapter 3 · Humanity's Biggest Killer

1. Wendy M. Chung, Christen M. Buseman, and Sibeso N. Joyner, "The 2012 West Nile Encephalitis Epidemic in Dallas, Texas," *JAMA Network* 310, no. 3 (July 17, 2013): 297–307.

2. Isaac Asimov and Jason A. Shulman, eds., *Isaac Asimov's Book of Science and Nature Quotations* (New York: Weidenfield and Nicolson, 1988), 80.

3. Donald G. McNeil Jr., "Tick and Mosquito Infections Spreading Rapidly, C.D.C. Finds," *New York Times,* May 1, 2018.

4. Jason Puckett and David Tregde, "Verify: Are Mosquitos Really the Deadliest Animals on Earth?," K5News, July 27, 2018 (updated July 31, 2018), https://www.king5.com/article/news/local/verify/verify-are -mosquitoes-really-the-deadliest-animals-on-earth/507-578093577.

5. WHO, "Dengue and Severe Dengue," https://www.who.int/en/news-room /fact-sheets/detail/dengue-and-severe-dengue.

6. Michael J. Conway, Tonya M. Colpitts, Erol Fikrig, et al., "Role of the Vector in Arbovirus Transmission," *Annual Review of Virology* 1 (2014): 71–88, http://www.annualreviews.org/doi/full/10.1146/annurev-virology -031413-085513.

7. CDC, "Arboviral Diseases, Neuroinvasive and Non-neuroinvasive 2015 Case Definition," https://wwwn.cdc.gov/nndss/conditions/arboviral-diseases -neuroinvasive-and-non-neuroinvasive/case-definition/2015/.

8. WHO, "Yellow Fever—Brazil," April 18, 2019, https://www.who.int/csr /don/18-april-2019-yellow-fever-brazil/en/.

9. WHO, "Yellow Fever—Key Facts," May 1, 2018, https://www.who.int/news-room/fact-sheets/detail/yellow-fever.

10. Mark D. Gershman, Kristina M. Angelo, Julian Ritchey, et al., "Addressing a Yellow Fever Vaccine Shortage: United States, 2016–2017," *Morbidity and Mortality Weekly* 66, no. 17 (2017): 457–459, https://www.cdc.gov/mmwr/volumes/66/wr/mm6617e2.htm.

11. WHO, "Dengue Fever—Sri Lanka," July 19, 207, https://www.who.int/csr/don/19-july-2017-dengue-sri-lanka/en/.

12. Euan McKirdy, "Unprecedented Outbreak of Dengue Fever Plagues Sri Lanka," CNN, July 25, 2017.

13. May O. Lwin, Santosh Vijaykumar, Vajira Sampath Rathnayake, et al., "A Social Media mHealth Solution to Address the Needs of Dengue Prevention and Management in Sri Lanka," *Journal of Medical Internet Research* 18, no. 7 (2016): e419, https://www.ncbi.nlm.nih.gov/pmc/articles/PMC4947191/.

14. "Campaign against Dengue," *Financial Express* (India), May 10, 2017.

15. José Lourenço, Warren Tennant, Nuno R. Faria, et al., "Challenges in Dengue Research: A Computational Perspective," Wiley Online Library, September 20, 2017, http://doi.org/10.1111/eva.12554.

16. Anna Beltrame, Andrea Angheben, Zeno Bisoffi, et al., "Imported Chikungunya Infection, Italy," *Emerging Infectious Diseases* 13, no. 8 (2007): 1264–1266.

17. SixunYang, Doran Fink, Andrea Hulse and R. Douglas Pratt, "Regulatory Considerations in Development of Vaccines to Prevent Disease Caused by Chikungunya Virus," *Vaccine* 35, no. 37 (2017): 4851–4858.

18. Lecia Bushak, "Brief History of Zika Virus, from Its Discovery in the Zika Forest to the Global Outbreak Today," *Medical Daily,* April 8, 2016, https://www.medicaldaily.com/zika-virus-outbreak-history-381132.

19. WHO, "Malaria: Information for Travelers," updated January 15, 2020, https://www.who.int/malaria/travellers/en/.

20. WHO, *World Malaria Report 2019* (Geneva: WHO, 2019), 11, https://www.who.int/publications-detail/world-malaria-report-2019.

21. WHO, "Malaria: Information for Travelers," xii.

22. WHO, "Malaria: Information for Travelers," xii.

23. WHO, *World Malaria Report 2019,* 7, 9.

24. Dan Garisto, "Genetically Modified Plant May Boost Supply of a Powerful Malaria Drug," *Science News,* April 24, 2018.

25. James Gallagher, "Alarm as 'Super Malaria' Spreads in Southeast Asia," BBC News, September 22, 2017.

26. José A. Nájera, Matiana González-Silva, and Pedro L. Alonso, "Some Lessons for the Future from the Global Malaria Eradication Programme (1955–1969)," *PLOS Medicine,* January 25, 2011, https://journals.plos.org/plosmedicine/article?id=10.1371/journal.pmed.1000412.

27. Roll Back Malaria Partnership, *Progress and Impact Series, Number 8: Eliminating Malaria: Learning from the Past, Looking Ahead* (Geneva, WHO, 2011).

28. WHA, Resolution WHA 68.28, "Global Technical Strategy for Malaria 2016–2030," January 22, 2016.
29. WHA, Resolution WHA 68.28.
30. Bill and Melinda Gates Foundation, "From Aspiration to Action: What Will It Take to End Malaria?," http://endmalaria2040.org/.
31. Stephen Eisenhammer, "Brazil's Rousseff Declares War on Mosquito Spreading Zika Virus," Reuters, January 27, 2016.
32. WHO, *Dengue Guidelines for Diagnosis, Treatment, Prevention and Control* (Geneva: WHO, 2009), 65.
33. WHO, *Indoor Residual Spraying: An Operational Manual for Indoor Residual Spraying (IRS) for Malaria Transmission and Elimination* (Geneva: WHO, 2015), 3.
34. WHO, "Malaria Prevention Works: Let's Close the Gap," Geneva, 2017, 15.
35. WHO, *Dengue Guidelines for Diagnosis*, 63.
36. WHO, *Malaria Elimination: Guide for Participants* (Geneva: WHO, 2016), 53.
37. WHO, *Dengue Guidelines for Diagnosis*, 70.
38. WHO, "The Use of DDT in Malaria Vector Control: WHO Position Statement," Geneva, 2011.
39. WHO, *Stockholm Convention on Persistent Organic Pollutants* (2001), entered into force May 17, 2004.
40. WHO, "WHO Releases New Guidance on Insecticide-Treated Mosquito Nets," August 16, 2007, https://www.who.int/mediacentre/news/releases /2007/pr43/en/.
41. WHO, *Global Technical Strategy for Malaria 2016–2030* (Geneva: WHO, June 2015).
42. WHO, *World Malaria Report 2017* (Geneva: WHO, 2017), 12.
43. WHO, "Conditions for Deployment of Mosquito Nets Treated with a Pyrethroid and Piperonyl Butoxide: Recommendations," Geneva, September 2017; revised December 2017.
44. Douglas G. Paton, Lauren M. Childs, Maurice A. Itoe, et al., "Exposing *Anopheles* Mosquitos to Antimalarials Blocks *Plasmodium* Parasite Transmission," *Nature* 567 (2019): 239–243.
45. Shibadas Biswal, Humberto Reynales, Xavier Saez-Llorens, et al., "Efficacy of a Tetravalent Dengue Vaccine in Children and Adolescents," *NEJM* 381(2019): 2009; WHO, "Q&A on the Malaria Vaccine Implementation Programme (MVIP)," January 2020, https://www.who.int/malaria/media /malaria-vaccine-implementation-qa/en/.
46. WHO, "Background Paper on Dengue Vaccines Prepared by the SAGE Working Group on Dengue Vaccines and WHO Secretariat," Geneva, April 18, 2018, 3.
47. Helen Branswell, "3 Global Health Challenges to Watch in 2019," Statnews, December 24, 2018.

48. Matthias Blamont and Julie Steenhuysen, "WHO Recommends Testing before Use of Sanofi's Dengue Vaccine," Reuters, April 19, 2018.

49. WHO, "Q&A on Malaria Vaccine Implementation Programme (MVIP)," January 2020, https://www.who.int/malaria/media/malaria-vaccine -implementation-qa/en/.

50. Maggie Fox, "Malaria Vaccine Mosquirix Approved by European Regulators," NBC News, July 24, 2015.

51. WHO, "Q&A on Malaria Vaccine."

52. NIH, "NIH Begins Study of Vaccine to Protect against Mosquito-Borne Diseases," February 21, 2017, https://www.nih.gov/news-events/news-releases /nih-begins-study-vaccine-protect-against-mosquito-borne-diseases.

53. NIH, "NIH Begins Study."

54. "CRISPER Use Creates Malaria-Resistant Mosquitos," *Genetic Engineering & Biotechnology News*, March 9, 2018, https://www.genengnews.com/topics /translational-medicine/crispr-use-creates-malaria-resistant-mosquitoes/.

55. Kyros Kyrou, Andrew M. Hammond, Roberto Galizi, et al., "A CRISPR–Cas9 Gene Drive Targeting *Doublesex* Causes Complete Population Suppression in Caged *Anopheles gambiae* Mosquitoes," *Nature Biotechnology* 36 (2018): 1062–1066.

56. Kyrou et al., "CRISPR–Cas9," 1062–1066.

57. Kyrou et al., "CRISPR–Cas9," 1062–1066.

58. Cinnamon S. Bloss, Justin Stoler, Kimberly C. Brouwer, et al., "Public Response to a Proposed Field Trial of Genetically Engineered Mosquitoes in the United States," *JAMA* 318, no. 7 (2017): 662–664.

59. Bloss et al., "Public Response," 662–664.

60. Givemore Menhenga, "South Africa Investigates Sterilising Mosquitoes in Anti-Malaria Drive," *The Conversation,* November 7, 2018, https:// theconversation.com/south-africa-investigates-sterilising-mosquitoes-in-anti -malaria-drive-106368; Givemore Munhenga, Basil D. Brooke, Jeremie R. L. Gilles, Kobus Slabbert, et al., "Mating Competitiveness of Sterile Genetic Sexing Strain Males (GAMA) under Laboratory and Semi-field Conditions: Steps towards the Use of the Sterile Insect Technique to Control the Major Malaria Vector *Anopheles arabiensis* in South Africa," *Parasites & Vectors* 9 (2016): 122.

## Chapter 4 · Disease by Decision

1. FBI, "Amerithrax Fact Sheet," September 2006, https://www.fbi.gov /history/famous-cases/amerithrax-or-anthrax-investigation.

2. National Research Council (NRC), Committee on Review of the Scientific Approaches Used during the FBI's Investigation of the 2001 Bacillus Anthracis Mailings, *Review of the Scientific Approaches Used during the FBI's Investigation of the 2001 Anthrax Letters* (Washington, DC: National Academies Press, 2011), https://www.nap.edu/read/13098/chapter/1.

3. NRC, *Review.*

4. Government Accountability Office, "Anthrax: Agency Approaches to Validation and Statistical Analysis Could Be Improved," December 19, 2014, https://www.gao.gov/products/gao-15-80.

5. NRC, *Understanding Biosecurity: Protecting against the Misuse of Science in Today's World* (Washington DC: National Academies Press, 2010), 8.

6. Helen Branswell, "CDC Made a Synthetic Ebola Virus to Test Treatments. It Worked," *STAT,* July 9, 2019, https://www.statnews.com/2019/07/09 /lacking-ebola-samples-cdc-made-a-synthetic-virus-to-test-treatments-it -worked/.

7. Lawrence O. Gostin, Alexandra Phelan, Michael A. Stoto, et al., "Virus Sharing, Genetic Sequencing, and Global Health Security," *Science* 345 (2014): 1295–1296.

8. NIH, "U.S. Government Gain-of-Function Deliberative Process and Research Funding Pause on Selected Gain-of-Function Research Involving Influenza, MERS, and SARS Viruses," October 17, 2014, https://www.phe .gov/s3/dualuse/Documents/gain-of-function.pdf; Motoko Araki and Tetsuya Ishii, "International Regulatory Landscape and Integration of Corrective Genome Editing into in Vitro Fertilization," *Reproductive Biology and Endocrinology* 12 (2014): 108, https://rbej.biomedcentral.com/articles/10 .1186/1477-7827-12-108.

9. Julian Borger, "Mike Pompeo: Enormous Evidence Coronavirus Came from Chinese Lab," *Guardian,* May 3, 2020.

10. Carl Zimmer, "Scientists Are Retooling Bacteria to Cure Disease," *New York Times,* September 4, 2018.

11. Tania Rabesandratana, "European Funders Detail Their Open-Access Plan," *Science,* November 26, 2018.

12. Jeronimo Cello, Aniko Paul, and Eckward Wimmer, "Chemical Synthesis of Poliovirus cDNA: Generation of Infectious Virus in the Absence of Natural Template," *Science* 297 (2002): 1016–1018.

13. James Randerson, "Did Anyone Order Smallpox?," *Guardian,* June 23, 2006.

14. WHO, "FAQs: H5N1 Influenza," https://www.who.int/influenza/human _animal_interface/avian_influenza/h5n1_research/faqs/en/.

15. David M. Morens, Kanta Subbarao, and Jeffrey K. Taubenberger, "Engineering H5N1 Avian Influenza Viruses to Study Human Adaption," *Nature* 486 (2012): 335–340.

16. Poh Lian Lim, Asok Kurup, Gowri Gopalakrishna, et al., "Laboratory Acquired Severe Acute Respiratory Syndrome," *NEJM* 350 (2004): 1740–1745.

17. Jarunee Siengsanan-Lamont and Stuart Blacksell, "A Review of Laboratory-Acquired Infections in the Asia Pacific: Understanding Risk and the Need for Improved Biosafety for Veterinary and Zoonotic Diseases," *Tropical Medicine and Infectious Diseases* 3 (2018): 36, https://www.ncbi.nlm.nih.gov /pmc/articles/PMC6073996/.

18. Gigi Kwik Gronvall, "A Biosafety Agenda to Spur Biotechnology Development and Prevent Accidents," *Health Security* 15 (2017): 25–27, https://www.liebertpub.com/doi/pdf/10.1089/hs.2016.0095.

19. Deputy Secretary of Defense, US Department of Defense, "Implementation of the Recommendations in the Comprehensive Review Report: Inadvertent Shipment of Live *Bacillus anthracis* (Anthrax) Spores by Department of Defense," July 23, 2015, https://dod.defense.gov/Portals/1/features/2015/0615_lab-stats/docs/DSD-Memo-Implementation-of-Recommendations-in-Comprehensive-Review-Report.pdf.

20. Henri Braat, Pieter Rottiers, Daniel W. Hommes, et al., "A Phase I Trial with Transgenic Bacteria Expressing Interleukin-10 in Crohn's Disease," *Clinical Gastroenterology Hepatology* 4 (2006): 754–759.

21. Federal Select Agent Program, "Select Agents and Toxins List," https://www.selectagents.gov/SelectAgentsandToxinsList.html; HHS, *Biosafety in Microbial and Biomedical Laboratories,* 5th ed., HHS Publication No. (CDC) 21-1112, revised December 2009; HHS, *NIH Guidelines for Research Involving Recombinant or Synthetic Nucleic Acid Molecules,* April 2019, https://osp.od.nih.gov/wp-content/uploads/NIH_Guidelines.pdf.

22. UPMC Center for Health Security, "National Biosafety Systems: Case Studies to Analyze Current Biosafety Approaches and Regulations for Brazil, China, India, Israel, Pakistan, Kenya, Russia, Singapore, the United Kingdom, and the United States," July 2016, http://www.centerforhealthsecurity.org/our-work/pubs_archive/pubs-pdfs/2016/National%20Biosafety%20Systems.pdf.

23. Convention on Biological Diversity, The Cartagena Protocol on Biosafety (2000), entered into force September 11, 2003; CEN Workshop Agreement, *Laboratory Biorisk Management,* CWA 15793 (2011).

24. WHO, *Laboratory Biosafety Manual,* 3rd ed. (Geneva: WHO 2004); OIE, "Biological Threat Reduction Strategy: Strengthening Global Biological Security," October 2015, https://www.oie.int/scientific-expertise/biological-threat-reduction/.

25. WHA, "Enhancement of Laboratory Biosafety," WHA58.29, May 25, 2005, https://internationalbiosafety.org/wp-content/uploads/2019/08/World-Health-Assembly-Resolution-58-29.pdf.

26. WHO, "Summary of 2011 States Parties Report on IHR Core Capacity Implementation," WHO/HSE/GCR/2012.10 (2012), https://www.who.int/ihr/publications/WHO_HSE_GCR_2012.10_eng.pdf.

27. Global Health Security Agenda, "Biosafety and Biosecurity," https://ghsagenda.org/home/action-packages/biosafety-and-biosecurity/.

28. Emily Baumgaertner, "White House Hails Success of Disease-Fighting Program, and Plans Deep Cuts," *New York Times,* March 13, 2018.

29. Stefan Riedel, "Biological Warfare and Bioterrorism: A Historical Review," *Baylor University Medical Center Proceedings* 17 (2004): 400–406, https://www.ncbi.nlm.nih.gov/pmc/articles/PMC1200679/.

30. UN Office for Disarmament Affairs, "Biological Weapons," https://www.un .org/disarmament/wmd/bio/.
31. National Academies of Science, Engineering, and Medicine, "Biodefense in the Age of Synthetic Biology," Washington, DC: The National Academies Press, 2018.
32. Ryan S. Noyce, Seth Lederman, and David H. Evans, "Construction of an Infectious Horsepox Virus Vaccine from Chemically Synthesized DNA Fragments," *PLOS One* 13 (2018): e0188453.
33. Raymond S. Weinstein, "Should Remaining Stockpiles of Smallpox (Variola) Be Destroyed?," *Emerging Infectious Diseases* 17 (2011): 681–683.
34. Robert F. Massung, Li-Ing Liu, Jin Qui, et al., "Analysis of the Complete Genome of Smallpox Variola Major Virus Strain Bangladesh-1975," *Virology* 210 (1994): 215–240.
35. WHO, "Scientific Review of Variola Virus Research, 1999–2010," December 2010, https://www.who.int/publications/i/item/WHO-HSE-GAR-BDP -2010-3.
36. Science and Technology Policy Office, "U.S. Government Policy for Oversight of Life Sciences Dual Use Research of Concern," March 29, 2012, https://www.phe.gov/s3/dualuse/Documents/us-policy-durc-032812 .pdf.
37. Ronald J. Jackson, Alistair J. Ramsay, Carina D. Christensen, et al., "Expression of Mouse Interleukin-4 by a Recombinant Ectromelia Virus Suppresses Cytolytic Lymphocyte Responses and Overcomes Genetic Resistance to Mousepox," *Journal of Virology* 75 (2001): 1205–1210; Rachel Nowak, "Killer Mousepox Virus Raises Bioterror Fears," *New Scientist,* November 10, 2001.
38. NRC, *Biotechnology Research in an Age of Terrorism: Confronting the Dual Use Dilemma* (Washington DC: National Academies Press, 2004), https://www .nap.edu/resource/biotechnology_research/0309089778.pdf.
39. K. Satyanarayana, "Dual Use Research of Concern: Publish *and* Perish?," *Indian Journal of Medical Research* 133 (2011): 1–4, https://www.ncbi.nlm.nih .gov/pmc/articles/PMC3100136/.
40. NIH, "Implementation of the U.S. Government Policy for Institutional Oversight of Life Sciences DURC: Frequently Asked Questions," September 2014, https://www.phe.gov/s3/dualuse/Documents/durc-faqs.pdf.
41. HHS, "Framework for Guiding Funding Decisions about Proposed Research Involving Enhanced Potentially Pandemic Pathogens," 2017, https://www .phe.gov/s3/dualuse/Documents/p3co.pdf.
42. Jocelyn Kaiser, "White House Announces Review Process for Risky Virus Studies," *Science,* January 9, 2017.
43. Marc Lipsitch and Tom Inglesby, "The U.S. Is Funding Dangerous Experiments It Doesn't Want You to Know About," *Washington Post,* February 27, 2019.
44. John D. Kraemer and Lawrence O. Gostin, "The Limits of Government Regulation of Science," *Science* 335 (2012): 1047–1049.

45. *New York Times v. United States,* 403 U.S. 713 (1971).

46. Mark Enserink, "Dutch Appeals Court Dodges Decision on Hotly Debated H5N1 Papers," *Science,* July 16, 2015.

47. "Setting Up a Community Regime for the Control of Exports, Transfer, Brokering and Transit of Dual-Use Items," Council Regulation (EC) No. 428/2009, *Official Journal of the European Union,* May 5, 2009, https://eur -lex.europa.eu/LexUriServ/LexUriServ.do?uri=OJ:L:2009:134:0001:0269:e n:PDF.

48. Mark Enserink, "Flu Researcher Ron Fouchier Loses Legal Fight over H5N1 Studies," *Science,* September 25, 2013.

49. HHS, *United States Government Policy for Institutional Oversight of Life Sciences Dual Use Research of Concern,* September 24, 2014, https://www.phe .gov/s3/dualuse/Documents/durc-policy.pdf.

50. European Commission, "Dual-Use Trade Controls," http://ec.europa.eu /trade/import-and-export-rules/export-from-eu/dual-use-controls/.

51. The Australia Group, http://australiagroup.net/en/.

52. Covington, "Export Control Reform Act Is Finalized in Congress," *Covington Alert,* July 30, 2018, https://www.cov.com/en/news-and-insights /insights/2018/07/export-control-reform-act-is-finalized-in-congress.

53. Piers D. Millett, "Gaps in the International Governance of Dual-Use Research of Concern," revised January 17, 2017, https://www.nap.edu/resource/24761 /Millett_Paper_011717.pdf.

54. Protocol for the Prohibition of the Use in War of Asphyxiating, Poisonous, or Other Gases, and of Biological Methods of Warfare (Geneva Protocol) (1925), entered into force February 8, 1928, https://unoda-web.s3-accelerate .amazonaws.com/wp-content/uploads/assets/WMD/Bio/pdf/Status _Protocol.pdf.

55. UN Office for Disarmament Affairs, "Biological Weapons," https://www.un .org/disarmament/wmd/bio/.

56. Convention on the Prohibition of the Development of Bacteriological (Biological) and Toxin Weapons and on Their Destruction (Biological Weapons Convention), 1972.

57. UN Office for Disarmament Affairs, *Guide to Participating in the Confidence-Building Measures of the Biological Weapons Convention* (Geneva: United Nations, 2015), https://unoda-web.s3-accelerate.amazonaws.com/wp -content/uploads/assets/publications/more/cbm-guide/cbm-guide-2015.pdf.

58. Jennifer Mackby, "Disputes Mire BWC Review Conference," Arms Control Association, January/February 2017, https://www.armscontrol.org/act/2017 -01/news/disputes-mire-bwc-review-conference.

59. David P. Fidler, "Outcome of the Sixth Review Conference of the Biological Weapons Convention," *ASIL Insights* 11, no. 3 (2007), https://www.asil.org /insights/volume/11/issue/3/outcome-sixth-review-conference-biological -weapons-convention-november.

60. Millett, "Gaps."

61. UN Office for Disarmament Affairs, "UN Security Council Resolution 1540 (2004)," https://www.un.org/disarmament/wmd/sc1540/.

62. UN, "Security Council Adopts Resolution 2325 (2015), Calling for Framework to Keep Terrorists, Other Non-State Actors from Acquiring Weapons of Mass Destruction," December 15, 2016, https://www.un.org/press/en /2016/sc12628.doc.htm.

63. UN Security Council (S.C.), "Non-proliferation of Weapons of Mass Destruction," S.C. Res. 2325, December 15, 2016, http://unscr.com/en /resolutions/doc/2325.

64. WHO, *Responsible Life Sciences Research for Global Health Security* (Geneva: WHO, 2010), https://www.ncbi.nlm.nih.gov/books/NBK305043/.

65. WHO, *Report on Technical Consultation on H5N1 Research Issues* (Geneva: WHO, 2012), https://www.who.int/influenza/human_animal_interface /mtg_report_h5n1.pdf.

66. WHO, "Report of the WHO Informal Consultation on Dual Use Research of Concern," February 2013, https://www.who.int/csr/durc/durc_feb2013 _full_mtg_report.pdf.

## Chapter 5 · Antimicrobial Resistance

1. NIH, "NIH Uses Genome Sequencing to Help Quell Bacterial Outbreak in Clinical Center," August 22, 2012, https://www.nih.gov/news-events/news -releases/nih-uses-genome-sequencing-help-quell-bacterial-outbreak -clinical-center.

2. Debora MacKenzie, "Resistance to Last-Resort Antibiotic Has Now Spread across Globe," *New Scientist,* December 7, 2015, https://www.newscientist .com/article/dn28633-resistance-to-last-resort-antibiotic-has-now-spread -across-globe/.

3. MacKenzie, "Resistance to Last-Resort Antibiotic."

4. Review on Antimicrobial Resistance, "Tackling Drug-Resistant Infections: Final Report and Recommendations (May 2016)," https://amr-review.org /sites/default/files/160525_Final%20paper_with%20cover.pdf.

5. Fergus Walsh, "Superbugs to Kill 'More than Cancer' by 2050," BBC News, December 11, 2014.

6. Walsh, "Superbugs."

7. Sara Reardon, "Antibiotic Treatment for COVID-19 Complications Could Fuel Resistant Bacteria," *Science,* April 16, 2020.

8. Kelly Wroblewski, "Antibiotic Resistance: What Is It? Why Is It a Problem? What Is Being Done to Stop It?," Association of Public Health Laboratories, November 16, 2016, http://www.aphlblog.org/antimicrobial-resistance -what-is-it-why-is-it-a-problem-what-is-being-done-to-stop-it/.

9. Wanda C. Reygaert, "Insights on Antimicrobial Resistant Mechanisms in Bacteria," *Advances in Clinical and Medical Microbiology* 2, no. 1 (2016); "Intrinsic Resistance," Antimicrobial Resistance Learning Site, http://amrls

.cvm.msu.edu/microbiology/molecular-basis-for-antimicrobial-resistance /intrinsic-resistance; Georgina Cox and Gerald D. Wright, "Intrinsic Antibiotic Resistance: Mechanisms, Origins, Challenges and Solutions," *International Journal of Medical Microbiology* 303, no. 6–7 (2013): 287–292.

10. Frank Lowy, "Antibiotic Resistance," lecture note, Columbia University, New York, 2009, http://www.columbia.edu/itc/hs/medical/pathophys/id /2009/antibresiNotes.pdf.

11. Anthony R. M. Coates, Gerry Halls, and Yanmin Hu, "Novel Classes of Antibiotics or More of the Same?," *British Journal of Pharmacology* 163, no. 1 (2011): 184–194.

12. William Paul Hanage, Christophe Fraser, Jing Tang, et al., "Hyper-Recombination, Diversity, and Antibiotic Resistance in Pneumococcus," *Science* 324, no. 5923 (2009): 1454–1457.

13. Arunaloke Chakrabarti, "Drug Resistance in Fungi—An Emerging Problem," *Regional Health Forum* 15, no. 1 (2011): 97–102; David A. Fitzpatrick, "Horizontal Gene Transfer in Fungi," *FEMS Microbiology Letters* 329, no. 1 (2012): 1–8; James B. Anderson, "Evolution of Antifungal-Drug Resistance: Mechanisms and Pathogen Fitness," *Nature Reviews Microbiology* 3 (2005): 547–556.

14. Bhagya K. Wijayawardena, Dennis J. Minchella, and James Andrew DeWoody, "Hosts, Parasites, and Horizontal Gene Transfer," *Trends in Parasitology* 29, no. 7 (2013): 329–339.

15. Review on Antimicrobial Resistance, "Antimicrobial Resistance: Tackling a Crisis for the Health and Wealth of Nations (December 2014)," https://amr -review.org/sites/default/files/AMR%20Review%20Paper%20-%20 Tackling%20a%20crisis%20for%20the%20health%20and%20wealth%20 of%20nations_1.pdf.

16. Review on Antimicrobial Resistance, "Antimicrobial Resistance"; Marl-ieke E. A. de Kraker, Andrew J. Stewardson, and Stephan Harbarth, "Will 10 Million People Die a Year Due to Antimicrobial Resistance by 2050?," *PLOS Medicine* 13, no. 11 (2016): e1002184.

17. Haidong Wang, Moshen Naghavi, Christine Allen, et al., "Global, Re-gional, and National Life Expectancy, All-Cause Mortality, and Cause-Specific Mortality for 249 Causes of Death, 1980–2015: A Systematic Analysis for the Global Burden of Disease Study 2015," *Lancet* 388, no. 10053 (2016): 1459–1544.

18. Review on Antimicrobial Resistance, "Antimicrobial Resistance"; European Centre for Disease Control and Prevention, "33,000 People Die Every Year Due to Infections from Antibiotic-Resistant Bacteria," November 6, 2018, https://www.ecdc.europa.eu/en/news-events/33000-people-die-every-year -due-infections-antibiotic-resistant-bacteria; CDC, "Antibiotic / Antimicro-bial Resistance: Biggest Threats," September 10, 2018, https://www.cdc.gov /drugresistance/biggest_threats.html.

19. Review on Antimicrobial Resistance, "Antimicrobial Resistance."

20. "WHO Names 12 Bacteria That Pose the Greatest Threat to Human Health," *Guardian* (UK), February 27, 2017.

21. Richard Smith and Joanna Coast, "The True Cost of Antimicrobial Resistance," *BMJ* 346 (2013): 1493.

22. Nele Brusselaers, Dirk Vogelaers, and Stijn Blot, "The Rising Problem of Antimicrobial Resistance in the Intensive Care Unit," *Annals of Intensive Care* 1, no. 47 (2011).

23. Carolin Fleischmann, Andre Sherag, Neill K. J. Adhikari, et al., "Assessment of Global Incidence and Mortality of Hospital-Treated Sepsis: Current Estimates and Limitations," *American Journal of Respiratory and Critical Care Medicine* 193, no. 3 (2016): 259–272; Konrad Reinhart, Ron Daniels, Niranjan Kissoon, et al., "Recognizing Sepsis as a Global Health Priority—A WHO Resolution," *NEJM* 377 (2017): 414–417.

24. WHO, *Global Tuberculosis Report 2019*, 59, https://apps.who.int/iris /bitstream/handle/10665/329368/9789241565714-eng.pdf.

25. WHO, *Global Tuberculosis Report 2019*, 59.

26. Aditya Sharma, Andrew Hill, Ekaterina Kurbatova, et al., "Estimating the Future Burden of Multidrug-Resistant and Extensively Drug-Resistant Tuberculosis in India, the Philippines, Russia, and South Africa: A Mathematical Modelling Study," *Lancet Infectious Diseases* 17, no. 7 (2017): 707–715.

27. WHO, *Global Tuberculosis Report 2019*, 63.

28. WHO, *Global Tuberculosis Report 2019*, 102, 105.

29. "New Center to Reinforce Battle against TB in Peru," Partners in Health (blog), September 15, 2016, http://www.pih.org/blog/new-center-to -reinforce-battle-against-tb-in-peru.

30. Donald G. McNeil Jr., "Cure Found for Deadliest Strain of Tuberculosis," *New York Times*, August 15, 2019.

31. Stop TB Partnership, *The Paradigm Shift, 2016–2020: Global Plan to End TB* (Geneva: Stop TB Partnership, 2015), http://www.stoptb.org/assets /documents/global/plan/GlobalPlanToEndTB_TheParadigmShift_2016 -2020_StopTBPartnership.pdf.

32. WHO, "WHO Interim Guidance on the Use of Delamanid in the Treatment of MDR-TB," October 28, 2014, http://www.who.int/tb/features _archive/delamanid/en/.

33. Médecins Sans Frontières, "Médecins Sans Frontières Response to the World Health Organization Global Tuberculosis Report," October 30, 2017, https://www.msfaccess.org/about-us/media-room/press-releases/m%C3%A9decins -sans-fronti%C3%A8res-response-world-health-organization.

34. Guido V. Bloemberg, Sebastien Gagneux, and Erik C. Bottger, "Acquired Resistance to Bedaquiline and Delamanid in Therapy for Tuberculosis," *NEJM* 373, no. 20 (2015):1986–1988.

35. McNeil, "Cure Found."

36. WHO, "Frequently Asked Questions about the Implementation of the New WHO Recommendation on the Use of the Shorter MDR-TB Regimen under

Programmatic Conditions," December 20, 2016, http://www.who.int/tb/areas
-of-work/drug-resistant-tb/treatment/FAQshorter_MDR_regimen.pdf;
WHO, *WHO Treatment Guidelines for Drug-Resistant Tuberculosis* (Geneva:
WHO, 2016), http://apps.who.int/iris/bitstream/handle/10665/250125
/9789241549639-eng.pdf.

37. "Inadequate Treatment," TB Alliance, https://www.tballiance.org/why-new
-tb-drugs/inadequate-treatment.

38. Huda Munir, "Drug Resistant Tuberculosis," Health Units (blog), December
20, 2016, https://healthunits.com/tuberculosis/mdr-tb-treatment/; Puneet
Bhardwaj, Atul Manoharrao Deshkar, and Rahul Verma, "Side Effects
Encountered in Treatment of Multidrug-Resistant Tuberculosis: A 3-Year
Experience at First Dots Plus Site of Chhattisgarh," *International Journal of
Scientific Study* 3, no. 5 (2015): 104–107.

39. WHO, *Global Tuberculosis Report 2016*.

40. Suzanne M. Marks, Jennifer Flood, Barbara Seaworth, et al., "Treatment
Practices, Outcomes, and Costs of Multidrug-Resistant and Extensively
Drug-Resistant Tuberculosis, United States, 2005–2007," *Emerging Infec-
tious Diseases* 20, no. 5 (2014): 812–821.

41. Anonymous, email to Eric A. Friedman, May 23, 2017.

42. Marcel Tanner and Don de Savigny, "Malaria Eradication Back on the
Table," *Bulletin of the World Health Organization* 86, no. 2 (2008): 81–160.

43. CDC, "Drug Resistance in the Malaria-Endemic World," September 22,
2015, https://www.cdc.gov/malaria/malaria_worldwide/reduction/drug
_resistance.htm; WHO, *Global Plan for Artemisinin Resistance Containment*
(Geneva: WHO, 2011), http://www.who.int/malaria/publications/atoz
/artemisinin_resistance_containment_2011.pdf.

44. Danielle Renwick, "Can Malaria Be Eradicated?," Council on Foreign
Relations, October 5, 2016, https://www.cfr.org/backgrounder/can-malaria
-be-eradicated; Christopher J. L. Murray, Lisa C. Rosenfeld, Stephen S.
Lim, et al., "Global Malaria Mortality between 1980 and 2010: A Systematic Analysis," *Lancet* 379, no. 9814 (2012): 413–431.

45. WHO, *World Malaria Report 2019* (Geneva: WHO, 2019), 11, https://www
.who.int/publications-detail/world-malaria-report-2019.

46. "History of Malaria," Wikipedia, https://en.wikipedia.org/wiki/History_of
_malaria#Antimalarial_drugs_2.

47. T. K. Mutabingwa, "Artemisinin-Based Combination Therapies (ACTs):
Best Hope for Malaria Treatment but Inaccessible to the Needy!," *Acta
Tropica* 95, no. 3 (2005): 305–315.

48. "Artemisinin-Based Combination Therapy," Malaria Consortium,
http://www.malariaconsortium.org/pages/112.htm.

49. WHO, *Global Plan for Artemisinin Resistance Containment*.

50. Mallika Imwong, Tran T. Hien, Nguyen T. Thuy-Nhien, et al., "Spread of a
Single Multidrug Resistant Malaria Parasite Lineage (*PfPailin*) to Vietnam,"
*Lancet Infectious Diseases* 17, no. 10 (2017): 1022–1023.

51. Kate Kelland, "Multi-Drug Resistant Malaria Spreading in Southeast Asia: Study," Reuters, July 22, 2019.
52. WHO, *World Malaria Report 2019,* 35.
53. Frankline M. Onchiri, Patricia B. Pavlinac, Benson O. Singa, et al., "Frequency and Correlates of Malaria Over-Treatment in Areas of Differing Malaria Transmission: A Cross-Sectional Study in Rural Western Kenya," *Malaria Journal* 14 (2015): art. 97.
54. Bertrand Graz, Merlin Willcox, Thomas Szeless, and André Rougemont, "'Test and Treat' or Presumptive Treatment for Malaria in High Transmission Situations? A Reflection on the Latest WHO Guidelines," *Malaria Journal* 10 (2011): art. 136; Ambrose O. Talisuna, Peter Bloland, and Umberto D'Alessandro, "History, Dynamics, and Public Health Importance of Malaria Parasite Resistance," *Clinical Microbiology Reviews* 17, no. 1 (2004): 235–254.
55. Gaurvika M. L. Nayyar, Joel G. Breman, Paul N. Newton, et al., "Poor-Quality Antimalarial Drugs in Southeast Asia and Sub-Saharan Africa," *Lancet Infectious Diseases* 12, no. 6 (2012): 488–496.
56. Harparkash Kaur, Elizabeth Louise Allan, Ibrahim Mamadu, et al., "Quality of Artemisinin-Based Combination Formulations for Malaria Treatment: Prevalence and Risk Factors for Poor Quality Medicines in Public Facilities and Private Sector Drug Outlets in Enugu, Nigeria," *PLOS One* 10, no. 5 (2015): e0125577; Magdalena Mis, "Substandard Drugs, Not Fakes, Undermine Fight against Malaria," Reuters, April 20, 2015.
57. WHO, *World Malaria Report 2019,* 72–73.
58. WHO, *Consolidated Guidelines on the Use of Antiretroviral Drugs for Treating and Preventing HIV Infection: Recommendations for a Public Health Approach* (Geneva: WHO, 2016); WHO, "Statement on DTG," May 18, 2018, http://www.who.int/medicines/publications/drugalerts/Statement_on_DTG_18May_2018final.pdf.
59. WHO, "WHO Recommends Dolutegravir as Preferred HIV Treatment Option in All Populations," July 22, 2019, https://www.who.int/news-room/detail/22-07-2019-who-recommends-dolutegravir-as-preferred-hiv-treatment-option-in-all-populations.
60. WHO, *Consolidated Guidelines on the Use of Antiretroviral Drugs.*
61. WHO, "WHO Publishes List of Bacteria for Which New Antibiotics Are Urgently Needed," February 27, 2017, http://www.who.int/mediacentre/news/releases/2017/bacteria-antibiotics-needed/en/; CDC, "Antibiotic/Antimicrobial Resistance: Biggest Threats," September 10, 2018, https://www.cdc.gov/drugresistance/biggest_threats.html.
62. Krisztina M. Papp-Wallace, Andrea Endimiani, Magdalena A. Taracila, et al., "Carbapenems: Past, Present, and Future," *Antimicrobial Agents and Chemotherapy* 55, no. 11 (2011): 4943–4960.
63. CDC, "Carbapenem-Resistant Enterobacteriaceae (CRE) Infection: Patient FAQs," https://www.cdc.gov/hai/organisms/cre/cre-patientfaq.html; CDC,

"Carbapenem-Resistant Enterobacteriaceae in Healthcare Settings," February 23, 2015, https://www.cdc.gov/hai/organisms/cre/index.html.

64. CDC, "Action Needed to Prevent Spread of Deadly Bacteria," March 5, 2013, https://www.cdc.gov/media/releases/2013/p0305_deadly_bacteria .html.

65. European Centre for Disease Control and Prevention, "Rapid Risk Assessment: Carbapenem-Resistant Enterobacteriaceae—First Update," June 7, 2018, https://www.ecdc.europa.eu/en/publications-data/rapid-risk -assessment-carbapenem-resistant-enterobacteriaceae-first-update.

66. CDC, *Antibiotic Resistance Threats in the United States 2019* (Atlanta: CDC, 2019), 71–72, https://www.cdc.gov/drugresistance/pdf/threats-report/2019 -ar-threats-report-508.pdf; National Institute for Health and Care Excellence, "Clostridium Difficile Infection: Risk with Broad-Spectrum Antibiotics," March 2015, https://www.nice.org.uk/advice/esmpb1/chapter/key -points-from-the-evidence.

67. CDC, "Nearly Half a Million Americans Suffered from Clostridium Difficile Infections in a Single Year," February 25, 2015, https://www.cdc .gov/media/releases/2015/p0225-clostridium-difficile.html; CDC, "Antibiotic / Antimicrobial Resistance: Biggest Threats," September 10, 2018, https://www.cdc.gov/drugresistance/biggest_threats.html.

68. Zhong Peng, Dazhi Jin, Hyen Bum Kim, et al., "Update on Antimicrobial Resistance in *Clostridium difficile:* Resistance Mechanisms and Antimicrobial Susceptibility Testing," *Journal of Clinical Microbiology* 55, no. 7 (2017): 1998–2008.

69. Patrizia Spigaglia, "Recent Advances in the Understanding of Antibiotic Resistance in *Clostridium difficile* Infection," *Therapeutic Advances in Infectious Disease* 3, no. 1 (2016): 23–42.

70. CDC, *Antibiotic Resistance Threats in the United States 2019*, 85.

71. Tristan O'Driscoll and Christopher W. Crank, "Vancomycin-Resistant Enterococcal Infections: Epidemiology, Clinical Manifestations, and Optimal Management," *Infection and Drug Resistance* 8 (2015): 217–220; Wondwossen Abebe, Mengistu Endris, Moges Tiruneh, and Feleke Moges, "Prevalence of Vancomycin Resistant *Enterococci* and Associated Risk Factors among Clients with and without HIV in Northwest Ethiopia: A Cross-Sectional Study," *BMC Public Health* 14 (2014): art. 185.

72. O'Driscoll and Crank, "Vancomycin-Resistant Enterococcal Infections."

73. Madeleine G. Sowash and Anne-Catrin Uhlemann, "Community-Associated Methicillin-Resistant *Staphylococcus aureus* Case Studies," *Methods in Microbiology* 1085 (2013):25–69.

74. CDC, *Antibiotic Resistance Threats in the United States 2019*, 17, 95–96; Sepsis Alliance, "MRSA," https://www.sepsis.org/sepsisand/mrsa/.

75. C. Lee Ventola, "The Antibiotic Resistance Crisis: Part I: Causes and Threats," *Pharmacy and Therapeutics* 40, no. 4 (2015): 277–283.

76. CDC, *Antibiotic Resistance Threats in the United States 2019*, 96.

77. Sam Wong, "MRSA's Resistance to Antibiotics Is Broken," *New Scientist*, March 9, 2016, https://www.newscientist.com/article/2080180-mrsa -superbugs-resistance-to-antibiotics-is-broken/.

78. CDC, "Fast Facts about Antibiotics," December 22, 2016, https://www.cdc .gov/getsmart/community/about/fast-facts.html.

79. Bashir Gaash, "Irrational Use of Antibiotics," *Indian Journal for the Practicing Doctor* 5, no. 1 (2008).

80. Eili Y. Klein, Thomas P. Van Boeckel, Elena M. Martinez, et al., "Global Increase and Geographic Convergence in Antibiotic Consumption between 2000 and 2015," *PNAS* 115, no. 15 (2018): e3463–e3470.

81. Günther Fink, Valérie D'Acremont, Hannah H. Leslie, and Jessica Cohen, "Antibiotic Exposure among Children Younger than 5 Years in Low-Income and Middle-Income Countries: A Cross-Sectional Study of Nationally Representative Facility-Based and Household-Based Surveys," *Lancet Infectious Diseases* 20, no. 2 (2020): 179–187.

82. Agence France-Presse, "WHO Maps Dangerous Misuse of Antibiotics," *France 24*, November 12, 2018, https://www.france24.com/en/20181112 -who-maps-dangerous-misuse-antibiotics.

83. Review on Antimicrobial Resistance, "Rapid Diagnostics: Stopping Unnecessary Use of Antibiotics (October 2015)," https://amr-review.org /sites/default/files/Paper-Rapid-Diagnostics-Stopping-Unnecessary -Prescription-Low-Res.pdf.

84. Gaash, "Irrational Use of Antibiotics."

85. Ron Sender, Shai Fuchs, and Ron Milo, "Revised Estimates for the Number of Human and Bacteria Cells in the Body," *PLOS Biology* 14, no. 8 (2016): e1002533.

86. "Antibiotic Resistance: Delaying the Inevitable," Understanding Evolution, http://evolution.berkeley.edu/evolibrary/article/medicine_03.

87. Pete Todd and Rein Houben, "New Estimate Suggests a Quarter of the World's Population Has Latent Tuberculosis," *The Conversation*, October 25, 2016, https://theconversation.com/new-estimate-suggests-a-quarter-of-the -worlds-population-has-latent-tuberculosis-65456.

88. Kathleen Anne Holloway, "Promoting the Rational Use of Antibiotics," *Regional Health Forum* 15, no. 1 (2011): 122–130.

89. Review on Antimicrobial Resistance, "Rapid Diagnostics," 1.

90. "Antibiotic Resistance: New Findings, Approaches to a Public Health Crisis," AMN Healthcare, August 19, 2012, https://www.amnhealthcare .com/latest-healthcare-news/327/1033/.

91. Jean Carlet, Vincent Jarlier, Stephan Harbarth, et al., "Ready for a World without Antibiotics? The Pensières Antibiotic Resistance Call to Action," *Antibiotic Resistance and Infection Control* 1 (2012): art. 11.

92. WHO, *Antibiotic Resistance: Multi-Country Public Awareness Survey* (Geneva: WHO, 2015), http://apps.who.int/medicinedocs/documents/s22245en /s22245en.pdf.

93. Peter Schwartzstein, "The Syrian Civil War Could Spell the End of Antibiotics," *Newsweek,* September 14, 2016; Carrie Lee Teicher, Jean-Baptiste Ronat, Rasheed M. Fakri, et al., "Antimicrobial Drug-Resistant Bacteria Isolated from Syrian War-Injured Patients, August 2011– March 2013," *Emerging Infectious Diseases* 20, no. 11 (2014): 1949–1951.

94. WHO, Regional Office for Europe, "Pharmacists Have Decisive Role in Combating Antibiotic Resistance, Says New WHO European Survey," November 13, 2014, http://www.euro.who.int/data/assets/pdf_file/0003 /263109/Press-release,-Pharmacists-have-decisive-role-in-combating -antibiotic-resistance,-says-new-WHO-European-survey.pdf.

95. Carl Lolr and Josep Maria Cots, "The Sale of Antibiotics without Prescription in Pharmacies in Catalonia, Spain," *Clinical Infectious Diseases* 48, no. 10 (2009): 1345–1349.

96. Review on Antimicrobial Resistance, "Rapid Diagnostics."

97. WHO, *Antibiotic Resistance: Multi-Country Public Awareness Survey.*

98. Lolr and Cots, "The Sale of Antibiotics."

99. Luca Garofalo, Gabriella Di Giuseppe, and Italo F. Angelillo, "Self-Medication Practices among Parents in Italy," *BioMed Research International* 2015 (2015).

100. Review on Antimicrobial Resistance, *Rapid Diagnostics.*

101. WHO, *Antibiotic Resistance: Multi-Country Public Awareness Survey.*

102. KwaZulu-Natal Provincial Council on AIDS, "Understanding Factors Contributing to Treatment Non Adherence in Patients on Anti-Retroviral Therapy (2012)," http://www.kznonline.gov.za/hivaids/councils/Provincial -Councils-on-AIDS/2012/PCA%20Treatment%20Access%20Concept%20 Paper%20-%20DR%20MNDAWENI.pdf.

103. American Heart Association, "Medication Adherence: Taking Your Meds as Directed," September 2, 2016, http://www.heart.org/HEARTORG /Conditions/More/ConsumerHealthCare/Medication-Adherence—Taking -Your-Meds-as-Directed_UCM_453329_Article.jsp#.WcBR5U2ovct; V. G. Bhat, M. Ramburuth, M. Singh, et al., "Factors Associated with Poor Adherence to Anti-Retroviral Therapy in Patients Attending a Rural Health Centre in South Africa," *European Journal of Clinical Microbiology and Infectious Diseases* 29, no. 8 (2010): 947–953.

104. Lawrence O. Gostin, Gillian J. Buckley, and Patrick W. Kelley, "Stemming the Global Trade in Falsified and Substandard Medicines," *JAMA* 309, no. 16 (2013):1693–1694.

105. UN Office on Drugs and Crime (UNODC), *Transnational Trafficking and the Rule of Law in West Africa: A Threat Assessment* (Vienna: UNODC, July 2009), https://www.osservatoriodiritti.it/wp-content/uploads/2017/05 /traffico-esseri-umani-africa.pdf.

106. WHO, "Substandard, Spurious, Falsely Labelled, Falsified and Counterfeit (SSFFC) Medical Products," Fact Sheet, January 31, 2018, http://www.who .int/mediacentre/factsheets/fs275/en/.

107. WHO, "1 in 10 Medical Products in Developing Countries Is Substandard or Falsified," November 28, 2017, http://www.who.int/mediacentre/news /releases/2017/substandard-falsified-products/en/.

108. A. N. Khan and R. K. Khar, "Current Scenario of Spurious and Substandard Medicines in India: A Systematic Review," *Indian Journal of Pharmaceutical Sciences* 77, no. 1 (2015): 2–7.

109. Gardiner Harris, "Medicines Made in India Set Off Safety Worries," *New York Times,* February 14, 2014.

110. Institute of Medicine, *Countering the Problem of Falsified and Substandard Drugs* (Washington, DC: National Academies Press, 2013).

111. NIH, "Global Pandemic of Fake Medicines Poses Urgent Risk, Scientists Say," April 20, 2015, https://www.nih.gov/news-events/news-releases/global -pandemic-fake-medicines-poses-urgent-risk-scientists-say.

112. Harris, "Medicines Made in India."

113. Review on Antimicrobial Resistance, "Infection Prevention, Control and Surveillance: Limiting the Development and Spread of Drug Resistance (March 2016)," https://amr-review.org/sites/default/files/Health%20 infrastructure%20and%20surveillance%20final%20version_LR_NO%20 CROPS.pdf.

114. FDA, "Antibacterial Soap? You Can Skip It—Use Plain Soap and Water," September 2, 2016, https://www.fda.gov/consumers/consumer-updates /antibacterial-soap-you-can-skip-it-use-plain-soap-and-water.

115. Alexandra Sifferlin, "How to Cut Antibiotic Use in Animals," *Time,* September 28, 2017.

116. Michaeleen Doucleff, "For the Love of Pork: Antibiotic Use on Farms Skyrockets Worldwide," NPR, March 20, 2015.

117. Thomas P. Van Boeckel, Emma E. Glennon, Dora Chen, et al., "Reducing Antimicrobial Use in Food Animals," *Science* 357, no. 6358 (2017): 1350–1352.

118. Thomas P. Van Boeckel, Charles Brower, Marius Gilbert, et al., "Global Trends in Antimicrobial Use in Food Animals," *PNAS* 122, no. 18 (2015): 5649–5654.

119. Charu Bahri, "Antibiotics Used in India's Poultry Farms Endangering Human Lives, Says Expert," *Hindustan Times,* August 6, 2017, http://www .hindustantimes.com/health/antibiotics-use-by-india-s-poultry-farms -endangering-human-lives-says-expert/story-6W6b10gfdUKhOkrTSscDlL .html.

120. Van Boeckel et al., "Reducing Antimicrobial Use in Food Animals."

121. Rosine Manishimwe, Kizito Nishimwe, and Lonzy Ojok, "Assessment of Antibiotic Use in Farm Animals in Rwanda," *Tropical Animal Health and Production* 49, no 6 (2017): 1101–1106.

122. Maureen Ogle, "Riots, Rage, and Resistance: A Brief History of How Antibiotics Arrived on the Farm," Scientific American (blog), September 3,

2013, https://blogs.scientificamerican.com/guest-blog/riots-rage-and
-resistance-a-brief-history-of-how-antibiotics-arrived-on-the-farm/.

123. President's Council of Advisors on Science and Technology (PCAST),
"Report to the President on Combating Antibiotic Resistance (September 2014)," https://obamawhitehouse.archives.gov/sites/default/files
/microsites/ostp/PCAST/pcast_amr_jan2015.pdf.

124. Scott Weathers, Sophie Hermanns, and Scott Bittman, "Health Leaders
Must Focus on the Threats from Factory Farms," *New York Times*, May 21,
2017.

125. Fiona Harvey, Andrew Wasley, Madlen Davies, and David Child, "Rise of
Mega Farms: How the US Model of Intensive Farming Is Invading the
World," *Guardian* (UK), July 18, 2018.

126. Qiuzhi Chang, Weike Wang, Gili Regev-Yochay, et al., "Antibiotics in
Agriculture and the Risk to Human Health: How Worried Should We Be?,"
*Evolutionary Applications* 8 (2015): 240–245.

127. Chang et al., "Antibiotics in Agriculture."

128. Compassion in World Farming, "Antibiotics in Animal Farming: Public Health
and Animal Welfare (2011)," https://www.ciwf.org.uk/media/3758863
/Antibiotics-in-Animal-Farming-Public-Health-and-Animal-Welfare.pdf;
Matthew Perrone, "Does Giving Antibiotics to Animals Hurt Humans?,"
*Seattle Times*, April 20, 2012; Ellen P. Carlin, "The Use of Antibiotics
in Farm Animals," letter to the editor, *New York Times*, August 5,
2014.

129. FDA, "Guidance for Industry: The Judicious Use of Medically Important
Antimicrobial Drugs in Food-Producing Animals," April 13, 2012,
https://www.fda.gov/media/79140/download.

130. Compassion in World Farming, "Antibiotics in Animal Farming"; Mark
Woolhouse, Melissa Ward, Bram van Bunnik, et al., "Antimicrobial
Resistance in Humans, Livestock and the Wider Environment," *Philo-
sophical Transactions of the Royal Society B: Biological Sciences* 370, no. 1670
(2015).

131. Environmental Working Group, "Superbugs Invade America's Supermarket
Meat," April 15, 2013, http://www.ewg.org/release/superbugs-invade
-america-s-supermarket-meat#.WdfrGE2ovcs.

132. FDA, "Guidance for Industry."

133. FDA, "Guidance for Industry."

134. Coates, Halls, and Hu, "Novel Classes of Antibiotics"; Gene Stowe and
Marissa Gebhard, "Notre Dame Chemists Discover New Class of Antibiotics," Notre Dame News, March 6, 2014, https://news.nd.edu/news/notre
-dame-chemists-discover-new-class-of-antibiotics/; Laura J. V. Piddock,
"Teixobactin, the First of a New Class of Antibiotics Discovered by iChip
Technology?," *Journal of Antimicrobial Chemotherapy* 70, no. 10 (2015):
2679–2680; "Researchers Identify New Class of Antibiotics with Potential

to Fight 'Superbugs,'" Brown University, March 28, 2018, https://news
.brown.edu/articles/2018/03/mrsa; Arlene Weintraub, "Nematodes Inspire
New Class of Antibiotic," FierceBiotech, April 9, 2018, https://www
.fiercebiotech.com/research/nematodes-inspire-new-class-antibiotic.

135. Sarah Knapton, "First New Antibiotic in 30 Years Discovered in Major
Breakthrough," *Telegraph,* January 7, 2016.

136. Coates, Halls, and Hu, "Novel Classes of Antibiotics."

137. "Resistance to Antibiotics: The Spread of Superbugs," briefing, *Economist,*
March 31, 2011.

138. Ed Yong, "The Plan to Avert Our Post-Antibiotic Apocalypse," *Atlantic,*
May 19, 2016.

139. Daniel Becker, Matthias Selbach, Claudia Rollenhagen, et al., "Robust
*Salmonella* Metabolism Limits Possibilities for New Antimicrobials," *Nature*
440, no. 7082 (2006): 303–307; Anthony Coates, Yanmin Hu, Richard Bax,
and Clive Page, "The Future Challenges Facing the Development of New
Antimicrobial Drugs," *Nature Reviews Drug Discovery* 1 (2002): 895–910.

140. Coates, Halls, and Hu, "Novel Classes of Antibiotics."

141. Andrew Jacobs, "Deadly Germs, Lost Cures: Crisis Looms in Antibiotics as
Drug Makers Go Bankrupt," *New York Times,* December 25, 2019.

142. Review on Antimicrobial Resistance, "Rapid Diagnostics."

143. Craig R. Fox, Jeffrey A. Linder, and Jason N. Doctor, "How to Not Prescribe Antibiotics," *New York Times,* March 25, 2016.

144. Scott W. Olesen, Michael L. Barnett, Derek R. MacFadden, et al., "Trends
in Outpatient Antibiotic Use and Prescribing Practice among US Older
Adults, 2011–15: Observational Study," *BMJ* 362 (2018): k3155.

145. WHO, "Stop Using Antibiotics in Healthy Animals to Stop the Spread of
Antibiotic Resistance," November 7, 2017, https://www.who.int/en/news
-room/detail/07-11-2017-stop-using-antibiotics-in-healthy-animals-to
-prevent-the-spread-of-antibiotic-resistance.

146. "Working with Women," Farm Africa, https://www.farmafrica.org/us/what
-we-do-1/working-with-women.

147. Institute of Medicine, *Countering the Problem.*

148. Review on Antimicrobial Resistance, "Securing New Drugs for Future
Generations: The Pipeline of Antibiotics (May 2015)," https://amr-review
.org/sites/default/files/SECURING%20NEW%20DRUGS%20FOR%20
FUTURE%20GENERATIONS%20FINAL%20WEB_0.pdf.

149. Coates, Halls, and Hu, "Novel Classes of Antibiotics."

150. Chantal M. Morel and Elias Mossialos, "Stocking the Antibiotic Pipeline,"
*BMJ* 340 (2010): c2115; PCAST, "Report to the President."

151. Review on Antimicrobial Resistance, "Securing New Drugs."

152. PCAST, "Report to the President."

153. Review on Antimicrobial Resistance, "Securing New Drugs."

154. Review on Antimicrobial Resistance, "Securing New Drugs."

155. "All Trials Registered; All Results Reported," AllTrials, http://www.alltrials
.net/find-out-more/all-trials/.

156. WHO, *Global Action Plan on Antimicrobial Resistance* (Geneva: WHO, 2015), http://apps.who.int/iris/bitstream/10665/193736/1/9789241509763 _eng.pdf.

157. WHO, *WHO Guidelines on Use of Medically Important Anti-Microbials in Food-Producing Animals* (Geneva: WHO, 2017), http://apps.who.int/iris /bitstream/10665/258970/1/9789241550130-eng.pdf.

158. Ann Versporten, Peter Zarb, Isabelle Caniaux, et al., "Antimicrobial Consumption and Resistance in Adult Hospital Inpatients in 53 Countries: Results of an Internet-Based Global Point Prevalence Survey," *Lancet Global Health* 6 (2018): e619–e629.

159. Food and Agricultural Organization of the UN, "Codex Alimentarius: Code of Practice to Minimize and Contain Antimicrobial Resistance, CAC / RCP 61-2005 (2005)," http://www.fao.org/fao-who -codexalimentarius/codex-texts/codes-of-practice/en/.

160. Food and Agricultural Organization of the UN, "Codex Alimentarius: Code of Practice."

161. World Organisation for Animal Health, "The OIE Strategy on Antimicrobial Resistance and the Prudent Use of Antimicrobials (November 2016)," http://www.oie.int/fileadmin/Home/eng/Media_Center/docs/pdf /PortailAMR/EN_OIE-AMRstrategy.pdf.

162. UN, *Political Declaration of the High-Level Meeting of the General Assembly on Antimicrobial Resistance* (General Assembly, New York, October 5, 2016), http://www.who.int/antimicrobial-resistance/interagency-coordination -group/UNGA-AMR-RES-71-3-N1631065.pdf.

163. UN Secretary-General, "Interagency Coordination Group on Antimicrobial Resistance," March 17, 2017, https://www.un.org/sg/en/content/sg/personnel -appointments/2017-03-17/interagency-coordination-group-antimicrobial -resistance.

164. Interagency Coordination Group on Antimicrobial Resistance, "No Time to Wait: Securing the Future from Drug-Resistant Infections (April 2019)," https://www.who.int/antimicrobial-resistance/interagency-coordination -group/IACG_final_report_EN.pdf?ua=1.

165. G7, *Annex to the Leaders' Declaration* (G7 Summit, Schloss Elmau, Germany, June 7–8, 2015), http://www.g8.utoronto.ca/summit/2015elmau/2015-G7 -annex-en.pdf; G7, *G7 Ise-Shima Vision for Global Health* (Ise-Shima, Japan, May 26–27, 2016), http://www.mofa.go.jp/files/000160273.pdf.

166. "About the Global Health Security Agenda," Global Health Security Agenda (GHSA), https://www.ghsagenda.org/.

167. "Action Packages," GHSA, https://ghsagenda.org/home/action-packages/; Bonnie Jenkins, "The Global Health Security Agenda (GHSA)," Conference Presentation at the Association of Public Health Laboratories, Albuquerque, New Mexico, June 6, 2016, https://www.aphl.org/conferences/proceedings /Documents/2016/Annual_Meeting/03Jenkins.pdf.

168. "Antimicrobial Resistance," GHSA, https://ghsagenda.org/home/action -packages/antimicrobial-resistance/.

169. Hellen Gelband, "Antimicrobial Resistance: Public Policy Implications," PowerPoint presentation, Center for Disease Dynamics, Economics & Policy, March 23, 2017, http://www.aplu.org/projects-and-initiatives /agriculture-human-sciences-and-natural-resources/antibiotics-and -agriculture/gelband_presentation_march_2017.pdf.

170. Sharon Levy, "Reduced Antibiotic Use in Livestock: How Denmark Tackled Resistance," *Environmental Health Perspectives* 122, no. 6 (2014): A160–A165.

171. D. C. Speksnijder, D. J. Mevius, C. J. Bruschke, and J. A. Wagenaar, "Reduction of Veterinary Antimicrobial Use in the Netherlands: The Dutch Success Model," *Zoonoses and Public Health* 62, suppl. 1 (2014): 79–87.

172. E. I. Schippers, M. J. van Rijin, A. M. Dijksma, and W. J. Mansveld, *Appendix 1 of the Letter to Parliament on the Approach to Antibiotic Resistance,* Government of the Netherlands, June 24, 2015, https://www.government.nl /documents/parliamentary-documents/2015/06/24/appendix-1-of-the-letter -to-parliament-on-the-approach-to-antibiotic-resistance.

173. Coates, Halls, and Hu, "Novel Classes of Antibiotics"; PCAST, "Report to the President."

174. "Actinobacteria," Wikipedia, https://en.wikipedia.org/wiki/Actinobacteria.

175. Angelika Gründling, "New Class of Antibiotics Discovered," *The Conversation,* January 9, 2015.

176. Wolfgang Wohlleben, Yvonne Mast, Evi Stegmann, and Nadine Ziemert, "Antibiotic Drug Discovery," *Microbial Biotechnology* 9, no. 5 (2016): 541–548.

177. Robert Lee Hotz, "Scientists Unearth Hope for New Antibiotics," *Wall Street Journal,* February 13, 2018.

178. Wohlleben et al., "Antibiotic Drug Discovery."

179. Donald G. McNeil Jr., "In a Dragon's Blood, Scientists Discover a Potential Antibiotic," *New York Times,* April 18, 2017.

180. Tori Rodriguez, "Essential Oils Might Be the New Antibiotics," *Atlantic,* January 16, 2015.

181. Peter I. O'Daniel, Zhihong Peng, Hualiang Pi, et al., "Discovery of a New Class of Non-β-lactam Inhibitors of Penicillin- Binding Proteins with Gram-Positive Antibacterial Activity," *Journal of American Chemical Society* 136 (2014): 3664–3672.

182. Victoria Corless, "In Silico Screening as an Effective Tool in Drug Discovery," Organic & Biomolecular Chemistry (blog), December 15, 2017, http://blogs.rsc.org/ob/2017/12/15/in-silico-screening-as-an-effective-tool -in-drug-discovery/.

183. Maria Temming, "Superbugs May Meet Their Match in These Nanoparticles," *ScienceNews,* October 9, 2017, https://www.sciencenews.org/article /superbugs-may-meet-their-match-these-nanoparticles; Colleen M. Courtney, Samuel M. Goodman, Toni A. Nagy, et al., "Potentiating Antibiotics in Drug-Resistant Clinical Isolates via Stimuli-Activated Superoxide Generation," *Science Advances* 3, no. 10 (2017): e1701776.

184. Heidi Ledford, "Hundreds of Antibiotics Built from Scratch," *Nature,* May 18, 2016.

185. "'Ancientbiotics' Researchers Look for Old Fixes to Modern Ailments," NPR, April 23, 2017.

186. Sara Reardon, "Phage Therapy Gets Revitalized," *Nature,* June 3, 2014; "Pitting Viruses against Bacteria to Combat Antibiotic Crisis," *Science Friday,* March 9, 2018, https://www.sciencefriday.com/segments/pitting -viruses-against-bacteria-to-combat-the-antibiotic-crisis/.

187. Sara Reardon, "Modified Viruses Deliver Death to Antibiotic Resistant Bacteria," *Nature,* June 21, 2017.

188. David Bikard and Rodolphe Barrangou, "Using CRISPR-Cas Systems as Antimicrobials," *Current Opinion in Microbiology* 37 (2017): 155–160.

189. Department of Health and Social Care and Prime Minister's Office, 10 Downing Street, "UK and China Start Global Fund to Tackle Drug Resistant Infections," GOV.UK, October 23, 2015, https://www.gov.uk /government/news/uk-and-china-start-global-fund-to-tackle-drug-resistant -infections; Department of Health and Social Care, "Expert Advisory Board to Support the Global AMR Innovation Fund," GOV.UK, November 29, 2016, https://www.gov.uk/government/news/expert-advisory-board-to -support-the-global-amr-innovation-fund.

190. Joe Larsen, "BARDA Seeks to Launch a Novel Partnership, a Product Accelerator to Address Antimicrobial Resistance," ASPR (blog), February 19, 2016, http://www.phe.gov/ASPRBlog/pages/BlogArticlePage.aspx?PostID =176.

191. "About GARDP," Global Antibiotic Research and Development Partnership, https://www.gardp.org/.

192. Review on Antimicrobial Resistance, *Tackling Drug-Resistant Infections.*

193. Review on Antimicrobial Resistance, *Tackling Drug-Resistant Infections.*

194. "Reinvigorating Antibiotic and Diagnostic Innovation Act of 2017," H.R. 1840 (115th Cong.), introduced March 30, 2017, https://www.congress.gov /bill/115th-congress/house-bill/1840.

195. "Reinvigorating Antibiotic and Diagnostic Innovation Act of 2017."

196. David Shlaes, "REVAMP: Congress Considers a Fix for Antibiotic Resistance," American Council on Science and Health, July 11, 2018, https://www.acsh.org/news/2018/07/11/shlaes-711-13179; Lisa Schnirring, "Bipartisan Bill Proposes New 'Pull' Incentives for Priority Antibiotics," CIDRAP, June 29, 2018, http://www.cidrap.umn.edu/news-perspective /2018/06/bipartisan-bill-proposes-new-pull-incentives-priority -antibiotics.

197. PCAST, "Report to the President"; Review on Antimicrobial Resistance, *Tackling Drug-Resistant Infections.*

198. Mitchell J. Schwaber, Boaz Lev, Avi Israeli, et al., "Containment of a Country-Wide Outbreak of Carbapenem-Resistant *Klebsiella pneumoniae* in Israeli Hospitals via a Nationally Implemented Intervention," *Clinical Infectious Disease* 52, no. 7 (2011): 848–855.

199. Silas Webb, "A Bitter Pill to Swallow: The Problem of, and Solutions to, Sub-Saharan Africa's Counterfeit Pharmaceutical Trade," *Journal of Global Health*, November 1, 2014.
200. Marlieke E. A. de Kraker, Andrew J. Stewardson, and Stephan Harbarth, "Will 10 Million People Die a Year Due to Antimicrobial Resistance by 2050?," *PLOS Medicine* 13, no. 11 (2016): e1002184.

## Chapter 6 · The Climate Crisis

1. Editorial Board, "Wake Up, World Leaders: The Alarm Is Deafening," *New York Times*, October 9, 2018.
2. Somini Sengupta, "U.S. Midwest Freezes, Australia Burns: This Is the Age of Weather Extremes," *New York Times*, January 29, 2019.
3. Meera Subrahmanian, "India's Terrifying Water Crisis," *New York Times*, July 16, 2019.
4. Rutger Willem Hofste, Paul Reig, and Leah Schleifer, "17 Countries, Home to One-Quarter of the World's Population, Face Extremely High Water Stress," World Resources Institute blog, August 6, 2019, https://www.wri .org/blog/2019/08/17-countries-home-one-quarter-world-population-face -extremely-high-water-stress.
5. Christopher Flavelle, "The Food Supply Is at Dire Risk, U.N. Experts Say," *New York Times*, August 8, 2019.
6. Somini Sengupta, "In India, Summer Heat May Soon Be Literally Unbear-able," *New York Times*, July 18, 2018.
7. NASA, "2020 Tied for Warmest Year on Record, NASA Analysis Shows," January 14, 2021, https://www.nasa.gov/press-release/2020-tied-for -warmest-year-on-record-nasa-analysis-shows.
8. John Schwartz and Nadja Popovich, "It's Official: 2018 Was the Fourth-Warmest Year on Record," *New York Times*, February 6, 2019.
9. Sam Wong, "So Far 2019 Has Set 35 Records for Heat and 2 for Cold," *New Scientist*, January 30, 2019, https://www.newscientist.com/article/2192369 -so-far-2019-has-set-35-records-for-heat-and-2-for-cold/.
10. Patrick May and Maggie Angst, "Which Bay Area Cities Are Setting New Records for High Temperatures?," *Mercury News*, June 10, 2019 (updated June 11, 2019), https://www.mercurynews.com/2019/06/10/these-bay-area -cities-setting-new-records-for-high-temperatures/; CBS News, "Alaska Hit With Record High Temperatures and Wildfires," WDEF, July 5, 2019, https://wdef.com/2019/07/05/alaska-hit-record-high-temperatures-wildfires/.
11. Jon Henley, Angelique Chrisafis, and Sam Jones, "France Records All-Time Highest Temperature of 45.9°C," *Guardian* (UK), June 28, 2019.
12. Jon Henley, "All-Time Temperature Records Tumble Again as Heatwave Sears Europe," *Guardian* (UK), July 26, 2019.
13. Milken Institute School of Public Health, "Ascertainment of the Estimated Excess Mortality from Hurricane Maria in Puerto Rico," Milken Institute

School of Public Health, George Washington University, 2018, 9, https://publichealth.gwu.edu/sites/default/files/downloads/projects/PRstudy/Acertainment%20of%20the%20Estimated%20Excess%20Mortality%20from%20Hurricane%20Maria%20in%20Puerto%20Rico.pdf.

14. Lancet Commission on Pollution and Health, "Executive Summary," *Lancet,* October 19, 2017.

15. WHO, "9 Out of 10 People Worldwide Breathe Polluted Air, but More Countries Are Taking Action," May 2, 2018, https://www.who.int/news-room/detail/02-05-2018-9-out-of-10-people-worldwide-breathe-polluted-air-but-more-countries-are-taking-action.

16. CDC, "Climate Effects on Health: Air Pollution," December 11, 2014, https://www.cdc.gov/climateandhealth/effects/air_pollution.htm.

17. Intergovernmental Panel on Climate Change (IPCC), "Climate Change 2013: The Physical Science Basis; The Working Group I Contribution to the Fifth Assessment Report of the Intergovernmental Panel on Climate Change" (IPCC, 2013), 5, https://www.ipcc.ch/site/assets/uploads/2018/02/WG1AR5_all_final.pdf.

18. IPCC, "Climate Change 2013," 161.

19. NOAA National Centers for Environmental Information, "State of the Climate: Global Climate Report for Annual 2017," January 2018, https://www.ncdc.noaa.gov/sotc/global/201713.

20. NOAA, "State of the Climate."

21. IPCC, "Special Report: Global Warming of 1.5° C—Summary for Policymakers," 2018, https://www.ipcc.ch/site/assets/uploads/sites/2/2019/05/SR15_SPM_version_report_LR.pdf.

22. IPCC, "Climate Change 2013," 7, 15.

23. IPCC, "Climate Change 2013," 11.

24. IPCC, "Climate Change 2013," 126–127.

25. IPCC, "Climate Change 2014: Synthesis Report; Contribution of Working Groups I, II and III to the Fifth Assessment Report of the Intergovernmental Panel on Climate Change" (IPCC, 2014), 8, https://www.ipcc.ch/site/assets/uploads/2018/05/SYR_AR5_FINAL_full_wcover.pdf.

26. IPCC, "Climate Change 2014," 8.

27. IPCC, "Climate Change 2014," 10.

28. Adrian E. Raftery, Alec Zimmer, Dargan M. W. Frierson, Richard Startz, et al., "Less Than 2°C Warming by 2100 Unlikely," *Nature Climate Change* 7 (2017): 637.

29. Paris Agreement, UN Doc. FCCC/CP/2015/10/Add.1, December 12, 2015, entered into force November 4, 2016.

30. IPCC, "Special Report," 4, 6.

31. IPCC, "Climate Change 2013," 20.

32. IPCC, "Climate Change 2014," 60–62.

33. IPCC, "Climate Change 2014," 42.

34. IPCC, "Climate Change 2013," 11.

35. Lijing Cheng, John Abraham, Zeke Hausfather, and Kevin E. Trenberth, "How Fast Are the Oceans Warming?," *Science* 363 (2019): 128–129.

36. Gerald A. Meehl, Aixue Hu, Claudia Tebaldi, and Julie M. Arblaster, "Relative Outcomes of Climate Change Mitigation Related to Global Temperature versus Sea-Level Rise," *Nature Climate Change* 2 (2012): 576–580.

37. IPCC, "Climate Change 2014," 53.

38. IPCC, "Climate Change 2014," 53.

39. Wei Mei and Shang-Ping Xie, "Intensification of Landfalling Typhoons over the Northwest Pacific since the Late 1970s," *Nature Geoscience* 9 (2016): 753–756.

40. IPCC, "Climate Change 2013," 20–23.

41. IPCC, "Climate Change 2014," 69.

42. UN, Address of Roosevelt Skerrit, Prime Minister of the Commonwealth of Dominica, UNifeed (September 23, 2017), https://www.unmultimedia.org/tv/unifeed/asset/1978/1978084/.

43. Kirk R. Smith, Alistair Woodward, Diarmid Campbell-Lendrum, et al., "Human Health: Impacts, Adaptation, and Co-Benefits," in IPCC, "Climate Change 2014," 709–754.

44. Smith et al., "Human Health," 721–722.

45. Smith et al., "Human Health," 732–733.

46. Smith et al., "Human Health," 733.

47. Smith et al., "Human Health," 717–718.

48. Smith et al., "Human Health," 717.

49. Griff Witte, "New UN Report Says World's Refugee Crisis Is Worse than Anyone Expected," *Washington Post*, June 18, 2015.

50. Nick Cumming-Bruce, "Number of People Fleeing Conflict Is Highest aince World War II, UN Says," *New York Times*, June 16, 2019.

51. UN High Commissioner for Refugees, "Climate Change and Disaster Displacement," https://www.unhcr.org/climate-change-and-disasters.html; Internal Displacement Monitoring Center, "Global Report on Internal Displacement 2018," https://www.internal-displacement.org/global-report/grid2018/.

52. David M. Morens and Anthony S. Fauci, "Emerging Infectious Diseases: Threats to Human Health and Global Stability," *PLOS Pathogens* 9, no. 7 (2013): 1, https://journals.plos.org/plospathogens/article/file?id=10.1371/journal.ppat.1003467&type=printable.

53. Morens and Fauci, "Emerging Infectious Diseases."

54. M. Gilbert, J. Slingenbergh, and X. Xiao, "Climate Change and Avian Influenza," *Scientific and Technical Review of the Office International des Epizooties* 27, no. 2 (2008): 459–466, https://doc.oie.int/seam/resource/directMedia/PWtWAJQAEsStQW_q-z6bDR8EXTv62okk;jsessionid=afdbe4926bc9f79d9b98f27f7ad0?binaryFileId=9895&cid=815.

55. WHO, "Review of Latest Available Evidence on Potential Transmission of Avian Influenza (H5N1) through Water and Sewage and Ways to Reduce

the Risks to Human Health," 2006, 7, https://www.who.int/water_sanitation_health/emerging/h5n1background.pdf.

56. WHO, "Ground Zero in Guinea: The Ebola Outbreak Smoulders—Undetected—for More than 3 Months," http://www.who.int/csr/disease/ebola/ebola-6-months/guinea/en/.

57. Jesús Olivero, John E. Fa, Raimundo Real, et al., "Recent Loss of Closed Forests Is Associated with Ebola Virus Disease Outbreaks," *Scientific Reports* 7 (2017): 1.

58. Roddy Sheer and Doug Moss, "Deforestation and Its Extreme Effect on Global Warming," *Scientific American*, November 13, 2012, https://www.scientificamerican.com/article/deforestation-and-global-warming/.

59. WHO, *Global Vector Control Response, 2017–2030* (Geneva: WHO, 2017); Mackenzie Kwak, "Forget Ebola, SARS and Zika: Ticks Are the Next Global Health Threat," *Guardian* (UK), January 25, 2018.

60. WHO, *Global Vector Control Response.*

61. Kwak, "Forget Ebola."

62. Rebecca Ellis, "Chart: Where Disease-Carrying Mosquitoes Will Go in the Future," NPR, March 28, 2019.

63. Smith et al., "Human Health," 722.

64. WHO, *World Malaria Report 2019* (Geneva: WHO, 2019), 5, https://www.who.int/publications-detail/world-malaria-report-2019.

65. David Alonso, Menno J. Bouma, and Mercedes Pascual, "Epidemic Malaria and Warmer Temperatures in Recent Decades in an East African Highland," *Proceedings of the Royal Society B* 278 (2011): 1661–1669, https://royalsocietypublishing.org/doi/pdf/10.1098/rspb.2010.2020.

66. Krijn P. Paaijmans, Simon Blanford, Andrew S. Bell, et al., "Influence of Climate on Malaria Transmission Depends on Daily Temperature Variation," *PNAS* 107, no. 34 (2010): 15135–15139, https://www.pnas.org/content/pnas/107/34/15135.full.pdf.

67. Paaijmans et al., "Influence of Climate."

68. Kostas Danis, Annick Lenglet, Maria Tseroni, et al., "Malaria in Greece: Historical and Current Reflections on a Re-Emerging Vector Borne Disease," *Travel Medicine and Infectious Disease* 11, no. 1 (2013): 8–14, https://reader.elsevier.com/reader/sd/pii/S1477893913000033?token=CE82B12126ABB057132CCCA5F552C5AE126C3EC1D528EC6369993F055DE4D47D4CE3231EF823937FCBD235122A610E02.

69. Hassan M. Khormi and Lalit Kumar, "Climate Change and the Potential Global Distribution of *Aedes aegypti:* Spatial Modelling Using Geographical Information System and CLIMEX," *Geospatial Health* 8, no. 2 (2014): 405–415, https://geospatialhealth.net/index.php/gh/article/view/29/29.

70. Cyril Caminade, Jolyon M. Medlock, Els Ducheyne, et al., "Suitability of European Climate for the Asian Tiger Mosquito *Aedes albopictus:* Recent Trends and Future Scenarios," *Journal of the Royal Society Interface* 9 (2012): 2708–2717, https://royalsocietypublishing.org/doi/pdf/10.1098/rsif.2012.0138.

71. Sadie J. Ryan, Jolyon M. Medlock, Els Ducheyne, et al., "Global Expansion and Redistribution of *Aedes*-Borne Virus Transmission Risk with Climate Change," *PLOS Neglected Tropical Diseases,* March 28, 2019, https://journals .plos.org/plosntds/article?id=10.1371/journal.pntd.0007213.

72. Ricardo Parreira and Carla A. Sousa, "Dengue Fever in Europe: Could There Be an Epidemic in the Future?," *Expert Review of Anti-infective Therapy* 13, no. 1 (2015): 29–40.

73. WHO, "Disease Outbreak News: Dengue Fever—Sri Lanka," July 19, 2017, http://www.who.int/csr/don/19-july-2017-dengue-sri-lanka/en/.

74. WHO, "Disease Outbreak News: Dengue Fever—Burkina Faso," November 6, 2017, http://www.who.int/csr/don/6-november-2017-dengue-burkina -faso/en/.

75. WHO, "Disease Outbreak News: Dengue Fever—Côte d'Ivoire," August 4, 2017, http://www.who.int/csr/don/04-august-2017-dengue-cote-d-ivoire/en/.

76. David J. Rogers and Simon Hay, "Technical Report: The Climactic Suit-ability for Dengue Transmission in Continental Europe," European Centre for Disease Prevention and Control (2012), https://ecdc.europa.eu/sites /portal/files/media/en/publications/Publications/TER-Climatic-suitablility -dengue.pdf.

77. Karen Levy, Andrew P. Woster, Rebecca S. Goldstein, et al., "Untangling the Impacts of Climate Change on Waterborne Diseases: A Systematic Review of Relationships between Diarrheal Diseases and Temperature, Rainfall, Flooding, and Drought," *Environmental Science & Technology* 50 (2016): 4906, https://pubs.acs.org/doi/pdf/10.1021/acs.est.5b06186.

78. Institute for Health Metrics and Evaluation (IHME), "GBD Results Tool," http://ghdx.healthdata.org/gbd-results-tool.

79. IHME, "GBD Results Tool."

80. Levy et al., "Untangling the Impacts,"4906.

81. Smith et al., "Human Health," 722.

82. David Fidler, "From International Sanitary Conventions to Global Health Security: The New International Health Regulations," *Chinese Journal of International Law* 4, no. 2 (September 5, 2005): 325–392, https://doi.org/10 .1093/chinesejil/jmi029.

83. Mohammad Ali, Allyson R. Nelson, Anna Lena Lopez, and David A. Sack, "Updated Global Burden of Cholera in Endemic Countries," *PLOS Neglected Tropical Diseases* 9, no. 6 (2015): 1–13, https://www.ncbi.nlm.nih.gov/pmc /articles/PMC4455997/.

84. WHO Regional Office for the Eastern Mediterranean, "Yemen Cholera Response: Weekly Epidemiological Bulletin (Dec 25–Dec 31)," January 4, 2018, http://www.emro.who.int/images/stories/yemen/Yemen_Cholera _Response_-_Weekly_Epidemiological_Bulletin_-_W52_2017_28Dec_25 -Dec_3129.pdf.

85. Guillaume Constantin de Magny and Rita R. Colwell, "Cholera and Climate: A Demonstrated Relationship," *Transactions of the American Clinical*

*and Climatological Association* 120 (2009): 119–128, https://www.researchgate
.net/publication/26825605_Cholera_and_Climate_A_Demonstrated
_Relationship.

86. Shlomit Paz, "Impact of Temperature Variability on Cholera Incidence in
    Southeastern Africa, 1971–2006," *EcoHealth* 6, no. 3 (2009): 340–345,
    https://www.researchgate.net/publication/40806042_Impact_of
    _Temperature_Variability_on_Cholera_Incidence_in_Southeastern_Africa
    _1971-2006.
87. Constantin de Magny and Colwell, "Cholera and Climate," 19–128.
88. Smith et al., "Human Health," 722.
89. Levy et al., "Untangling the Impacts," 4916.
90. Spencer R. Weart, *The Discovery of Global Warming* (Cambridge, MA:
    Harvard University Press, 2003), 146.
91. Weart, *Discovery of Global Warming,* 146.
92. World Climate Programme, World Meteorological Organization, "Report
    of the International Conference on the Assessment of the Role of Carbon
    Dioxide and of Other Greenhouse Gases in Climate Variations and
    Associated Impacts," Villach, Austria, October 9–15, 1985 (World Meteo-
    rological Organization, 1986), 1, https://library.wmo.int/pmb_ged/wmo
    _661_en.pdf.
93. IPCC, "History of the IPCC," https://www.ipcc.ch/about/history/.
94. United Nations Framework Convention on Climate Change, May 9, 1992,
    entered into force March 21, 1994.
95. Framework Convention on Climate Change, art. 3.3.
96. Paris Agreement, preamble.
97. Paris Agreement, preamble.
98. Jing Liu-Helmersson, Mikkel Quam, Annelies Wilder-Smith, et al.,
    "Climate Change and Aedes Vectors: 21st Century Projections for Dengue
    Transmission in Europe," *EBioMedicine* 7 (2016): 267–277, at 276,
    https://www.ebiomedicine.com/article/S2352-3964(16)30133-5/pdf.
99. IPCC, "Special Report."
100. IPCC, "Special Report."
101. IPCC, "Special Report."
102. Paris Agreement, art. 3.
103. Paris Agreement, art. 4.
104. IPCC, "Special Report."
105. IPCC, "Climate Change 2013."
106. Joeri Rogelj, Michel den Elzen, Niklas Höhne, et al., "Paris Agreement
    Climate Proposals Need a Boost to Keep Warming Well Below 2°C,"
    *Nature* 534 (2016): 631–639.
107. NAH Editorial Staff, "To Protect Our Health, We Have to Protect the
    Earth," *Nutrition Action,* October 12, 2018, https://www.nutritionaction
    .com/daily/food-safety/to-protect-our-health-we-have-to-protect-the
    -earth/.

## Chapter 7 · Governing Global Health Security

1. The White House, "President Donald J. Trump Is Demanding Account-ability from the World Health Organization," April 8, 2020, https://www.whitehouse.gov/briefings-statements/president-donald-j-trump-demanding-accountability-world-health-organization/.

2. Donald G. McNeil Jr., "U.S. Intends to Redirect Funds Owed to W.H.O.," *New York Times,* September 3, 2020.

3. Ian Norton, "Ebola Diaries: Bringing Help to Those in Desperate Need," WHO, 2015, http://www.who.int/features/2015/ebola-diaries-norton/en/.

4. Helen Branswell, "WHO Declares Ebola Outbreak an International Health Emergency," STATNEWS, July 17, 2019, https://www.statnews.com/2019/07/17/who-declares-ebola-outbreak-an-international-health-emergency/.

5. Lawrence Gostin, Alexandra Phelan, Alex Godwin Coutinho, et al., "Ebola in the Democratic Republic of the Congo: Time to Sound a Global Alert?," *Lancet* 393, no. 10172 (2019): 617–620; Lawrence O. Gostin, Neil R. Sircar, and Eric A. Friedman, "Fighting Novel Diseases amidst Humanitarian Crises," *Hastings Center Report* 49, no.1 (2019) 1: 6–9, https://doi.org/10.1002/hast.970; Lawrence O. Gostin, Matthew M. Kavanagh, and Eliza-beth Cameron, "Ebola and War in the Democratic Republic of Congo: Avoiding Failure and Thinking Ahead," *JAMA* 321, no. 3 (2019): 243–244.

6. Lawrence O. Gostin, J. T. Monahan, Kenny Kaldor, Mary DeBartolo, et al., "The Legal Determinants of Health: Harnessing the Power of Law for Global Health and Sustainable Development," *Lancet* 393, no. 10183 (2019): 1857–1910.

7. Steven J. Hoffman, Clarke B. Cole, and Mark Pearcey, "Mapping Global Health Architecture to Inform the Future Chatham House," Centre on Global Health Security, January 2015, https://www.chathamhouse.org/sites/files/chathamhouse/field/field_document/20150120GlobalHealthArchitectureHoffmanColePearceyUpdate.pdf.

8. Benjamin Mason Meir and Lawrence O. Gostin, eds., *Human Rights in Global Health: Rights-Based Governance for a Globalizing World* (Oxford: Oxford University Press, 2018).

9. WHO, Constitution of the World Health Organization, 1948, art. 2.

10. WHO, "WHO—Organizational Structure," https://www.who.int/about/who-we-are/structure.

11. WHA, Declaration of Eradication of Smallpox, WHA 33.3, May 8, 1980.

12. WHA, Global Eradication of Poliomyelitis by the Year 2000, WHA 41.28, May 13, 1988.

13. Leslie Roberts, "Polio Vaccination Campaigns Restart after Modelers Warn about Risk of 'Explosive' Outbreaks," *Science,* July 21, 2020, https://www.sciencemag.org/news/2020/07/polio-vaccination-campaigns-restart-after-modelers-warn-about-risk-explosive-outbreaks.

14. Lawrence O. Gostin, *Global Health Law* (Cambridge, MA: Harvard University Press, 2014), 99.

15. Lawrence O. Gostin and Eric A. Friedman, "Ebola: A Crisis in Global Health Leadership," *Lancet* 384, no. 9951 (2014): 1323–1325, at 1323; Lawrence O. Gostin and Eric A. Friedman, "A Retrospective and Prospective Analysis of the West African Ebola Virus Disease Epidemic: Robust National Health Systems at the Foundation and an Empowered WHO at the Apex," *Lancet* 385, no. 9980 (2015) 1902–1909, 1902, 1904; Vivienne Walt, "The World Health Organization Comes Under Fire for Failure to Stop Ebola," *Time*, October 30, 2014, https://time.com/3547831/who-ebola/.

16. Sheri Fink, "W.H.O. Leader Describes the Agency's Ebola Operations," *New York Times*, September 4, 2014.

17. WHO, *2018 Global Progress Report on Implementation of the WHO Framework Convention on Tobacco Control* (Geneva: WHO, 2018), 13, https://www.who.int/fctc/reporting/WHO-FCTC-2018_global_progress_report.pdf.

18. Gostin, *Global Health Law,* 131–132.

19. WHA, International Health Regulations (2005), WHA 58.3, May 23, 2005.

20. Permanent Mission of the United States to the United Nations Office and Other International Organizations in Geneva, Letter of IHR Reservation and Understanding, December 13, 2006, https://www.who.int/ihr/usa.pdf.

21. Lawrence O. Gostin, Mary C. DeBartolo, and Rebecca Katz, "The Global Health Law Trilogy: Towards a Safer, Healthier, and Fairer World," *Lancet* 390, no. 10105 (2017): 1918–1926.

22. WHO, "Concept Note: Development, Monitoring and Evaluation of Functional Core Capacity for Implementing the International Health Regulations," 2005, http://www.who.int/ihr/publications/concept_note_201407.pdf.

23. WHO, "Joint External Evaluation Missions Update: Week of January 16, 2017," https://www.who.int/ihr/procedures/mission-reports/en/.

24. US Department of Health and Human Services (HHS), "HHS Officials Deliver Remarks at the Fifth Annual Global Health Security Agenda Ministerial Meeting," November 7, 2018, https://www.hhs.gov/about/news/2018/11/07/hhs-officials-deliver-remarks-at-the-fifth-annual-global-health-security-agenda-ministerial-meeting.html.

25. Gostin and Friedman, "Ebola: A Crisis"; WHO, "2014 Ebola Virus Disease Outbreak and Follow-Up to the Special Session of the Executive Board on Ebola: Options for a Contingency Fund to Support WHO's Emergency Response Capacity: Report of the Programme, Budget and Administration Committee," 2018, https://apps.who.int/iris/handle/10665/253140.

26. WHO, "2014 Ebola Virus Disease Outbreak and Follow-up to the Special Session of the Executive Board on Ebola: Options for a Contingency Fund to Support WHO's Emergency Response Capacity: Report by the Director-General," WHA 68.26, May 12, 2015, http://apps.who.int/gb/ebwha/pdf_files/WHA68/A68_26-en.pdf.

27. WHO, "Contingency Fund for Health Emergencies," https://www.who.int/emergencies/funding/contingency-fund/en/.

28. WHO, *Contingency Fund for Emergencies: Report of the WHO Health Emergencies Programme* (Geneva: WHO, 2017).

29. Anne Gulland, "WHO to Set Up Emergencies Program," *BMJ* 353 (2016): i3052.

30. Médecins Sans Frontières, "Place of Safety Needed for 356 People Rescued in Central Mediterranean," August 13, 2019, https://www.msf.org/place -safety-needed-356-people-rescued-central-mediterranean; WHO, Independent Oversight and Advisory Committee for the WHO Health Emergencies Program: Terms of Reference, http://who.int/about/who_reform /emergency-capacities/oversight-committee/Terms-of-Reference -Independent-Oversight-Committee.pdf.

31. WHO, "Global Health Emergency Workforce: Report by the Director-General," WHA 68.27, May 15, 2015, http://apps.who.int/gb/ebwha/pdf _files/WHA68/A68_27-en.pdf.

32. WHO, "2014 Ebola Virus Disease Outbreak and Issues Raised: Follow-Up to the Special Session of the Executive Board on the Ebola Emergency (Resolution EBSS3.R1) and the Sixty-Eighth World Health Assembly (Decision WHA68(10)): Update on the 2014 Ebola Virus Disease Outbreak and Secretariat Response and Other Issues Raised: Report by the Director-General," EB 132.22, January 22, 2016, http://apps.who.int/gb/ebwha/pdf _files/EB138/B138_27-en.pdf.

33. "WHO's New Emergencies Programme Bridges Two World," *Bulletin of the World Health Organization* 95, no. 1 (2017): 8–9. https://www.ncbi.nlm.nih .gov/pmc/articles/PMC5180344/.

34. Sarah Boseley, "World Health Organisation Admits Botching Response to Ebola Outbreak," *Guardian* (UK), October 17, 2014.

35. Devi Sridhar and Lawrence O. Gostin, "Reforming the World Health Organization," *JAMA* 305, no. 15 (2011): 1585–1586.

36. WHA, Programme Budget 2018–2019, WHA 70.5, May 26, 2017.

37. WHO, "Overview of Financial Situation: Programme Budget 2018–2019," WHA 74.34, May 13, 2014, http://apps.who.int/gb/ebwha/pdf_files /WHA72/A72_34-en.pdf.

38. Somini Sengupta, "Effort on Ebola Hurt W.H.O. Chief," *New York Times*, January 6, 2015.

39. WHA, Framework of Engagement with Non-State Actors, WHA 69.10, May 28, 2016.

40. WHO, "Principles Governing Relations with Nongovernmental Organizations," https://www.who.int/governance/civilsociety/principles/en/.

41. Christophe Lanord, "A Study of WHO's Official Relations System with Nongovernmental Organizations," WHO, 2002, https://apps.who.int/iris /handle/10665/279938; Thomas Schwarz, "A Stronger Voice for Civil Society at the World Health Assembly?," Medicus Mundi International Network, June 2010, https://www.medicusmundi.org/contributions/reports /2010/a-stronger-voice-of-civil-society-at-the-world-health-assembly.

42. UN, "Sustainable Development Goals," https://sustainabledevelopment.un .org/?menu=1300.
43. UN, "Sustainable Development Goals."
44. Gostin, Sircar, and Friedman, "Fighting Novel Diseases."
45. Julian Borger, "US Blocks Vote on UN's Bid for Global Ceasefire over Reference to WHO," *Guardian*, May 8, 2020.
46. UN, "With Spread of Ebola Outpacing Response, Security Council Adopts Resolution 2177 (2014) Urging Immediate Action, End to Isolation of Affected States," September 18, 2014, https://www.un.org/press/en/2014 /sc11566.doc.htm.
47. UN, "Adopting Resolution 2439 (2018), Security Council Condemns Attacks by Armed Groups in Democratic Republic of Congo Jeopardizing Responses to Ebola Outbreak," October 30, 2018, https://www.un.org/press /en/2018/sc13559.doc.htm.
48. WTO, WTO Agreement on the Application of Sanitary and Phytosanitary Measures, 1994, https://www.wto.org/english/tratop_e/sps_e/spsagr_e.htm.
49. Ruby Prosser Scully, "WHO Declares International Emergency over DRC Ebola Outbreak," *New Scientist*, July 18, 2019, https://www.newscientist .com/article/2210430-who-declares-international-emergency-over-drc-ebola -outbreak/.
50. OIE, "The World Animal Health Information System," http://www.oie.int /animal-health-in-the-world/the-world-animal-health-information-system /the-oie-data-system/.
51. Tyson Wanjura, "International Standards for Managing Emerging and Re-emerging Zoonoses of Public Health Significance: A Call for Horizontal Collaboration between Intergovernmental Organizations," *International Lawyer* 41, no. 3 (2007): 975–999, https://scholar.smu.edu/cgi/viewcontent .cgi?article=1148&context=til.
52. Food and Agriculture Organization of the United Nations, "Emergency Management Centre for Animal Health," http://www.fao.org/emergencies /how-we-work/prepare-and-respond/cmc-animal-health/en/.
53. Wanjura, "International Standards."
54. Laurie Garrett, "Dr. Kim and the World Bank's Health Role," Council on Foreign Relations Expert Brief, April 13, 2012, https://www.cfr.org/expert -brief/dr-kim-and-world-banks-health-role.
55. Gostin, *Global Health Law*.
56. World Bank, "Health: Overview," http://www.worldbank.org/en/topic /health/overview.
57. World Bank, *Annual Report 2016* (Washington, DC: World Bank, 2017).
58. World Bank, "Understanding Poverty," http://www.worldbank.org/en/topic /pandemics/overview#2.
59. World Bank, "World Bank Launches First-Ever Pandemic Bonds to Support $500 Million Pandemic Emergency Financing Facility," June 28, 2017, https://www.worldbank.org/en/news/press-release/2017/06/28/world

-bank-launches-first-ever-pandemic-bonds-to-support-500-million
-pandemic-emergency-financing-facility.

60. World Bank, "Ebola Escalated Response: US$80 Million Commitment to the Democratic Republic of the Congo," February 28, 2019, https://www .worldbank.org/en/news/press-release/2019/02/28/ebola-escalated-response -us80-million-commitment-to-the-democratic-republic-of-the-congo.

61. World Bank, "PEF Allocates US$195 Million to More than 60 Low-Income Countries to Fight COVID-19," April 27, 2020, https://www .worldbank.org/en/news/press-release/2020/04/27/pef-allocates-us195 -million-to-more-than-60-low-income-countries-to-fight-covid-19.

62. Lawrence O. Gostin, Oyewale Tomori, Suwit Wibulpolprasert, et al., "Towards a Common Secure Future: Four Global Commissions in the Wake of the Ebola," *PLOS Medicine* 13, no.5 (2016): e1002042, https://doi .org/10.1371/journal.pmed.1002042; Bangin Brim and Clare Wenham, "Pandemic Emergency Financing Facility: Struggling to Deliver on Its Innovative Promise," *BMJ* (2019) 367:l5719.

63. Center for Global Development, *Does the IMF Constrain Health Spending in Poor Countries? Evidence and Agenda for Action* (Washington, DC: Center for Global Development, 2007), https://www.cgdev.org/publication/does-imf -constrain-health-spending-poor-countries-evidence-and-agenda-action.

64. Sanjeev Gupta, "Response to 'The International Monetary Fund and the Ebola Outbreak,'" *Lancet Global Health* 3, no. 2 (2015): e78, https://www .sciencedirect.com/science/article/pii/S2214109X14703456?via%3Dihub; Alexander Kentikelenis, Thomas Stubbs, and Lawrence King, "Did the IMF Actually Ease Up on Structural Adjustment? Here's What the Data Say," *Washington Post,* June 2, 2016.

65. IMF, "Questions and Answers: The IMF's Response to COVID-19," https://www.imf.org/en/About/FAQ/imf-response-to-covid-19.

66. WTO and WHO, *WTO Agreements and Public Health—A Joint Study by the WHO and WTO Secretariat* (Geneva: WTO and WHO, 2002).

67. WTO, "WTO Agreement on the Application of Sanitary and Phytosanitary Measures, 1994," https://www.wto.org/english/tratop_e/sps_e/spsagr_e.htm.

68. Tim K. Mackey and Bryan A. Liang, "Lessons from SARS and H1N1/A: Employing a WHO-WTO Forum to Promote Optimal Economic Public Health Pandemic Response," *Journal of Public Health Policy* 33, no. 1 (2012): 119–130; WHO, "Emergency Preparedness, Response: Pandemic (H1N1) 2009: Meeting Reports," https://www.who.int/csr/disease/swineflu/meetings/en/.

69. Bradley Condon and Tapen Sinha, "The Effectiveness of Pandemic Prepara-tions: Legal Lessons from the 2009 Influenza Epidemic" *Florida Journal of International Law* 22, no. 1 (2010): 1–30.

70. Mackey and Liang, "Lessons from SARS and H1N1/A."

71. Global Fund to Fight AIDS, Tuberculosis and Malaria (GFATM), *35th Board Meeting: The Global Fund's Sustainability, Transition and Co-Financing Policy* (Geneva: GFATM, 2016).

72. World Bank, *International Development Association* (Washington, DC: World Bank Group, 2018), http://ida.worldbank.org/sites/default/files/pdfs /1-ida_brochure_2018.pdf.; GFATM, "Eligibility List 2019," https://www .theglobalfund.org/media/8340/core_eligiblecountries2019_list_en.pdf.

73. The Global Fund, "COVID-19 Situation Report—8 May 2020," https://www.theglobalfund.org/media/9631/covid19_2020-05-08-situation _report_en.pdf?u=637245329620000000.

74. Gavi, "Support Guidelines," https://www.gavi.org/support/process/apply/.

75. Gavi, "How the Pneumococcal AMC Works," https://www.gavi.org /investing/innovative-financing/pneumococcal-amc/how-the-pneumococcal -amc-works/.

76. Gavi, "Gavi's Proposal for an Advance Market Commitment for COVID-19 Vaccines," https://www.gavi.org/sites/default/files/covid/Gavi-proposal -AMC-COVID-19-vaccines.pdf.

77. Gavi, "Cash Receipts," https://www.gavi.org/investing/funding/donor -contributions-pledges/cash-receipts/.

78. Karin Strohecker and Tommy Wilkes, "Analysis: Vaccine Bond Sales to Soar to Fund COVID-19 Shots for Poor Countries," *Reuters,* December 22, 2020.

79. Gavi, "The Gavi Matching Fund," https://www.gavi.org/investing/innovative -financing/matching-fund/.

80. Gavi, "Loan Buydown," https://www.gavi.org/investing/innovative-financing /loan-buydown/.

81. Gavi, "INFUSE," https://www.gavi.org/investing/infuse/.

82. Unitaid, "About Us," https://unitaid.org/about-us/#en.

83. Unitaid, Unitaid Constitution, adopted July 6, 2011, as amended June 21, 2018, https://unitaid.org/assets/UNITAID-Constitution-revised-version-15 -June-2018.pdf.

84. Unitaid, "About Us"; WHO, *WHO Country Cooperation Strategy, 2017–2021* (Geneva: WHO, 2017), https://www.afro.who.int/publications/who-country -cooperation-strategy-2017-2021.

85. Unitaid, *Impact Story: Medicine Patent Pool: Voluntary Licenses Can Make Medicines More Accessible* (Geneva: Unitaid, 2017), https://unitaid.org/assets /impact-story_medicines-patent-pool.pdf; Unitaid, "The Medicines Patent Pool Adds New Suppliers from South Africa and South Korea to Its Growing Manufacturing Network," May 2, 2018, https:// medicinespatentpool.org/mpp-media-post/the-medicines-patent-pool-adds -new-suppliers-from-south-africa-and-south-korea-to-its-growing-generic -manufacturing-network/.

86. Coalition for Epidemic Preparedness Innovations (CEPI), Articles of Association, 2018, https://cepi.net/wp-content/uploads/2019/01/CEPI -Articles-of-Association_v3.0_final.pdf.; CEPI, "Creating a World in Which Epidemics Are No Longer a Threat to Humanity," https://cepi.net /about/whyweexist/.

87. CEPI, "Priority Diseases," https://cepi.net/research_dev/priority-diseases/.

88. CEPI, "Our Portfolio," https://cepi.net/research_dev/our-portfolio/.

89. CEPI, "CEPI Launches New Funding Opportunity to Accelerate COVID-19 Vaccine Development and Production," May 5, 2020, https://cepi.net/news_cepi/cepi-seeks-to-expand-covid-19-vaccine-portfolio-focusing-on-speed-and-global-manufacturing/.

90. WHO, "Stronger Collaboration, Better Health," https://www.who.int/sdg/global-action-plan.

91. WTO, "Agreement between the World Trade Organization and the Office International des Epizooties," July 8, 1998, WT / L / 272.

92. Stop TB Partnership, http://www.stoptb.org.

93. David Garmaise, "The Global Fund Should Move Now to Expand the Non-CCM Window," *Aidspan,* November 15, 2010, http://www.aidspan.org/gfo_article/global-fund-should-move-now-expand-non-ccm-window.

94. WHO, "Neglected Tropical Diseases," https://www.who.int/neglected_diseases/diseases/en/; Report for the All-Party Parliamentary Group on Malaria and Neglected Tropical Diseases, *The Neglected Tropical Diseases: A Challenge We Could Rise To—Will We?* (London: APPMG, 2010), https://www.who.int/neglected_diseases/diseases/NTD_Report_APPMG.pdf.

95. WHO, *A Healthier Humanity: The WHO Investment Case for 2019–2023* (Geneva: WHO, 2018), https://apps.who.int/iris/bitstream/handle/10665/274710/WHO-DGO-CRM-18.2-eng.pdf.

96. Patrick Vinck, Phuong N. Pham, Kenedy K. Bindu, et al., "Institutional Trust and Misinformation in the Response to the 2018–19 Ebola Outbreak in North Kivu, DR Congo: A Population-Based Survey," *Lancet Infectious Diseases* 19, no.5 (2019): 529–536, https://www.thelancet.com/journals/laninf/article/PIIS1473-3099(19)30063-5/fulltext.

## Chapter 8 · International Pathogen Sharing and Global Health Equity

1. Endang R. Sedyaningsih et al., "Towards Mutual Trust, Transparency and Equity in Virus Sharing Mechanism: The Avian Influenza Case of Indonesia," *Annals Academy of Medicine Singapore* 37, no 6 (2008): 482–487.

2. Lawrence O. Gostin et al., "Virus Sharing, Genetic Sequencing, and Global Health Security," *Science* 345, no. 6202 (2004): 1295–1296.

3. Gostin et al., "Virus Sharing."

4. David P. Fidler, "Negotiating Equitable Access to Influenza Vaccines: Global Health Diplomacy and the Controversies Surrounding Avian Influenza H5N1 and Pandemic Influenza H1N1," *PLOS Medicine* 7, no. 5 (2010): 1–4, https://journals.plos.org/plosmedicine/article?id=10.1371/journal.pmed.1000247.

5. WHO, "Pandemic Influenza Preparedness Framework for the Sharing of Influenza Viruses and Access to Vaccines and Other Benefits," WHA 64.8, May 24, 2011, https://www.who.int/influenza/resources/pip_framework/en/.

6. Emily Baumgaertner, "China Has Withheld Samples of a Dangerous Flu Virus," *New York Times,* August 27, 2018.

7. Jon Cohen, "Chinese Researchers Reveal Draft Genome of Virus Implicated in Wuhan Pneumonia Outbreak," *Science Magazine,* January 11, 2020.

8. Associated Press, "China delayed releasing coronavirus info, frustrating WHO," *PBS,* June 2, 2020.

9. Helen Branswell, "CDC Made a Synthetic Ebola Virus to Test Treatments. It Worked," STAT, July 9, 2019, https://www.statnews.com/2019/07/09/lacking -ebola-samples-cdc-made-a-synthetic-virus-to-test-treatments-it-worked/.

10. A. Danielle Iuliano et al., "Estimates of Global Seasonal Influenza-Associated Respiratory Mortality: A Modelling Study," *Lancet* 391, no. 10127 (2018): 1285–1300.

11. CDC, "How the Flu Virus Can Change: 'Drift' and 'Shift,'" September 27, 2017, https://www.cdc.gov/flu/about/viruses/change.htm.

12. CDC, "How Flu Spreads," August 27, 2018, https://www.cdc.gov/flu/about /disease/spread.htm.

13. WHO, "Emergency Preparedness, Response: Pandemic Influenza Vaccine Manufacturing Process and Timeline," August 6, 2009, https://www.who .int/csr/disease/swineflu/notes/h1n1_vaccine_20090806/en/.

14. WHO, "Pandemic Influenza Preparedness and Response: A WHO Guidance Document," 2009, 1–64, https://apps.who.int/iris/bitstream /handle/106651/494123/9789241547680_eng.pdf.

15. Michael Dumiak, "Push Needed for Pandemic Planning," *Bulletin of the World Health Organization* 90, no. 11 (2012): 800–801, https://www.who.int /bulletin/volumes/90/11/12-021112.pdf.

16. WHO, "Global Pandemic Influenza Action Plan to Increase Vaccine Supply," 2006, 1–24, https://apps.who.int/iris/bitstream/handle/10665 /69388/WHO_IVB_06.13_eng.pdf.

17. WHO, "Report of the Second WHO Consultation on the Global Action Plan for Influenza Vaccines (GAP)," 2012, 1–43, https://www.who.int /influenza_vaccines_plan/resources/gap2consultationreport.pdf; WHO, "The Ten Years of the Global Action Plan for Influenza Vaccines: Report to the Director-General from the GAP Advisory Group," 2016, 1–4, https://www.who.int/influenza/GAP_AG_report_to_WHO_DG.pdf.

18. Thedi Ziegler, Awandha Mamahit, and Nancy J. Cox, "65 Years of Influenza Surveillance by a World Health Organization-Coordinated Global Network," *Influenza and Other Respiratory Viruses* 12, no. 5 (2018): 558–565, at 559; WHO, "Fact Sheet: Global Influenza Surveillance and Response System (GISRS)," https://www.who.int/influenza/gisrs_laboratory/updates /gisrs_one_pager/en/.

19. Ziegler, Mamahit, and Cox, "65 Years of Influenza Surveillance," 564.

20. Jason Carter, "WHO's Virus Is It Anyway? How the World Health Organization Can Protect against Claims of 'Viral Sovereignty,'" *Georgia Journal of International and Comparative Law* 38 (2010): 717–740, 719.

21. WHO, "Fact Sheet."

22. Arielle Sloan, "IP Neutrality and Benefit Sharing for Seasonal Flu: An Argument in Favor of WHO PIP Framework Expansion," *Chicago-Kent Journal of Intellectual Property* 17, no. 2 (2018): 296–321, at 305, 318.

23. Kenneth A. McLean et al., "The 2015 Global Production Capacity of Seasonal and Pandemic Influenza Vaccine," *Vaccine* 34, no. 45 (2016): 5410–5413, at 5412.

24. McLean et al., "2015 Global Production Capacity," 5412.

25. Mark R. Eccleston-Turner, "The Pandemic Influenza Preparedness Framework: A Viable Procurement Option for Developing States?," *Medical Law International* 17, no. 4 (2017): 227–248, at 239, http://eprints.keele.ac.uk /3932/; Sloan, "IP Neutrality," 306.

26. Fidler, "Negotiating Equitable Access," 1, https://journals.plos.org/plosmedicine /article?id=10.1371/journal.pmed.1000247.

27. Carter, "WHO's Virus Is It Anyway?," 719.

28. WHO, "Pandemic Influenza Preparedness."

29. David P. Fiddler and Lawrence O. Gostin, "The WHO Pandemic Influenza Preparedness Framework: A Milestone in Global Governance for Health," *JAMA* 306, no. 2 (2011): 200–201; Nicole Jefferies, "Levelling the Playing Field? Sharing of Influenza Viruses and Access to Vaccines and Other Benefits," *Journal of Law and Medicine* 20, no. 1 (2012): 59–73.

30. WHO, "Summary of Benefit Sharing Options," 2016, https://www.who.int /influenza/pip/benefit_sharing/SMTA2BenefitSharingOptions.pdf.

31. WHO, "Category A: SMTA2 with Vaccine & Antiviral Manufacturers," May 2019, https://www.who.int/influenza/pip/smta2/SMTA2_catA _23may2019.pdf.

32. WHO, "Category A."

33. Phillip R. Dormitzer et al., "Synthetic Generation of Influenza Vaccine Viruses for Rapid Response to Pandemics," *Scientific Translational Medicine* 5, no. 185 (2013): 1–12, http://www.tolonenlab.org/Presentations/MSSB /Exam2013/dormitzer2013.pdf.

34. WHO, "Category A."

35. WHO, "Approaches to Seasonal Data and Genetic Sequence Data under the PIP Framework: Analysis" (Geneva: WHO, December 14, 2018), 18, https://www.who.int/influenza/pip/WHA70108b_Analysis.pdf.

36. Technical Expert Working Group on Genetic Sequence Data, "Final Report to the PIP Advisory Group," WHO, May 15, 2014, revised October 10, 2014, 6–8, https://www.who.int/influenza/pip/advisory_group/PIP_AG _Rev_Final_TEWG_Report_10_Oct _2014.pdf.

37. Convention on Biological Diversity, June 5, 1992, entered into force December 29, 1993, 3, https://www.cbd.int/doc/legal/cbd-en.pdf.

38. Nagoya Protocol on Access to Genetic Resources and the Fair and Equitable Sharing of Benefits Arising from Their Utilization to the Convention on Biological Diversity, October 29, 2010, entered into force October 12, 2014, 4, https://www.cbd.int/abs/doc/protocol/nagoya-protocol-en.pdf.

39. Michelle Rourke, "Viruses for Sale: All Viruses Are Subject to Access and Benefit-Sharing Obligations under the Convention on Biological Diversity," *European Intellectual Property Review* 39, no. 2 (2017): 79–89, at 86.

40. Krishna Ravi Srinivas, "Regimes in Conflict? Controversies over Access and Benefit Sharing and Sharing of Virus Samples," *European Journal of Risk Regulation* 8, no. 3 (2017): 573–579, at 575, https://www.cambridge.org/core/journals/european-journal-of-risk-regulation/article/regimes-in-conflict-controversies-over-access-and-benefit-sharing-and-sharing-of-virus-samples/C50272311C0B5CDAD03844248EF8B1DE/core-reader.

41. WHO Secretariat, "Implementation of the Nagoya Protocol and Pathogen Sharing: Public Health Implications," 2016, https://www.who.int/influenza/pip/2016-review/NagoyaStudyAdvanceCopy_full.pdf.

42. Conference of the Parties on the Convention on Biological Diversity, "Specialised International Access and Benefit Sharing Instruments in the Context of Article 4, Paragraph 4, of the Nagoya Protocol," CBD/NP-MOP/3/L.3, November 22, 2018, https://www.cbd.int/doc/c/7a3f/b000/f7c46f51a09dc6b9e2fc95a5/np-mop-03-l-03-en.pdf.

43. Marie Wilke, "A Healthy Look at the Nagoya Protocol: Implications for Global Health Governance," in Elisa Morgera, Matthias Buck, and Elsa Tsioumani, eds., *The 2010 Nagoya Protocol on Access and Benefit-Sharing in Perspective* (Boston: Martinus Nijhoff, 2012), 123–148, at 143.

44. WHO, "Approaches to Seasonal Data," 9.

45. Conference of the Parties on the Convention on Biological Diversity, "Specialised International Access."

46. Elisa Morgera, Stephanie Switzer, and Elsa Tsioumani, "Study into Criteria to Identify a Specialized International Access and Benefit-Sharing Instrument, and a Possible Process for Its Recognition," CBD/SBI/2/INF/17, May 29, 2018, 1–27, at 6, https://www.cbd.int/doc/c/9376/a644/1bed20a1837af8e3d1edc5f9/sbi-02-inf-17-en.pdf.

47. UN General Assembly, "Transforming Our World: The 2030 Agenda for Sustainable Development," UN G.A. Res. 70/1, September 25, 2015, https://www.un.org/ga/search/view_doc.asp?symbol=A/RES/70/1&Lang=E.

48. "Regulation (EU) No. 511/2014 of the European Parliament and of the Council of 16 April 2014," *Official Journal of the European Union* (May 5, 2014): L150/59–L150/71, https://www.dsmz.de/fileadmin/Bereiche/Microbiology/Dateien/EU_Regulation_511-2014_EN_TXT.pdf.

49. Conference of the Parties on the Convention on Biological Diversity, "Specialised International Access."

50. Influenza Pandemic Preparedness Framework Advisory Group, "Meeting of the Influenza Pandemic Preparedness Advisory Group: Report to the Director-General," WHO, November 8–10, 2017, https://www.who.int/influenza/pip/AG_Nov2017.pdf.

51. Influenza Pandemic Preparedness Framework Advisory Group, "Meeting of the Influenza Pandemic Preparedness Advisory Group."

52. UN, "Protecting Humanity from Future Health Crises: High-Level Panel on the Global Response to Health Crises," 2016, 62, http://www.un.org /News/dh/infocus/HLP/2016-02-05_Final_Report_Global_Response_to _Health_Crises.pdf.

53. Michael Shear, "The Lost Month: How a Failure to Test Blinded the U.S. to Covid-19," *New York Times*, March 28, 2020.

54. Jane Bradley, "In Scramble for Coronavirus Supplies, Rich Countries Push Poor Aside," *New York Times*, April 9, 2020.

## Chapter 9 · Universal Health Coverage

1. John Donnelly, "Maternal Death Stalks Malawi's Rural Poor," GlobalPost, June 26, 2011, https://www.pri.org/stories/2011-06-26/maternal-death -stalks-malawi-s-rural-poor.

2. "Health Systems Situation in Guinea, Liberia and Sierra Leone," paper presented at WHO Ebola and Health Systems Meeting, Geneva, December 10–11, 2014, https://www.who.int/csr/disease/ebola/health-systems/health -systems-ppt1.pdf.

3. Kim J. Brolin Ribacke, Alex J. van Duinen, Helena Nordenstedt, et al., "The Impact of the West Africa Ebola Outbreak on Obstetric Health Care in Sierra Leone," *PLOS One* 11, no. 2 (2016): e0150080, https://journals.plos .org/plosone/article?id=10.1371/journal.pone.0150080.

4. Tedros Adhanom Ghebreyesus, "All Roads Lead to Universal Health Coverage," *Lancet Global Health* 5, no. 9 (2017): e839–e840.

5. Karin Stenberg, Odd Hanssen, Tessa Tan-Torres Edejer, et al., "Financing Transformative Health Systems towards Achievement of the Health Sustainable Development Goals: A Model for Projected Resource Needs in 67 Low-Income and Middle-Income Countries," *Lancet Global Health* 5, no. 9 (2017): e875–e887.

6. Denise Grady, "Suspected Cases of Ebola Rise to 29 in Democratic Republic of Congo," *New York Times*, May 18, 2017.

7. Mark J. Siedner, Lawrence O. Gostin, Hilarie H. Cranmer, et al., "Strengthening the Detection of and Early Response to Public Health Emergencies: Lessons from the West African Ebola Epidemic," *PLOS Medicine* 12, no. 3 (2015): e1001804, http://doi:10.1371/journal. pmed.1001804.

8. Paul E. M. Fine, "Herd Immunity: History, Theory, Practice," *Epidemiologic Reviews* 15, no. 2 (1993): 265–301, http://op12no2.me/stuff/herdhis.pdf.

9. WHO, "Alert, Response, and Capacity Building under the International Health Regulations (IHR)," http://www.who.int/ihr/preparedness/en/.

10. WHO, "Surveillance," http://www.who.int/ihr/surveillance/en/.

11. Lawrence O. Gostin, *Global Health Law* (Cambridge, MA: Harvard University Press, 2014).

12. Lawrence Gostin and Devi Sridhar, "Global Health and the Law," *New England Journal of Medicine* 370, no. 18 (2014): 1732–1740.

13. Gostin, *Global Health Law* (2014).

14. UN General Assembly, "Transforming Our World: The 2030 Agenda for Sustainable Development," UN G.A. Res. 70/1, September 25, 2015, https://www.un.org/ga/search/view_doc.asp?symbol=A/RES/70/1&Lang=E.

15. WHO and World Bank, *Tracking Universal Health Coverage: First Global Monitoring Report* (Geneva: WHO, 2015), https://apps.who.int/iris/bitstream/handle/10665/174536/9789241564977_eng.pdf.

16. Jim Kim, "Speech by World Bank Group President Jim Yong Kim at the Government of Japan–World Bank Conference on Universal Health Coverage," December 6, 2013, http://www.worldbank.org/en/news/speech/2013/12/06/speech-world-bank-group-president-jim-yong-kim-government-japan-conference-universal-health-coverage.

17. "Declaration of Astana, Global Conference on Primary Health Care: From Alma-Ata towards Universal Health Coverage and the Sustainable Development Goals," Asanta, Kazakhstan, October 25–26, 2018, https://www.who.int/docs/default-source/primary-health/declaration/gcphc-declaration.pdf.

18. WHO, *Primary Health Care on the Road to Universal Health Coverage: 2019 Monitoring Report*, 2019, 2, https://www.who.int/docs/default-source/documents/2019-uhc-report.pdf.

19. New York Times, Editorial Board, "The Coronavirus Crisis Is Poised to Get Much, Much Worse," *New York Times*, April 13, 2020.

20. Thomas J. Bollyk, Krycia Cowling, and Diana Schoder, "Three More Billboard on the Long Road to Global Quality Health Care," *Health Affairs* blog, October 15, 2018, https://www.healthaffairs.org/do/10.1377/hblog20181011.858188/full/.

21. Universal Declaration of Human Rights, UN G.A. Res. 217A (III), December 10, 1948.

22. International Covenant on Economic, Social and Cultural Rights, December 16, 1966, entered into force January 3, 1976; International Covenant on Civil and Political Rights, December 16, 1966, entered into force March 23, 1976.

23. Committee on Economic, Social and Cultural Rights, "General Comment No. 14: The Right to the Highest Attainable Standard of Health," UN Doc. E/C.12/2000/4 (August 11, 2000).

24. Jody Heymann, Adèle Cassola, Amy Raub, and Lipi Mishra, "Constitutional Rights to Health, Public Health and Medical Care: The Status of Health Protections in 191 Countries," *Global Public Health* 8, no. 6 (2013): 639–653.

25. Constitution of Brazil (1988) (with amendments through 2014), https://www.constituteproject.org/constitution/Brazil_2014.pdf.

26. Constitution of Haiti (1987) (with amendments through 2012), https://www.constituteproject.org/constitution/Haiti_2012.pdf.

27. Leonardo Cubillos, Maria-Luisa Escobar, Sebastian Pavlovic, and Roberto Lunes, "Universal Health Coverage and Litigation in Latin America," *Journal of Health Organization and Management* 26, no. 3 (2012): 390–406.

28. International Covenant on Economic, Social and Cultural Rights, art. 2.

29. Lawrence Gostin, Oyewale Tomori, Suwit Wibulpolprasert, Ashish K. Jha, et al., "Toward a Common Secure Future: Four Global Commissions in the Wake of Ebola," *PLOS Medicine* 13, no. 5 (2016):1–15, https://journals.plos.org/plosmedicine/article?id=10.1371/journal.pmed.1002042.

30. WHO, "Implementation of the International Health Regulations (2005): Report of the Review Committee on Second Extensions for Establishing National Public Health Capacities and on IHR Implementation: Report by the Director General," A68/22 Add. 1, March 27, 2015, http://apps.who.int/gb/ebwha/pdf_files/WHA68/A68_22Add1-en.pdf.

31. CDC, "Spotlight: International Health Regulations," 2015, http://www.cdc.gov/globalhealth/ihr/.

32. WHO, "Implementation of the International Health Regulations (2005): Report of the Review Committee on the Role of the International Health Regulations (2005) in the Ebola Outbreak and Response," WHO Doc. A69/21, http://apps.who.int/gb/ebwha/pdf_files/WHA69/A69_21-en.pdf.

33. WHO, "Concept Note: Development, Monitoring and Evaluation of Functional Core Capacity for Implementing the International Health Regulations," 2005, https://www.who.int/ihr/publications/concept_note_201507/en/.

34. WHO, *Joint External Evaluation Tool: International Health Regulations (2005)* (Geneva: WHO, 2016), http://apps.who.int/iris/bitstream/10665/204368/1/9789241510172_eng.pdf.

35. WHO, "Joint External Evaluation (JEE) Mission Reports," https://www.who.int/ihr/procedures/mission-reports/en/.

36. Uganda Ministry of Health, *Annual Health Sector Performance Report System for Financial Year 2015/16,* Republic of Uganda, Ministry of Health, http://www.health.go.ug/sites/default/files/AHSPR%202015_16.pdf.

37. Darren Taylor, "Inside South Africa's Rural Healthcare Crisis," *Voice of America,* April 30, 2012, http://www.voanews.com/a/inside-south-africas-rural-healthcare-crisis-149690295/370015.html.

38. Anja Schoeps, Sabine Gabrysch, Louis Niiamba, et al., "The Effect of Distance to Health-Care Facilities on Childhood Mortality in Rural Burkina Faso," *American Journal of Epidemiology* 173, no. 5 (2011): 492–498.

39. Zoe M. McLaren, Cally Ardington, and Murray Leibbrandt, "Distance Decay and Persistence Health Care Disparities in South Africa," *BMC Health Services* 14 (2014): 541, http://www-personal.umich.edu/~zmclaren/mclaren_distancedecay.pdf.

40. Roger A. Rosenblatt and L. Gary Hart, "Physicians and Rural America," *Western Journal of Medicine* 173, no. 5 (2002): 348–351.

41. Karen Anderson and Kevin Rothstein, "Rural Massachusetts County Short on Resources Hit Hard by COVID-19," WCVB ABC, April 16, 2020, https://www.wcvb.com/article/rural-massachusetts-county-short-on-resources-hit-hard-by-covid-19/32176689.

42. Justine I. Blanford, Supriya Kumar, Wei Luo, et al., "It's a Long, Long Walk: Accessibility to Hospital, Maternity and Integrated Health Centers in Niger," *International Journal of Health Geographics* 11 (2012): 24.

43. Rupa Chinai, "Getting Health Care to Vulnerable Communities," *Bulletin of the World Health Organization* 83, no. 11 (2005): 804–805, http://www.who .int/bulletin/volumes/83/11/news11105/en/.

44. WHO, "Factors That Contributed to Undetected Spread of the Ebola Virus and Impeded Rapid Containment," January 2015, http://www.who.int/csr /disease/ebola/one-year-report/factors/en/.

45. Brolin Ribacke et al., "Impact of the West Africa Ebola Outbreak," e0150080.

46. Alyssa S. Parpia et al., "Impact of the 2014–2015 Ebola Outbreak on Malaria, HIV, and Tuberculosis in West Africa," *Emerging Infectious Diseases* 22, no. 3 (2016): 433–441, https://wwwnc.cdc.gov/eid/article/22/3/15-0977 _article.

47. Aniruddha Ghosal and Victoria Milko, "Coronavirus Could Erode Global Fight against Other Diseases," *The Star,* April 16, 2020, https://www.thestar .com/news/world/asia/2020/04/16/coronavirus-could-erode-global-fight -against-other-diseases.html.

48. Jane Bradley, "In Scramble for Coronavirus Supplies, Rich Countries Push Poor Aside," *New York Times,* April 9, 2020.

49. Brolin Ribacke et al., "Impact of the West Africa Ebola Outbreak," e0150080.

50. Ernest Tambo, Emmanuel Chidiebere Ugwu, and Jeane Yonkeu Ngogang, "Need of Surveillance Response Systems to Combat Ebola Outbreaks and Other Emerging Infectious Diseases in African Countries," *Infection Diseases of Poverty* 3, no. 29 (2014), https://www.ncbi.nlm.nih.gov/pmc /articles/PMC4130433/.

51. Martin N. Adokiya and John K. Awoonor-Williams, "Ebola Virus Disease Surveillance and Response Preparedness in Northern Ghana," *Global Health Action* 9, no. 1 (2016), http://dx.doi.org/10.3402/gha.v9.29763.

52. Adokiya and Awoonor-Williams, "Ebola Virus Disease Surveillance."

53. Organization for Economic Co-operation and Development, "Hospital Beds," https://data.oecd.org/healtheqt/hospital-beds.htm.

54. Graeme Wood, "Think 168,000 Ventilators Is Too Few? Try Three," *Atlantic,* April 10, 2020.

55. Lydia Namubiru, "Cancer Is on the Rise in Africa Just as Some of the Few Radiotherapy Centers Fall Apart," *Quartz Africa,* May 27, 2016, https://qz .com/692584/cancer-is-on-the-rise-in-africa-just-as-some-of-the-few -radiotherapy-centers-fall-apart/.

56. Hannah McNeish, "Health Clinics Already Hit by 'Catastrophic' Global Gag Rule," *News Deeply,* February 2, 2017, https://www.newsdeeply.com /womenandgirls/articles/2017/02/02/health-clinics-already-hit-catastrophic -global-gag-rule.

57. UNICEF, "Delivery Care," https://data.unicef.org/topic/maternal-health/delivery-care/.

58. WHO, "Global Health Workforce Shortage to Reach 12.9 Million in Coming Decades," November 11, 2013, https://www.who.int/mediacentre/news/releases/2013/health-workforce-shortage/en/.

59. WHO, "Addressing the 18 Million Health Worker Shortfall—35 Concrete Actions and 6 Key Messages," May 28, 2019, https://www.who.int/hrh/news/2019/addressing-18million-hw-shortfall-6-key-messages/en/.

60. WHO, "Global Health Workforce Shortage."

61. WHO, "Ebola Situation Report—4 November 2015," November 4, 2015, http://apps.who.int/iris/bitstream/10665/192654/1/ebolasitrep_4Nov2015_eng.pdf.

62. Eric Reguly, "Italian Doctors' Fatalities Reach Tragic Levels as They Fight COVID-19 in Overburdened Hospitals," *Globe and Mail* (April 3, 2020), https://www.theglobeandmail.com/world/article-italian-doctors-fatalities-reach-tragic-levels-as-they-fight-covid-1/.

63. WHO, *World Health Organization Model List of Essential Medicines: 21st List, 2019* (Geneva: WHO, 2019), https://apps.who.int/iris/handle/10665/325771.

64. WHO, "Essential Medicines," http://www.who.int/topics/essential_medicines/en/.

65. Sheila Mysorekar, "Silent Murder," *D & C e-Paper* no. 4 (2013): 136, https://www.dandc.eu/en/article/medicines-are-too-expensive-poor-people-developing-countries-local-production-could-make.

66. Marion Hart, "Team Vaccine: Immunizing Every Child Is a Global Group Effort," UNICEF, April 22, 2019, https://www.unicefusa.org/stories/team-vaccine-immunizing-every-child-global-group-effort/26851.

67. International Working Group on Financing Preparedness, *From Panic and Neglect to Investing in Health Security: Financing Pandemic Preparedness at a National Level* (Washington, DC: World Bank Group, 2017), http://documents.worldbank.org/curated/en/979591495652724770/From-panic-and-neglect-to-investing-in-health-security-financing-pandemic-preparedness-at-a-national-level.

68. Nathalie Van de Maele, David B. Evans, and Tessa Tan-Torres, "Development Assistance for Health in Africa: Are We Telling the Right Story?," *Bulletin of the World Health Organization* 91, no. 7 (2013): 483–490, https://www.who.int/bulletin/volumes/91/7/12-115410.pdf.

69. Institute for Health Metrics and Evaluation (IHME), *Financing Global Health 2010: Development Assistance and Country Spending in Economic Uncertainty* (Seattle: IHME, 2010), http://www.healthdata.org/sites/default/files/files/policy_report/2010/FGH2010/IHME_FGH201 0_Chapter4.pdf.

70. WHO, *A Healthier Humanity: The WHO Investment Case for 2019–2023* (Geneva: WHO, 2018), http://www.who.int/docs/default-source/investment-case/who-ic-healthier-humanity.pdf.

## Chapter 10 · Global Medical War Chest

1. Nicole Lurie, Melanie Saville, Richard Hatchett, and Jane Halton, "Developing Covid-19 Vaccines at Pandemic Speed," *NEJM* 382 (2020): 1969–1973, https://www.nejm.org/doi/full/10.1056/NEJMp2005630, March 30, 2020.

2. "Moderna's Work on a Potential Vaccine against COVID-19," Moderna, https://www.modernatx.com/modernas-work-potential-vaccine-against-covid-19.

3. Jonathan Corum, Denise Grady, Sui-Lee Wee, and Carl Zimmer, "Coronavirus Vaccine Tracker," https://www.nytimes.com/interactive/2020/science/coronavirus-vaccine-tracker.html.

4. WHO, "Timeline of the Ebola Outbreak Response in Democratic Republic of the Congo 2018," http://www.who.int/ebola/drc-2018/timeline/en/.

5. Jon Cohen, "Congo's Ebola Outbreak Is All but Over: Did an Experimental Vaccine Help?," *Science,* July 18, 2018.

6. Ana Maria Henao-Restrepo, Ira M. Longini, Matthias Egger, et al., "Efficacy and Effectiveness of an rVSV-vectored Vaccine Expressing Ebola Surface Glycoprotein: Interim Results from the Guinea Ring Vaccination Cluster Randomized Trial," *Lancet* 386, no. 9996 (2015): 857–866.

7. Steven M. Jones, Heinz Feldman, Ute Stöher, et al., "Live Attenuated Recombinant Vaccine Protects Nonhuman Primates against Ebola and Marburg Viruses," *Nature Medicine* 11 (2005): 786–790; Patent WO2004011488 A2, Recombinant Vesicular Stomatitis Virus Vaccines for Viral Hemorrhagic Fevers, Application Number PCT/CA2003/001125; Denise Grady, "Ebola Vaccine, Ready for Test, Sat on the Shelf," *New York Times,* October 23, 2014.

8. Jason A. Regules, John H. Beigel, Kristopher M. Paolino, et al., "A Recombinant Vesicular Stomatitis Virus Ebola Vaccine," *NEJM* 376, no. 4 (2017): 330–341.

9. Elizabeth Payne, "The Story of 'the Canadian Vaccine' That Beat Back Ebola," *National Post,* September 4, 2016.

10. F. E. André, "How the Research-Based Industry Approaches Vaccine Development and Establishes Priorities," *Developments in Biologicals* 110 (2002): 25–29.

11. Nick Chapman, Lisette Abela-Oversteegen, Anna Doubell, et al., *Neglected Disease Research and Development: A Pivotal Moment for Global Health* (Sydney: Policy Cures Research, 2017), 6, https://www.policycuresresearch.org/wp-content/uploads/2019/01/Y9-GFINDER-full-report-web.pdf.

12. Chapman et al., *Neglected Disease Research,* 4, 6.

13. Jon Cohen, "Research during Ebola Vaccine Trial: It's Complicated," *Science,* May 25, 2018.

14. WHO, "WHO Supports Ebola Vaccination of High Populations in the Democratic Republic of the Congo," May 21, 2018, http://www.who.int

/news-room/detail/21-05-2018-who-supports-ebola-vaccination-of-high
-risk-populations-in-the-democratic-republic-of-the-congo.

15. WHO, *2018 Annual Review of Diseases Prioritized Under the Research and Development Blueprint,* Meeting Report, Geneva, Switzerland, February 6–7, 2018, http://origin.who.int/emergencies/diseases/2018prioritization-report .pdf.

16. CEPI, *Coalition for Epidemic Preparedness Innovations, Preliminary Business Plan 2017–2021* (Washington, DC: CEPI, 2016), 14, 54, https://cepi.net/wp -content/uploads/2019/02/CEPI-Preliminary-Business-Plan-061216_0.pdf.

17. Aaron E. Carroll, "$2.6 Billion to Develop a Drug? New Estimate Makes Questionable Assumptions," *New York Times,* November 18, 2014.

18. Katarzyna Smietana, Marcin Siatlowski, and Mortin Møller, "Trends in Clinical Success Rates," *Nature Reviews Drug Discovery* 15, no. 6 (2016): 379–380; Chi Heem Wong, Kien Wei Siah, and Andrew W Lo, "Estimation of Clinical Trial Success Rates and Related Parameters," *Biostatistics* 20, no.2 (2019): 273–286.

19. Christopher J. Elias, *Policies and Practices to Advance Global Health Technologies* (Washington, DC: CSIS, 2009), https://csis-website-prod.s3.amazonaws .com/s3fs-public/legacy_files/files/media/csis/pubs/090420_elias_policies practices.pdf.

20. CEPI, *Preliminary Business Plan, 2017–2021,* https://cepi.net/wp-content /uploads/2019/02/CEPI-Preliminary-Business-Plan-061216_0.pdf.

21. Theresa Wizemann, Sally Robinson, and Robert Giffin, *Breakthrough Business Models: Drug Development for Rare and Neglected Diseases and Individualized Therapies* (Washington, DC: National Academies Press, 2009), https://www .ncbi.nlm.nih.gov/books/NBK50977/pdf/Bookshelf_NBK50977.pdf.

22. FDA, "FDA Approves First Treatment for COVID-19," news release, October 22, 2020, https://www.fda.gov/news-events/press-announcements /fda-approves-first-treatment-covid-19#:~:text=Today%2C%20the%20U.S .%20Food%20and,of%20COVID%2D19%20requiring%20hospitalization.

23. FDA, "FDA Issues Emergency Use Authorization for Convalescent Plasma as Potential Promising COVID-19 Treatment, Another Achievement in Administration's Fight Against Pandemic," news release, August 23, 2020, https://www.fda.gov/news-events/press-announcements/fda-issues -emergency-use-authorization-convalescent-plasma-potential-promising -covid-19-treatment.

24. Trial Site News, "National Convalescent Plasma EUA Results: Not Sufficient Evidence for Claim that Convalescent Plasma Reduces COVID-19 Death Rate," August 15, 2020, https://www.trialsitenews.com/national -convalescent-plasma-eua-results-not-sufficient-evidence-for-claim-that -convalescent-plasma-reduces-covid-19-death-rate/.

25. Johns Hopkins Center for Health Security, "Vaccine Platforms: State of the Field and Looming Challenges," https://www.centerforhealthsecurity.org /our-work/pubs_archive/pubs-pdfs/2019/190423-OPP-platform-report.pdf.

26. Lena H. Sun, "Global Response to Ebola Marked by Lack of Coordination and Leadership, Experts Say," *Washington Post*, September 11, 2014.

27. WHO, "ACT-Accelerator Update," news release, June 26, 2020, https://www.who.int/news-room/detail/26-06-2020-act-accelerator -update.

28. Rebecca Weintraub, Asaf Bitton, and Mark L. Rosenberg, "The Danger of Vaccine Nationalism," *Harvard Business Review*, May 22, 2020.

29. HHS, "Fact Sheet: Explaining Operation Warp Speed," June 16, 2020, https://www.hhs.gov/about/news/2020/06/16/fact-sheet-explaining -operation-warp-speed.html.

30. "Sanofi and GSK Selected for Operation Warp Speed to Supply United States Government with 100 Million Doses of COVID-19 Vaccine," GlaxoSmithKline plc., July 31, 2020, https://www.gsk.com/en-gb/media /press-releases/sanofi-and-gsk-selected-for-operation-warp-speed-to-supply -united-states-government-with-100-million-doses-of-covid-19-vaccine/.

31. Government of France, "European Initiative for the Covid-19 Vaccine," June 5, 2020, https://www.gouvernement.fr/en/european-initiative-for-the -covid-19-vaccine.

32. Duke Global Health Innovation Center, "Launch and Scale Speedometer: COVID-19: December 18, 2020: Weekly Vaccine Research Update," updated December 18, 2020, https://launchandscalefaster.org/COVID-19.

33. Emily Baumgaertner and Patrick J. McConnell, "Seeking to Expand Their Influence, China and Russia Market Coronavirus Vaccines around the World," *LA Times*, October 28, 2020.

34. Oliver Holmes, "Brazil, Saudi Arabia and Morocco 'Told of Delay in Covid Jabs From India,'" *The Guardian* (UK), March 21, 2021, https://www .theguardian.com/world/2021/mar/21/brazil-saudi-and-morocco-told-of -delay-in-covid-jabs-from-india.

35. Gavi,, "COVID-19 Vaccine Global Access (COVAX) Facility," June 11, 2020, https://www.keionline.org/wp-content/uploads/COVAX-Facility -Preliminary-technical-design-061120-vF.pdf.

36. WHO, "More than 150 Countries Engaged in COVID-19 Vaccine Global Access Facility," news release, July 15, 2020, https://www.who.int/news -room/detail/15-07-2020-more-than-150-countries-engaged-in-covid-19 -vaccine-global-access-facility; WHO, *ACT-Accelerator Prioritized Strategy & Budget for 2021* (Geneva: WHO, March 2021), 45, https://www.who.int /initiatives/act-accelerator.

37. Gavi, "G7 Backs Gavi's COVAX Advance Market Commitment to Boost COVID-19 Vaccines in World's Poorest Countries," February 19, 2021, https://www.gavi.org/news/media-room/g7-backs-gavis-covax-amc-boost -covid-19-vaccines-worlds-poorest-countries.

38. WHO, *ACT-Accelerator Prioritized Strategy & Budget for 2021*, 47.

39. Chapman et al., *Neglected Disease Research*, 8, 74.

40. Chapman et al., *Neglected Disease Research*, 68.

41. Commission on Global Health Framework for the Future, *Neglected Dimension of Global Security: A Framework to Counter Infectious Disease Crises* (Washington, DC: National Academies Press, 2016), 7.

42. Robert Hecht, Paul Wilson, and Amrita Palriwala, "Innovative Health R&D Financing for Developing Countries: A Menu of Innovative Policy Options," *Health Affairs* 28, no.4 (2009): 974–985.

43. USAID, "USAID Invests Over $15 Million to Accelerate Development and Deployment of 21 Innovations to Combat the Spread of Zika," August 10, 2016, https://2012-2017.usaid.gov/news-information/press-releases/aug-10 -2016-usaid-announces-initial-results-grand-challenge-combat-zika.

44. Alexander Gaffney, Michael Mezher, and Zachary Brennan, "Regulatory Explainer: Everything You Need to Know about FDA's Priority Review Vouchers," *Regulatory Affairs Professionals Society,* February 25, 2020, https://www.raps.org/regulatory-focus/news-articles/2017/12/regulatory -explainer-everything-you-need-to-know-about-fdas-priority-review-vouchers.

45. HHS, "Fact Sheet: Explaining Operation Warp Speed."

46. CEPI, "COVAX: Ensuring Fair Allocation of a COVID-19 Vaccine," June 26, 2020, https://cepi.net/news_cepi/covax-ensuring-fair-allocation-of -a-covid-19-vaccine/.

47. Gavi, "Gavi Launches Innovative Financing Mechanism for Access to COVID-19 Vaccines," June 4, 2020, https://www.gavi.org/news/media-room /gavi-launches-innovative-financing-mechanism-access-covid-19-vaccines.

48. Center for Global Development, *Making Markets for Vaccines: Ideas to Action* (Washington, DC: Center for Global Development, 2005), 14.

49. Gavi, "Positive Impact of Advance Market Commitment Highlighted in Report," February 26, 2016, https://www.gavi.org/library/news/press -releases/2016/positive-impact-of-advance-market-commitment-highlighted -in-report/.

50. Gavi, "How the Pneumococcal AMC Works," https://www.gavi.org /investing-gavi/innovative-financing/pneumococcal-amc/how-it-works.

51. Allie Nawrat, "Access to Covid-19 Vaccines: Deep Dive into Gavi's COVAX AMC," *Pharmaceutical Technology,* July 27, 2020, https://www .pharmaceutical-technology.com/features/gavi-covax-amc-covid-19/.

52. Gavi, "Gavi Launches Innovative Financing Mechanism."

53. COVAX, "COVAX Announces Additional Deals to Access Promising COVID-19 Vaccine Candidates; Plans Global Rollout Starting Q1 2021," December 18, 2020, https://www.gavi.org/news/media-room/covax -announces-additional-deals-access-promising-covid-19-vaccine-candidates -plans.

54. WHO, "Solidarity Call to Action," https://www.who.int/emergencies /diseases/novel-coronavirus-2019/global-research-on-novel-coronavirus -2019-ncov/covid-19-technology-access-pool/solidarity-call-to-action/docs /default-source/coronaviruse/solidarity-call-to-action/solidarity-call-to -action-01-june-2020.

55. WHO, "Endorsements of the Solidarity Call to Action," https://www.who
.int/emergencies/diseases/novel-coronavirus-2019/global-research-on-novel
-coronavirus-2019-ncov/covid-19-technology-access-pool/endorsements-of
-the-solidarity-call-to-action.

56. Ed Silverman, "Pharma Leaders Shoot Down WHO Voluntary Pool for
Patent Rights on Covid-19 Products," STAT, May 28, 2020. https://www
.statnews.com/pharmalot/2020/05/28/who-voluntary-pool-patents-pfizer/.

57. WHO, "The Doha Declaration on the Trips Agreement and Public Health,"
https://www.who.int/medicines/areas/policy/doha_declaration/en/.

58. AstraZeneca, "AstraZeneca Takes Next Steps towards Broad and Equitable
Access to Oxford University's Potential COVID-19 Vaccine," June 4, 2020,
https://www.astrazeneca.com/media-centre/articles/2020/astrazeneca-takes
-next-steps-towards-broad-and-equitable-access-to-oxford-universitys
-potential-covid-19-vaccine.html.

59. National Academy of Sciences, Engineering, and Medicine (NASEM),
*Integrating Clinical Research into Epidemic Response: The Ebola Experience*, ed.
Emily R. Busta, Michelle Mancher, Patricia A. Cuff, et al. (Washington,
DC: National Academies Press, 2017), 40.

60. NASEM, *Integrating Clinical Research,* 46.

61. Joyanthi Wolf, Samantha Bruno, Michael Eichberg, et al., "Applying
Lessons from the Ebola Vaccine Experience for SARS-CoV-2 and Other
Epidemic Pathogens," *Npj Vaccines* 5, no. 51 (2020).

62. Andrew Joseph, "'A Huge Experiment': How the World Made So Much
Progress on a Covid-19 Vaccine So Fast," STAT, July 30, 2020, https://www
.statnews.com/2020/07/30/a-huge-experiment-how-the-world-made-so
-much-progress-on-a-covid-19-vaccine-so-fast/.

63. Joseph, "'A Huge Experiment.'"

64. Knvul Sheikh, "Pfizer Begins Human Trials of Possible Coronavirus
Vaccine," *New York Times,* May 5, 2020.

65. FDA, "Coronavirus (COVID-19) Update: FDA Takes Action to Help
Facilitate Timely Development of Safe, Effective COVID-19 Vaccines,"
June 30, 2020, https://www.fda.gov/news-events/press-announcements
/coronavirus-covid-19-update-fda-takes-action-help-facilitate-timely
-development-safe-effective-covid.

66. Suerie Moon, Jennifer Leigh, Liana Woskie, et al., "Post Ebola Reforms:
Ample Analysis, Inadequate Action," *BMJ* 356, no. 280 (2017): j280.

67. Vincent Ahonkhai, Samuel F. Martins, Alexandre Portet, et al., "Speeding
Access to Vaccines and Medicines in Low- and Middle-Income Countries:
A Case for Change and a Framework for Optimized Product Market
Authorization," *PLOS One* 11, no.11 (2016): e0166515.

68. Ahonkhai et al., "Speeding Access."

69. COVID-19 Vaccine Global Access Facility, "Preliminary Technical Design,"
discussion document, June 11, 2020, https://www.keionline.org/wp-content
/uploads/COVAX-Facility-Preliminary-technical-design-061120-vF.pdf.

70. Ahonkhai et al., "Speeding Access."
71. Ahonkhai et al., "Speeding Access."
72. Ahonkhai et al., "Speeding Access."
73. WHO, *Research Ethics in International Epidemic Response* (Geneva: WHO, 2009), https://www.who.int/ethics/gip_research_ethics_.pdf.
74. NASEM, *Integrating Clinical Research*, 75.
75. Jon Cohen and Kai Kupferschmidt, "Ebola Vaccine Trials Raise Ethical Issues," *Science* 346, no. 6207 (2014): 289–290.
76. Clement Adebamowo, Oumou Bah-Sow, Fred Binka, et al, "Randomised Controlled Trials for Ebola: Practical and Ethical Issues," *Lancet* 384, no. 9952 (2014): 1423–1424.
77. NASEM, *Integrating Clinical Research*, 64.
78. Annelies Wilder-Smith, Stefan Flasche, and Peter G. Smith, "Vaccine-Attributable Severe Dengue in the Philippines," *Lancet* 394, no. 10215 (2019): P2151–2152.
79. Wilder-Smith, Flasche, and Smith, "Vaccine-Attributable Severe Dengue."
80. Jon Cohen, "Russia's Approval of a COVID-19 Vaccine Is Less than Meets the Press Release," *Science,* August 11, 2020.
81. Lawrence Gostin, "Russia's Covid-19 Vaccine Breaches Crucial Scientific and Ethical International Standards," *Moscow Times,* August 12, 2020.
82. NIH, "Phase 3 Clinical Trial of Investigational Vaccine for COVID-19 Begins," July 27, 2020, https://www.nih.gov/news-events/news-releases/phase-3-clinical-trial-investigational-vaccine-covid-19-begins.
83. Cohen, "Russia's Approval."
84. FDA, "Coronavirus (COVID-19) Update: FDA Revokes Emergency Use Authorization for Chloroquine and Hydroxychloroquine," June 15, 2020, https://www.fda.gov/news-events/press-announcements/coronavirus-covid-19-update-fda-revokes-emergency-use-authorization-chloroquine-and.
85. Olivia Benecke and Sarah Elizabeth DeYoung, "Anti-Vaccine Decision-Making and Measles Resurgence in the United States," *Global Pediatric Health* 6, no. 2333794X19862949 (2019).
86. Shannon Mullen O'Keefe, "One in Three Americans Would Not Get COVID-19 Vaccine," *Gallup,* August 7, 2020, https://news.gallup.com/poll/317018/one-three-americans-not-covid-vaccine.aspx.
87. Jon Cohen, "Top U.S. Scientists Left Out of White House Selection of COVID-19 Vaccine Short List," *Science,* June 4, 2020.
88. Letter to FDA, CSPI, August 5, 2020, https://cspinet.org/sites/default/files/COVID_Vaccine_Letter_to_FDA_8.5.2020.pdf.

## In and beyond the Age of COVID-19: What Does the Future Hold?

1. Radley Balko, "Stopping Covid-19 behind Bars Was an Achievable Moral Imperative: We Failed," *Washington Post,* May 1, 2020, https://www.nytimes.com/2020/04/08/nyregion/coronavirus-disabilities-group-homes.html;

Danny Hakim, "'It's Hit Our Front Door': Homes for the Disabled See a Surge of Covid-19," *New York Times,* April 8, 2020.

2. Olivia Heffernan, "Farmworkers Continue to Work with Little Protection," *Documented,* April 27, 2020, https://documentedny.com/2020/04/27 /farmworkers-continue-to-work-with-little-protection/; Shashank Bengali, "From 'Gold Standard' to a Coronavirus 'Explosion': Singapore Battles New Outbreak," *Los Angeles Times,* April 14, 2020.

3. Paul Davidson, "Unemployment Soars to 14.7%, Job Losses Reach 20.5 Million in April as Coronavirus Pandemic Spreads," *USA Today,* May 8, 2020; Neha Poonia, "How COVID-19 Is Inflaming India's Social and Religious Tensions," PBS News Hour, aired May 7, 2020; Sifiso Zulu, "SA's Unemployment Rate Could Reach 40% Due to COVID-19—Mogajane," *Eyewitness News,* May 4, 2020, https://ewn.co.za/2020/05/04/sa-s -unemployment-rate-could-possibly-reach-40-due-to-covid-19-mogajane.

4. Amanda Taub, "A New Covid-19 Crisis: Domestic Abuse Rises World-wide," *New York Times,* April 6, 2020.

5. "The Post-COVID World: A Fareed Zakaria GPS Special," CNN, aired May 10, 2020.

6. Julia Hollingsworth, "How New Zealand 'Eliminated' Covid-19 after Weeks of Lockdown," CNN, April 28, 2020.

7. "In Memoriam: Healthcare Workers Who Have Died of COVID-19," Medscape, April 1, 2020, https://www.medscape.com/viewarticle/927976.

8. Jonathan Safran Foer, "Meat Is Not Essential: Why Are We Killing for It?," *Washington Post,* May 11, 2020.

9. Michelle Harven, "Coronavirus: Should Wet Markets Be Shut Down?," WAMU 88.5, May 12, 2020.

10. James Gorman, "China's Ban on Wildlife Trade a Big Step, but Has Loopholes, Conservationists Say," *New York Times,* February 27, 2020.

11. Rachel Nuwer, "Stop Wildlife Trade to Prevent Next Epidemic, Conservationists Say," *New York Times,* February 20, 2020.

12. "Illegal Wildlife Trade," US Fish & Wildlife Service, https://www.fws.gov /international/travel-and-trade/illegal-wildlife-trade.html.

13. AP, "UN: Live Animal Markets Shouldn't Be Closed Despite Virus," *WTOP News,* May 8, 2020, https://wtop.com/europe/2020/05/un-market -where-virus-may-have-started-shouldnt-be-closed/.

14. USAID, "Pandemic Influenza and Other Emerging Threats," Fact Sheet, April 2013, https://www.usaid.gov/news-information/fact-sheets/emerging -pandemic-threats-2-program; Kristin Burns, "PREDICT Receives Extension for COVID-19 Pandemic Emergency Response," *UC Davis News,* April 3, 2020, https://www.vetmed.ucdavis.edu/news/predict-receives-extension -covid-19-pandemic-emergency-response.

15. Lawrence O. Gostin and Eric A. Friedman, "Imagining Global Health with Justice: Transformative Ideas for Health and Well-Being while Leaving No One Behind," *Georgetown Law Journal* 108 (2020): 1535–1606.

16. CEPI, "CEPI Policy Documentation," https://msfaccess.org/sites/default /files/2018-09/CEPIoriginalPolicy_2017.pdf.

17. Gostin and Friedman, "Imagining Global Health with Justice" (proposing a Framework Convention on Global Health, Right to Health Capacity Fund, and health equity programs of action as part of the post-COVID-19 global health infrastructure).

18. UN, "68% of the World Population Projected to Live in Urban Areas by 2050, Says UN," May 16, 2018, https://www.un.org/development/desa/en /news/population/2018-revision-of-world-urbanization-prospects.html.

19. Christina Goldbaum, "Subway Shutdown: New York Closes System for First Time in 115 Years," *New York Times,* May 6, 2020.

20. "COVID-19 Crisis Drives Changes in eCommerce Purchasing Behaviors, ACI Worldwide Research Reveals," AP News, April 7, 2020.

21. James Melton, "Grocery Retailers Adapt as Coronavirus Upends Shopping Patterns," *Digital Commerce 360,* April 24, 2020, https://www .digitalcommerce360.com/article/coronavirus-impact-online-retail/.

22. Laura Dyrda, "Telehealth May See Big Long-Term Gains Due to COVID-19: 10 Observations," *Becker's Hospital Review,* April 17, 2020, https://www .beckershospitalreview.com/telehealth/telehealth-may-see-big-long-term -gains-due-to-covid-19-10-observations.html.

23. Max Roser, "Tourism (2020)," Our World in Data, https://ourworldindata .org/tourism.

## Appendix: Tabletop Exercises to Prepare for the Impact

1. WHO, *Development, Monitoring and Evaluation of Functional Core Capacity for Implementing the International Health Regulations (2005)* (Geneva: WHO, 2015), 3.

2. WHO, *WHO Simulation Exercise Manual* (Geneva: WHO, 2017).

3. This scenario is taught at Georgetown University Law Center by Professors Lawrence O. Gostin and Michael Stoto. Our gratitude goes to Prof. John Kraemer and Alexandra Phelan for crafting this Tabletop Exercise.

4. CDC, "How the Flu Virus Can Change: 'Drift' and 'Shift,'" September 27, 2017, https://www.cdc.gov/flu/about/viruses/change.htm.

5. WHO, "Emergency Preparedness, Response: Pandemic Influenza Vaccine Manufacturing Process and Timeline," August 6, 2009, https://www.who .int/csr/disease/swineflu/notes/h1n1_vaccine_20090806/en/.

6. CDC, "How Flu Spreads," August 27, 2018, https://www.cdc.gov/flu/about /disease/spread.htm; CDC, "Flu Symptoms & Complications," February 26, 2019, https://www.cdc.gov/flu/consumer/symptoms.htm; Heidi Goldman, "How Long Does the Flu Last?," Harvard Health Publishing, updated January 16, 2018, https://www.health.harvard.edu/staying-healthy/how -long-does-the-flu-last.

7. WHO, "Cholera: Key Facts," January 17, 2019, https://www.who.int/en /news-room/fact-sheets/detail/cholera.

8. WHO, "Global Epidemics and Impact of Cholera," https://www.who.int/topics/cholera/impact/en/; WHO, "Cholera: Key Facts," January 17, 2019, https://www.who.int/en/news-room/fact-sheets/detail/cholera.

9. WHO, "Cholera: Key Facts," January 17, 2019, https://www.who.int/en/news-room/fact-sheets/detail/cholera.

10. Sara Jerving, "Why Governments Tiptoe around the Word 'Cholera,'" *Devex*, March 21, 2018, https://www.devex.com/news/why-governments-tiptoe-around-the-word-cholera-92348.

11. UN Office for the Coordination of Humanitarian Affairs, "Haiti: Cholera Figures: As of 26 December 2018," https://reliefweb.int/sites/reliefweb.int/files/resources/ocha-hti-cholera-figures-2018123_en.pdf.

12. WHO Regional Office for the Eastern Mediterranean, "Disease Outbreaks in Eastern Mediterranean Region (EMR), January to December 2018," *Weekly Epidemiological Monitor* 11, no. 52 (2018): 1.

13. Communications Team, "Mystery of Yemen Cholera Epidemic Solved," *Wellcome Sanger Institute*, January 2, 2019, https://www.sanger.ac.uk/news/view/mystery-yemen-cholera-epidemic-solved.

14. WHO, "Cholera: Key Facts," January 17, 2019, https://www.who.int/en/news-room/fact-sheets/detail/cholera.

15. "Outrage over Cholera Screening," *The Herald* (Zimbabwe), September 20, 2018, https://www.herald.co.zw/outrage-over-cholera-screening/.

16. David Brunnstrom, "Obama Announces Lifting of U.S. Sanctions on Myanmar," *Reuters*, October 7, 2016, https://www.reuters.com/article/us-usa-myanmar-sanctions/obama-announces-lifting-of-u-s-sanctions-on-myanmar-idUSKCN127262.

# Acknowledgments

It is with enormous gratitude that I acknowledge the leaders and fellows of the O'Neill Institute for National and Global Health Law at Georgetown University, and especially Linda and Timothy O'Neill, whose remarkable generosity and ongoing intellectual guidance have enabled our Institute to flourish. Bill Treanor, Georgetown Law's dean, and Katie Gottschalk, the Institute's executive director, never failed to support this ambitious book project.

The O'Neill Institute team with whom I have worked intensely are some of the most intelligent, insightful, and hardworking colleagues I have ever had the privilege of learning from. They researched, drafted, edited, and conceptualized the book from the onset and throughout. They are the ones who provided the intellectual firepower that fueled the ideas and the prose in this book. Two colleagues at the O'Neill Institute worked tirelessly to make this book possible: Eric A. Friedman is the Institute's Global Health Justice Scholar and the project leader for the Platform for a Framework Convention on Global Health (FCGH). Sarah Wetter is an Associate at the Institute. This book would not have been possible without Eric and Sarah's dedication and intelligence. My gratitude to Eric and Sarah is beyond measure.

I also had invaluable support from O'Neill Institute fellows and staff for key chapters in the book: Katharina Ó Cathaoir (now at the Faculty of Law, University of Copenhagen), Margherita Cinà (O'Neill Institute), Sarah Duranske (SI-Bone, Inc.), Nareh Ghalustians (MaRS Discovery District), Sibel Ozcelik (University of Pennsylvania Law School), Alexandra Phelan (Center for Global Health Science and Security, Georgetown University), Tom Vincent (Evidera), and Heather Whiteside (Fasken Martineau DuMoulin LLP). This team deserves all the credit and all of the gratitude I can muster. I also want to extend my gratitude to research assistants who have supported this book—Rebecca Dittrich, Jingyi Xu (who also provided important contributions to the index), Benny Chan, Han-Hsi (Indy) Liu, Jiawen (Elyssa) Liu, Julie McCardy, and Aejin Noh—and to Alexandra Finch (O'Neill Institute) for critical contributions to the index.

I also want to express my deep gratitude to my editor at Harvard University Press. Janice Audet phoned me five years ago when I was living in Buenos Aires, giving me the idea for this book project. She has nurtured this project intellectually throughout this process, with invaluable support as well from Emeralde Jensen-Roberts, Stephanie Vyce, and the rest of the Harvard University Press team.

As any author knows, writing a book of this magnitude takes a personal toll. My family has been wonderful, loving, and supportive. This book is for my wife, Jean, sons Bryn and Kieran, and their loving partners Jen and Isley. I have two amazing grandchildren, Aviva and Ellis, who mean the world to me. Aviva and Ellis lived through this pandemic and will tell the tales of the hardships of the Great Coronavirus Pandemic of 2020 to their children and grandchildren.

# Index